The Institutional Framework of Russian Serfdom

Russian rural history has long been based on a 'Peasant Myth', originating with nineteenth-century Romantics and still accepted by many historians today. In this book, Tracy Dennison shows how Russian society looked from below, and finds nothing like the collective, redistributive, and market-averse behaviour often attributed to Russian peasants. On the contrary, the Russian rural population was as integrated into regional and even national markets as many of its west European counterparts. Serfdom was a loose garment that enabled different landlords to shape economic institutions, especially property rights, in widely diverse ways. Highly coercive and backward regimes on some landlords' estates existed side by side with surprisingly liberal approximations to a rule of law. This book paints a vivid and colourful picture of the everyday reality of rural Russia before the 1861 abolition of serfdom.

TRACY DENNISON is Associate Professor of Social Science History at the California Institute of Technology. Her work has received numerous prizes, including the Pollard Prize awarded by the Institute for Historical Research at the University of London, and the Economic History Association's Alexander Gerschenkron Prize.

Cambridge Studies in Economic History

Editorial Board

PAUL JOHNSON *La Trobe University*
SHEILAGH OGILVIE *University of Cambridge*
AVNER OFFER *All Souls College, Oxford*
GIANNI TONIOLO *Università di Roma 'Tor Vergata'*
GAVIN WRIGHT *Stanford University*

Cambridge Studies in Economic History comprises stimulating and accessible economic history which actively builds bridges to other disciplines. Books in the series will illuminate why the issues they address are important and interesting, place their findings in a comparative context, and relate their research to wider debates and controversies. The series will combine innovative and exciting new research by younger researchers with new approaches to major issues by senior scholars. It will publish distinguished work regardless of chronological period or geographical location.

A complete list of titles in the series can be found at:
www.cambridge.org/economichistory

The Institutional Framework of Russian Serfdom

Tracy Dennison

CAMBRIDGE UNIVERSITY PRESS

CAMBRIDGE UNIVERSITY PRESS
Cambridge, New York, Melbourne, Madrid, Cape Town,
Singapore, São Paulo, Delhi, Tokyo, Mexico City

Cambridge University Press
The Edinburgh Building, Cambridge CB2 8RU, UK

Published in the United States of America by Cambridge University Press,
New York

www.cambridge.org
Information on this title: www.cambridge.org/9780521194488

First published 2011

Printed in the United Kingdom at the University Press, Cambridge

A catalogue record for this publication is available from the British Library

Library of Congress Cataloguing in Publication data
Dennison, T. K. (Tracy K.), 1970–
The institutional framework of Russian serfdom / T. K. Dennison.
  p.   cm. – (Cambridge studies in economic history)
Includes bibliographical references and index.
ISBN 978-0-521-19448-8 (hardback)
1. Serfdom – Russia – History.   2. Peasants – Russia – Economic conditions.
3. Peasants – Russia – Social conditions.   4. Russia – Rural
conditions.   5. Russia – Economic conditions – To 1861.
6. Russia – Commerce – History.   7. Land tenure – Russia – History.
8. Right of property – Russia – History.   9. Agriculture – Economic aspects –
Russia – History.   10. Agriculture – Social aspects – Russia –
History.   I. Title.   II. Series.
HD714.D46   2011
306.3′650947–dc22
                                                            2010043705

ISBN 978-0-521-19448-8 Hardback

It is a very bad policy to want to change by laws what should be changed by customs.

—Article XXIX of Catherine II's *Nakaz*

This article seems to make norms (*moeurs*) independent of laws. I think that norms derive from laws . . . Norms are good when the laws which are observed are good and bad when the laws which are observed are bad. There are no norms when good or bad laws are not observed.

—Diderot on Article XXIX of the *Nakaz*

Contents

Figures and tables

Figure

Tables

Preface

The revolutionary popular movements that led to the collapse of the Soviet empire, and eventually of the Soviet Union itself, began about two decades ago. These events were accompanied, for the first few years, by millenial hopes on both sides of the former Iron Curtain. Such hopes for changes in the real world have, of course, been more and more disappointed since then, but that very disappointment has left one deep and lasting change in the intellectual world. In the subdiscipline of development economics, and in a number of subfields connected with it, a lesson has been learned. It has been recognised that institutions matter; indeed, this has become a slogan repeated by many who have little interest in the fate of eastern Europe or the particular problems of transition associated with that part of the world.

The presumed lesson has been to remind us of the degree to which the assumptions made by development economists were not so much assumptions about human behaviour as such, but rather assumptions about human behaviour in an institutional structure that guaranteed property rights and contract enforcement. ('Remind' since of course these conditions had been spelled out long ago by David Hume and Adam Smith at the dawn of classical economics.) This reminder has been very fruitful and has led research in development economics, political economy, and economic history in many new and interesting directions. This book can be regarded as one product of this general trend.

But it also differs from many other products of this trend, in one critical respect: it makes no attempt to develop, or even to test, any new or interesting theory of institutions or institutional development. On the contrary, it was driven to some degree by a certain frustration with the lack of connection between such theories as we have and anything concrete or identifiable. This book has nothing of the sublimity of theory. Instead, it takes a worm's eye view of institutions, looking at them through the eyes of provincial villagers in all their boring drudgery and everyday concerns. It sketches its view of pre-Emancipation Russia on 'two inches of ivory' rather than painting a grand panorama on a large canvas.

It should be emphasised that this book shares the concerns of Hume, Smith, and the new institutional economics to understand how institutions shape economic and social life. It is inspired by the same questions. They are what motivated its subject: Russia before the Emancipation Act of 1861 – the paradigm of a society lacking the institutions of private property and judicial rule of law. But it approaches this subject without any prior assumptions about the categories in which to locate what it finds. Of course, it is impossible to escape preconceptions; if ever there was a society veiled in massive accretions of ideological fog, it is Russia. This is impossible to ignore; nearly all the literature we have on this society is coloured by these preconceptions, especially the one I call the 'Peasant Myth' and, try as we might, we historians find it impossible to leave our predecessors behind altogether. But this book does its best to let the voices of the villagers themselves penetrate this modern fog. It seeks to develop categories that are as close to the immediate sources as possible, without assuming that we already know what a commune was, for instance, or what serfdom meant in a specific local context.

The aim of this book, then, is not to solve the grand problems this field is wrestling with, but to put some solid ground under our feet. It is widely assumed that we know exactly what we are talking about when we use terms like 'serfdom', 'credit', 'commune', or 'family' (or even 'institution'), but in fact, things get rather vague once the generalities are left behind and specific situations are addressed. There is little agreement on what we are actually supposed to be explaining, how the societies in question actually worked, on the ground, or how they developed over time. So it is hardly surprising that, as things stand now, the institutional, geographical, and cultural explanations contending for researchers' attention are often not empirically distinguishable. They co-exist side by side, often in uneasy combinations, without being related to sufficiently concrete cases to enable us to relate their theoretical predictions with empirically robust concepts and categories.

This confused state of affairs is, in my view, due to the ideological myths mentioned above, especially the 'Peasant Myth', a hydra-headed monster that has fed generations of Russian and eastern European nationalisms and served a variety of political masters over the years without being subjected to serious empirical scrutiny. The urgent need to cut this undergrowth away before we can get a clear view explains the focus on that myth in parts of this book. Not only does the book attempt to sharpen up this hazy myth – very much against the grain of its historical articulations – into a group of empirical theories, but it also uses its findings, in the course of investigating the different aspects of pre-Emancipation rural life, to refute those theories. This focus reflects the dominance of the Peasant Myth specifically in the historiography of Russia and eastern Europe. (If some other unexamined tradition had been so dominant, that would undoubtedly have been the focus of specification and refutation.) To get the facts across, it has to be made clear that they are sharply at variance with what has been largely taken for granted up to now.

It was fortunate that the time when I became interested in the institutional structure of Russia coincided with the time when Russian archives were becoming more accessible to foreign researchers. Until fairly recently, foreign scholars were not even allowed unrestricted access to the archive catalogues. This alone would have made it difficult to carry out a local study of the sort undertaken here. But while Russian archives are more accessible than they once were, they still pose certain challenges to the foreign researcher. There are, for example, stringent limits on the amount of material one can photocopy and/or microfilm. This is particularly unfortunate since random closings and countless public holidays significantly reduce the time one can spend in the archive reading room. But these and other challenges of Russian life were more than compensated by the many people – more than I can list here – who helped to make my research time in Russia both pleasant and productive. The following should be singled out for their significant contributions to this research: Svetlana Romanovna Dolgova and the staff at the Russian State Archive for Old Documents (RGADA) in Moscow; Yevgenii Leonidovich Guzanov and the staff at the State Archive of Yaroslavl' Province (GAYaO); Yuri Aleksandrovich Tikhonov, who often acted as a surrogate advisor in Moscow; Boris Nikolaevich Mironov, who assured me many years ago that a project like this one could be done; and Igor Fedyukin, who cheerfully accompanied me on a long, cold journey to the former Voshchazhnikovo estate in October 2002. The Russian State University for the Humanities provided institutional support for numerous archive trips.

Special thanks are due to the late Charles Feinstein for his guidance and support when I was in the earliest stages of planning this project. I am sorry that I cannot present him with this evidence that his encouragement was put to good use. In Cambridge, the History Faculty's Ellen MacArthur Fund provided much appreciated research funding, as did an Earhart Studentship and the IHR/EHS Postan Fellowship. I have also benefited from a research fellowship at the Centre for History and Economics and Robinson College. I am grateful to colleagues at both institutions for memorable conversations and good advice, in particular to Bernhard Fulda, William O'Reilly, Emma Rothschild, Gareth Stedman-Jones, and Chris Ward. Ian Blanchard provided much more than his statutory external perspective. The Cambridge Department of Slavonic Studies offered a welcoming home during the academic year 2004–5. And

I am grateful to the Economic History Association for recognising an earlier version of this book with the Alexander Gerschenkron Prize in 2004.

The Cambridge Group for the History of Population and Social Structure provided a stimulating and supportive environment for graduate research. I have especially profited from conversations with Chris Briggs, André Carus, Peter Kitson, John Landers, Alysa Levene, Julie Marfany, Beatrice Moring, Sheilagh Ogilvie, Roger Schofield, Leigh Shaw-Taylor, Rhiannon Thompson, Richard Wall, Paul Warde, and Tony Wrigley. Jim Oeppen and Ros Davies were generous with much-appreciated methodological advice. The late Peter Laslett was characteristically enthusiastic about my initial Russian household findings, and would equally have appreciated this book; I am grateful to him, Tony Wrigley, and Roger Schofield for instigating the Cambridge Group to begin with. The ideal apprenticeship in its research ethos and exacting standards was provided by my dissertation advisor, Richard Smith, who was an invaluable source of guidance and encouragement, thereby balancing out the bracingly rigorous treatment he meted out to my ideas and drafts.

This book was completed in California – far from Russia and England, where it was begun. Caltech has proven the ideal environment for an interdisciplinary project of this sort; the book has benefited enormously from discussions with my colleagues in the Division of Humanities and Social Sciences, and with those in the wider California economic history community. In particular, I should like to thank Warren Brown, Jean Ensminger, Philip Hoffman, Morgan Kousser, and Robert Rosenstone. I am especially grateful to Jean-Laurent Rosenthal and Sheilagh Ogilvie, both of whom generously provided detailed comments on a penultimate draft. Thanks are also owed to Tom Willard, who provided invaluable assistance in generating a map. Others who have provided helpful suggestions along the way include Timothy Guinnane, Hubertus Jahn, Naomi Lamoreaux, Steven Nafziger, Matti Polla, Douglas Smith, the participants in the meetings of the Caltech Early Modern Group, and two anonymous readers for Cambridge University Press.

A note on the value of the rouble

A number of different kinds of roubles circulated in imperial Russia in this period, posing a considerable challenge to the historian wishing to undertake a longitudinal study of prices and wages.[1] Although no such attempt is made in this book, another, not unrelated problem has presented itself. It has been surprisingly difficult to determine which of the two currencies in use in rural Russia in this period – the silver rouble and the paper rouble (*assignat*) – is being referred to in the estate documents. It is especially surprising given how large the difference was: the official exchange rate from 1839 was 3.5 *assignat* to 1 silver rouble (the real exchange rate at the local level is unclear). Feudal levies were set in silver roubles, as explicitly noted in the estate instructions. But no other prices were systematically recorded in a specific currency. Some cases – casual references to salaries of communal officials, disputes over loans, and prices for goods – refer explicitly to *assignat*, while other references to similar things refer explicitly to silver. In more than half of the cases cited in this book, it is not clear which rouble is being used.

I have decided against educated guesses, since there are ambiguous cases, where either value is plausible in the context. Instead, I have reported the values as given in the documents, specifying the currency where known and referring only to 'roubles' where unknown. This has in a few cases been somewhat inconvenient, as I have been careful to avoid any claims that might have depended on this difference. However, it is a serious issue that requires close attention before historians can adequately address questions of standards of living or changes in real incomes in rural Russia, and especially comparisons of pre- and post-Emancipation conditions.

Some baseline figures are offered below, to provide some context for the price and wage data given in the text.

---

[1] For more on the different roubles and the problems they present, see the discussion in T. Owen, 'A standard ruble of account for Russian business history 1769–1914: a note', *Journal of Economic History* 49 (1989), pp. 699–706.

- In the nineteenth century, the soul tax stood at 86 silver kopecks per year.[2]
- Quitrent levies (*obrok*) per *tiaglo* of land remained at 15 silver roubles per year thoughout the period under investigation.[3]
- In the 1796 instructions, Sheremetyev notes that a female labourer in the textile industry could earn 15 to 25 silver roubles per year.[4]

---

[2] J. Blum, *Lord and peasant in Russia from the ninth to the nineteenth century* (Princeton, NJ, 1961), p. 434.
[3] RGADA, f. 1287, op. 3, ed. khr. 2320, l. 3 ('Descriptions of estates, 1858').
[4] RGADA, f. 1287, op. 3, ed. khr. 555, l. 26 ('Instructions, 1796–1800').

A note on transliteration

Russian words have been transliterated in accordance with the Library of Congress system with certain exceptions for conventional English usage. Quotations from archival sources have been transliterated exactly as they appear in the original documents, which were written before the standardisation of spelling and punctuation.

Abbreviations

GAYaO	Gosudarstvennyi Arkhiv Yaroslavskoi Oblasti (State Archive of Yaroslavl' Oblast')
RGADA	Rossisskii Gosudarstvennyi Arkhiv Drevnikh Aktov (Russian State Archive of Old Documents)
f.	*fond*
op.	*opis*
ed. khr.	*edinitsa khraneniia*
d.	*delo*
l.	*list*

Glossary

barshchina	corvée labour; feudal obligations in labour services
obrok	quitrent; feudal obligations in money or kind

Land units

desiatina	roughly equal to 2.7 acres
sazhen'	roughly equal to 2.134 meters
tiaglo	conventional measure referring to the amount of land that could be cultivated by a male–female work unit with one horse

Weights and measures

pood	roughly equal to 16.38 kilograms
funt'	1/40 *pood* (roughly equal to 409.5 grams)
chetvert'	8 *poods* (roughly equal to 130 kilograms)
chetverik	1/8 *chetvert'*

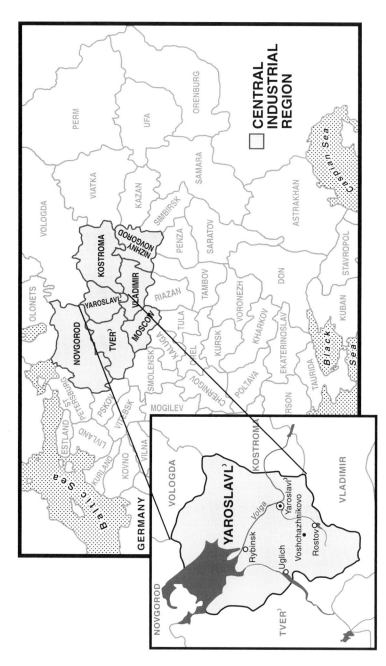

Yaroslavl' and surrounding provinces

1 Why is Russia different? Culture, geography, institutions

Russia has long been viewed as fundamentally different from western Europe. This difference was not only among the main preoccupations of nineteenth-century Russian novelists and social thinkers, but it has often been invoked by historians to explain the failure of economic reforms in the nineteenth and early twentieth centuries, and also to account for the peculiarities of the Soviet experiment. This view of Russia as different has persisted and is now often adduced to explain the failure of the Russian transition to a modern democratic state. Thus the rule of law, for instance, has failed to take hold in post-Soviet Russia because it is a peculiarly western idea, while Russians have deeply rooted anti-legalistic attitudes.[1] The transition to a market economy has faltered due to the incompatibility of western incentives and Russian culture.[2] And parliamentary democracy has failed to take root because Russians have always preferred authoritarianism.[3]

But which differences exactly are relevant here, and can account for such strikingly divergent outcomes? The most popular answer to this question, both inside and outside of Russia, and perhaps the most prevalent among historians, is that the differences in question here are ultimate and irreducible. They are rooted in folk memory and folk culture, and are reflected perhaps most obviously in the organisation of rural society before industrialisation. Russian peasants, this view holds, were culturally imbued with fundamentally different behaviour patterns from western or central European tillers of the soil. Konstantin Levin, the idealistic landlord in L. N. Tolstoy's *Anna Karenina*, gives classic expression to this view when, after various attempts to improve productivity on his estate, he

---

[1] M. Newcity, 'Russian legal tradition and the rule of law', in J. Sachs and K. Pistor (eds.), *The rule of law and economic reform in Russia* (Boulder, 1997), pp. 41–53.

[2] U. Procaccia, *Russian culture, property rights, and the market economy* (Cambridge, 2007).

[3] N. P. Popov, *The Russian people speak: democracy at the crossroads* (Syracuse, 1995), esp. pp. 123–6. Even Herzen saw Russians as fundamentally illiberal (see, for instance, his essay 'The Russian people and socialism: an open letter to Jules Michelet', reprinted in *From the other shore & The Russian people and socialism* (repr. Oxford, 1979).

concludes that European approaches to agriculture are of no use in Russia. English ploughs are 'useless' in the hands of Russian peasants (p. 320), and European works on political economy are inapplicable to the Russian case (p. 342).[4] Russian peasant society has its own logic – a logic that has little in common with that of Europe. For this reason Levin decides that European books on agricultural methods 'had nothing to tell him'.

> He saw that Russia had splendid soil and splendid labourers, and that in some cases . . . the labourers and land produced much: but in the majority of cases, when capital was expended in the European way, they produced little, and that this happened simply because the labourers are only willing to work and work well, in the way natural to them, and that their opposition was not accidental but permanent, being rooted in the spirit of the people. (p. 342)

The spirit of the Russian people, on this view, is reflected in practices that were more 'collectivist' than those in western societies. Communal justice, it is claimed, substituted for a formal system of courts.[5] Collective responsibility for taxes, feudal dues, and village maintenance outweighed the importance of individual obligations to landlords, state officials, and the community.[6] Extended-family households and kinship networks played a more central role in the culture and economy of rural Russia than nuclear families and individual contractual relations.[7] Land, above all, was held in communal rather than individal tenure. Thus Alexander Herzen, one of many nineteenth-century admirers of the peasant commune, noted that Russian peasants, unlike those in western Europe, had a strong aversion to private property and legal formalities; '[c]ontracts and written agreements', he claimed, 'were [among Russian peasants] quite unheard of'.[8]

The 'spirit of the people' or *mentalité* thus described becomes an ultimate court of explanatory appeal in this approach to Russian difference; we can trace the history of that fundamental difference but it is a black box whose inner workings remain invisible. Uriel Procaccia, in a recent book, argues that this mentality has deep cultural roots: Russia, he claims, is an inherently collectivist society, steeped in Orthodox beliefs which are

---

[4] These page numbers refer to the Oxford Paperbacks edition, translated by Louise and Aylmer Maude, repr. 1992.

[5] See discussion in chapter 1 of J. Burbank, *Russian peasants go to court: legal culture in the countryside, 1905–1917* (Bloomington, 2004).

[6] An overview of *krugovaia poruka* can be found in D. Moon, *The Russian peasantry: 1600–1930: the world the peasants made* (London, 1999), pp. 207–11.

[7] For a comparison of the Russian and 'European' household formation systems, see J. Hajnal, 'Two kinds of preindustrial household formation system', *Population and Development Review* 8 (1982), pp. 449–94.

[8] Herzen, 'The Russian people and socialism', p. 183.

hostile to western-style legality, and especially to contractual exchange, while western Europe is inherently individualistic and legalistic.[9] Similarly, Michael Newcity argues that lawlessness in modern Russia has its roots in Russian culture and Orthodox values, which 'long pre-date the [1917] Revolution'.[10]

But this is not the only way of explaining the obvious differences between Russia and the west. Another approach invokes the vast expanses of Russia, even European Russia, in comparison to the relatively small land areas of European states, and explains the attributes reviewed above by reference to the differences in soil productivity, the problems of state formation over such a large area, and the challenge to the development of unified markets under conditions of high transportation and communication costs. L. V. Milov, for instance, sees such geographical factors as the main determinants of Russia's historical 'peculiarities' (*osobennosti*), including serfdom and communal land tenure.[11] This view is also shared by Jeffrey Sachs, who maintains that Russia's size and climate have shaped its fate. Sachs notes that

> Russia is a high-latitude country, marked by short growing seasons and an often forbidding climate. Population densities throughout Russian history have been low because food production per hectare has also tended to be low. As a result, during most of Russian history more than 90 per cent of the population lived as farmers in sparsely populated villages, producing food with very low yields. Cities were few and far between. The division of labor that depends on urban life and international trade were never dominant features of social life.[12]

This geographical view makes the differences between Russia and the west just as fundamental and unbridgeable as the cultural one; geography, presumably, cannot be changed.

A third approach takes a more sceptical view of cultures and mentalities, regarding them as artefacts, not of geography, but of underlying institutional differences. Tolstoy's 'spirit of the people', in this view, is not a deep-rooted cultural invariant, but the result of incentive structures brought about by contingent, sometimes unintended, and comparatively recent political developments. Unlike the deep and immobile cultural roots of Russian difference posited by the first view, then, and the iron

---

[9] Procaccia, *Property rights*, see pp. 1–31 for an overview of the argument.
[10] Newcity, 'Russian legal tradition', p. 45.
[11] L. V. Milov, *Velikorusskii pakhar' i osobennosti rossiiskogo istoricheskogo protsessa* (Moscow, 1998).
[12] J. Sachs, *The end of poverty: economic possibilities for our time* (New York, 2005), pp. 146–7. Geographical explanations are also discussed in D. Engerman, *Modernization from the other shore: American intellectuals and the romance of Russian development* (Cambridge, MA, 2003), esp. pp. 3–4.

geographical determinism of the second view, this third approach does not regard Russian difference as written in stone; it is historically contingent. In other words, the differences are bridgeable; there is nothing fundamental about the differences between Russia and other places. This view is, in recent historiography, associated mainly with the economic historian Alexander Gerschenkron, who attributed Russia's economic 'backwardness' to institutional constraints imposed by serfdom in the period before 1861, and then to the codification of communal land tenure in the post-reform period. According to Gerschenkron, these institutions constrained labour mobility and undermined the development of private property, which in turn hindered industrial development in the pre-revolutionary period.[13] This view was never the dominant one in the historical literature for reasons outlined below, but since Gerschenkron's death in 1978 it has even more thoroughly fallen from favour.

This book seeks to revive the institutional approach, but from a perspective not available to Gerschenkron himself, one that involves, above all, a different empirical understanding of the pre-Emancipation Russian countryside.[14] Even Gerschenkron, it will emerge, was too willing to accept the account of the pre-1861 Russian peasantry he had inherited from his predecessors – essentially the view associated above with Herzen and Tolstoy. He accepted, for instance, that Russian peasants did not engage in markets, that they had only 'very vague views of proprietary rights',[15] and that for either 'religious reasons or because of tenacity of collective memories carried over from the pre-serfdom era, the peasants regarded the land as under no human ownership ("the land is God's")'.[16] The primary flaw of the 1861 Emancipation Act, according to Gerschenkron, was its failure to introduce modern economic concepts, such as private property, into the Russian rural economy. But as we will see, such concepts were amply in evidence among the serf population before 1861, wherever there was institutional scope for them, and 1861 appears to have been not just a missed opportunity, as Gerschenkron thought, but possibly even a step *backwards* in this respect. Still, this book will make the case that

[13] A. Gerschenkron, esp. *Economic backwardness in historical perspective* (Cambridge, MA, 1962), and *Continuity in history and other essays* (Cambridge, MA, 1968).

[14] This is not meant to imply that only Gerschenkron held this view or even that he was first to express it. There were certainly critics of serfdom and the commune in pre-Emancipation Russia and, as noted in the preface, many modern-day social scientists are concerned about the role of institutions. But in the more recent Russian historiography, Gerschenkron was among the most prominent proponents of the view that rural institutions hindered industrialisation and economic development.

[15] A. Gerschenkron, 'Russia: agrarian policies and industrialization, 1861–1914', in *Continuity in history*, p. 157.

[16] *Ibid.*, p. 157.

Gerschenkron's stress on institutions as the primary determinants of Russian difference is more in accord with available evidence, especially the evidence that has come to light since his death, than the explanatory frameworks that have enjoyed the limelight for so long.

All debates on Russian economic development ultimately come back to the question of communal land tenure – the feature of Russian rural society that has widely been held to distinguish it most sharply from western rural society, and perhaps in some way to underlie all the other differences. While peasants in western Europe held their land in individual tenure, Russian peasants lived in 'repartitional communes', where arable land was held in collective tenure by the community and allocated to member households on the basis of their production capabilities and consumption needs. The amount of land allocated to a household was supposed to be adjusted, or 'repartitioned', in response to life cycle changes. When a son married and brought his wife into the household, additional land was allocated to it by the commune. When an adult male died, land was taken away and allocated to a household whose labour force had grown. This communal allocation of land is supposed to have enabled peasant households to balance their land and labour requirements without the use of markets. Herzen, like many of his contemporaries, thought the land commune would enable Russia to avoid the sort of 'proletarianisation' experienced in England and Europe during industrialisation,[17] by making it possible for Russian peasants to remain self-sufficient. There was no need to engage in labour markets, since allotments were adjusted in accordance with household size, and there was no need to engage in land markets, as land was provided to all. Furthermore, communal allotments could not be sold by individual households, making it very difficult for a peasant to cut his ties to the land. Even if a peasant were to leave the commune temporarily to work elsewhere, he was supposed to have retained his rights to a share of the communal land. As a result of such practices, wrote Herzen, 'a rural proletariat was not possible'.[18] Moreover, because the land was held communally and all member households were, in principle, entitled to some portion, he saw this system as more egalitarian than that found in western Europe. The repartitional commune, he argued, provided peasants with a guaranteed minimum subsistence. In Herzen's words, the 'economic principle of the commune

---

[17] A. Herzen, 'O sel'skoi obshchine v Rossii', in *Sochineniia v deviati tomakh* (Moscow, 1956).

[18] *Ibid.*, p. 509. This strongly echoes the view of Haxthausen, as discussed in T. K. Dennison and A. W. Carus, 'The invention of the Russian rural commune: Haxthausen and the evidence', *Historical Journal* 46, 3 (2003), pp. 561–82.

[was] entirely at odds with the renowned views of Malthus: the commune extended to everyone, without exception, a place at its table'.[19]

Gerschenkron can hardly be blamed for accepting this account, especially of the pre-Emancipation Russian peasantry, because it was accepted by just about everyone else. It was hardly questioned; it had acquired the status (which it still maintains, to a surprising degree) of a set of hard stylised facts, taken for granted as the starting point of any inquiry. One of the aims of this book is to question this mythical peasant culture, which sets the economic, social, and demographic behaviour of peasants apart from that of other groups in a society. Such an apparently narrow focus, in a book devoted to the entire institutional structure of pre-Emancipation Russia, becomes more easily comprehensible as a response to the thoroughgoing institutional reductionism prevalent among historians who follow in the footsteps of Tolstoy's 'cultural' approach to Russian rural society.[20] Major components of the pre-Emancipation institutional structure, even including serfdom itself, are often brushed aside as, in the words of one historian, 'merely something draped over an ecology, a demographic regime or social order, a thin, translucent cover sufficient only to distort our view of the inner workings of Russian peasant society'.[21] To understand the role and workings of the commune within the overall institutional configuration of Russian serf society before 1861, we must first understand the degree to which nearly all empirical work to date on this period has been deeply coloured by the 'Peasant Myth', as it will be referred to henceforth. The task of freeing ourselves from the grip of this nineteenth-century ideology, and gaining a more empirical perspective on the institutional configuration of this society, requires certain very specific kinds of evidence, and a very specific approach to them. In the two sections that follow, this myth and a method for addressing it are highlighted in turn.

1.1   The Peasant Myth

The overwhelming popularity of Tolstoy's and Herzen's cultural explanation of Russian difference has deep roots in nineteenth-century debates about land reform and the organisation of rural society in the post-Emancipation period. The new legal framework created by the Emancipation Act of 1861 was designed to preserve the Russian peasant

---

[19] Herzen, 'O sel'skoi obshchine v Rossii', p. 508.
[20] See, for instance, the discussion below on the cultural determinism implicit in the work of the 'moral economy' school of peasant studies.
[21] S. L. Hoch, 'The serf economy and the social order in Russia', in M. L. Bush (ed.), *Serfdom and slavery: studies in legal bondage* (London and New York, 1996), p. 311.

commune, which was seen by many reformers as an organic institution with a long history.[22] The authors of the Act assumed, like Herzen (and perhaps partly due to his influence), that Russian peasant society before Emancipation had been organised around the commune, essentially as Herzen had described it. Its functions included the allocation of communal resources among member households, the provision of relief for the indigent, and the administration of justice on the basis of communal customs and norms. Worried that these institutions, perceived as ancient and deeply rooted in peasant culture, might break down as a result of Emancipation, the authors of the Act decided to turn the commune into a formal legal entity, on which they conferred many of the powers granted previously to landlords.[23] This codification of communal institutions was designed to ensure that the integration of former serfs into market society was a gradual process. By retaining organic peasant institutions such as the commune, the authors of the Act hoped to avoid the 'proletarianisation' that had characterised agrarian reform in western Europe.[24]

Since 1861, the terms of the Act and its impact on various aspects of Russian rural society have been hotly debated by historians and other social scientists. Even before the Act came into existence, its terms had been passionately thrashed out in the Russian press. Reformers across the political spectrum, though they disagreed about the pace at which changes should be made to the rural constitution, had uniformly discouraged too sudden a disruption to the existing communal order and communal ownership.[25] 'Everything we see, hear, and know in our villages rests on this principle', was a typical claim, 'Its abolition would require a transformation of nearly the whole of Russia.'[26] The outpouring of opinion from all

---

[22] C. Goehrke, *Die Theorien über Entstehung und Entwicklung des 'Mir'* (Wiesbaden, 1964); J. von Keussler, *Zur Geschichte und Kritik des bäuerlichen Gemeindebesitzes in Rußland*, 3 vols. (Riga, Moscow, and Odessa, 1876–87), vol. I; S. G. Pushkarev, *Krest'ianskaia pozemel'no-peredel'naia obshchina v Rossii* (repr. Newtonville, MA, 1976); V. I. Semevksii, *Krest'ianskii vopros v Rossii v XVIII v pervoi polovine XIX veka* (St Petersburg, 1888).

[23] See the discussion in C. Gaudin, *Ruling peasants: village and state in late imperial Russia* (DeKalb, IL, 2007).

[24] T. Emmons, *The Russian landed gentry and the peasant Emancipation of 1861* (Cambridge, 1968), p. 55; D. Saunders, *Russia in the age of reaction and reform, 1801–1881* (London, 1992), pp. 226–30.

[25] This is not to imply there were no dissenting voices. The liberal 'westernisers', the most renowned of whom is probably Chicherin, were vocally opposed to the retention of communal land tenure; e.g. G. M. Hamburg, 'Peasant emancipation and Russian social thought: the case of B. N. Chicherin', *Slavic Review* 50 (1991), pp. 890–904. But this group lost the debate, whose somewhat mysterious course is the subject of my current research.

[26] A. Koshelev in his commentary on an article by the Slavophile Beliaev of 1856, quoted by Keussler, *Gemeindebesitz*, vol. I, p. 114.

quarters on this subject in 1857–9,[27] though, was characterised by an almost complete absence of empirical evidence. Johannes von Keussler, surveying this literature in the 1870s, regretted that 'it completely lacks *any basis in positive facts*. In great detail and sleep-inducing repetition, the same abstract arguments [on both sides] are brought forward again and again … But there are no *facts* on the basis of which a judgment could be formed about what the effects of communal ownership, especially the economic ones, really are.'[28]

The status of the rural commune was one of the central questions in Russian politics between 1861 and 1917. Lenin himself notoriously weighed in with his anti-populist book of 1899 on *The development of capitalism in Russia*, as well as a number of later analyses that targeted the programme of the Socialist-Revolutionary Party, which repaid him and other Bolsheviks in kind. Once again, all sides in these vituperative, and not terribly fact-oriented, debates took for granted that the institutional framework codified by the Emancipation Act had existed throughout rural Russia before 1861. Indeed, this is still taken for granted, more than a century after Lenin's book. The evidence for the nature and role of communal institutions in the pre-Emancipation Russian countryside remains largely unexamined. As B. N. Mironov has pointed out, much of the enormous literature on the rural commune is focused on some specific aspect of communal life, such as land repartition or *krugovaia poruka* (collective responsibility for taxes and dues), rather than the broader context in which communes were situated.[29] Without knowledge of this larger institutional context, it is impossible to form a just appraisal of the impact of the Emancipation Act on Russian society. And without evidence for the nature of the *status quo ante*, we are in no position to say what the 1861 Act actually changed.

This book will argue that we still have only very limited information about pre-1861 Russian rural institutions; the knowledge that has almost universally been taken for granted consists largely of a politically convenient nineteenth-century myth and rests on very little solid evidence.[30] The book is an attempt to begin filling this void by providing some positive evidence for one particular region of rural Russia, and, on the basis of this evidence, sketching an account of the rural institutional framework, which might provide a kind of benchmark to which future studies of

---

[27] *Ibid.*, pp. 113–81.   [28] *Ibid.*, p. 143.

[29] B. N. Mironov, 'The peasant commune after the reforms of the 1860s', in B. Eklof and S. Frank (eds.), *The world of the Russian peasant: post-Emancipation culture and society* (Boston, 1990), p. 33 (n. 4).

[30] Dennison and Carus, 'The invention'.

other regions can index their findings. No claim for definitiveness would be appropriate in such a first attempt, especially in a country as huge and regionally differentiated as imperial Russia. This study is intended, rather, to make a beginning, in the hope that further studies of other regions can complement, complicate, and possibly even refute the findings reported here.

Still, it is reasonable to ask whether long-held views of the Russian peasantry can be discredited on the basis of a single local study. The answer to this question has two sides: first, in the remainder of this section, to show that the Peasant Myth, despite its venerable pedigree, has no solid empirical foundation; second, in the following section, to understand how a local study can be brought to bear microcosmically on larger and more general questions about the structure of Russian rural society.

To call something a myth that generations of social thinkers, legislators, scholars, historians, and literary figures have believed is, admittedly, to make a strong claim. Yet the political motivations of the Peasant Myth, in its first incarnation, were as clear as the evidence for it was flimsy. The Peasant Myth was not a folk tradition; it was imported to Russia from outside by the tsarist government. It was formulated in the 1840s by a German Romantic social writer, August von Haxthausen, a Catholic nobleman known up to then mainly as a favourite of the Prussian crown prince (later Wilhelm IV) and the Prussian agrarian conservatives. His writings had argued for the preservation of traditional forms of ownership and customary law. He was invited to travel through rural Russia by the tsar, in the hopes he would write a book to counter the negative propaganda of the Marquis de Custine[31] and give a positive spin to rural institutions then still widely regarded in the west as barbaric and reactionary. In this public relations project, the tsar's government succeeded beyond its wildest hopes.[32] Haxthausen's book not only gave a vivid picture of a country largely unknown to western Europeans (or even to educated Russians), but glorified the Russian village commune as an ideal for the rest of the world.[33] According to Haxthausen, Russia had no need of Saint-Simon or other utopian schemes, as its existing rural society already realised the ideals expressed in such utopias. He saw in the Russian peasantry the simplicity and integrity he thought northern Germany was in danger of losing to western-style industrialisation and urbanisation, and he wished

---

[31] Whose book *Russia in 1839* (also called *Letters from Russia*) was published in 1843, though rumours of its likely contents circulated in Russia before this date.

[32] P. Blickle, *Kommunalismus: Skizzen einer gesellschaftlichen Organisationsform*, 2 vols. (Munich, 2000).

[33] More details on Haxthausen's trip and his book can be found in Dennison and Carus, 'The invention'.

to save the Russian countryside from a fate like Germany's. His book was received with great enthusiasm by Russian intellectuals across the political spectrum, from Slavophiles like Aksakov to Socialists like Herzen, who welcomed it for widely different, indeed incompatible, reasons.[34] None paused to note the slender basis of evidence on which Haxthausen's wide-ranging claims rested. Though he had spent more than a year in Russia, Haxthausen had only been on serf estates for a few days during that time. He knew no Russian, relied on interpreters for all his information, was under constant government surveillance (unbeknownst to him), and had come to Russia with a strong predisposition to find there precisely the institutions he already associated, before his trip, with a primordial 'Slavic' village settlement and property-holding pattern he had previously projected on to parts of Germany – though he had been able to find no more than anecdotal evidence for them there, either.[35] Because his story was so convenient to so many different political programmes in Russia, though, it was in no one's interest to subject Haxthausen's theory of rural institutions to even the most superficial cross-examination. A hard set of stylised facts had been launched into circulation. This new stylised account of the Russian peasantry quickly displaced an earlier tradition of Russian writing about rural society, exemplified by the *Encyclopédie*-inspired St Petersburg Free Economic Society.[36] In this way, the publication of Haxthausen's book represents a major discontinuity. Herzen would later remark that 'it took a German to discover the Russia of the people, which before him was as unknown as America before Columbus'.[37]

The Peasant Myth did not remain confined to a small group of social and political commentators. It soon became a central preoccupation among Russian literary figures. Haxthausen's book was avidly discussed among the dissident intellectuals of the Petrashevsky Circle in St Petersburg; Dostoevsky, for instance, thought it very important.[38] The best-known literary manifestation of the Peasant Myth is to be found, as we have seen, in the writings of Tolstoy,[39] whence it reached a western audience far larger than Haxthausen's book had ever had. Its acceptance among literary figures, though very widespread, was not universal. I. A. Goncharov's

---

[34] Goehrke, *Theorien*, pp. 23–5, 29–41.

[35] Dennison and Carus, 'The invention', pp. 566–7.

[36] M. Confino, *Domaines et seigneurs en Russie vers la fin du XVIIIe siècle: études de structure agraires et de mentalités économiques* (Paris, 1963), esp. chapter 1.

[37] Quoted by Goehrke, *Theorien*, p. 25.

[38] J. Frank, *Dostoevsky: the seeds of revolt, 1821–1849* (Princeton, 1976), pp. 255–6.

[39] Konstantin Lieven (*Anna Karenina*) is the most obvious mouthpiece for this view. But in other novels, too – e.g.*War and Peace*, or *A Landlord's Morning* – Tolstoy portrayed Russian peasants as exemplars of a better and more harmonious life than any model available under western capitalism.

depiction, in his novel *Oblomov* (1859), for instance, of the (superficially) idyllic village of Oblomovka can be viewed as savage parody of an idealisation that had by then become commonplace.

Meanwhile, events moved swiftly, and the Emancipation Act had made irrelevant (at least as an issue of current politics) the question whether, in fact, rural institutions before 1861 had corresponded to the Peasant Myth. It is entirely possible that the Act itself had the effect of bringing about a rural society that corresponded more closely to the Peasant Myth than what had existed before 1861, especially as the provisions of the Act were motivated by the desire to 'preserve' institutions associated with the Peasant Myth.[40] But this question is beyond the scope of the present study, whose focus is confined to Russian rural institutions before 1861. Those institutions continued to be implicitly discussed in accounts of the Peasant Myth in the later nineteenth century, though, which almost uniformly assumed that the rural commune of that period originated in, and was substantially unchanged from, a much earlier time. This was especially true of the views among traditionalist Slavophile intellectuals and the growing populist movement. N. G. Chernyshevsky, one of the leading figures in the latter,[41] was an ardent supporter of the idea that the ancient, organically grown rural commune (the *obshchina*, as the Populists called it) could provide the basis for a special Russian path to socialism that avoided the violence and class struggle of western revolutionary movements. He also published the first extracts from Haxthausen's book to appear in Russian translation.[42]

Populism largely died out after its suppression in the wake of the populist-inspired assassination of Alexander II in 1881. Its ideas remained alive, though, and were transmitted directly to the Socialist-Revolutionary Party that revived in the late 1890s under the leadership of Viktor Chernov.[43] This party increasingly became the Bolsheviks' foremost political competition, and thus maintained, in contrast to Lenin, a strong emphasis on the peasant commune as the basis for future 'socialisation' of the land. Lenin's polemic, and the thrust of his argument that capitalism had undermined the traditional commune, was directed mainly against the

[40] The implications of this are the subject of Corinne Gaudin's illuminating study *Ruling peasants*.

[41] F. Venturi, *Roots of revolution: a history of the populist and socialist movements in nineteenth-century Russia* (Chicago, 1960); I. Berlin, 'Russian Populism', in his *Russian thinkers* (London and New York, 1978), pp. 216–37.

[42] W. Bobke, 'August von Haxthausen: eine Studie zur Ideengeschichte der politischen Romantik', unpublished Ph.D. dissertation (Munich, 1954), p. 237.

[43] M. Perrie, *The agrarian policy of the Russian Social-Revolutionary Party from its origins through the revolution of 1905–1907* (Cambridge, 1976), Part I, 'From Populism to the SR party (1881–1901)'.

platform of this party.[44] Both sides in this struggle shared the assumption that the Peasant Myth best described Russian rural society before 1861, but the Socialist Revolutionaries naturally emphasised it more, as they stood for less centralisation and a greater degree of continuity than the Bolsheviks. However, they were also severely weakened by the Stolypin reform programme (begun in 1906), which they had strongly opposed because it undermined the basis of the repartitional commune as it had existed since 1861.[45]

The most influential restatement of the Peasant Myth for later historians, however, was made by the Russian agronomist A. V. Chayanov in his theory of peasant economy. Chayanov argued that standard economic assumptions were not applicable to peasants, since peasants were not integrated into markets and could therefore not calculate costs and benefits in terms of money. Because all labour inputs on the peasant farm were provided by household members, peasants were 'unacquainted with the categories of wage labour and wages'.[46] And since 'there [was] no social phenomenon of wages, the social phenomenon of profit [was] also absent. Thus, it [was] impossible to apply the capitalist profit calculation.'[47] Instead, peasants had to calculate net benefit in qualitative terms, directly comparing the proceeds of their crop with the disutility of physical labour:

It is obvious that with the increase in produce obtained by hard work, the subjective valuation of each newly gained rouble's significance for consumption decreases, but the drudgery of working for it which will demand an ever greater amount of self-exploitation will increase ... As soon as the equilibrium point is reached continuing work becomes pointless ... Farm size and composition and the urgency of its demands determine the consumption evaluation ... The significance of each rouble of gross income for consumption is increased in a household burdened with members incapable of work. This makes for increased self-exploitation of family labour power ... Thus the objective arithmetical calculation of the highest possible net profit in the given market situation does not determine the whole activity of the family unit: this is done by the internal confrontation of *subjective evaluations*.[48]

For Chayanov the 'family economy' meant that the traditional rationality assumptions of classical economics were not valid for peasants. Peasants did not maximise profits, but sought other things, like security; their

---

[44] E. Kingston-Mann, *Lenin and the problem of Marxist peasant revolution* (Oxford, 1983), pp. 77–9.

[45] Perrie, *Agrarian policy*, pp. 177–84.

[46] A. V. Chayanov, *The theory of peasant economy*, ed. D. Thorner, B. Kerblay, and R. E. F. Smith (Homewood, IL, 1966), p. 1.

[47] *Ibid.*, p. 5.

[48] Chayanov, quoted by Kerblay in T. Shanin (ed.), *Peasants and peasant societies* (Oxford, 1987), p. 179; also in Chayanov, *Theory of peasant economy*, pp. 6–7.

aversion to risk and work effort dominated their desire to increase money income so as to increase consumption of market goods. Peasants were, in short, differently rational from participants in urban or industrial economies, where market transactions were more common. In this way Chayanov characterised peasant rationality in very much the same terms as those employed in the traditional Peasant Myth of Haxthausen and the Populists.[49]

Among Russian scholars, Chayanov fell out of favour because his theory contradicted Lenin's insistence on the capitalist character of post-1861 agriculture. (Indeed, Chayanov himself fell afoul of the regime, and was censored, imprisoned, and executed.) After 1930, his writings, even his name, were off limits for Soviet historians. Nonetheless, they were unable, despite their fundamentally different orientation, to overcome the Peasant Myth. There were two probable reasons for this. First, they were forced to adhere to a narrow interpretation of Lenin's theory of pre-1861 development, which consigned that period to the category of 'feudalism'. For them, as for Lenin, feudalism largely excluded the involvement of peasants in markets, and was thus at least consistent with the Peasant Myth. Second, they were not permitted to confront the Chayanov–Haxthausen or the Socialist-Revolutionary versions of the Peasant Myth openly and directly. Lenin's view was the established one, and no subsequent refutation of Socialist-Revolutionary ideology was considered necessary or desirable, so the target of Lenin's diatribe was simply ignored.

After 1945, historians and development economists in Europe and the United States discovered Chayanov, and in this way the Peasant Myth reached what will probably remain the zenith of its worldwide influence. During the 1950s it was believed that Chayanov's theory of a separate 'peasant economics' applied not just to Russian peasants but to all peasantries everywhere, including those in sub-Saharan Africa, in Southeast Asia, and in pre-industrial Europe. (This is somewhat ironic, given that the original version of this view, as put forth by Herzen and his contemporaries, was intended to *distinguish* the Russian peasantry from others.) Within development economics, this idea, though not entirely

---

[49] This is perhaps not surprising when one considers that Chayanov, like Haxthausen, Herzen, and other Russian intellectuals, was strongly influenced by German Romanticism. He, too, spent some part of his student years in Germany. And, in addition to his work in agronomy, he wrote a number of Romantic novellas in the style of E. T. A. Hoffmann. More information on the life and work of Chayanov can be found in the Chayanov archive in the Russian State Archive of the Economy (RGAE) in Moscow. His novellas and other early manuscripts were shown recently (2004) at an RGAE exhibition. On the German influence, see F. Bourgholtzer, *Aleksandr Chayanov and Russian Berlin* (London and New York, 1999).

abandoned even now, began to fall out of favour in the 1960s after attempts at policy based on these ideas failed, and a new approach, pioneered by T. W. Schultz, began to take hold.[50] Within the historiography of pre-industrial Europe, it was a slower process, but here, too, the Peasant Myth has been receding from its once-dominant position. But however clearly historians of Europe may realise that the Peasant Myth (at least in its Haxthausen–Chayanov form) does not apply to their countries in the past, it is even now still thought that the Chayanovian formulation holds true for Russia, the society on which Chayanov's theory was based. For example, a recently published book on late medieval English agrarian society notes that those aspects of Chayanov's theory – such as the absence of rural land and labour markets – which cannot be applied to pre-industrial England are still relevant to pre-revolutionary rural Russia.[51]

Still, this approach, in its Chayanovian formulation, though not nearly as dominant as it was in its post-war heyday, was not discarded altogether by those working on non-Russian societies. It evolved into a newer version of the cultural approach, based on the fundamental (Chayanovian) assumption that peasant rationality is different from that of people in modern, market societies. This assumption is, for instance, at the basis of the widely held 'moral economy' view, put forward by James C. Scott in the 1970s.[52] The moral economy view was explicitly presented as an extension of Chayanov's theory of the peasant.[53] Like Chayanov, Scott maintains that 'the peasant household has little scope for the profit maximization calculus of traditional neoclassical economics'.[54] Because the peasant farmer lives 'close to the subsistence margin and [is] subject to the vagaries of weather and the claims of outsiders', he seeks to minimise risk rather than maximise profit; this, in Scott's view, is what distinguishes him from the capitalist farmer. According to Scott, 'the peasant cultivator seeks to avoid the failure that will ruin him rather than attempting a big, risky killing'.[55] The moral economy of the peasant is based on what Scott calls the 'subsistence ethic', or the notion that all members of the community have a 'right to subsistence'. On this view, the 'subsistence ethic' is the operating principle behind the collectivist risk-minimisation strategies we observe in

---

[50] T. W. Schultz, *Transforming traditional agriculture* (New Haven, 1964). Chapter 2, especially, addresses the problems of cultural approaches to questions of agricultural development. On separate 'peasant' economic sectors and the shortcomings of this approach, see I. M. D. Little, *Economic development: theory, policy, and international relations* (New York, 1982), esp. pp. 86–97, 104–7.

[51] J. Whittle, *The development of agrarian capitalism: land and labour in Norfolk, 1440–1580* (Oxford, 2000), pp. 88, 92–7.

[52] J. C. Scott, *The moral economy of the peasant: rebellion and subsistence in Southeast Asia* (New Haven, 1976).

[53] *Ibid.*, esp. chapter 1.   [54] *Ibid.*, p. 4.   [55] *Ibid.*, p. 4.

pre-industrial societies. Scott himself uses the Russian commune as an example. 'The right to subsistence', he says, 'took concrete form ... in the practice of the Russian *mir* whose members redistributed land at regular intervals in accordance with family size.'[56] This view was subsequently adopted by historians of the Russian peasantry. Mironov has recently argued that 'the right to a minimum level of subsistence' was one of the 'principles of communal life' in rural Russia.[57] Peasants, he maintained, 'valued stability over efficiency, and reliability over progress'.[58] J. Pallot notes that in Russian peasant studies 'the emphasis is on survival strategies, risk minimization, and the primacy in peasant motivation of securing household and community reproduction. These contrast with the profit-maximizing, risk-taking behaviours that, with industrial advance, began to dominate urban society in the second half of the nineteenth century.'[59]

A new component of the Peasant Myth in this recent version is that it does not merely fail, as Chayanov does, to provide a model of change over time or in response to external forces, but actually adopts a stance of cultural determinism: the distinct peasant rationality it discerns in certain societies is the fundamental basis or determinant of social, economic, demographic, and political behaviour. This new stance is possibly due to the fact that this most recent version is largely the work of anthropologists, such as Scott and Eric Wolf. The new view neatly (though never, it seems, quite explicitly) inverts Marx's notion that economic relations form the basis of social, political, and cultural formations, which are regarded as 'superstructure' to that basis. The 'moral economy' version of the Peasant Myth regards *institutions* as superstructure, and the effects of landlords' policies on social and economic behaviour as negligible. In this view, peasant behaviour is not seen as a response to particular institutional constraints, but as an expression of certain underlying universal, cultural norms. This is made quite explicit in the moral economy version, where peasant revolts, for instance, are regarded as desperate attempts to defend traditional society against encroaching urbanisation and marketisation.[60]

The notion of a special peasant culture, largely impervious to external constraints, has been taken for granted by historians of pre-Emancipation Russia. And, in the spirit of the moral economy version of the Peasant Myth, this culture is taken as the fundamental basis for all social and economic behaviour in the society. This has important implications for

---

[56] *Ibid.*, p. 177.
[57] B. N. Mironov, *Sotsial'naia istoriia Rossii perioda imperii (XVIII–nachalo XX v.)*, 2 vols. (St Petersburg, 1999), vol. I, p. 453.
[58] *Ibid.*, p. 455.   [59] J. Pallot, *Land reform in Russia, 1906–1917* (Oxford, 1999), p. 16.
[60] E. Wolf, *Peasants* (Englewood Cliffs, NJ, 1966), pp. 106–9; Scott, *The moral economy*, pp. 10–11, and chapters 5 and 7.

the study of serfdom in pre-revolutionary Russia, since, in this framework, serfdom is viewed as superstructure, which had very little effect on the 'underlying' peasant culture. In the words of the historian Daniel Field:

> Peasant custom determined the configuration of the village and the fields and the phases of the cycle of cultivation; it dictated the choice of crops and of tools, for the plows, sickles, carts, and horses all belonged to the peasants. The most important characteristic of the estate was the insignificance of the proprietor's imprint on the pattern of life and work.[61]

Similarly, Steven Hoch has argued that the institution of serfdom was merely 'draped over' an underlying peasant culture, of familism and patriarchy, which were more significant to the development (or under-development) of the Russian rural economy than serfdom. Serfdom, he maintains, came and went, and left the peasant economy much as it had always been.[62] A modified version of this view has been put forward for certain other serf societies. For example, Andrejs Plakans and Charles Weatherell have argued, in their work on the Baltic estate of Pinkenhof, that serfs had a great deal of autonomy within the feudal framework, and were thus able to pursue their own 'moral economy' objectives, despite the constraints imposed by landlords.[63] A similar view exists in work on central European societies that experienced the 'second serfdom'.[64]

Still, for all these applications of the Peasant Myth in its myriad forms to other serf societies and present-day peasant populations, its home turf remains Russia, its country of origin; the Russian peasantry before 1861 is still the classical case. A study of this case is therefore optimally positioned to grasp the Peasant Myth by the roots. But casting doubt on its origins is not enough to pull it up. Subversive genealogy gives us a certain amount of leverage, but only the accumulation of empirical evidence can ulti-mately do the job. The following section will discuss the kinds of evidence and the method that can best be applied to, and adjudicate among, the three rather vaguely formulated alternative approaches discussed above: cultural, geographical, and institutional.

The outcomes to be explained are the observed differences between Russian and western rural societies, as well as among different Russian

---

[61] D. Field, *The end of serfdom: nobility and bureaucracy in Russia, 1855–1861* (Cambridge, MA, 1976), p. 22.

[62] *Ibid.*, pp. 311–22.

[63] A. Plakans and C. Weatherell, 'Family and economy on an early nineteenth-century Baltic serf estate', in R. Rudolph (ed.), *The European peasant family and society* (Liverpool, 1995), pp. 165–87.

[64] See the discussion of this 'communal autonomy' view in S. C. Ogilvie, 'Communities and the second serfdom in early modern Bohemia', *Past and Present* 187 (2005), esp. pp. 73–4.

localities, during the pre-Emancipation period. So the kind of evidence we need is twofold. First, we need to get a better picture of what differences between Russia and the west are in fact observable. Given the above account of the origins of the Peasant Myth, it would be unwise to begin with the assumption that this view can be regarded as a reliable guide to what might actually be observable when we go into archives to have a look. We need independent evidence from that provided by this long tradition. But that is only a beginning. We also want evidence, secondly, that can be brought to bear on the appraisal of the cultural, geographical, and institutional accounts of whatever differences are revealed by that first sort of evidence.

This is not as straightforward as it might sound. Not only are the three approaches, as described above, rather vague; they are also not as easy to distinguish as might appear. In fact, none of the three approaches entirely neglects the other two considerations; the differences among them are mainly a matter of emphasis and intersubordination. Culture, geography, and institutions are each, respectively, regarded as fundamental, while the other two are seen, in each case, as having a subordinate place within a complete explanation.

The present book follows this same pattern. It takes its inspiration and starting point from the recent work of development economists and economic historians persuaded that institutions are the fundamental determinants of social and economic outcomes,[65] and makes no pretence of treating the three kinds of explanation with disinterested impartiality. It fully acknowledges that culture and geography had important roles to play, but its goal is to push the institutional approach to its limits, i.e. to explain as much as possible of what is observed on the basis of institutions, without reference to culture or geography. The concluding chapter will return to a more detailed consideration of the respective merits and short-comings of the cultural and geographical approaches compared to the institutional approach.

1.2   Why a local study?

One reason for the survival of the Peasant Myth is the difficulty of studying the institutional structure of past rural societies. Even as institutions have

---

[65] A wide spectrum of such work is represented in such collections as J. Drobak and J. Nye (eds.), *The frontiers of the new institutional economics* (San Diego and London, 1997); J. Knight and I. Sened, *Explaining social institutions* (Ann Arbor, 1995); and C. Ménard and M. Shirley, *Handbook of new institutional economics* (Berlin, 2008). Serviceable overviews, now a bit dated, are to be found in T. Eggertsson, *Economic behavior and institutions* (Cambridge, 1990), and M. Rutherford, *Institutions in economics: the old and the new institutionalism* (Cambridge, 1994).

made a comeback in development economics and economic history, there is little agreement over how to study them. The method dominant among empirical economists has been the cross-country regression model. While the resulting studies have shown that a certain combination of institutions makes a significant difference to long-run growth, the drawback of this method, as Rohini Pande and Christopher Udry point out in their review of this literature,[66] is that it provides no way to refine or explain these findings. The comparable institution measures used are too coarse (and too biased to the urban and formal sector of what are often largely rural and informal economies) to bring the study of institutions beyond this extremely vague and general finding to the more interesting question of exactly which features of what institutions result in what kinds of social and economic outcomes.[67] Pande and Udry suggest that

---

[66]   R. Pande and C. Udry, 'Institutions and development: a view from below', in R. Blundell, W. K. Newey, and T. Persson (eds.), *Advances in economics and econometrics: theory and applications, Ninth World Congress* (Cambridge, 2006), vol. II, pp. 349–412. The five 'core papers' they cite (pp. 352–3) as having established the cross-country method are D. Acemoglu, S. Johnson, and J. A. Robinson, 'The colonial origins of comparative development: an empirical investigation', *American Economic Review* 91 (2001), pp. 1369–401; R. E. Hall and C. I. Jones, 'Why do some countries produce so much more output per worker than others?', *Quarterly Journal of Economics* 114 (1999), pp. 83–116; S. Knack and P. Keefer, 'Institutions and economic performance: cross-country tests using alternative institutional measures', *Economics and Politics* 7 (1995), pp. 207–27; R. La Porta, F. Lopez-de Silanes, A. Schleifer, and R. Vishny, 'The quality of government', *Journal of Law, Economics, and Organization* 15 (1999), pp. 222–79; and P. Mauro, 'Corruption and growth', *Quarterly Journal of Economics* 110 (1995), pp. 681–712.

[67]   Pande and Udry also detail a number of other serious problems with this literature; most tellingly, in the present context, what they say about Africa applies *a fortiori* to almost any pre-modern society: 'A common distinction in the cross-country institutions literature has been between political institutions (as measured by, say, expropriation risk) and institutions which determine contractual form (as measured by, say, legal origins). However, the real world is much more complicated, and in particular, this distinction is treacherous when considering land rights in Africa. Indigenous tenure principles are implemented and arbitrated by authorities (chiefs, lineage heads, elders) whose legitimacy is typically drawn from a local political process. Their authority over land allocation is political power, since it enables them to give or refuse a farmer the right to cultivate or to settle . . . Thus, political and contractual institutions seem to be fundamentally intertwined for land tenure processes in Africa. Importantly, the nature of such intertwining varies significantly across countries. This again suggests heterogeneity in the effect of institutions across countries . . . We conclude that the extraordinary diversity of institutional practices across and within countries places natural constraints on the usefulness of cross-country analyses for understanding the specific channels through which institutions affect economic outcomes, and how these institutions, in turn, respond to economic, demographic, political, and social forces.' Pande and Udry, 'Institutions and development', pp. 377–8. See also D. Acemoglu, 'Constitutions, politics, and economics', *Journal of Economic Literature* 43 (2005), pp. 1025–48, as well as J. C. Brown and T. Guinnane, 'Regions and time in the European fertility transition: problems in the Princeton Project's statistical methodology', *Economic History Review* 60 (2007), pp. 574–95, on the pitfalls and limitations of cross-sectional regressions in this particular application.

only an approach from 'below' – from the micro-level – can bring further progress.

Among historians, historical anthropologists, and historical sociologists, there is even less agreement on the right approach for answering questions of this kind, only islands of consensus among like-minded practitioners of particular research programmes. For a well-studied, relatively small country, with easily accessible archives, like early modern England, such pluralism can be stimulating, as research done from different perspectives can sometimes be pieced together into a more or less coherent account. Those working within one programme can often arrive at some way of triangulating on the results of other programmes and thus relating them meaningfully to their own framework. This can lead to genuine competition among research programmes, as each is to some degree able to judge the results reached by others, and to gauge their usefulness or fruitfulness in answering its own questions by its own standards.

It is this convergence among different research traditions that led, eventually, to a widespread rejection of the Peasant Myth as a way of explaining the behaviour of medieval and early modern English villagers. Empirical research, especially associated with the Cambridge Group for the History of Population and Social Structure, undermined the belief – present in the work of Henry Maine, as well as in Marx, Maitland, and other nineteenth-century researchers, and still widespread in the twentieth century – that English villagers before the industrial revolution possessed not just a different culture, different resource constraints, and different technologies from present-day English people, but a different rationality altogether. In a number of other European countries, a similar confluence among research traditions has led to the gradual discrediting of the Peasant Myth as a key to the explanation of their pre-industrial pasts, especially in the Netherlands, in France, and in parts of Germany.[68]

For Russia, the dominant research programme underlying most research on the rural economy over the past century has been largely based on the Peasant Myth, and is therefore not suitable for subjecting the myth itself to empirical scrutiny. Furthermore, the existing research is mostly of an unsuitable nature to yield such a test, even if there were agreement on methods and research programmes. Most existing studies of the Russian peasantry (in both Russian and English) are large-scale studies based on cross-sectional data for a substantial number of different

---

[68] See, for instance, J. de Vries, *The Dutch rural economy in the golden age* (New Haven, 1974); P. T. Hoffman, *Growth in a traditional society: the French countryside 1450–1815* (Princeton, 1996); S. Ogilvie, *State corporatism and proto-industry: the Württemberg Black Forest 1580–1797* (Cambridge, 1997).

communities. In these studies, isolated pieces of information taken from a number of different societies are aggregated and employed to address specific, usually quite narrowly focused, questions about rural society in Russia. The aim is to maximise the amount of data about the particular phenomenon being investigated. This was the approach used in the early twentieth century by Chayanov and Lenin, and in the Soviet period, by economic historians such as V. A. Fyodorov, I. D. Koval'chenko, and Yu. A. Tikhonov.[69]

This approach has not only been used to study more specifically economic phenomena. It has also been used to study institutions such as serfdom or the peasant commune. The work of K. N. Shchepetov, for instance, investigates 'serfdom on the Sheremetyev estates', using data drawn from some thirty-five Sheremetyev holdings in Russia between the years 1650 and 1861.[70] L. S. Prokof'eva also used data from numerous Sheremetyev holdings in the eighteenth and nineteenth centuries to investigate the workings of the rural commune.[71] And in what is perhaps the most comprehensive study of the rural commune in the Russian language, V. A. Aleksandrov employed data 'from over 50 landlords' estates and 500 sets of communal resolutions' covering the period from 1600 to 1850.[72]

Such large-scale cross-sectional studies, like the cross-country regressions by economists and political scientists, discussed above, have their uses. They can raise questions, and point to regularities that demand explanation. But they share the weaknesses and limitations of the cross-country regression studies. They are insensitive to any cultural variation there may be across the population whose data are aggregated; so they cannot in themselves define the boundaries of what it makes sense to call a 'given society' for the purposes of focus and relevance. At their best, they can show what is typical in a given society (provided we have some independent way of delimiting the 'given society'). In very exceptional

---

[69] Chayanov, *Theory of peasant economy*; V. I. Lenin, *The development of capitalism in Russia* (repr. Moscow, 1964); V. A. Fyodorov, *Pomeshchich'i krest'iane tsentral'no-promyshlennogo raiona Rossii kontsa XVIII–pervoi poloviny XIX v.* (Moscow, 1974); I. D. Koval'chenko, *Russkoe krepostnoe khoziastvo v pervoi polovine XIX veka* (Moscow, 1967); Yu. A. Tikhonov, *Pomeshchich'i krest'iane v Rossii: feodal'naia renta v XVII–nachale XVIII v.* (Moscow, 1974). Other examples of macro studies by Soviet historians include E. I. Indova, *Krepostnoe khoziastvo v nachale XIX veka po materialam votchinnogo arkhiva Vorontsovakh* (Moscow, 1955); L. V. Milov, *Velikorusskii pakhar' i osobennosti rossiiskogo istoricheskogo protsessa* (Moscow, 1998); N. A. Rubinshtein, *Sel'skoe khoziastvo Rossii vo vtoroi polovine XVIII v.* (Moscow, 1957); K. V. Sivkov, *Ocherki po istorii krepostnogo khoziastvo i kres'tianskogo dvizheniia v Rossii v pervoi polovine XIX veka* (Moscow, 1951).

[70] K. N. Shchepetov, *Krepostnoe pravo v votchinakh Sheremetyevykh* (Moscow, 1947).

[71] L. S. Prokof'eva, *Krest'ianskaia obshchina v Rossii vo vtoroi polovine XVIII–pervoi polovine XIX v.* (Leningrad, 1981).

[72] V. A. Aleksandrov, *Sel'skaia obshchina v Rossii, XVII–nachalo XIX vv.* (Moscow, 1976).

circumstances, where the isolated data points or variables they focus on are uniformly present over an extended time period in each of the localities being aggregated together, they can give a general sense of the development over time of the specific phenomenon of interest.

What a large-scale cross-sectional study cannot do, even at its best, is make visible the context of even a specified, narrowly defined phenomenon within the society in which it is embedded. This means that, unless an exceptionally clear pattern emerges across the communities so aggregated, the phenomenon itself remains ill-defined, since we have no *ex ante* reason to think that its context is uniform across all the communities in question. For example, we have no reason to believe that the concept of 'compulsory military service' was used uniformly across regions, landlords, classes of peasant, types of holding (e.g. state serfs vs. church serfs), and other variables. In some of these cases, military service may have been a form of social control or punishment by the landlord, in other cases it may have been a form of taxation, in others a form of currying favour with the tsar or certain military officials, and in yet others a form of population control. There is no way to know in advance which of these it might – relevantly – be in each instance. Thus the concept itself, 'compulsory military service' is quite ill-defined, until more tightly constrained by context, making it problematic to study it cross-sectionally. It might make more sense to study forms of punishment or taxation cross-sectionally, but again there is no way of knowing in advance what other institutions within an estate might be involved in such a wide-ranging category of behaviour. A more concrete example concerns arrears in feudal quitrent dues on Russian estates in the eighteenth and nineteenth centuries. This was a preoccupation of Soviet historians, a number of whom examined averages in arrears across a wide range of estates in central Russia.[73] They interpreted rising arrears in feudal dues as evidence of a crisis in agriculture, marked by rising obligations and falling standards of living for serfs. But, as we will see in later chapters, there are alternative explanations for arrears in dues. On the estate studied in these pages, some serfs allocated their income to consumer goods, such as new clothes, instead of paying their quitrent dues, inspiring the landlord to attempt to regulate the consumption habits of his serfs.[74] Such important processes are quite invisible in large-scale cross-sectional comparisons.

[73] One such example is the study by I. D. Koval'chenko and L. V. Milov, 'Ob intensivnosti obrochnoi ekspluatatsii krest'ian tsentral'noi Rossii v kontse XVIII – pervoi polovine XIX v.', *Istoriia SSSR*, 4 (1966), pp. 55–80.

[74] RGADA, f. 1287, op. 3, ed. khr. 1615 ('Decree, 1843').

Because of the shortcomings of historical data sets,[75] cross-sectional studies have tended to focus on a particular variable or phenomenon of interest, and not relate it to other possible variables. This makes it hard to advance from mere description to actual explanation. A study that focuses on a particular community, on the other hand, makes it possible to understand what role a given institution is playing in that local context. Indeed, more fundamentally, it is only on a local level, as Hans Medick has pointed out, that we can even give any concrete meaning or empirical content to abstract terms such as 'law', 'state', 'family', or 'property', let alone 'capitalism', and so on.[76] These concepts may or may not have a more precise content in our modern vernacular, but there is no *prima facie* reason to think this concept will be applicable in just that form to a given past society. In a society about which we know as little as pre-Emancipation Russia, it would be especially unrealistic to think that such abstract categories could have any meaning apart from their observed application in particular situations. And the only context in which we can indeed observe their application is at the local level, in a particular community, where we have sufficient context to understand how a market, for instance, or property institutions, are functioning.

Another advantage of a micro-historical approach to the study of institutions is that it enables us to combine quantitative and qualitative approaches.[77] In recent years, there has been increased criticism of quantitative methods in history. Quantitative studies, it has been argued, reduce human populations to 'a faceless mass without individual concerns and tastes'.[78] Instead, many scholars prefer the use of ethnographic materials, which they see as better reflections of human beings' subjective experiences, to the exclusion of quantitative methods. Such criticisms are, of course, quite justified, as we saw, in relation to many cross-sectional studies, especially those on relatively data-poor areas such as

---

[75] Pande and Udry have argued that modern cross-country regressions suffer from similar problems; the apparently reassuring homogeneity of the data on 'institutional quality' provided by organisations such as Political Risk Services and its *International country risk guide* can mask significant heterogeneity in the actual interpretation of these numbers.

[76] H. Medick, *Weben und Überleben in Laichingen, 1650–1900: Lokalgeschichte als allgemeine Geschichte* (Göttingen, 1996), pp. 20–1.

[77] This is especially true of the 'micro-exemplary' approach, as it has recently been called to distinguish it from other 'micro-historical' approaches: A. W. Carus and S. Ogilvie, 'Turning qualitative into quantitative evidence: a well-used method made explicit', *Economic History Review* 62 (2009), pp. 893–925. The present study falls squarely into the tradition of the 'well-used method' described there.

[78] C. Worobec, 'Victims or actors? Russian peasant women and patriarchy', in E. Kingston-Mann and T. Mixter (eds.), *Peasant economy, culture, and politics of European Russia, 1800–1921* (Princeton, 1991), p. 182.

Russia. But a local study can employ quantitative approaches without losing the deeper understanding brought by qualitative information about individuals. It is precisely in a local study, as Medick points out, that we can begin to understand the *interaction* between the uniquely individual experience and the typical, representative experience of the society at large – that we can see the individual in interaction with the institutions and the social context.[79]

A micro-level study is thus the ideal way to subject the Peasant Myth, or any of its components, to empirical scrutiny, since this approach aims to encompass as many aspects of the entire social, demographic, and economic context as possible, to form a picture of each institution in its overall context. This is especially important in a study of the vague abstraction known as 'serfdom'. In the past, serfdom has been approached in one of two ways. On the one hand is the macro-level, Aleksandrov-style, study of estate regulations or communal resolutions from a large number of holdings. This approach, however, captures only the juridical aspects of serfdom – it cannot tell us how these regulations actually affected economic and social life on the estate in real life. The other approach involves looking at one particular aspect of serfdom, such as rents levied on estate land or the role of the commune in estate management, across a large number of estates.[80] But whatever this may tell us about specific aspects, it says little about serfdom itself, which was not a monolithic institution, but a set of policies which varied – within bounds that only an accumulation of local studies can begin to establish – from landlord to landlord and region to region. Moreover, these landlord policies were, in each case, embedded in a larger institutional environment within a particular locality. We need to see how estate policies interacted with other local institutions if we are to understand their effects on the rural population.

Micro-history has often been criticised for focusing too narrowly on one particular community and not looking at the society as a whole. What can the history of Terling or of Kirby Lonsdale tell us about the history of England?[81] But a local study carried out in the way Medick suggests is not just a local study; it essentially studies institutions that are *not* unique to a particular community. Indeed, it is the only way to study such national or regional institutions, as we can only observe them in action at the local

[79] Medick, *Weben und Überleben*, p. 27.
[80] As in Tikhonov, *Pomeshchich'i krest'iane*; Aleksandrov, *Sel'skaia obshchina*; Prokof'eva, *Krest'ianskaia obshchina*.
[81] This kind of question was asked for instance, by G. R. Elton in 'Happy families', *New York Review of Books* (14 June 1984), pp. 39–41; see also his *Return to essentials: some reflections on the present state of historical study* (Cambridge, 1991), p. 117.

level.[82] Regional property, labour, and credit markets, national or international markets for goods, and long-distance labour migration are only some of the most obvious ways in which a tiny community interacts with the wider world, and studying it gives us a window on the entire social and economic world with which it was intertwined. In this way, a local study can, as M. M. Postan once noted, be 'microcosmic' rather than 'microscopic'.[83]

While such micro-historical approaches have been used to study a number of pre-industrial societies in England and western Europe, very little such research has so far been carried out on Russian localities. A few pioneering studies, such as those by Peter Czap and Edgar Melton, have used local evidence to examine specific aspects of Russian rural society. Czap, for instance, used evidence from household listings and parish registers for the serf estate of Mishino to test theories about household size and structure in the nineteenth century.[84] Melton has used data for the serf estate of Baki, in Kostroma province, to examine questions about the role of rural industry in the serf economy and intra-communal conflict on serf estates.[85] Rodney Bohac, too, has used local evidence, from the Manuilovskoe estate, to address questions about migration, remarriage, and military conscription.[86] Steven Hoch's work on the serf estate of

---

[82] I. de Madariaga has made a similar point with regard to the study of state policies affecting serfs and nobles under Catherine II, noting that in order to understand the implications of such policies, we need knowledge of how they were actually implemented and enforced in particular localities. See 'Catherine II and the serfs: a reconsideration of some problems', in *idem*, *Politics and culture in eighteenth-century Russia* (London, 1998), pp. 124–49.

[83] M. Postan, *Fact and relevance: essays on historical method* (Cambridge, 1971), pp. 20–21. See Carus and Ogilvie, 'Qualitative into quantitative', for a more detailed exploration of this idea.

[84] P. Czap, 'The perennial multiple-family household, Mishino, Russia, 1782–1858', *Journal of Family History* (Spring 1982), pp. 5–26.

[85] H. E. Melton, 'Proto-industrialisation, serf agriculture, and agrarian social structure: two estates in nineteenth-century Russia', *Past and Present* 115 (1987), pp. 73–87; *idem*, 'Household economies and communal conflicts on a Russian serf estate, 1800–1817', *Journal of Social History* 26 (1993), pp. 559–85; and *idem*, 'The magnate and her trading peasants: Countess Lieven and the Baki estate, 1800–1820', *Jahrbücher für Geschichte Osteuropas* 47 (1999), pp. 40–55.

[86] R. Bohac, 'Agricultural structure and the origins of migration in central Russia 1810–1850', in G. Grantham and C. S. Leonard (eds.), *Agrarian organization in the century of industrialization: Europe, Russia and North America*, Research in Economic History Supplement 5 Part B (Greenwich, CT, and London, 1989), pp. 369–88; *idem*, 'The "mir" and the military draft', *Slavic Review* 47 (1988), pp. 652–66; *idem*, 'Widows and the Russian serf community', in B. E. Clements, B. A. Engel, and C. D. Worobec (eds.), *Russia's women: accommodation, resistance, transformation* (Berkeley and Los Angeles, 1991), pp. 95–112. Much of this work derives from his more comprehensive doctoral study of Manuilovskoe estate: R. Bohac, 'Family, property, and socioeconomic mobility: Russian peasants on Manuilovskoe estate, 1810–1861', unpublished Ph.D. dissertation (University of Illinois at Champaign-Urbana, 1982).

Petrovskoe in Tambov province is a more comprehensive micro-history.[87] Hoch has used estate evidence to address questions about demographic behaviour and household structure, the role of village patriarchs, the activities of landlords and bailiffs, and forms of social control.

That so few micro-exemplary studies have been undertaken for Russia is probably at least partly due to the difficulties involved in doing archival research in the Soviet Union. It is only since the 1990s that Russian archives – federal and provincial – have been made fully accessible to foreign scholars. Until then, most foreign scholars were not even allowed unrestricted access to the archive catalogues. Furthermore, Soviet scholars had few opportunities to learn about the methodologies being used by their western colleagues. The possibilities for collaboration and exchange are of course much greater now, and the micro-historical approach is one of those which has more recently made its way to Russia, as evident in the 2004 publication of V. L. Nosevich's historical account of the Koren estate in Belorus.[88] This research builds on these pioneering works, and also expands on them, by focusing explicitly on larger questions about the institutional structure of Russian serfdom.

The source materials used in this study are for the estate of Voshchazhnikovo, a Sheremetyev family holding in Yaroslavl' province. This estate was chosen for three reasons. First, it was located in the Central Industrial Region of European Russia, rather than in the Central Black Earth Region. The best-known micro-level research for Russia, such as that of Czap and Hoch, has been undertaken for societies in the Central Black Earth region, and, as a result, many historians have assumed that the findings from these studies apply to all peasant societies in imperial Russia. Using data for an estate in another part of Russia, where there were different economic characteristics and institutional configurations, has made it possible to test this assumption. Second, the estate belonged to a landowner (the Sheremetyev family) other than the Gagarin family. The estates studied by Hoch, Czap, and Bohac were all Gagarin family holdings. An in-depth look at the way rural society functioned on a *different* landlord's estate may help to cast new light on the effects of landlords' policies and estate administration on peasant behaviour. Finally, and most importantly, the Voshchazhnikovo estate administration generated a wide variety of sources, including inventories of households (*podvornye opisi*), soul revisions (*revizskie skazki*), parish registers (*metricheskie knigi*), communal resolutions (*mirskie prigovory*), serf petitions (*proshcheniia*), landlords' instructions and decrees (*instruktsii i prikazy*), parish and communal account books (*prikhodo-rasskhodnye knigi tserkvei, mirskie prikhodo-rasskhodnye knigi*), correspondence between various branches of the Sheremetyev administration as well as between estate authorities and local government authorities (*perepiski*), reports from bailiffs and other estate officials to the Sheremetyevs (*raporty i donosheniia*), lists of serfs to whom passports were issued (*spiski pachportov*), serf wills (*zaveshchaniia*), inventories (*opisi imeniia*), and serf contracts (*dogovory*). By comparison with other estates, this is an incredibly broad range of sources. The range of documents available for the Petrovskoe estate, for example, is relatively narrow. The inventories of households (*podvornye opisi*) used by Hoch are remarkably rich in detail, as are the various estate reports, but they appear to provide little information about the internal workings of the commune, dispute resolution at the manorial level, or the larger economic context (rural factor markets, output markets, consumption). The existence of so many different types of documents for Voshchazhnikovo makes this estate ideal for an investigation into the workings of rural institutions in pre-Emancipation Russia.

The source material for Voshchazhnikovo is not, however, without its flaws. The main problem is that, although a wide array of sources exists, none spans the whole of the period under examination. We know that in some cases annual records were kept by the estate management (this was true for documents such as communal resolutions, account books of various kinds, and passport lists); however, many of these documents have been destroyed or lost over the years, and those that have survived cover only a few scattered years between 1750 and 1860. For instance, while it is clear from the archival record that lists of out-migrants from the Voshchazhnikovo estate (passport lists) were compiled annually for the period 1706–1861, only a few (for the years 1760, 1762, 1825, 1832, 1834, 1859, and 1860) have survived. Contracts for the transfer of property, the provision of credit, and other formal agreements were also recorded annually, but these have survived only for the years 1759, 1793, 1831, 1832, and 1840. Similarly, we have only scattered examples of annual account books, serf petitions, wills, and communal resolutions. Because no set of documents has survived for the whole period, it has not been possible to obtain a rigorous quantitative depiction of change over time for this community. (Household structure is the exception, since soul revisions and household listings for the period 1816–58 make it possible to examine changes across the first part of the nineteenth century.) This does not mean that the picture of rural society at Voshchazhnikovo portrayed by the surviving source materials is unreliable. As we shall see, there is no reason to think that the data provided in the documents that have survived are inaccurate. Their scattered, incomplete nature, however, does impose certain constraints on quantitative analysis.

Despite what has been said about the indispensability of the micro-exemplary method for the study of institutional configurations, it will inevitably be asked how 'representative' such an estate is of Russian serfdom, or of the Central Industrial Region, or even of Sheremetyev holdings. Can the evidence from such an estate tell us anything about Russia as a whole? Were the Sheremetyevs not rather exceptional landlords who ran their estates in a quite untypical way?

This is a fair question, but it has a good answer. Voshchazhnikovo serfs do indeed appear to have been better off than most serfs in Russia, on average. But as we will see in the course of this book, it is just this excep-tional situation that makes the Voshchazhnikovo estate an ideal microcosm for the interaction of institutions within rural Russia as a whole. Precisely because it was in some respects more 'western' than many other Russian estates, Voshchazhnikovo enables us to see why other estates, whose populations shared the same underlying culture and the same wider insti-tutional constraints (serfdom, military conscription, corruption, etc.) were not able to overcome these barriers. Because Voshchazhnikovo is in some ways more familiar, from a western or central European point of view, it makes starkly visible the differences in the surrounding background society. This is partly because the Voshchazhnikovo evidence enables us to observe interactions between the estate population and the regional, even national, economy (including migration in and out, regional labour markets, regional credit markets, consumption of goods imported from far and wide, as well as far-flung land purchases). We know, therefore, that the institutional configuration we observe in Voshchazhnikovo was not isolated or self-contained, but at least regional (though it is far too early to make confident pronouncements about its ultimate extent).

More importantly, though, what the case of Voshchazhnikovo reveals is that the whole idea of a 'representative' Russian estate is a mirage. The unique value of this case is that it enables us to see that the Russian countryside was a far more complex and variegated cultural and economic landscape than has been suspected. Just as the quest for a 'representative' German or Italian village before about 1800 would be futile, because the assumption of homogeneity in some early modern entity called 'Germany' or 'Italy' is obviously defective, so the present study of a particular village enables us to see that any such assumption of homogeneity is equally misleading for imperial Russia. The most important lesson of this study, therefore, beyond the doubt it may cast on the Peasant Myth and the positive knowledge it contributes about a particular local society, is to reveal how little we still know about the Russian countryside in this period. This may sound like a negative or pessimistic message, but it can also be regarded in a positive light. For there can be no progress in understanding the pre-Emancipation peasantry until we dispose of the illusion that it is a single, uniform, homogeneous entity. If this book achieves nothing beyond casting doubt on that illusion, it will have contributed significantly to our knowledge of Russia and whether it is really so different.

2 Voshchazhnikovo: a microcosm of nineteenth-century Russia

The Voshchazhnikovo estate was given to Field Marshal Boris Petrovich Sheremetyev in 1706 by Peter the Great as a reward for outstanding service during the Great Northern War with Sweden (1700–21).[1] The Sheremetyev family, who descended from a long line of Muscovite aristocrats,[2] was one of the largest landholding families in Russia. Boris Petrovich Sheremetyev had already acquired several estates through inheritance and military service by the time he was given the Voshchazhnikovo holding. By 1708, he held nineteen estates in at least seven different provinces, on which lived approximately 40,000 serfs.[3] The family's holdings were expanded by his son, Pyotr Borisovich, who, through marriage, purchase, and service to the crown, acquired a number of additional holdings. By 1765, the Sheremetyevs held over thirty estates in seventeen provinces and roughly 170,000 serfs.[4] This expansion continued into the next century, so that by the time serfdom was abolished in 1861, the Sheremetyev family held some 300,000 serfs.[5] These holdings put the Sheremetyevs – along with other families such as the Gagarins, Iusupovs, Vorontsovs, and Orlovs – among that small group of landholders, who, although they comprised only 1 per cent of total landholders in Russia, held over 30 per cent of the serf population.[6]

The Voshchazhnikovo estate was located in Yaroslavl' province, in the Central Industrial Region of European Russia. A number of important towns were established here in the early medieval period, including Yaroslavl', Vladimir, Moscow, and Nizhnyi Novgorod. In the eighteenth

---

[1] Shchepetov, *Krepostnoe pravo*, p. 11. Before 1706 the estate was a holding of the crown.
[2] The family of Boris Petrovich Sheremetyev was descended from boyars, an elite group of aristocrats who served the grand prince of Muscovy. On the boyars, see N. S. Kollman, *Kinship and politics: the making of the Muscovite political system, 1345–1547* (Stanford, 1987); the Sheremetyev family, in particular, appears on pp. 115–16.
[3] Shchepetov, *Krepostnoe pravo*, p. 18.   [4] *Ibid.*, pp. 19–21.   [5] *Ibid.*, p. 26.
[6] Blum, *Lord and peasant*, p. 386. The convention in imperial Russia was to measure the wealth of landowners in terms of the number of souls in their possession. There was a good reason for this: serfs were valuable assets against which many Russian nobles borrowed. This peculiar practice and its more absurd implications are the subject of Nikolai Gogol's *Dead souls*.

century, when the system of *guberniia* (provinces) and *uezdy* (districts or counties) was introduced, the Central Industrial Region was divided into seven different provinces: Kaluga, Kostroma, Moscow, Nizhnyi Novgorod, Tver', Vladimir, and Yaroslavl'. According to data collected for the General Land Survey[7] in the second half of the eighteenth century, roughly 60 per cent of the land owned by the Sheremetyevs was located in the Central Industrial Region,[8] and the region was home to just over half of the family's serfs.[9]

Yaroslavl' province had a total population of 976,866 in the nineteenth century (c. 1858), of which 557,525 (57 per cent) were proprietary serfs.[10] The proportion of proprietary peasants was higher in Yaroslavl' than that for the empire as a whole, where it was roughly 38 per cent, but it was in keeping with figures for other provinces of the Central Industrial Region, where the proportion ranged from 51 to 62 per cent.[11] There were 2,810 serf-owning landlords in Yaroslavl' province at this time, only 26 of whom held more than 1,000 serfs. The majority of proprietors in this province (2,200) held under 100 serfs.[12] The Sheremetyev family held nearly 24,000 serfs in Yaroslavl' (and may thus have been the largest serf-holders in the province), and, according to the General Land Survey, some 84,569 *desiatin* (228,330 acres) of land (8.5 per cent of the total Sheremetyev holdings). Of these 24,000 serfs, over 20,000 lived on the Iukhotskoe estate in Uglich district, in the southwestern part of the province. The others resided at Voshchazhnikovo.[13]

---

[7] On the General Land Survey, see L. V. Milov, *Issledovanie ob ekonomicheskikh primechaniiakh k general'nomu mezhevaniiu* (Moscow, 1965). The survey was carried out over a number of years beginning in the 1760s. The figures cited here are mostly from the 1770s and 1780s.

[8] According to the survey figures, the Sheremetyevs held roughly 2.7 million acres, 1.6 million of which were located in the Central Industrial Region. See Shchepetov, *Krepostnoe pravo*, pp. 296–347 (Table 4). We should bear in mind that this figure probably includes land that was in fact owned by serfs, since, for most of the period under investigation here, serfs could only purchase land in the name of their lords. Serf landholding will be discussed in greater detail in chapter 5.

[9] At the time of the General Land Survey, the Sheremetyevs held approximately 196,000 serfs of both sexes, roughly 99,000 of whom lived on estates in the Central Industrial Region. (Calculated from figures provided in Shchepetov, *Krepostnoe pravo*, pp. 296–347.)

[10] Not all Russian peasants in this period were serfs. Other categories included free peasants, state peasants (those bound to crown estates), and factory peasants. On the eve of emancipation, the total population of European Russia was roughly 60 million, of which 22.5 million were proprietary serfs. A. Troinitskii, *The serf population in Russia according to the 10th national census*, ed. E. Domar (Newtonville, MA, 1982), pp. 107–8. For Yaroslavl' figures, see p. 62.

[11] *Ibid.*, pp. 61–2. Moscow province was the exception, due to a large urban population. Serfs comprised only 39 per cent of the population in Moscow province.

[12] *Ibid.*, p. 56.

[13] Figures from Shchepetov, *Krepostnoe pravo*, pp. 322–6.

Table 2.1. *Villages on the Voshchazhnikovo estate, 1834, 1850*

| Village | Number of households | |
	1834	1850
Arkhipovo	15	14
Chernets	26	22
Dem'ian	19	19
Denis'evo	23	22
Fodos'ino	10	11
Frolovo	8	8
Gavrino	9	10
Golubkovo	21	19
Iurenino	14	14
Kanditovo	12	13
Ketskovo	14	15
Kulelevo	6	5
Lykhino	23	21
Malakhovo	14	14
Moiseyevo	11	11
Musorovo	15	15
Popovo	3	2
Pukesovo	9	6
Stomar'evo	10	10
Strel'ki	15	17
Sysoevo	5	5
Sytino	11	11
Tomakovo	28	27
Zadubrov'e	9	8
Nikola na Berioznikakh	**16**	**14**
Nikola na Pen'e	**29**	**29**
Semionovskoe	**38**	**38**
Uslavtsevo	**37**	**39**
Vioska	**38**	**38**
Voshchazhnikovo	**201**	**193**
Total households	689	670

Source: RGADA, f. 1287, op. 3, ed. khr. 2553 ('Soul revision, 1834'), and ed. khr. 1941 ('Soul revision, 1850').

Voshchazhnikovo was located in Rostov district, in the southeastern part of the province, roughly 20 miles northwest of Rostov Velikii (pop. 5,508 in 1825) and 35 miles southwest of the provincial capital, Yaroslavl' (pop. 20,271 in 1825).[14] The Voshchazhnikovo estate spanned some

---

[14] T. S. Fedor, *Patterns of urban growth in the Russian empire during the nineteenth century* (Chicago, 1975), p. 203.

12,000 *desiatin* (32,400 acres), roughly 4,500 *desiatin* (12,150 acres) of which was arable; the remaining area consisted of forest, meadowland, wasteland, and serfs' garden plots. According to data compiled for the descriptions of estates, the total serf population on the estate in 1858 was 3,553.[15] This population was distributed among thirty villages, ranging in size from 2 households to over 200. The largest of these was the village of Voshchazhnikovo, from which the estate took its name. Table 2.1 provides the names of the estate villages and the number of serf households recorded for each in the 1834 and 1850 soul revisions (villages with churches are shown in boldface).

There were six parishes on the estate, named for the villages which contained churches. Each of the thirty estate villages belonged to one of these six parishes. Parish groupings are not shown in the table, since none of the estate documents provides information about parish boundaries. The only sources that do offer such information are the parish registers (*metricheskie knigi*), and these, unfortunately, are only available for Voshchazhnikovo parish.[16] According to the registers, the villages Lykhino, Tomakovo, Kulelevo, Frolovo, and Zadubrov'e were all part of Voshchazhnikovo parish.[17] It has not so far been possible to determine precisely which villages belonged to the other five parishes.

2.1   Local ecology and economy

The Central Industrial Region was characterised by sandy soils, low-lying marshlands, and large tracts of forest land. Ecological conditions in this region are thought to have made it somewhat less suitable for agriculture than those in the Central Black Earth Region to the south, where the soil was rich and fertile. As a result, very few estates in this region specialised in grain production. Some estates – such as Voshchazhnikovo – had no demesne land; the owners of such estates collected rents from their serfs in cash or kind (*obrok*), instead of labour services (*barshchina*). On the eve of Emancipation, some 60 per cent of serfs in the Central Industrial Region paid dues in cash or kind, compared to only 30 per cent in the Central Black Earth Region.[18] It is generally maintained that harsh ecological conditions made it difficult for peasants in the Central Industrial

---

[15] RGADA, f. 1287, op. 3, ed. khr. 2320 (1858). The 'Descriptions of estates' were compiled in the later 1850s in preparation for emancipation.

[16] Registers for some of the other parishes have survived, but because they are damaged and awaiting restoration, they are not currently available to researchers. The surviving registers are all located in the Yaroslavl' provincial archive (GAYaO), f. 230.

[17] GAYaO, f. 230, op. 11, d. 1588 ('Parish registers for Voshchazhnikovo parish, 1786–1826').

[18] I. I. Ignatovich, *Pomeshchich'i krest'iane nakanune osvobozhdeniia* (Moscow, 1925), pp. 70–6.

Region to make a living from farming alone. They are thus supposed to have engaged in a wide variety of non-agricultural activities – crafts, trade, manufacture, service – to supplement inadequate returns to agriculture and enable them to meet their state and feudal obligations. As a result, manufacturing and proto-industry are thought to have been more widespread in this area (hence the name 'Central Industrial Region') than in the agricultural zone to the south.

The ecological conditions at Voshchazhnikovo were indeed less than favourable for agriculture. The estate was situated in a low-lying, marshy part of Yaroslavl' province. The estate fields were bounded by the rivers Ust'e and Mogza, which flow into the river Kotorosl', a tributary of the Volga. In addition, a network of smaller streams flowed across the estate territory, connecting the larger rivers to Lake Nero[19] and the river Volga. The combination of low altitude and rocky, clay soil meant frequent flooding, especially after a particularly wet spring, when drainage problems associated with melting snow were exacerbated by heavy rains. This was the case in 1843, when the estate bailiff noted that the harvest was 'considerably worse in the fields that were steeped in stagnant water, which had built up over the winter and spring'.[20]

Such inhospitable local conditions were further complicated by the vagaries of the Russian climate. Long, cold winters were often followed by hot, dry summers. According to the documents for Voshchazhnikovo, these dry summers posed as great a threat to local harvests as wet springs. In September 1845 the bailiff noted that 'there was very little rain this past summer and a drought ensued, which resulted in poor grass ... as for the grain, it has, due to the drought, turned out poorly'.[21] In 1850, the region experienced another drought – though somewhat milder than that of 1845 – and again the harvest was poor.[22] On the other hand, wet summers, like that of 1844, were also problematic for grain cultivation. In a report to the estate administration, the bailiff claimed that 'excessive moisture during the summer had ruined a substantial portion of the wheat'.[23]

---

[19] The town Rostov Velikii is located on the northwest bank of Lake Nero, roughly 25 kilometres from the Voshchazhnikovo estate.

[20] '[urozhai khleba] okazal'sa vykhodom ... bolee khud na mnogikh neizmennykh v poliakh mestakh ot zimniago i vesiniago zastoia vody', in RGADA, f. 1287, op. 3, ed. khr. 1568, l. 7 ('Report on grain harvests, 1842–54').

[21] 'v proshedshei leta vesma malo bylo dozhdia i prodolzhalas' bol'shaia zasukha ot chego urozhai trav vesma mal ... o zimnoi khlebe ... ot zasukhi zdelalis' khudy', in ibid., l. 9.

[22] Ibid., ll. 23–4.

[23] 'nemalaia chast' kolos'ev [khleba] ot mochlivosti leta byli pustye', in ibid., l. 7.

These harsh climatic conditions made for a relatively short growing season. Fields could not usually be sown until mid-May, when the snow had melted and the ground had thawed.[24] The grain was then harvested during late July (winter grains) and early August (spring grains). Animals had to be kept indoors during the cold winter months; in many parts of Russia, they were only let out to graze in late April.[25]

The land cultivated by Voshchazhnikovo serfs was communal land. Although these serfs, like many serfs in the Central Industrial Region, paid their feudal dues in mainly cash and kind (*obrok*), they were still obligated to cultivate their communal allotments. The communal land, while officially estate land, was not demesne land; it was land owned by the landlord but allotted to the serfs in return for a cash payment.[26] The landlord insisted that this land be cultivated as a form of 'insurance' so that 'a serf could be sure his household would not be without subsistence, even if he were to suffer some misfortune in his commercial activities'.[27] This rule was to be enforced by imposing a fine of at least 10 roubles on those who failed to cultivate their land.[28]

Communal land at Voshchazhnikovo was measured in *tiagly*. The *tiaglo* was a conventional measure usually defined as the amount of land that could be cultivated by one husband-and-wife work unit. Each *tiaglo* consisted of a combination of arable, pasture, and forest land. In 1858, a *tiaglo* at Voshchazhnikovo consisted of 10.5 acres of arable, 3.25 acres of pasture, and 9.45 acres of forest.[29] Serfs were charged a set fee of 15 silver roubles for every *tiaglo* they held.[30] In addition to this cash payment, the landlord demanded that serfs provide, for each *tiaglo* held, 1.5 *chetverik* of rye and 0.5 *chetverik* of oats for the estate granary.[31] The allocation of *tiagly* among member households was the responsibility of the estate commune and the village communes.

---

[24] Milov, *Velikorusskii pakhar'*, pp. 118–19; Moon, *The Russian peasantry*, p. 124.

[25] Moon, *The Russian peasantry*, pp. 139–40.

[26] The cash rents attached to land allotments were only one of the serfs' *obrok* obligations. Other taxes and obligations will be discussed below.

[27] 'khotia v torgu kakoe i neshchastie s nim by sluchilos' to on mozhet byt' nadezhnym chto doma bez propitaniia neostanetsia', in RGADA, f. 1287, op. 3, ed. khr. 555, l. 23 ('Instructions, 1796/1800', point 8).

[28] *Ibid.*, l. 24. As we will see, serfs working in non-agricultural occupations often hired labourers to cultivate their communal lands for them.

[29] RGADA, f. 1287, op. 3, ed. khr. 2320, l. 11 ('Descriptions of estates, 1858').

[30] This charge does not appear to have changed during the nineteenth century. It is noted as the set fee per *tiaglo* in the 1796 instructions (ed. khr. 555, l. 22) and then again in the 1858 'Descriptions of estates' (ed. khr. 2320, l. 10).

[31] RGADA, f. 1287, op. 3, ed. khr. 1774, l. 1 ('Contributions to the estate granary, 1847').

Table 2.2. *Seed/yield ratios for the Voshchazhnikovo estate, 1841–54*

Crop	1841–2	1842–3	1843–4	1844–5	1850–1	1851–2	1853–4
Rye	4	3	3	2	3	5	2
Oats	4	4	4	1.6	3	3	2
Barley	3	3	3	2	5	3	3
Wheat	2	2	3	2	2	3	3
Flax	2.5	2.5	2	1.5	3	3	2

Source: RGADA, f. 1287, op. 3, ed. khr. 1568 ('Report on grain harvests, 1842–54').

As in most parts of European Russia, winter-sown rye, or *rozh'*, was the main crop cultivated on these communal lands.[32] In addition, there were several spring-sown grains – barley, wheat, and oats – along with a small amount of flax grown each year. The documents for Voshchazhnikovo provide no information about the estate's crop rotation system, though it is generally believed that the three-field system was still prevalent in this part of Russia during this period.[33] Table 2.2 shows seed/yield ratios for the crops grown at Voshchazhnikovo, as recorded by estate officials between 1841 and 1854.

The figures recorded for Voshchazhnikovo are broadly consistent with those recorded for other parts of central Russia during this period.[34] Seed/yield ratios were notoriously low in pre-Emancipation Russia, even in areas more fertile than Yaroslavl' province. Figures recorded for the Central Black Earth Region during this period suggest average seed/yield ratios of 1:5 (oats) or 1:6 (rye).[35] While such ratios were not unheard of in nineteenth-century western Europe, they were probably near the lower end of the range.[36] At the upper end were ratios of 1:20 and higher,

[32] According to R. E. F. Smith, rye was always the staple grain for peasants in European Russia. References to rye can be found in sources dating back as far as the thirteenth century. In R. E. F. Smith, *Peasant farming in Muscovy* (Cambridge, 1977), pp. 33–4. See also R. E. F. Smith and D. Christian, *Bread and salt: a social and economic history of food and drink in Russia* (Cambridge, 1984), pp. 255–6.

[33] M. Confino, *Systèmes agraires et progrès agricole: l'assolement triennal en Russie aux XVIIIe–XIXe siècles* (Paris, 1969), pp. 37–40; Milov, *Velikorusskii pakhar'i*, pp. 60–6.

[34] A. Kahan, *Russian economic history: the nineteenth century* (Chicago and London, 1989), p. 128; idem, *The plow, the hammer, and the knout: an economic history of eighteenth-century Russia* (Chicago and London, 1985), p. 49; N. A. Rubinshtein, *Sel'skoe khoziaistvo Rossii vo vtoroi polovine XVIII v.* (Moscow, 1957), pp. 355–6, 444–84.

[35] Hoch, *Serfdom and social control*, p. 29.

[36] Yields at Voshchazhnikovo are similar to those reported for parts of German-speaking central Europe in this same period. See S. Ogilvie, M. Küpker, and J. Maegraith, *Community characteristics and demographic development: three Württemberg communities, 1558–1914*, Cambridge Working Papers in Economics (2009), pp. 174–88.

achieved by farmers in England and the Netherlands well before the mid-nineteenth century.[37] However, it is important to note that, in contrast to England or western Europe, land was abundant in imperial Russia, making it possible – at least in theory – to increase total agricultural output by bringing more land under cultivation instead of improving seed/yield ratios. It has been suggested that this strategy was employed by landlords in the Central Black Earth Region during the early nineteenth century.[38] There is, however, no evidence to suggest that new land was brought under cultivation on the Voshchazhnikovo estate during the period examined here. In fact, the data we have indicate a decline in the amount of estate land under cultivation between 1796 and 1858. In a set of landlord's instructions from 1796, the amount of estate arable was recorded as roughly 4,645 *desiatin*[39] (12,542 acres); in a document from 1858, the figure was 4,339 *desiatin*[40] (11,715 acres). It seems unlikely, therefore, that total output at Voshchazhnikovo was increasing despite low seed/yield ratios. The evidence presented in subsequent chapters suggests that low yields were probably not entirely due to inhospitable geographical conditions, but rather to the lack of incentive for serfs to invest in agricultural production.[41] Returns to labour were evidently higher in other occupations, and, as we will see in chapter 8, grain was available locally at affordable prices.

It is interesting that, despite a number of years with harvests described by officials as 'poor', there is no indication in the documents that serfs at Voshchazhnikovo experienced subsistence crises. There are no references to grain or seed shortages, no petitions from serfs requesting famine-related relief, no references to – or evidence of – famine-related mortality or migration, and no special instructions to bailiffs regarding crop failures. Furthermore, the years described as poor by the Voshchazhnikovo estate bailiff do *not* coincide with those noted elsewhere in Russia as years of crisis. For instance, according to statistics gathered by the Russian central government, spring frosts in 1847 had deleterious effects on harvests across central Russia, to the extent that grain had to be imported into the region.[42] At Voshchazhnikovo, however, the bailiff called the 1847 harvest 'good' and made no reference to harvest failure of any kind.[43]

---

[37] B. H. Slicher van Bath, *The agrarian history of western Europe A.D. 500–1850* (London, 1963), pp. 330.

[38] P. Gatrell, *The tsarist economy 1850–1917* (London and New York, 1986), p. 129.

[39] RGADA, f. 1287, op. 3, ed. khr. 555, l. 21 ('Instructions, 1796/1800').

[40] RGADA, f. 1287, op. 3, ed. khr. 2320, l. 10 ('Descriptions of estates, 1858').

[41] Even Haxthausen (*Studien über die innern Zustände, das Volksleben und insbesondere die ländlichen Einrichtungen Rußlands*, 3 vols. (Hannover, 1847–52), vol. I, p. 123) reports that this was a widespread view in the region.

[42] Kahan, *Russian economic history*, p. 140.

[43] RGADA, f. 1287, op. 3, ed. khr. 1568 ('Report on grain harvests, 1842–54'), ll. 10–11.

Similarly, the same national statistics indicate that in 1852, a cold, rainy spring resulted in low yields across the country.[44] But on the Voshchazhnikovo estate, the 1852 yields were at the upper end of the 'normal' range.[45] Voshchazhnikovo thus appears to have been unaffected by some of the so-called regional calamities of this period. While we cannot draw any firm conclusions about the nature of subsistence crises without more rigorous evidence – especially time-series data for burials and grain price indices[46] – the data we do have suggest that there was a great deal of variation in local economic conditions, even within loosely defined regions such as the Central Industrial Region.

Although obligated to cultivate their communal lands, very few serfs on the Voshchazhnikovo estate actually lived from their communal allotments. Unlike many inhabitants of Rostov district, these peasants did not engage in *ogorodnichestvo*, the intensive cultivation of garden produce for sale in nearby towns and cities.[47] According to an inventory of households carried out in 1832, only 10 per cent of serf households in the village of Voshchazhnikovo were at that time 'living primarily from agriculture'.[48] In the 1838 inventory, this figure had fallen to 5 per cent.[49] The figures for livestock ownership in this village are consistent with a low level of specialisation in agriculture. In 1832, roughly one quarter of the households in Voshchazhnikovo (46 of 203) held no livestock.[50] Most households that

---

[44] Kahan, *Russian economic history*, p. 140.

[45] RGADA, f. 1287, op. 3, ed. khr. 1568 ('Report on grain harvests, 1842–54'), l. 30.

[46] Ideally one would want to undertake the kind of study Hoch has done for Borshevka, a parish in Tambov province, in the Central Black Earth Region. Interestingly, his analysis of burials and grain price series suggests that mortality patterns in this parish did not coincide with periods of dearth. S. Hoch, 'Famine, disease, and mortality patterns in the parish of Borshevka, Russia, 1830–1912', *Population Studies* 52 (1998), pp. 357–68.

[47] Garden farming became a very profitable enterprise in Rostov district in the nineteenth century. Peasants supplied local towns with fruits and vegetables, and even travelled as far as Moscow and St Petersburg to market their produce. V. A. Fyodorov, 'Vozniknovenie torgovogo ogorodnichestva v rostovskom uezde Yaroslavskoi gubernii (konets XVIII–pervaia polovina XIX veka)', *Vestnik moskovskogo universiteta* 6 (1962), pp. 49–68.

[48] 22 out of 203 households were noted as earning their living 'ot odnogo zemliapashestva' or 'from agriculture alone'. However, living 'primarily from agriculture' is probably a more accurate translation than 'from agriculture alone', since the *podvornye opisi* tell us only about male occupations (female occupations are only mentioned in records for all-female households). It is possible that female members of these households were engaged in some kind of wage labour.

[49] 10 of 184 households were living primarily from agriculture.

[50] Most of these households did not specialise in agriculture. They were not, however, as Koval'chenko might predict, the poorest households on the estate. 16 were described as 'good', 20 were 'poor' and the remaining 10 were 'average'. See the discussion in Koval'chenko, *Russkoe krepostnoe khoziaistvo*, pp. 183–4. The Voshchazhnikovo findings are more consistent with those of Sivkov for Iusupov holdings in the southern central provinces, where the agricultural households also tended to be the poorer ones. Sivkov, *Ocherki po istorii krepostnogo khoziaistva*, pp. 167–8.

owned animals had cows. According to the 1832 inventory, 117 house-holds in the village had at least one cow, though only 53 of these also owned a horse (all households that owned horses also had at least one cow). Only 14 of 203 households owned more than one horse (and only two of these owned more than two horses). Only 5 households in Voshchazhnikovo owned sheep. This is a very different pattern to the one described for the Central Black Earth Region, where many more serfs are thought to have specialised in agricultural production, and live-stock holdings were more substantial.[51]

The majority of Voshchazhnikovo serfs were engaged in non-agricultural activities, including crafts (smiths, cobblers, glaziers), trade, small-scale manufacturing, and live-in service in cities. This was not an unusual pattern for Yaroslavl' province, where there were numerous manufactories, markets, and fairs, many of which were in Rostov district.[52] On the estate itself, there were seven serf-owned manufactories in the nineteenth century: two leather manufactories, one paper manufactory, one brickworks, one candleworks, and two distilleries.[53] A second paper manufactory was formally owned by the Sheremetyev family but leased to the serf Dmitri Slasnikov in the 1830s for an annual fee.[54] There was also a local textile manufactory, which is only rarely mentioned in the documents. There are references to the distribution of flax to estate women for spin-ning, as well as to women's earnings in the textile industry (15–25 roubles per year in 1796), but these are few and far between, and no records for the manufactory itself appear to have survived.[55] According to the Soviet historian Shchepetov, the manufactory employed the so-called 'household serfs' (*dvorovye liudi*), and produced napkins and other kinds of thin cloths.[56] A best guess is that this was a holdover from the seventeenth

---

[51] Hoch, *Serfdom and social control*, pp. 46–7.
[52] Morrison, *'Trading peasants' and 'urbanization' in eighteenth-century Russia: the Central Industrial Region* (New York and London, 1987), pp. 265–72.
[53] RGADA, f. 1287, op. 3, ed. khr. 1119 ('Report on estate manufactories').
[54] *Ibid.*, ll. 3–4. It is not clear whether this factory had been leased to others before it was let to Slasnikov or whether another serf household took over when Slasnikov's lease expired.
[55] On the distribution of flax to estate females for spinning see RGADA, f. 1287, op. 3, ed. khr. 103 ('On the distribution of flax, 1744–6'). The reference to average earnings of female textile workers is in RGADA, f. 1287, op. 3, ed. khr. 555, l. 26 ('Instructions, 1796/1800', point 23). These documents are for the mid- to late eighteenth century as are Shchepetov's (see n. 56 below). It is not clear whether the estate continued to produce textiles in the nineteenth century.
[56] 'Household serfs' were proprietary serfs who worked in the landlord's household as servants rather than on the demesne. The reference to textile work is in K. N. Shchepetov, *Iz zhizni krepostnykh krest'ian Rossii XVIII–XIX vekov: po materialam Sheremetyevskikh votchin* (Moscow, 1963), p. 17. Unfortunately, Shchepetov provides no archival references in his discussion of the Voshchazhnikovo textile industry.

century, when the state peasants at Voshchazhnikovo, before becoming serfs of the Sheremetyev family, were active in the textile industry.[57] It is unlikely that textiles dominated the local economy in the period under investigation here, as Voshchazhnikovo was not considered one of the Sheremetyev's proto-industrial estates like Ivanovo (textiles) or Pavlovo (metal industry).[58] Furthermore, the data we do have indicate that Voshchazhnikovo serfs engaged in a wide variety of economic activities on the estate itself and across the wider region.

The serf population on this estate was highly stratified. The Sheremetyevs acknowledged this in a system of progressive taxation, whereby serf households were divided into three groups: those with assets worth under 500 roubles, those with assets worth 500 to 1,000 roubles, and those with assets worth over 1,000 roubles.[59] As we will see, most fees and fines were levied in accordance with household wealth. For instance, if a household from the poorest, or 'third' rank (*tret'ia stat'ia*), was caught hiring labourers from outside the estate without officially registering them, a fine of 20 roubles was to be levied. For a middling household, the fine was 50 roubles, and for a household of the first rank, the fine was 100 roubles.[60] A similar system was applied to fines for the unauthorised cutting of wood, the unauthorised division of households, the failure to cultivate communal allotments, and a variety of other transgressions.

Voshchazhnikovo was neither the largest nor the smallest of the Sheremetyev holdings. Estates such as Iukhotskoe (also in Yaroslavl') and Alekseyevka (in Voronezh) were home to over 20,000 serfs, while Molodoi Tud in Tver' and Ivanovo in Vladimir had 7,000 to 8,000 serfs. The Nikol'skoe estate in Moscow province had fewer than 1,000 serfs, as did Sergeyevskoe in Riazan. As noted, the Voshchazhnikovo estate, unlike the proto-industrial estates of Ivanovo or Pavlovo, had no particular specialism. Voshchazhnikovo was not the wealthiest of the Sheremetyev holdings, nor was it the poorest. Figures for the early part of the nineteenth century (1800–15) suggest that there were proportionately more wealthy serfs (those with income and assets worth more than 10,000 roubles) on the larger estates, such as Iukhotskoe and Pavlovo, and even

---

[57] This guess is based on the discussion in L. L. Murav'eva, *Derevenskaia promyshlennost' tsentral'noi Rossii vtoroi poloviny XVII v.* (Moscow, 1971), esp. pp. 79–80.

[58] For a detailed discussion of proto-industry on the Sheremetyev estates, see K. Gestwa, *Proto-Industrialisierung in Russland: Wirtschaft, Herrschaft und Kultur in Ivanovo und Pavlovo, 1741–1932* (Göttingen, 1999).

[59] RGADA, f. 1287, op. 3, ed. khr. 555, ll. 22–3, 49–50 ('Instructions 1796/1800'). 'Assets' were not clearly defined in the instructions; they are referred to vaguely as 'property and capital' (*imeniia i kapitaly*).

[60] RGADA, f. 1287, op. 3, ed. khr. 555, l. 22 ('Instructions 1796/1800').

Molodoi Tud, than there were at Voshchazhnikovo.[61] Because it was neither big nor small, neither rich nor poor, and had no particular economic specialisation, Voshchazhnikovo was probably more representative of (the larger) serf estates in the Central Industrial Region than many other Sheremetyev holdings in this area.[62] It does, for instance, seem to bear certain similarities to the Baki estate in Kostroma province (studied by Melton) and the Manuilovskoe estate in Tver' province (studied by Bohac).[63]

2.2   Estate structure

The Sheremetyevs, like many large landholders, were absentee landlords. They spent most of their time at court in St Petersburg, and paid only the occasional visit to their rural estates. It is not clear how often – if ever – they visited the Voshchazhnikovo estate. In the documents available for the years 1750–1860, which cover three generations of Sheremetyev landlords, there is not a single reference to a visit by a member of the Sheremetyev family. This does not mean the family ignored its holdings, content to let local bailiffs or serf officials run them as they pleased. In fact, quite the contrary seems to have been the case. In order to supervise the affairs of their many and disparate holdings, the Sheremetyevs developed a centralised system of administration, which was run from their St Petersburg residence.[64] This central office – the 'home office' (*domovaia konsulariia*) – was constantly in touch with officials from each of the estates, advising them on the day-to-day management of their respective holdings. It set out the rules and regulations by which the estates were to be governed, and, as we shall see in chapters 4–9, served as a manorial court for the settlement of disputes among serfs and the enforcement of

---

[61] Only a small number of households on the Voshchazhnikovo estate (5–10) were this wealthy. Information on assets can be found in documents such as the lists of serfs engaged in trade and their guild associations, RGADA, f. 1287, op. 3, ed. khr. 1391 ('List of trading peasants and guilds, 1838'). On the Pavlovo and Iukhot estates, see Shchepetov, *Krepostnoe pravo*, pp. 366–9. Data from Molodoi Tud can be found in Prokof'eva, *Krest'ianskaia obshchina*, p. 167. The Ivanovo estate, one of the largest and wealthiest, would surely have had an even greater number of wealthy serfs.

[62] Of course, Voshchazhnikovo would have been considered very large by comparison with the average Russian estate. As noted earlier, most estates in Russia were quite small, containing fewer than 100 serfs. However, we have very little information about such holdings, since they seem to have generated far fewer records.

[63] Though there were also substantial differences, which will be highlighted in subsequent chapters.

[64] A number of large landholders developed centralised administrative systems of this sort. Not surprisingly, estates that were part of these large, centralised systems generated the best source materials.

contracts. Moreover, all decisions taken at the local level had to be first approved by officials in the landlord's home office.

The Voshchazhnikovo estate had its own administrative office (the *voshchazhnikovskoe votchinnoe pravleniie*), which was located in the village of Voshchazhnikovo, in a separate building designed specifically for administrative purposes. It was here that communal meetings (discussed in chapter 4) took place, and that serfs had to pay their taxes and quitrent dues. The building also served as the estate gaol, where punishments were meted out to those arrested by estate authorities. The Voshchazhnikovo estate administration usually consisted of a bailiff (*prikazchik*),[65] an elder (*starosta*), at least one selectman (*vybornyi*), at least one clerk (*zemskii*), a scribe (*pisar'*), a churchwarden (*tserkovnyi starosta*), several tax collectors (*zborshchiki*), an accountant (*prikhodo-raskhodchik*), and several constables (*sot'skie*). The bailiff was the most powerful official on the estate; he reported directly to the landlord's officials in St Petersburg. For most of the period under investigation, the Voshchazhnikovo bailiff was not a serf, but an outside official hired by the landlord to run the estate.[66] The bailiff was responsible for keeping the St Petersburg office informed about day-to-day affairs on the estate, and for the implementation of decrees and instructions from the centre. He presided over communal meetings, and supervised all aspects of the estate management. He also served as the landlord's representative to the local government, handling all correspondence and interaction with district and provincial officials. The other estate officers provided administrative support to the bailiff. These were supposed to be elected by serfs from among the local serf population, and to report directly to the bailiff himself (their responsibilities are outlined in chapter 4). The salaries of these officials were paid from communal funds, while the bailiff's salary was paid by the landlord.

The Voshchazhnikovo estate was a serf estate; all of its peasants belonged to the legal category 'serf' (*krespostnoi krest'ianin*). There has been much debate among historians as to what the term serf actually meant in practice. One thing we have learned from the detailed local research done for serf societies in medieval England and western Europe, as well as for societies that experienced the 'second serfdom', is that serfdom was not a monolithic institution. It was, in the words of

---

[65] To be more precise, the *prikazchik* seems to have been something like a combination of bailiff and steward. He did preside over communal meetings and judicial proceedings, but he was also responsible for all the day-to-day affairs of the estate, including, on *barshchina* estates, supervising work on the demesne.

[66] At certain points in this period, local serfs served as bailiffs. For instance, in the early 1800s Ivan Slasnikov, a serf from one of the wealthier families on the estate, held the post of *prikazchik*.

Hoch, 'not a system, but a widely varying set of practices'.[67] This set of practices varied not only across political entities, but within them as well. In other words, serfdom was no more a uniform system in medieval England or France than it was in eighteenth-century Russia. Practices varied from landlord to landlord, across space and over time. The most we can say about serfdom as a system is that it implied a certain kind of legal subject status. The serf was the subject of his landlord, and was required to submit to the lord's jurisdiction. What this meant in practice, though, varied enormously.

In Russia, the process of enserfment occurred gradually across the sixteenth, seventeenth, and eighteenth centuries.[68] From a legal point of view, two significant events were the Muscovite Law Code (*Ulozhenie*) of 1649, which formally made it illegal for serfs to leave their lords' estates without permission, and the decree of 1767 that formally denied serfs the right to bring petitions against their landlords before the tsar.[69] The *Ulozhenie* officially placed serfs under the jurisdiction of their lords; the 1767 legislation formally denied them legal recourse beyond that jurisdiction (though even before 1767, there was nothing in Russia like the royal courts of medieval England, where serfs could in some instances appeal beyond their local manorial courts). It is not clear how the Russian petition process in place prior to 1767 actually worked in practice, or indeed whether serfs made regular use of it. There are no references in the Voshchazhnikovo records (which begin around 1708) to any such practice; in none of the surviving documents did serfs threaten to take complaints to the tsar. On the whole, Russian serfs seem to have had even fewer formal rights *vis-à-vis* their landlords – especially after 1767 – than serfs in medieval England or in some central European serf societies.[70]

---

[67] Hoch, 'The serf economy', p. 320.

[68] On the process of enserfment in Russia, see R. Hellie, *Enserfment and military change* (Chicago, 1971) and *idem, The Muscovite Law Code (Ulozhenie) of 1649* (Irvine, CA, 1988); R. E. F. Smith (ed.), *The enserfment of the Russian peasantry* (Cambridge, 1968); Blum, *Lord and peasant*, esp. pp. 247–76.

[69] Blum, *Lord and peasant*, p. 440.

[70] On medieval England, see D. Crook, 'Freedom, villeinage and legal process: the dispute between the abbot of Burton and his tenants of Mickleover, 1280', *Nottingham Medieval Studies* 44 (2000), pp. 123–40; C. Dyer, 'Memories of freedom: attitudes toward serfdom in England, 1200–1350', in M. L. Bush (ed.), *Serfdom and slavery: studies in legal bondage* (Harlow, 1996), pp. 277–95. A particularly informative account of serfdom and extra-manorial jurisdiction in medieval England can be found in C. D. Briggs, 'Manor court procedures, debt litigation levels, and rural credit provision in England c. 1290–1380', *Law and History Review* 24 (2006), pp. 519–58; peasants in German-speaking central Europe were also able to bring cases against their lords. See W. Hagen, *Ordinary Prussians* (Cambridge, 2002), pp. 541–59; S. C. Ogilvie, 'The state in Germany: a non-Prussian view', in J. Brewer and E. Hellmuth (eds.), *Rethinking Leviathan: the eighteenth-century*

One area, in particular, where Russian landlords seem to have enjoyed greater powers than landlords in other serf societies was in their scope for levying feudal rents. Unlike medieval English landlords, the rent-exaction powers of Russian lords were not constrained by 'custom'. Although English lords may have, in theory, enjoyed legal powers of taxation similar to those of Russian landlords, in practice there were limits on their ability to raise existing rents or levy new ones. English serfs, through the manorial courts – as well as, on occasion, the royal courts – had some protection from landlords who tried to exact rents beyond those customarily associated with a holding.[71] Similar constraints existed in other serf societies. On the Stavenow estate in Prussia, feudal obligations were set out in a formal contract, changes to which could be legally challenged by serfs.[72] As far as we can tell (we still know very little about what serfdom in Russia meant in practice), this was not the case on Russian estates. None of the larger, macro-level studies on feudal rents or customary law refers to customary rents on peasant holdings. There do not seem to have been customary rents on the Petrovskoe estate studied by Hoch, nor are there any references to any such thing in the documents for Voshchazhnikovo. Some serfs at Voshchazhnikovo did occasionally petition the estate administration against specific obligations (such as the dues in kind they were required to provide in addition to cash rents).[73] But they did not cite custom as a defence against new levies; none of the petitions in the archive refers to customary obligations of any sort. Of course in both the English and Prussian cases, the ability to challenge the landlord – to enforce the contract – would have been critical. Without this right, the contract implied by custom would only have been as good as the word of the landlord himself.

The Sheremetyevs imposed a broad array of feudal obligations on their Voshchazhnikovo serfs. First, there were the rents attached to estate landholdings. These were set at 15 silver roubles per *tiaglo*, and seem to have remained constant across the nineteenth century (at least between 1796

---

state in Britain and Germany (Oxford, 1999), pp. 167–202; G. Sreenivasan, *The peasants of Ottobeuren 1487–1726: a rural society in early modern Europe* (Cambridge, 2004), chapter 1, esp. pp. 35–6.

[71] J. Hatcher, 'English serfdom and villeinage: towards a reassessment', *Past and Present* 90 (1981), pp. 3–39; J. Kanzaka, 'Villein rents in thirteenth-century England: an analysis of the Hundred Rolls of 1279–1280', *Economic History Review* 56 (2002), pp. 593–618. On use of the royal courts for custom disputes, see Crook, 'Freedom, villeinage, and legal process'; and Dyer, 'Memories of freedom'.

[72] Hagen, *Ordinary Prussians*, pp. 524–5.

[73] See, for instance, the report in RGADA, f. 1287, op. 3, ed. khr. 555 ('Instructions, 1796/ 1800'), where Sheremetyev agrees to consider the serfs' arguments against their feudal obligation to provide oats for the estate stables.

and 1858).[74] In addition to these, there were feudal levies on marriage, migration, land and property transactions, the registration of petitions, the formalisation of contracts, and the use of estate mills. Monopoly rights to the market square and estate fisheries were granted to the highest bidders, and the serfs who won these rights could in turn extract fees from those who traded in the square or fished in the rivers. The Sheremetyevs also levied an annual income tax on earnings from non-agricultural activities. Those serfs who practised a craft, for instance, had to pay a tax of 1 rouble per year.[75] Those who engaged in trade in St Petersburg and Moscow paid a tax of 10 roubles per year.[76] Serfs of the middle and upper strata (roughly 75 per cent of the population) were required to pay a wealth tax of 0.5 per cent annually on the value of their total assets exceeding 500 roubles.[77] In addition, the Sheremetyevs raised money with fines levied for breaking estate rules. Some examples include fines for the late payment of taxes and dues, for the unauthorised use of wood from estate forests, for marrying an outsider without permission, for establishing an independent household without permission, and for failing to register a household servant or labourer brought in from outside the estate. Finally, Voshchazhnikovo serfs were required to pay a communal tax (*mirskie sbory*), the proceeds of which were put toward certain communal expenses, such as the repair of roads, bridges, or fences, the billeting of soldiers, the support of parish churches, and the delivery of feudal dues to the St Petersburg office. All of these levies and their effects on serfs' economic behaviour will be discussed in greater detail in the following chapters.

That Russian landlords had great freedom in levying rents does not necessarily mean that they imposed rents beyond what their serfs could afford. Landlords wanted their estates to be economically viable; there was a point beyond which increasing rents could have diminishing returns. Also, the state imposed certain constraints on rent-levying by holding landlords liable for their serfs' obligations to the crown. The

---

[74] The *tiaglo* was a conventional measure roughly equal to the amount of land that could be worked by one male–female (usually husband–wife) work team. References to measurements other than this rarely appear in the Voshchazhnikovo documents. Dues on feudal lands are recorded in RGADA, f. 1287, op. 3, ed. khr. 555, ll. 22–3 ('Instructions, 1796/1800'), and ed. khr. 2320, l. 12 ('Descriptions of estates, 1858').

[75] RGADA, f. 1287, op. 3, ed. khr. 555, ll. 22–3 ('Instructions, 1796/1800').

[76] *Ibid.*, l. 49.

[77] The existence of an asset tax may have offered an incentive to under-report the value of goods when possible. For this reason, estimates of serf wealth reported in these pages may be underestimates. More will be said about this taxation system in the following chapters. Information on this and on the asset tax is in RGADA, f. 1287, op. 3, ed. khr. 555, ll. 22–3, 49–50 ('Instructions, 1796/1800').

annual poll tax, levied on male serfs, stood in the nineteenth century at roughly 86 silver kopecks per male soul.[78] When serfs were unable to pay, their landlords were required to provide the tax money from their own funds. In addition, landlords were held responsible for the state's annual recruitment levies (a number of conscripts were taken each year from among the serf population), as well as any fines levied on the serf population by the state (such as those imposed for hiding souls in the state tax censuses).[79] It was therefore in landlords' interests to ensure that their serfs could meet their obligations to the state. This is not to say that landlords *never* imposed rents that their serfs were unable to pay, or that no Russian landlord taxed his serfs to the point of impoverishment. There were certainly landlords who managed their estates badly. Still, we should not assume that, because the Russian legal system granted landlords certain theoretical powers over their serfs, this power was, in practice, completely unconstrained.

The documents for Voshchazhnikovo illustrate how the power of Russian landlords was, in fact, constrained to some degree not only by their own self-interest, but also by external institutions. Landlords' estates were, after all, part of a larger institutional environment; there were competing – and in many cases overlapping – local and regional jurisdictions. The landlord had the power of the state behind him, but so did the district and provincial officials, the higher clergy, and other competing interest groups, such as merchant guilds. Because these, too, were powerful groups, the landlord could not always protect his serfs against their demands. Local government officials could, for instance, conscript serfs to build or repair roads, buildings, and bridges.[80] Higher church officials could decide who had permission to trade on the estate church grounds.[81] Merchant guilds could demand that serfs wishing to engage in trade purchase guild licences.[82] All of these demands cut into landlords'

---

[78] Blum, *Lord and peasant*, p. 464.

[79] RGADA, f. 1287, op. 3, ed. khr. 59 ('Instructions for carrying out soul revisions, 1737'), ed. khr. 938 ('On the carrying out of the 7th revision, 1825'), ed. khr. 2266 ('On preparing for the 10th revision, 1857').

[80] As in the case where local government officials conscripted Voshchazhnikovo serfs to help build new bridges in Borisogleb district. In RGADA, f. 1287, op. 3, ed. khr. 2518, l. 5 ('Communal resolutions, 1791').

[81] As in the case where Mikhail Bacharnikov, a trader from outside Voshchazhnikovo, was given permission to open a trading stall on the grounds of the Voshchazhnikovo parish church. In RGADA, f. 1287, op. 3, ed. khr. 1643 ('Petition regarding trade dispute, 1844').

[82] As in the case where all Voshchazhnikovo serfs engaged in trade are informed that they must purchase guild licences or risk incurring fines (levied by the merchant guilds). In RGADA, f. 1287, op. 3, ed. khr. 1391, ll. 6–7 ('List of trading peasants and guilds, 1838').

revenues, since, when serfs were forced to pay rents to other groups (in cash, labour, or time), there was less available for expropriation by the lord. But the documents for Voshchazhnikovo suggest that there was little the landlord could do; fighting these groups, according to the Sheremetyev administration, 'would only result in considerable unpleasantness'.[83]

This is not to say that there was no jurisdictional hierarchy. Evidence for Voshchazhnikovo confirms that, in most instances, serfs came under the jurisdiction of their lords. Disputes among estate serfs over property, credit, inheritance, conscription, and other issues of this sort were handled by the landlord's officials. Only serfs who committed the most serious of crimes – murder or large-scale theft from a member of the landholding class – were tried in provincial courts. Even a serf who had a dispute with another landlord (not his own) was not likely to be tried in the civil courts. The Voshchazhnikovo documents suggest that in these cases it was left up to the two landlords to come to an agreement.[84] Voshchazhnikovo serfs actually had very little to do with government officials in any formal sense; they had very few formal rights before the law. It was the landlord, often represented locally by his official, the bailiff, who officially served as liaison between the state and his serfs.

One fundamental way in which the local institutional framework in Russian serf society seems to have differed from that in western European rual societies is in the role played by the church. At Voshchazhnikovo, the parish churches seem to have been almost entirely dependent on the landlord. The parish clergy on the estate were supported by communal funds, often at the insistence of the landlord. The parish churches were financed mainly by the landlord; there is no mention of a tithe – not even in the account books of the individual churches.[85]

---

[83] In a petition from 1844, two Voshchazhnikovo serfs requested that the landlord stop an outside trader from selling his wares on the estate. The landlord's administration declined to act, noting that the outsider had support from one of the merchant guilds and the church, and that fighting these groups would only bring trouble for estate officials, as well as the petitioners themselves. In RGADA, f. 1287, op. 3, ed. khr. 1643, ll. 2–4 ('Petition regarding trade dispute, 1844').

[84] As in the case where some Voshchazhnikovo serfs and a landlord from Borisoglebskii *uezd* were involved in a property dispute. The dispute was settled by the two landlords. In RGADA, f. 1287, op. 3, ed. khr. 480, l. 7 ('Instructions to Voshchazhnikovo officials, 1785'). Had they been unable to reach an agreement, the two nobles presumably could have taken the case to the civil courts.

[85] The closest things were the fees serfs were required to pay to receive sacraments and register vital events. In addition, serfs were fined for failure to attend services. A more detailed discussion can be found in G. Freeze, *The Russian Levites: parish clergy in the eighteenth century* (Cambridge, MA, 1977), pp. 164–5.

There was no church court on the estate. The consistorial courts, which were located in the provincial capital, mainly heard cases brought by higher clergymen (those above the parish level).[86] Serfs only appeared before these courts for issues relating to marriage – bigamy, in particular.[87] There are no references in the estate documents to the sorts of 'moral' issues – fornication, adultery, failing to attend church services, working on holy days – with which church courts in pre-modern western and central European societies were preoccupied. If such issues did arise on the Voshchazhnikovo estate, they must have been handled informally by the community (as discussed in chapter 4). As far as one can tell, the church was not involved in the provision of welfare; even the clergy sought relief from the commune or the landlord.[88] Serfs themselves do not appear to have given voluntarily to the church. Parish account records suggest that extremely small sums were taken in from the weekly collection plate. For the year 1793, the amount collected by Voshchazhnikovo parish ranged from 4 roubles 25 kopecks per month to 13 roubles 93 kopecks per month.[89] If we assume there were roughly 275 households in the parish, as the 1834 soul revision figures suggest, this means the parish collected, on average, between 1.5 and 5 kopecks per month from each household. In other words, each household donated between 18 and 60 kopecks per year, or 1 to 4 per cent of the minimum annual *obrok* payment of 15 roubles. These sums are remarkably small, especially considering that there were serfs on the estate who earned over 500 roubles annually (as we will see, even elected officials were paid at least 100 roubles per year). While it is not possible at this point to say how representative Voshchazhnikovo was, it is worth noting that Hoch's findings for Petrovskoe are broadly similar. According to Hoch, 'little mention is made [in the Petrovskoe documents] of peasant religious practices, festivals, or the role of the parish church'.[90] The references he does cite

---

[86] The church did not actually have jurisdiction over parishioners, who were laymen, making its local policies near impossible to enforce. Freeze, *Russian Levites*, p. 159.

[87] No cases concerning Voshchazhnikovo serfs were found in the records for the consistorial court in Rostov district. Records are in GAYaO, f. 230, op. 1 ('Records of the Yaroslavl' consistorial court and other ecclesiastical institutions').

[88] As in the case where the widow of the recently deceased priest of Voshchazhnikovo parish begged the landlord to provide relief for her family. The landlord agreed to provide 60 roubles per year. In RGADA f. 1287, op. 3., ed. khr. 1030, ll. 1–3 ('Petition regarding poor relief, 1830'). In 1832, the priest from Vioska parish petitioned Sheremetyev for funding for the parish church. Sheremetyev agreed to provide 1,300 roubles toward the maintenance of the church. In RGADA, f. 1287, op. 3, ed. khr. 1140, ll. 1, 12 ('Petition regarding maintenance of parish church, 1832').

[89] RGADA, f. 1287, op. 3, ed. khr. 608 ('Parish account books, 1793').

[90] Hoch, *Serfdom and social control*, p. 12.

suggest that the parish churches and the local clergy, as at Voshchazhnikovo, were dependent on the estate for financial support, and that the estate serfs were reluctant to subsidise them. Serfs at Petrovskoe, it seems, were often in conflict with the parish clergy over the allocation of local resources.[91] The findings for both Petrovskoe and Voshchazhnikovo are consistent with the more general description of Russian parish conditions described by Gregory Freeze in his work on the nineteenth-century parish clergy.[92]

The only thing over which the local parishes at Voshchazhnikovo seem to have retained some degree of independent control was the issuance of licences to trade on the church grounds. When some Voshchazhnikovo serfs petitioned in 1844 to have the stall of a non-estate trader removed from the church market, the landlord's administration expressed a very definite unwillingness to go up against church authorities.[93] Their response implies that, in cases such as this one, the local parish could count on higher authorities to support it against the landlord. Why this should have been the case is not clear from the documents; it may be that church authorities were more likely to intervene at the local level when revenues were at stake.[94] There is not yet a great deal of empirical evidence available pertaining to the role of the church in peasants' lives, but the evidence we do have, such as that for Petrovskoe and Voshchazhnikovo, suggests that the church probably played a significantly smaller independent role at the local level in Russia than it did in pre-industrial societies in western Europe.

This description of the local institutional framework has been intended to provide a general background to the more detailed account in the chapters that follow. This detailed investigation begins, in chapter 3, with an analysis of household structure and the serf family economy in the village of Voshchazhnikovo. Chapter 4 examines the rural commune, its major functions, and the role it played within the Sheremetyevs' administrative apparatus. Chapters 5–8 focus on the local economy, and include a discussion of factor and retail

---

[91] *Ibid.*, p. 148.

[92] G. Freeze, *The parish clergy in nineteenth-century Russia: crisis, reform, counter-reform* (Princeton, 1983), esp. pp. 55–9. They are also consistent with the account of the nineteenth-century Russian priest I. S. Belliustin: *The description of the clergy in rural Russia: the memoir of a nineteenth-century parish priest* (translated G. Freeze) (Ithaca, 1985).

[93] RGADA, f. 1287, op. 3, ed. khr. 1643 ('Petition regarding trade dispute, 1844').

[94] The trading stalls may have been on land the estate was required by law to provide to the parish. See the discussion in Freeze, *Russian Levites*, pp. 127–9. It is possible that revenues from the market were used to support the local clergy.

markets, consumption, and material life on the Voshchazhnikovo estate. The concluding chapter returns to the question of how the institution of serfdom actually manifested itself in a particular locality, and uses the evidence presented in chapters 3–8 to examine the implications of this institutional framework for economic and social life in rural Russia.

3   Household structure and family economy

The nature of the peasant household constitutes the most significant single characteristic of the peasantry as a specific social phenomenon and gives rise to the generic features displayed by peasantries all over the world. A peasant household is characterised by the extent of integration of the peasant family's life with its farming enterprise ... A Russian peasant household consisted typically of blood-relatives spanning two or three generations and their spouses. However, the basic determinant of household membership was not the actual kinship but the total participation in the life of the household ... This unity implied living together under the authority of the patriarchal head, close cooperation in day-to-day labour, a 'common purse', and the basic identification of a member with the household ... Generally, the head of the household was the father of the family or its oldest male member. His authority over other members and over household affairs implied both autocratic rights and extensive duties of care and protection ... Women, in spite of their heavy burden of labour, were ... nearly always placed under the authority of a male ... The scope of market and money relations was limited by the extent of the consumption-determined production, low rates of surplus, and a low level of professional specialisation and diversification of the rural population.

T. Shanin, *Russia as a 'developing society'* (New Haven and London, 1985), pp. 66–7.

3.1   Approaches to the Russian peasant household

This classical picture of 'peasantries all over the world', inherited from Haxthausen and Chayanov and cherished for many generations, has been questioned over the past few decades as a historical picture of pre-industrial Europe. Community studies by the Cambridge Group and the French Annales school first found it inadequate to England and northern France. Since then, other studies have found that it also fails to describe much of central Europe, the Netherlands, parts of Scandinavia, and many other societies in western Europe.[1]

---

[1] For a summary of the pioneering studies on household structure in English and European societies, see P. Laslett with R. Wall (eds.), *Household and family in past time* (Cambridge,

Nonetheless, this view is still accepted for Russia. The Russian peasantry is seen as the paradigm of 'traditional society', with large, multiple- or extended-family households headed by patriarchs, early and universal marriage, and low levels of permanent celibacy. This traditional household formation system is viewed as part of a larger, Chayanovian economic framework, where markets in land and labour were largely absent, leaving the household economy dependent on family members for labour inputs. Furthermore, a large household is thought to have been especially important in the context of the Russian land commune, since communally held land is supposed to have been allocated to a household proportionately to the size of its labour force. The large, extended-family peasant household is prevalent in the accounts of nineteenth-century travellers to Russia, as well as in the ethnographic literature, and has been widely accepted in the modern historical literature.[2] The pioneering work on serf households undertaken by historians Czap and Hoch has largely confirmed this picture for two of the Gagarin family estates in the Central Black Earth Region.[3] But the extent to which this pattern existed in other parts of Russia or among serfs on other landlords' estates is still not clear.

More recent research has suggested some degree of variation in household size and structure in imperial Russia. The findings of Aleksandrov, Mitterauer and Kagan, Melton, and Kolle indicate that households in the Central Industrial Region may have been smaller and less complex than those described for the Central Black Earth Region.[4] In most accounts, this variation is attributed to geography or culture.

1972); R. Wall, J. Robin, and P. Laslett (eds.), *Family forms in historic Europe* (Cambridge, 1983); R. Wall, T. Harevan, and J. Ehmer (eds.), *Family history revisited* (Newark and London, 2001). For a more recent survey of the field, see D. P. Kertzer and M. Barbagli (eds.), *The history of the European family*, 3 vols. (New Haven, 2001–3). Since the early work of the Cambridge Group and the Annales, family history has become a vibrant sub-field, with specialised journals, such as *History of the Family* and *Journal of Family History*, devoted to research in this area.

[2] One of the earliest formulations of this view is in Haxthausen, *Studien*. Haxthausen's view of peasant households was also adopted by Herzen. See 'The Russian people and socialism', esp. pp. 190–1. In the modern literature see O. Figes, *Natasha's dance: a cultural history of Russia* (New York, 2002), p. 258; B. N. Mironov, 'Traditsionnoe demograficheskoe povedenie krest'ian v XIX–nachale XX v.', in A. G. Vishnevskii (ed.), *Brachnost', rozhdaemost', smertnost' v Rossii i v SSSR* (Moscow, 1977), pp. 83–104; M. Mitterauer and R. Sieder, *Vom Patriarchat zur Partnerschaft: zum Strukturwandel der Familie* (Munich, 1991), p. 53; T. Shanin, *The awkward class: the political sociology of the peasantry in a developing society* (Oxford, 1972), pp. 66–7; C. Worobec, *Peasant Russia: family and community in the post-emancipation period* (DeKalb, IL, 1995), pp. 76–117.

[3] P. Czap, 'A large family, the peasant's greatest wealth: serf households in Mishino, Russia, 1814–1858', in R. Wall, J. Robin, and P. Laslett (eds.), *Family forms in historic Europe* (Cambridge, 1983), pp. 105–51; Hoch, *Serfdom and social control*.

[4] V. A. Aleksandrov, 'Typology of the Russian peasant family in the feudal period', *Soviet Studies in History* (1982), pp. 26–62; M. Mitterauer and A. Kagan, 'Russian and central European family structures: a comparative view', *Journal of Family History* (1982),

The geographical explanation sees a greater demand for large families in the Central Black Earth Region, where landowners often specialised in agriculture and peasant households required labour to cultivate demesne land and family plots. A large labour force was less critical in the Central Industrial Region, it is argued, since the land was less fertile, forcing peasants to seek income primarily from non-agricultural activities.[5] The geographical theory assumes the existence of the repartitional commune, but because the soil was less cultivable in the Central Industrial Region, households' incentives for maximizing allotment size are thought to have been weaker than in the Central Black Earth Region.

The cultural view sees peasants' demographic decisions primarily as expressions of traditional social norms.[6] Regional variation, according to this view, might be attributed to the weakening of traditional culture in more urbanised areas, where behaviour is supposed to have been more individualistic and market-oriented.[7] That said, most historians of Russia[8] would not see these approaches as so clearly distinguished from one another. The view that cultural norms determined demographic behaviour is fairly widespread in the literature on Russian peasants; the effects of local ecology, though acknowledged, are viewed as relatively marginal.

The geographical and cultural views underemphasise the effects of the institutional structure on demographic behaviour. Both tend to assume certain underlying features of peasant demographic behaviour, with institutions, such as serfdom, treated as superstructure, whose observed effects are comparatively trivial. In the words of one historian: 'when owners tried to change their serfs' social customs, they were likely to fail'.[9] The geographical approach goes somewhat further than the cultural in allowing for the effects of local economic conditions, but treats the local economy in any given place as an inevitable outcome of ecological conditions, without reference to the institutional context. In other words, estates in the Central Industrial Region operated within one sort of

---

pp. 103–31; Melton, 'Household economies and communal conflicts'; H. Kolle, *Social change in nineteenth-century Russia: family development in a proto-industrial community* (Bergen, 2006).

[5] See Kolle, *Social change*, summarised on pp. 287–95.

[6] As outlined in B. N. Mironov and B. Eklof, *The social history of imperial Russia, 1700–1917*, 2 vols. (Boulder, 1999), pp. 58–66 (on 'demographic mentality'); in the Russian original, *Sotsial'naia istoriia*, vol. I, pp. 160–7.

[7] C. Worobec notes that nineteenth-century observers held this view, *Peasant Russia*, p. 79; Mironov talks about a transition from 'traditional' to 'rational' forms of demographic behaviour in *Social History*, vol. I, p. 109 (in *Sotsial'naia istoriia*, pp. 209–10).

[8] Indeed, most western historians of any society since Montesquieu, who regarded culture (and hence political systems) as largely shaped by ecological and geographical conditions.

[9] J. Bushnell, 'Did serf owners control serf marriage?', *Slavic Review* 52 (1993), p. 445.

regional economy, while those in the Central Black Earth Region existed in another. There is little attempt to determine the extent to which local economy was itself shaped by manorial or communal practices.

In this chapter, the effects of institutions on serfs' demographic decisions will be examined using data for the village of Voshchazhnikovo, the largest of the Voshchazhnikovo estate villages. Nearly one third of estate households were located in Voshchazhnikovo. The data used here come primarily from two estate household listings (*podvornye opisi*) and four soul revisions (*revizskie skazki*).[10] The household listings were compiled by the estate management in 1832 and 1838, and provide information on the sex, age, and marital status of household members, as well as notes on the quantity of livestock and land in each household's possession, the feudal obligations of each, their sources of income, and descriptions of their dwellings.[11] The soul revisions, on the other hand, were state tax documents, used by the central government to assess the poll tax for which all male peasants in Russia were liable. Serfs were recorded by household in the revisions, and the name, age, sex, and marital status of each household member is provided. There were ten soul revisions carried out between 1719 and 1858, but only the last four, those for the years 1816, 1834, 1850, and 1858, have survived for Voshchazhnikovo.

In addition to the household listings and soul revisions, this chapter draws on information provided in landlords' 'instructions' (rules and regulations governing various estate procedures), estate passport lists (lists of estate peasants who had permission from the landlord to work elsewhere or non-estate peasants who had permission to work on the Voshchazhnikovo estate), land transactions contracts, and serf petitions to the landlord.

3.2   Methodological issues

The household listings and soul revisions, though rich in detail, are not without drawbacks as source materials for a study of this kind. First, the soul revisions are *de jure* lists, meaning they provide information about all serfs who were *legally* resident on the estate at the time of the count rather than those who were *actually* present. It is therefore possible that the soul revisions overstate the real size of households. The estate household

---

[10] The estate household listings can be found in RGADA, f. 1287, op. 3, ed. khr. 1143 (1832/8). Soul revisions for 1834 and 1850 are in RGADA, f. 1287, op. 3, ed. khr. 2553 (1834), and ed. khr. 1941 (1850); soul revisions for 1816 and 1858 are in GAYaO, f. 100, op. 8, d. 647 (1816), and d. 2656 (1858).

[11] It seems likely that such inventories were carried out more often, but only the listings for these years have survived.

listings provide a useful cross-check on them, however, since absentees are noted as such in the margins – making these, in a sense, both *de jure* and *de facto* listings.[12]

A second and potentially more serious problem involves the possibility of under-registration in the soul revisions. In examining the distribution of the Voshchazhnikovo population by age and sex (Table 3.1), we find a significant disparity in the number of males to females in this village. This imbalance appears in all four of the soul revisions, with the ratio of males per 100 females falling from a high of 86 in the 1816 revision to 78 in 1858. At first glance, under-registration of males seems the likely explanation. The revisions were, after all, originally compiled as tax documents; each male soul recorded was obligated to pay the state poll tax. Responsibility for the collection and delivery of the tax fell ultimately on the estate management (i.e. the landlord), creating a strong incentive for hiding souls where possible.[13]

There are, however, three problems with this interpretation. First, it seems unlikely that under-registration itself could account for such disparity. To produce sex ratios of this sort, the estate management would have had to have hidden some 15 to 20 per cent of the male serf population, and statistical studies of the revision data by the Soviet historian V. M. Kabuzan suggest that hidden souls comprised at most 3 per cent of the taxable population.[14] This is consistent with evidence for Voshchazhnikovo which suggests that revisions were carried out thoroughly and conscientiously. Estate documents indicate that estate and communal officials did their best to account for each and every serf.[15] They had a strong incentive: substantial fines were to be levied on the entire serf community for every soul missed.[16]

The second problem with this interpretation concerns the estate household listings (1832 and 1838), where the same disparity in sex ratios is evident. While it seems plausible that landlords (together with serfs) could have had an interest in hiding souls from the state tax collectors, it seems highly unlikely that landlords would under-report males in documents compiled for their own purposes. It also seems unlikely that, given the

---

[12] The overstatement in the soul revisions might, on the other hand, be offset by the fact that neither they nor the household listings provides information on live-in labourers and servants – a problem which will be discussed later on in this section.

[13] On hiding souls see V. M. Kabuzan, *Narodonaselenie Rossii v XVIII–pervoi polovine XIX v.* (Moscow, 1963); Troinitskii, *The serf population in Russia*, pp. vii–xxiii.

[14] Kabuzan, *Narodonaselenie Rossii*, p. 171.

[15] RGADA, f. 1287, op. 3, ed. khr. 714 ('Instructions regarding the soul revision, 1816') and 1942 ('Instructions regarding the soul revision, 1850').

[16] RGADA, f. 1287, op. 3, ed. khr. 714 ('Instructions regarding the soul revision, 1816').

Table 3.1. *Age structure, village of Voshchazhnikovo, 1816–58*

Age	1816 revision			1832 household list			1834 revision			1838 household list			1850 revision			1858 revision		
	M	F	T	M	F	T	M	F	T	M	F	T	M	F	T	M	F	T
00–4	61	54	115	51	46	97	50	52	102	45	55	100	47	49	96	49	43	92
05–9	46	55	101	46	41	87	54	43	97	45	47	92	36	48	84	37	32	69
10–14	44	70	114	46	41	87	52	47	99	45	45	90	38	58	96	30	46	76
15–19	74	56	130	43	38	81	36	32	68	48	37	85	41	43	84	32	46	78
20–4	41	43	84	31	46	77	29	51	80	26	32	58	43	45	88	28	44	72
25–9	37	51	88	27	42	69	28	41	69	25	39	64	37	32	69	38	42	80
30–4	21	32	53	36	54	90	28	46	74	20	36	56	27	31	58	32	37	69
35–9	30	47	77	34	36	70	38	44	82	32	41	73	27	30	57	26	22	48
40–4	24	52	76	32	39	71	32	29	61	25	32	57	21	34	55	21	21	42
45–9	28	31	59	14	14	28	15	26	41	22	36	58	15	30	45	15	28	43
50–4	17	21	38	18	38	56	18	34	52	11	15	26	22	30	52	15	30	45
55–9	22	17	39	11	31	42	10	36	46	11	33	44	13	20	33	14	26	40
60–4	13	13	26	13	28	41	11	25	36	7	20	27	12	16	28	10	20	30
65–9	9	9	18	12	12	24	17	13	30	9	15	24	7	17	24	10	16	26
70 plus	10	9	19	12	16	28	8	14	22	12	14	26	10	17	27	8	16	24
unknown	2	0	2	5	5	10	4	0	4	2	9	11	6	2	8	1	1	2
TOTAL	479	560	1,039	431	527	958	430	533	963	385	506	891	402	502	904	366	470	836

Sources: GAYaO, f. 100, op. 8, d. 647 ('Soul revision, 1816') and d. 2656 ('Soul revision, 1858'); RGADA, f. 1287, op. 3, ed. khr. 1143 ('Inventories of households, 1832/8'), ed. khr. 2553 ('Soul revision, 1834'), and ed. khr. 1941 ('Soul revision, 1850').

amount of detail in these listings, serfs themselves would have been able to hide significant numbers of male household members from estate authorities.

Finally, a closer look at the age/sex structure of the population indicates that the problem in Voshchazhnikovo was not so much a shortage of males as a *surplus of females*. The number of females in each age category does not begin to decline significantly until around age 40–50, suggesting that females in younger age groups were moving into the village at a fairly steady rate. It is unlikely that these were young women coming into Voshchazhnikovo as servants or inmates, since labourers from outside the estate were not included in the *de jure* revisions. Besides, as we will see in chapter 6, the lists kept by the landlord's administration of non-estate serfs resident in Voshchazhnikovo indicate that servants and labourers were more often male than female.

A more plausible explanation for the disparity in sex ratios is that women from outside the estate were coming into Voshchazhnikovo through marriage.[17] Unfortunately, this is a difficult theory to test given the nature of the available source materials. Marriage registers for Voshchazhnikovo parish show that local serfs did frequently bring wives into the village from outside; however, they do not tell us how many Voshchazhnikovo women left the village to marry serfs from other estates, making it impossible to determine whether the number of females marrying in was in fact greater than the number marrying out.[18] Still, there are several points that can be made in support of the theory that women were migrating into the village through marriage. First, this theory is consistent with the age and sex distribution of the population, where the number of females in younger age groups (15–30) remains roughly constant, and does not begin to taper off until after age 40. Second, if more women were marrying into the village than marrying out, we might expect to find an extraordinarily high proportion of never-married females in the population.[19] This was the case in the village Voshchazhnikovo, where up to 20 per cent of the female population remained unmarried in the period 1816–58 (see Table 3.10 below). Finally, the landlord himself expressed concern about the growing number of unmarried females on his estates,

---

[17] This practice has been observed for villages on the Sheremetyevs' Vykhino estate near Moscow. A discussion can be found in A. Avdeev, A. Blum, and I. Troitskaia, 'Peasant marriage in nineteenth-century Russia', *Population* 59 (2004), pp. 721–64.

[18] GAYaO, f. 230, op. 11, d. 1588 ('Parish registers for Voshchazhnikovo parish, 1786–1826'), and d. 1608 ('Parish registers for Voshchazhnikovo parish, 1850–61').

[19] If a substantial number of local men chose wives from outside the village, the marriage market for local women should have been highly competitive, with a significant proportion remaining unmarried.

and attributed it explicitly to male serfs' preference for non-estate brides.[20] Men, it seems, were much more likely to choose non-estate spouses than women, since the Sheremetyevs, like other Russian land-lords, charged local women a substantial fee for marrying non-estate serfs.[21] Serf men, on the other hand, were free to bring wives on to the estate without paying such a penalty.[22] The Sheremetyevs do not appear to have had an 'exchange' policy, as some landlords did, where the number of women marrying out was coordinated with the number marry-ing in.[23] Thus the imbalance in sex ratios noted here may have been at least partly due to disparities arising from estate policy.[24]

It is possible that this trend was further exacerbated by male out-migration in the region.[25] Since the soul revisions were *de jure* documents, the names of serfs who left the estate legally as migrant labourers (i.e. those who obtained passports from the estate administration) would still have been recorded in the listings, and their *de facto* absence would not have affected the sex ratio. It is possible, however, that there was some degree of illegal emigration on this estate. Unfortunately, illegal emigra-tion is nearly impossible to document, though there are signs that it occasionally occurred at Voshchazhnikovo. There are several entries in the estate household listings where members of households (always male) are noted as having 'disappeared without a trace' or as having 'run away'.[26] In two cases entire households are noted as missing, and notes in the margin read 'it is said that the family lives in St Petersburg, but this cannot be verified'.[27] These entries are not terribly surprising, considering

---

[20] RGADA, f. 1287, op. 3, ed. khr. 1318, l. 26 ('Instructions, 1800').

[21] This policy is discussed in greater detail in section 3.7 of this chapter. Feudal taxes on marriage were not unique to Russia. See R. M. Smith, 'Further models of medieval marriage: landlords, serfs and priests in rural England, c. 1290–1370', in C. Duhamel-Amado and G. Lobrichon (eds.), *Georges Duby: l'écriture de l'histoire* (Brussels, 1996), pp. 161–73.

[22] RGADA, f. 1287, op. 3, ed. khr. 555, l. 49 ('Instructions, 1796/1800').

[23] A discussion of this approach can be found in Bushnell, 'Did serf owners', p. 425.

[24] If all landlords implemented a similar policy, we might expect sex ratios to be more sym-metrical; however, there is no reason at this point to think this particular marriage policy was universal, even if it was widespread among the wealthier landlords. (See Bushnell, 'Did serf owners', pp. 422–6, for a discussion of landlords' approaches to off-estate marriage.) It is possible that serf men at Voshchazhnikovo were marrying women from among the state peasantry or, in rarer instances, from other legal categories (*sosloviia*).

[25] Low sex ratios have been noted for other societies with substantial male out-migration. See the discussion in L. Page Moch, *Moving Europeans: migration in western Europe since 1650* (Bloomington, 1992), pp. 68–83; also in C. B. Brettel, *Men who migrate, women who wait: population and history in a Portuguese parish* (Princeton, 1986), pp. 92–3; S. Ogilvie, *A bitter living: women, markets, and social capital in early modern Germany* (Oxford, 2003), chapter 2.

[26] 'propal bez vesti' or 'beglyi' in RGADA, f. 1287, op. 3, ed. khr. 1143 ('Inventories of households, 1832/8').

[27] *Ibid.*

the size of the territory; it would have been difficult to keep track of everyone, despite estate officials' best efforts. In light of such entries, it does seem possible that at least some young men from this region could have gone off to work in cities and disappeared there, never again returning to their estates of origin.[28]

Uneven sex ratios have been noted by other historians for various parts of the Central Industrial Region, and differential migration is usually cited as the cause, since urban areas were supposed to have exerted a stronger 'pull' on males in this part of Russia.[29] Unfortunately, it is not clear from existing studies whether this migration was *de jure* or *de facto*, since most of these (especially the ones for the pre-Emancipation period) are based on qualitative evidence rather than quantitative micro-level data. Very little work has been done on migration using nominal lists for specific localities, making it difficult to compare Voshchazhnikovo with other estates in the region.[30]

Another problem encountered in using soul revisions as sources for a study of household structure concerns the way 'household' was defined by those compiling the lists. The estate authorities in Voshchazhnikovo recognised two different definitions or levels of 'household'. The first of these was essentially that originally employed by Laslett and used in the present analysis: a co-resident domestic group, participating in the same domestic economy (or eating from a 'common pot').[31] The second of these treated the household as a tax unit: those collectively responsible for tax payments and feudal dues (including the provision of conscripts).

---

[28] Still, as with 'hidden souls', these numbers were probably marginal, and could hardly account by themselves for the great disparity in the number of males to females in Voshchazhnikovo.

[29] See, for instance, B. A. Engel, *Between the fields and the city: women, work, and family in Russia, 1861–1914* (Cambridge, 1996), pp. 34–63; J. Burds, *Peasant dreams and market politics: labour migration and the Russian village, 1861–1905* (Pittsburgh, 1998), pp. 17–39; B. B. Gorshkov, 'Serfs on the move: peasant seasonal migration in pre-reform Russia 1800–61', *Kritika: Explorations in Russian and Eurasian History* 1 (2000), esp. pp. 642–3.

[30] On the macro-level, it is perhaps worth noting that a similar trend is evident in the data collected for the Russian census of 1897. The published figures show that males consistently outnumbered females in urban areas and vice versa in rural areas (this is especially pronounced in the Central Industrial Region). See N. Troinitskii (ed.), *Naselenie imperii po perepisi 28-go ianvaria 1897 goda* (St Petersburg, 1897). This is the reverse of the situation in pre-modern western Europe. See discussions in R. Wall, 'The composition of households in a population of 6 men to 10 women: southeast Bruges in 1814', in R. Wall, J. Robin, and P. Laslett (eds.), *Family forms in historic Europe* (Cambridge, 1983), pp. 421–74; and, in the same volume, A. Fauve-Chamoux, 'The importance of women in an urban environment: the example of the Rheims household at the beginning of the industrial revolution', pp. 475–92.

[31] P. Laslett, 'Introduction: the history of the family', in P. Laslett with R. Wall (eds.), *Household and family in past time* (Cambridge, 1972), esp. pp. 23–8.

Often the two coincided, with those living together also dividing state and feudal burdens among themselves. It was also possible, however, to find two or three 'households' in the Laslett sense being assessed collectively – as one household – for tax purposes.

How did this work in practice? A serf in Voshchazhnikovo wishing to separate from his household of origin had to petition the estate authorities for permission. In some cases, a serf would request only that he (and, in most cases, his family) be allowed to live separately from his parents. If permission was granted, the serf might then later petition for permission to be assessed separately for taxes and dues (a formal division, or *formal'-nyi razdel*). In other instances, serfs would petition simultaneously for a separation from their household of origin and a formal household division. If the formal division was granted, the petitioner and his family would form a new, separate residence, while the landlord's officials would make the appropriate changes to the estate account books, and begin assessing the two households separately for feudal dues and taxes and, most importantly, conscripts. Alternatively, authorities might grant permission for serfs to establish separate residences, but deny them a full household division.[32] In this case, their positions in the account books would remain unchanged, though it would be noted in the margin that the tax unit now comprised several households.

How do we know which definition of household was being used in the household listings and soul revisions? Are these domestic groups or tax units?[33] This is not a serious problem with the estate household listings, since they are so detailed. We know that all those listed as members of a particular household were assessed together for feudal and communal dues and state taxes, because the amounts owed were recorded in the document. We also know that they lived under one roof, because a description of the dwelling is provided for each household. The soul revisions, however, are slightly more opaque. They were official tax listings, and as such it is reasonable to assume that they recorded taxation units rather than domestic groups. But there are several reasons to think that these two often coincided at Voshchazhnikovo. When compared with

---

[32] As in RGADA, f. 1287, op. 3, ed. khr. 1646, l. 10 ('Petition for household division, 1844'). A serf family was given permission to live separately ('otdelit' zhitel'stvom na osoboe semeistvo') though they would be assessed for feudal and communal dues and conscription obligations together ('po ocherednoi knige i po gospodskim i obshchestven-nom povinnostiam ostavit po prezhnemu').

[33] This problem is discussed in relation to soul revisions for Tambov province in V. Kanitschev, R. Kontchakov, Iu. Mizis, and E. Morozova, 'The development of the family structure in Tambov region, 1800–1917', in P. Kooij and R. Paping (eds.), *Where the twain meet again: new results of the Dutch-Russian project on regional development 1750–1917* (Groningen, 2004), pp. 239–62.

entries from estate account books, we find that those families noted as 'living separately' in the accounts were indeed recorded separately in the revisions and were given a different household number from that of the household(s) with which they paid taxes and dues. In addition, we know that the revision enumerators were instructed to go out into the villages and record information for members of each individual household, rather than simply copy out an existing tax list.[34] Finally, and most significantly, the soul revisions and the household listings match up very well, making it very likely that the same units were being recorded in each instance.

Another important methodological consideration concerns resident non-kin. Historians have long assumed that live-in servants and lodgers were unknown to rural Russia, since such persons are uniformly absent from soul revisions and household listings. However, domestic servants and live-in labourers *were* present in serf households in Voshchazhnikovo. We know they existed because there are annual passport lists for in-migrants which record the names of all non-estate serfs living at Voshchazhnikovo. These lists provide information on the labourers' place of origin, the length of their contracts, their occupations on the estate, and the names of their Voshchazhnikovo employers (i.e. those with whom they were living while on the estate). These people do not appear in household listings or soul revisions because, according to the landlord's instructions, they were counted with their households of origin.[35] Unfortunately, it is not possible to adjust the household listings to reflect the presence of servants and lodgers, since the years for which immigration lists have survived and those for which there are soul revisions do not coincide. Furthermore, there is very little information available regarding the role of such persons in the peasant household, making it impossible to speculate on the extent to which such residents were integrated into their host households.[36] In this respect, then, the household

---

[34] Instructions for carrying out revisions are among the estate papers which survived for Voshchazhnikovo. See RGADA, f. 1287, op. 3, ed. khr. 59 (for the year 1737), ed. khr. 714 (for the year 1816), ed. khr. 1942 and 1943 (for the year 1850).

[35] RGADA, f. 1287, op. 3, ed. khr. 555, l.22 ('Instructions, 1796/1800'). Point 4 in the instructions states that 'all serfs will be counted in the villages where they are registered (*propisan*), where they have homes and *tiagly*, and not where they may happen to be living at the time of the count'.

[36] It does not seem, on the basis of available data, that service was the same sort of life-cycle phenomenon in Voshchazhnikovo that it was in England/northwestern Europe. The servants at Voshchazhnikovo were usually male, and often married. Female servants were usually middle-aged widows or spinsters. These findings will be discussed in greater detail in chapter 6. Data come from RGADA, f. 1287, op. 3, ed. khr. 1143 ('Inventories of households, 1832/8'), and ed. khr. 271 ('Passport list, 1762').

sizes provided in the estate listings and soul revisions must be regarded as minima.

One final point concerns the nature of a cross-sectional analysis based on census-like source material. Cross-sectional analysis has been criticised by some social scientists as misleading, in that it provides a static view of household structure rather than a dynamic one.[37] In other words, a cross-sectional analysis can tell us how many simple-family households there were in a society at a given point in time, but it can not tell us how many of those households would eventually become complex households. Critics of cross-sectional studies argue that a census could have been compiled just before a son brought his wife into a household or before the birth of a grandchild. On this view, a cross-sectional analysis is more likely to reflect 'accidental demographic circumstances' than the true underlying household structure.[38]

That a census provides only a momentary snapshot rather than a continuous moving picture is of course true. The question is how representative the snapshot is of a hypothetical series for which it is the only sample. Unless there is some reason to think otherwise, 'accidental demographic circumstances' should be distributed equally across households, so a snapshot in time would have been just as likely to capture a complex household that was on the verge of becoming a simple one as a simple-family household that was about to become complex. To claim that the snapshot is not representative of the underlying structure, that it is an outlier from the hypothetical series would require evidence about that series or structure that is better than the snapshot itself. An *a priori* presumption based on anecdotal travellers' impressions is no substitute for such evidence.[39] Until such evidence is forthcoming, there is no reason to assume that a momentary snapshot is unrepresentative. The present study, like the household analyses of Czap and Hoch, is actually based on a series of snapshots for different points in time. Since none of these departs radically from the others, there is even less reason to doubt their representativeness in their locality and time period.[40]

---

[37] See the discussion in Moon, *The Russian peasantry*, pp. 164–5 and 179–80.

[38] *Ibid.*, p. 179. A thoughtful critique of this view can be found in T. Guinnane, *The vanishing Irish: households, migration, and the rural economy in Ireland, 1850–1914* (Princeton, 1997), pp. 143–6.

[39] Dennison and Carus, 'The invention', pp. 1–22.

[40] T. K. Dennison, 'Serfdom and household structure in central Russia: Voshchazhnikovo 1816–1858', *Continuity and Change* 18 (3) (2003), pp. 395–429.

3.3   Household size and structure

If the conventional view of Russian peasant household structure held for the Voshchazhnikovo estate, we would expect the household listings and soul revisions to reveal a distinctly non-European pattern, marked by large, complex, multiple-family households, such as those found by Czap and Hoch for estates in the Central Black Earth Region.[41]

Some basic descriptive statistics regarding household size in the village of Voshchazhnikovo are provided in Table 3.2. Mean household size (MHS) in four of the six household listings/revisions is under 5.0, while for the last two revisions it is only slightly higher than 5.0. Larger-scale studies of Russian household size based on aggregative data, such as that of Aleksandrov, have suggested that MHS may have been lower in the Central Industrial Region than in other parts of Russia, though the estimates from these studies are still higher than the MHS figures reported here.[42] The figures for Voshchazhnikovo are, however, consistent with those calculated by Mitterauer and Kagan for Yaroslavl' province in 1762–3.[43] Especially remarkable is the extent to which these figures differ from those of Czap's for Mishino (where MHS in the nineteenth century varied between 8.5 and 9.7) and Hoch's for Petrovskoe (where MHS varied between 7.7 and 9.0).[44]

While the range of household sizes in Voshchazhnikovo is certainly much greater than one would expect to find in pre-industrial England or Europe, it again differs from the figures for the Central Black Earth Region. We see in Table 3.2 that the minimum household size in each listing is 1 and the maximum varies between 14 and 20. On the Mishino estate, in particular, there were serf households with as many as 30 members; 14 would not have been considered unusual.[45] In Voshchazhnikovo, 14-member households were rare. In the listings for 1816 and 1832, there was only one 14-member household (in each case the next largest household had 10 members). In 1834, two 14-member households were recorded, 1838 had one 16-member household, 1850 recorded two

---

[41] Czap and Hoch derived their figures from soul revisions and inventories of households. Czap, 'A large family', pp. 110–12; Hoch, *Serfdom and social control*, pp. 66–7.

[42] Aleksandrov, for instance, estimates MHS for the Central Non-Black-Earth Region as having been around 7.4 in 1710, falling to 6.8 by 1858. In Aleksandrov, 'Typology', p. 42.

[43] Mitterauer and Kagan, 'Russian and central European family structures', p. 109. Their calculations for rural Yaroslavl' put MHS at 5.2.

[44] Czap, 'The perennial multiple-family'; Hoch, *Serfdom and social control*, p. 79. Chi-square tests were used to rule out the possibility that observed differences in household size between Voshchazhnikovo and the other two estates were due to random variation (the tests were significant at the .01 level).

[45] Czap, 'The perennial multiple-family', p. 11.

Table 3.2. *Mean household size, village of Voshchazhnikovo, 1816–58*

	1816	1832[a]	1834	1838[a]	1850	1858
Mean	4.57	4.77	4.93	4.82	5.27	5.19
Standard deviation	2.39	2.56	2.71	2.92	3.68	3.42
Median	4	4	5	4	5	4
Mode	4	2	5	2	1	1
Range	1–14	1–14	1–14	1–16	1–20	1–16
Total no. of households	227	201	195	184	172	160
Total population	1038	958	963	891	914	836
No. of households of 7–9	34	36	44	41	39	36
No. of households of 10+	8	11	8	11	17	19
No. of households of 15+	0	0	0	1	4	1

[a] Indicates estate household listing.
Sources: RGADA, f. 1287, op. 3, ed. khr. 1143 ('Inventories of households, 1832/8'), ed. khr. 2553 ('Soul revision, 1834'), ed. khr. 1941 ('Soul revision, 1850'), and GAYaO, f. 100, op. 8, d. 647 ('Soul revision, 1816'), and d. 2656 ('Soul revision, 1858').

households of 20 people, and 1858 had one 16-member household. In Mishino, the proportion of the population living in households of 9 persons or more varied from a low of 56.6 per cent in 1834 to a high of 76.6 per cent in 1795.[46] In Voshchazhnikovo, the proportion of households of 9 persons or more varied between 17 per cent (1832) and 37 per cent (1850). In Mishino, between 13 and 20 per cent of the population lived in households of more than 15 persons.[47] In Voshchazhnikovo, such households contained less than 2 per cent of the population, with the exception of 1850 where they contained 8 per cent. Furthermore, as we shall see shortly, there were significantly more single-person (solitary) households in Voshchazhnikovo than there were in either Mishino or Petrovskoe.

Although the MHS figures in Table 3.2 are lower than those found elsewhere in Russia, they do seem to be growing over time. Also remarkable are the changes in the modal value; by the end of this period solitary households have become the most numerous. That the characteristics of Voshchazhnikovo households exhibited significant change over time does suggest that household formation strategies responded to changes in incentives beyond geography and culture. Ecological and soil conditions in the Rostov district did not suddenly, in the mid-nineteenth century, begin to resemble those of the southern agricultural zone. And while

[46] *Ibid.*, p. 11. [47] *Ibid.*, p. 11.

cultural norms may evolve, it seems unlikely that they did so in the short space between soul revisions (maximum 16 years). Moreover, the change exhibited at Voshchazhnikovo is in the wrong direction: by the end of the period households were becoming more 'traditional' rather than more 'modern'.

While the documents for Voshchazhnikovo, as noted in chapter 1, do not allow us adequately to address change over time, they do allow some scope for speculation. The landlord's instructions, for instance, suggest that policies designed to regulate serfs' demographic behaviour did not remain constant over the period – new rules were introduced and old ones were sometimes waived.[48] It also appears that stricter landlord policies prohibiting household division were in effect by the middle of the nineteenth century.[49] According to landlords' instructions for Voshchazhnikovo from the year 1796, serf households were supposed to contain at least two male workers between the ages of 17 and 65.[50] The extent to which this was enforced, however, seems to have varied over time. There is evidence, in the form of serf petitions and individual land-lord decrees, to suggest that it was more strictly enforced in the later nineteenth century, with fines being levied more systematically.[51] Even stricter policies may have been implemented in the 1850s as a result of recruitment levies for the Crimean War.[52]

Another possibility is that the trend toward larger households was connected to an increase in emigration to urban areas. Although the households appear to be quite large in the revisions, it is possible that, given the substantial levels of emigration in earlier periods, many of those listed were not in fact living in the village (emigration would not have been reflected in the *de jure* soul revisions). If this were the case, members of

---

[48] For example, in a set of instructions for the year 1796, Count Sheremetyev, in response to serfs' requests, temporarily reduced by 50 per cent the fee levied on serf women for marrying non-estate serfs. RGADA, f. 1287, op. 3, ed. khr. 555, ll. 49–50 ('Instructions, 1796/1800'). In another example from 1800, the Count introduced new financial incentives for male serfs who chose local spouses instead of marrying non-estate females. RGADA, f. 1287, op. 2, ed. khr 1318, ll. 26–7 ('Instructions, 1800').

[49] Similar restrictions have been observed by M. Polla for households in northern Russia during this same period. M. Polla, *Vienankarjalainen perhelaitos 1600–1900* (Helsinki, 2001), pp. 641–2 of English summary. Also in M. Polla, 'Family systems in central Russia in the 1830s and 1890s', *History of the Family* 11 (2006), pp. 27–44.

[50] RGADA, f. 1287, op. 3, ed. khr. 555, l. 24 ('Instructions, 1796/1800').

[51] In a decree from the year 1847, Count Sheremetyev ordered estate officials to impose fines on those undertaking household divisions without his permission. RGADA, f. 1287, op. 3, ed. khr. 1766 ('On unauthorised household divisions, 1847').

[52] Landlords were obligated to provide serf conscripts for the Russian army. They usually preferred to take recruits from larger households, where male labourers were in greater supply. This issue will be discussed in greater detail in section 3.7 below.

extended- or multiple-family households may not have bothered filing petitions for formal divisions, since their *de jure* co-residents would have been already living elsewhere. But this theory is, unfortunately, difficult to test, since passport lists for this later period have not survived.

The increase in the number of solitaries – most of whom were widows between the ages of 45 and 65 – is especially noteworthy. Why did widowed females in later age groups become more likely to live alone as the nineteenth century progressed? There is nothing in the documents to suggest a change in authorities' attitudes toward widowed females in the later part of the period under investigation. It is particularly curious that the number of solitary females is increasing simultaneously with the number of complex households. It may be that estate officials were not especially concerned with the living arrangements of widows, since women were not eligible for military service. (As we will see, most of the policies that aimed to keep serfs together in larger domestic units seem to have been motivated by concerns about recruitment.) It is also possible that the increase in the number of solitary widows was an artefact of the increase in the total proportion of widowed females on the estate. Widows comprised only 15 per cent of the female population in 1816; by 1850, they were 18 per cent. Finally, it should be noted that wage work for women – especially in textiles – seems to have been widely available in this region. It may be that such employment opportunities made it possible for widows and never-married women to maintain independent households.[53]

In any case, households were clearly much smaller in Voshchazhnikovo than the few available studies on other parts of Russia would have led us to expect. But what does this tell us about household structure? It should be borne in mind that household size often reveals little about complexity. Large households can be quite simple in structure and small ones extremely complex. In Voshchazhnikovo, households were small, but were they also simple? Table 3.3 provides a summary of the types of households found in Voshchazhnikovo and the proportion of households in each category. For comparative purposes, the households have been categorised according to the Laslett–Hammel classification scheme. The categories used in this scheme can occasionally obscure the more interesting differences between Russian and western European households; however, these differences will become apparent in the discussion that follows.

---

[53] Sheremetyev himself claimed that 'since unmarried women were capable of earning a decent wage, they, too, could make *obrok* payments'. In RGADA, f. 1287, op. 3, ed. khr. 555, l. 26 ('Instructions, 1796/1800').

Table 3.3. *Household structure, village of Voshchazhnikovo, 1816–58*

Category	1816 N	1816 %	1832[a] N	1832[a] %	1834 N	1834 %	1838[a] N	1838[a] %	1850 N	1850 %	1858 N	1858 %
Solitaries	11	5	12	6	13	7	15	8	34	20	27	17
No family	14	6	7	3	9	5	11	6	6	3	13	8
Simple	106	47	82	41	68	35	68	37	32	19	36	23
Extended	43	19	59	30	53	27	50	27	46	27	37	23
Multiple	52	23	39	19	46	24	41	22	52	30	47	29
Indeterminate	0	0	2	1	6	2	0	0	2	1	0	0
Total	226	100	201	100	195	100	185	100	172	100	160	100

[a] Indicates estate household listing.
Sources: RGADA, f. 1287, op. 3, ed. khr. 1143 ('Inventories of households, 1832/8'), ed. khr. 2553 ('Soul revision, 1834'), ed. khr. 1941 ('Soul revision, 1850'); and GAYaO, f. 100, op. 8, d. 647 ('Soul revision, 1816'), and d. 2656 ('Soul revision, 1858').

The findings presented in this table are surprising. The proportion of simple-family households is significantly larger than anticipated and the proportion of extended- and multiple-family households significantly smaller. The widely accepted view of Russian household structure since Haxthausen maintains that extended- and multiple-family households were the norm in rural Russia. We might expect, then, that at least three-fourths of Russian peasant households were multiple- and/or extended-family ones, which is what both Czap and Hoch found for their respective estates. In Mishino, 80 to 90 per cent of households were either extended- or multiple-family ones; in Petrovskoe, the figure was 75 per cent. In Voshchazhnikovo, multiple- and extended-family households together are never much more than half of all households, ranging from 42 per cent in 1816 to 57 per cent in 1850.[54] Again, this is broadly consistent with the findings of Mitterauer and Kagan in their more general study of household structure in Yaroslavl' province in the late eighteenth century.[55]

Tables 3.4 and 3.5 reproduce Peter Czap's findings for the Mishino estate and Steven Hoch's findings for Petrovskoe. The figures for Mishino and Petrovskoe are broadly similar, while those for Voshchazhnikovo suggest a rather different pattern. In Mishino and Petrovskoe, multiple-family households comprised the greatest proportion of households on the

---

[54] These figures are still consistent with the features of a joint-family household formation system. See Hajnal, 'Two kinds'.

[55] Mitterauer and Kagan, 'Russian and central European family structures', pp. 110–11.

Table 3.4. *Household structure, Mishino, 1814–58*

Category	1814 N	1814 %	1831 N	1831 %	1834 N	1834 %	1843 N	1843 %	1850 N	1850 %	1858 N	1858 %
Solitaries	1	0.7	0	0.0	2	1.2	4	2.3	2	1.2	0	0.0
No family	0	0.0	1	0.6	2	1.2	2	1.1	7	4.2	2	2.1
Simple	10	7.6	15	9.8	20	12.1	19	10.8	23	13.8	21	12.2
Extended	14	10.8	14	9.1	24	14.5	12	6.7	11	6.6	20	11.6
Multiple	95	74.0	113	74.2	107	65.1	124	71.9	110	66.1	115	67.8
Indeterminate	8	6.0	9	5.9	9	5.4	11	6.3	13	7.8	11	6.5
Total	128	100.0	152	100.0	164	100.0	172	100.0	166	100.0	169	100.0

Source: Czap, 'The perennial multiple-family', p. 12. Figures are exactly as reported by Czap.

Table 3.5. *Household structure, Petrovskoe, 1814–56*

Category	1814 N	1814 %	1818 N	1818 %	1824 N	1824 %	1827 N	1827 %	1850 N	1850 %	1856 N	1856 %
Solitaries	1	2	0	0	2	3	1	1	7	7	11	9
No family	0	0	1	2	1	1	1	1	3	3	1	1
Simple	10	15	5	8	14	19	12	16	17	16	30	24
Extended	3	5	8	12	10	14	13	17	15	14	27	22
Multiple	51	78	50	78	47	64	49	64	62	60	56	45
Indeterminate	0	0	0	0	0	0	0	0	0	0	0	0
Total	65	100	64	100	74	101	76	99	104	100	125	101

Source: Hoch, *Serfdom and social control*, pp. 80–1. Figures are exactly as reported by Hoch.

estate; in Voshchazhnikovo, the largest proportion of households was the simple-family type, particularly in the earlier part of the period. Whereas roughly 60 to 70 per cent of households were the multiple-family type on the Central Black Earth estates, only 20 to 30 per cent of Voshchazhnikovo households were multiple-family ones. In addition, there were significantly more solitary households in Voshchazhnikovo than in either Mishino or Petrovskoe – especially toward the end of the period, as well as significantly more 'no-family' households (households without a conjugal unit, such as those consisting of co-resident siblings or cousins). Widow-headed households seem to have been much more common in Voshchazhnikovo than in Mishino or Petrovskoe. There were more households consisting of widows with children in

Voshchazhnikovo – 20 per cent of simple-family households – and widowed solitaries (most of whom were female) than at Mishino, where only 1 to 2 per cent of households were in these categories in the nineteenth century, or Petrovskoe, where these categories comprised only 3 to 4 per cent of households.[56]

Table 3.6 provides a more detailed breakdown of household types found in Voshchazhnikovo for the years covered by the household listings and soul revisions. Again, this analysis employs the Laslett–Hammel framework, with only a couple of minor changes made to the classification scheme. The 3(c) and 3(d) categories have been changed from 'widowers with children' and 'widows with children' to 'fathers with children' and 'mothers with children' in order to account for those households consisting of unmarried women with their illegitimate children (though these appear relatively infrequently in the listings). This also provides a way of accounting for those cases where a lone parent's marital status was not recorded, since the presence of children does not necessarily indicate that a woman had once been married (although illegitimate offspring were usually designated as such). Category 6, the 'indeterminate' group, includes only those households for which it was impossible to determine how the members of a co-resident group were related.

Even the complex families in Voshchazhnikovo were not as complex as those found on the estates in the Central Black Earth Region. As shown in Table 3.6, the majority of extended-family households were stem families, consisting of one conjugal family unit and a widowed parent, usually the husband's mother. The multiple-family households usually consisted of only two conjugal family units. In most cases the second unit was formed when an eldest son brought his wife into the household while both parents were still alive. In some instances, there were more than two families (a second son, for instance, and his wife), but this was not nearly so common as it was in Mishino and Petrovskoe. *Frérèches* – laterally extended households consisting of brothers and their families – were not especially prevalent in Voshchazhnikovo. Even in the later part of the period, when households were at their largest and most complex, *frérèches* comprised only about 3 per cent of all households and 10–12 per cent of multiple-family households. And while there are instances of households where grandnephews and nieces and great-grandchildren are present, they occur only rarely (only about two households per revision contained such distant relatives).

---

[56] Czap, 'A large family', pp. 128–9; Hoch, *Serfdom and social control*, pp. 80–1. At Petrovskoe, the proportion of solitary widows rises to 9 per cent by 1856, and the number of households consisting of widows with children rises from two to ten between 1827 and 1850.

Table 3.6. *Household structure, Voshchazhnikovo, 1816–58*

Category	1816 N	%	1832[a] N	%	1834 N	%	1838[a] N	%	1850 N	%	1858 N	%
1. Solitaries												
(a) widowed	5		8		5		8		18		18	
(b) single/unknown	6		4		8		7		16		9	
Total	11	5	12	6	13	7	15	8	34	20	27	17
2. No family												
(a) siblings	10		4		3		4		3		6	
(b) other relatives	2		3		4		7		3		7	
(c) not evidently related	2		0		2		0		0		0	
Total	14	6	7	3	9	5	11	6	6	3	13	8
3. Simple family												
(a) couple alone	19		14		16		15		4		2	
(b) couple with child	57		41		38		30		17		22	
(c) father with child	3		2		1		2		2		0	
(d) mother with child	27		25		13		21		9		12	
Total	106	57	82	41	68	35	68	37	32	19	36	23
4. Extended family												
(a) extended up	30		33		30		32		23		23	
(b) extended down	2		2		1		1		5		3	
(c) lateral	5		8		9		6		11		7	
(d) (a)–(c) combined	6		16		13		11		7		4	
Total	43	19	59	30	53	27	50	27	46	27	37	23
5. Multiple family												
(a) second units up	0		2		0		1		1		0	
(b) second units down	48		19		30		18		20		13	
(c) units all on one level	1		10		7		5		12		11	
(d) *frérèches*	1		3		0		6		5		6	
(e) other multiple	2		5		9		11		14		17	
Total	52	23	39	19	46	24	41	22	52	30	47	29
6. Indeterminate	0		2		6		0		2		0	
Total	0	0	2	1	6	2	0	0	2	1	0	0
TOTAL	226	100	201	100	195	100	185	100	172	100	160	100

[a] Indicates estate household listing.

Sources: RGADA, f. 1287, op. 3, ed. khr. 1143 ('Inventories of households, 1832/8'), ed. khr. 2553 ('Soul revision, 1834'), ed. khr. 1941 ('Soul revision, 1850'); and GAYaO, f. 100, op. 8, d. 647 ('Soul revision, 1816'), and d. 2656 ('Soul revision, 1858').

Change in household composition over time, as noted earlier, is also reflected in the distribution of households within each category in Table 3.6. The steep decline in the number of type 3(a) households (married couples alone) is consistent with the above speculation about the role of estate policies in the changes observed toward the end of this period, particularly the possibility that permission to partition became more difficult to obtain. This would fit with evidence from the revisions and household listings, which indicates that the number of complex households rose from 28.6 per cent in 1816 to 41.5 per cent in 1850. These new enforcement policies may account for the decline in the number of couples living alone, as well as the corresponding increase in the number of type 5 households and, in particular, type 5(e) households, most of which contain a fairly random assortment of relatives (usually people related through marriage).[57]

Household size and structure in Voshchazhnikovo seem to have differed substantially from those found in the Central Black Earth provinces of Riazan and Tambov. But how do they compare with those for other European societies? While households in Voshchazhnikovo were much more complex than those in pre-industrial northwest Europe,[58] they were actually less complex than some of those studied in parts of central and southern Europe. In northern and central Italy, for instance, the households of sharecroppers could be exceptionally large and complex. David Kertzer and Dennis Hogan, in their work on Casalecchio, found that over 70 per cent of sharecropping households in the late nineteenth and early twentieth centuries were of the multiple-family type.[59] In Voshchazhnikovo, multiple-family households made up only one quarter to one third of all households. And in Voshchazhnikovo there were slightly fewer multiple-family households – and far more solitary females – than in parts of the Polish-Lithuanian Commonwealth in the late eighteenth century.[60] The Transdanubian serf households studied by Rudolf

---

[57] Because widows would not have been eligible for military service and most solitaries were widowed females, the number of solitary widows is unlikely to have been affected by these policies.

[58] See the comparisons in P. Laslett, *Family life and illicit love in earlier generations* (Cambridge, 1977), pp. 20–3.

[59] D. P. Kertzer and D. I. Hogan, *Family, political economy, and demographic change: the transformation of life in Casalecchio, Italy, 1861–1921* (Madison, WI, 1989), pp. 53–5. Findings reported by Rebecca Jean Emigh for Tuscany in an earlier period indicate that landlords' policies strongly influenced tenants' household formation behaviour. R. J. Emigh, 'Labor use and landlord control: sharecropping and household structure in fifteenth-century Tuscany', *Journal of Historical Sociology* 11 (1) (1998), pp. 37–73.

[60] M. Szoltysek, 'Rethinking eastern Europe: household formation patterns in the Polish-Lithuanian Commonwealth and European family systems', *Continuity and Change* 23 (2008), pp. 389–427, see esp. p. 401.

Andorka and Tamás Faragó were also somewhat more complex than Voshchazhnikovo households; there were substantially more solitaries and 'no family' households in Voshchazhnikovo than in any of the Transdanubian villages.[61] In this way the evidence for Voshchazhnikovo casts doubt on the idea that there was a particularly 'eastern' (or Slavic) household formation pattern.[62]

The findings for Voshchazhnikovo appear, on the surface, consistent with a geographical explanation for variation in Russian household patterns. But, although the Voshchazhnikovo pattern is broadly similar to patterns reported for several other settlements in the Central Industrial Region, it does not at all resemble the one described by Bohac for Manuilovskoe estate in Tver' province. Tver' province bordered Yaroslavl' to the west (see map, p. xx), and had similar ecological characteristics. Serfs at Manuilovskoe, like those at Voshchazhnikovo, engaged in a variety of non-agricultural activities.[63] Yet household structure at Manuilovskoe more closely resembled that in Mishino and Petrovskoe than that in Voshchazhnikovo. In the period 1813–61, mean household size at Manuilovskoe varied between 7.1 and 8.7, and the proportion of complex households ranged from 70 to 90 per cent.[64] Tver' was not an agricultural province like Riazan or Tambov. However, Manuilovskoe did have one important feature in common with Mishino and Petrovskoe: it belonged to the Gagarin family. The implications of this will be discussed in greater detail in sections 3.6 and 3.7 below. But first we will examine more closely two specific aspects of the household formation system at Voshchazhnikovo, both of which figure prominently in existing accounts of the Russian peasant family: marriage and household headship.

3.4   Marriage

Marriage among Russian serfs is traditionally thought to have been early and universal, with very low levels of lifetime celibacy. This feature is supposed to have been characteristic of joint-family household formation systems, where marriage does not necessarily precipitate the establishment of a new and independent household.[65] In rural Russia, this pattern has been viewed as a deeply rooted cultural norm, which dovetailed with

[61] R. Andorka and T. Faragó, 'Pre-industrial household structure in Hungary', in R. Wall, J. Robin, and P. Laslett (eds.), *Family forms in historic Europe* (Cambridge, 1983), pp. 281–307.

[62] As discussed in Czap, 'A large family', pp. 145–6.

[63] Bohac, 'Family, property, and socioeconomic mobility', esp. chapter 3.

[64] *Ibid.*, pp. 140, 178.   [65] Hajnal, 'Two kinds'.

Table 3.7. *Singulate mean age at marriage, Mishino, 1782–1858*

	1782	1795	1814	1825	1834	1843	1850	1858
Males	19.0	19.4	17.0	18.0	19.7	19.5	18.9	18.0
Females	17.6	18.1	18.5	18.7	18.9	19.0	19.0	16.6

Source: Czap, 'The perennial multiple-family', p. 10.

Table 3.8. *Average age at first marriage, Petrovskoe, 1813–56*

	1813–27	1831	1850–6
Males	18.8	0.0	20.1
Females	18.4	19.1	19.5

Source: Hoch, *Serfdom and social control*, p. 76.

the communal land allocation system.[66] As noted in chapter 1, communal allotments were supposed to have been distributed to households on the basis of size; thus larger households would have been entitled to a larger share of the communal land, since they would have contained more labourers, as well as more consumers.

The joint-family pattern is reflected in the marriage ages calculated by Czap and Hoch for their respective Gagarin estates in the Central Black Earth Region (Tables 3.7 and 3.8). In each case, age at marriage was quite low for both women and men, increasing only very gradually across the period under investigation. The difference between age at first marriage for men and that for women was relatively small.

Table 3.9 presents figures for the singulate mean age at marriage (SMAM) for Voshchazhnikovo. SMAM is an estimate of the mean number of years lived by a given cohort before their first marriage, and is calculated from the proportion of unmarried males or females in successive age groups as provided in a census (or, in this case, soul revision or household listing).[67]

---

[66] Russian peasant women are sometimes said to have married as early as age 13; it has been maintained that age 16 was 'relatively old for a serf girl to marry'. Figes, *Natasha's dance*, p. 30. Early marriage has been viewed by some historians as a cultural norm, e.g. Bushnell, 'Did serf owners?'; Mironov, *Social history*, vol. I, pp. 59, 62 (*Sotsial'naia istoriia*, pp. 161, 163).

[67] J. Hajnal, 'Age at marriage and proportions marrying', *Population Studies* 7 (1953), pp. 111–36.

Table 3.9. *Singulate mean age at marriage, village of Voshchazhnikovo, 1816–58*

	1816	1832[a]	1834	1838[a]	1850	1858
Males	22.1	25.4	22.9	22.4	24.7	26.4
Females	22.0	20.7	18.5	18.3	21.1	20.3

[a] Indicates estate household listing.
Sources: RGADA, f. 1287, op. 3, ed. khr. 1143 ('Inventories of households, 1832/8'), ed. khr. 2553 ('Soul revision, 1834'), ed. khr. 1941 ('Soul revision, 1850'); and GAYaO, f. 100, op. 8, d. 647 ('Soul revision, 1816'), and d. 2656 ('Soul revision, 1858').

Again, the figures shown for Voshchazhnikovo suggest a pattern different from that found in Mishino and Petrovskoe. While the SMAM values indicate that marriage occurred earlier in Voshchazhnikovo than in pre-industrial western Europe[68] (at least for women), serfs on this estate did marry later than those in the Central Black Earth Region.[69] This is again broadly consistent with evidence for several other settlements in the Central Industrial Region. I. Shustrova and E. Sinitsyna, for instance, present similar findings for Archangelsky and Sandyrevsky parishes in Yaroslavl' province during this same period.[70] Kolle's data for Bun'kovskaia volost' in nineteenth-century Moscow province look considerably more like those for Voshchazhnikovo than those for Mishino or Petrovskoe.[71] And the Voshchazhnikovo pattern also looks very similar to that found for Sheremetyev holdings in Moscow province.[72] Similarities like these appear, on the surface, to support a geographical or ecological interpretation. Because the land in the Central Industrial Region was poor, one might argue, and serfs were unable to make a living in agriculture, there was less of an incentive to marry early and claim an additional communal allotment. But it will become clear in the discussion below (and especially in section 3.7) that local institutions – especially landlords'

---

[68] Hajnal, 'Two kinds', pp. 452–9; Laslett, *Family life*, pp. 26–7; E. A. Wrigley and R. S. Schofield, *The population history of England 1541–1871: a reconstitution* (Cambridge, 1981), p. 255.

[69] It should be noted that because the formula used to calculate SMAM assumes a closed population, the values for Voshchazhnikovo could be slightly inflated. Since Czap used the same methodology this is unlikely to affect the conclusions drawn.

[70] I. Shustrova and E. Sinitsyna, 'Demographic behaviour in the Yaroslavl' loamy area: the results of cohort analysis for two typical rural parishes', in P. Kooij and R. Paping, *Where the twain meet again: new results of the Dutch-Russian project on regional development 1750–1917* (Groningen, 2004), pp. 19–20.

[71] Kolle, *Social change*, pp. 186–94.

[72] Age at marriage on the Vykhino estate in this period ranged from 20 to 22.9 for men, and 19.3 to 20.9 for women. In Avdeev, Blum, and Troitskaia, 'Peasant marriage', pp. 733–4.

policies – could also affect marriage decisions, thereby complicating this seemingly straightforward relationship.

Men in Voshchazhnikovo seem to have married at a significantly later age than did women (particularly after 1816), where in Mishino and Petrovskoe the age at first marriage was similar for both sexes. Moreover, like household structure, marriage age at Voshchazhnikovo fluctuated considerably across the nineteenth century. It is not clear what was behind these changes. The fluctuations in the sex ratio noted for nineteenth-century Voshchazhnikovo would undoubtedly have had some effect on the marriage market, by narrowing or widening the pool of prospective spouses. In addition, marriage decisions would have been affected by changes in the local economy, though it is difficult to determine the extent to which this occurred, since the documents provide little information about fluctuations in local economic conditions.

Changes in estate policies may also have played a role. Estate instructions suggest that landlords' policies regarding serf marriage, like those regarding household structure, varied over time, often in response to changes in the overall economic position of the estate. There was, for instance, a temporary reduction in the levels of fines for marrying non-estate serfs, implemented in 1796 in response to serfs' complaints about their feudal burdens.[73] Petitions from the 1830s, however, indicate that by this time the fines had returned to their pre-1800 levels.[74] Similarly, in the same decree, the count temporarily waived the tax that had been levied on all unmarried serfs between the ages of 20 and 40.[75] Such changes in estate policy, in conjunction with fluctuations in local economic conditions, must have affected decisions serfs took about when to marry, and might at least partly explain the observed fluctuations in age at marriage.

Marriage is widely believed to have been universal in rural Russia, especially for women. In the words of one historian, '[t]he predominant marriage pattern among the Russian peasantry in all regions . . . was near-universal and early marriage'.[76] This view is supported by the evidence for Mishino and Petrovskoe, where, according to the findings of Czap and Hoch, only those with obvious physical or mental disabilities appear to have remained single.[77] Was this also the case at Voshchazhnikovo?

---

[73] RGADA, f. 1287, op. 3, ed. khr. 555, ll. 49–50 ('Instructions, 1796/1800').
[74] RGADA, f. 1287, op. 3, ed. khr. 1124, ll. 17, 41 ('Petitions regarding marriage, 1832').
[75] RGADA, f. 1287, op. 3, ed. khr. 555, l. 49 ('Instructions, 1796/1800').
[76] Moon, *The Russian peasantry*, p. 165.
[77] According to Czap, being 'never married' was so unusual for Mishino women that explanations were usually provided with such entries. Czap, 'A large family', pp. 120–1. And Hoch notes that in Tambov province, according to nineteenth-century ethnographers, 'only freaks and the morally depraved [did] not marry'. Hoch, *Serfdom and social control*, pp. 76–7.

Table 3.10. *Proportion of serfs never married, village of Voshchazhnikovo, 1816–58*

Age categories	1816		1832[a]		1834		1838[a]		1850		1858	
	F	M	F	M	F	M	F	M	F	M	F	M
15–19	75.0	94.6	92.1	95.3	81.3	97.2	83.3	95.8	83.7	92.7	97.8	100.0
20–4	30.2	43.9	54.3	61.3	43.1	48.3	26.6	33.3	26.6	62.8	54.5	85.7
25–9	17.7	2.7	21.4	29.6	26.8	10.7	20.5	4.2	12.5	27.0	14.3	39.5
30–4	15.6	4.8	13.0	16.7	15.2	3.6	15.6	0.0	6.5	11.1	10.8	3.1
35–9	12.8	3.3	11.1	5.9	4.5	0.0	7.5	9.7	13.3	0.0	4.5	0.0
40–4	9.6	0.0	12.8	0.0	13.8	0.0	3.3	4.3	17.6	0.0	9.5	0.0
45–9	3.2	3.6	14.3	0.0	23.1	0.0	20.6	0.0	10.0	0.0	17.9	0.0
50–4	4.8	0.0	21.1	0.0	20.6	0.0	14.3	0.0	6.6	0.0	16.6	0.0

[a] Indicates estate household listing.

Sources: RGADA, f. 1287, op. 3, ed. khr. 1143 ('Inventories of households, 1832/8'), ed. khr. 2553 ('Soul revision, 1834'), ed. khr. 1941 ('Soul revision, 1850'); and GAYaO, f. 100, op. 8, d. 647 ('Soul revision, 1816'), and d. 2656 ('Soul revision, 1858').

Table 3.10 shows proportions of Voshchazhnikovo serfs who never married. The figures for never-married females are extremely high for a society with a non-European marriage pattern, but they are not inconsistent with what we know about the sex ratio in Voshchazhnikovo during the nineteenth century.[78] It is possible that the shortage of males on this estate made it impossible for all women to marry. As mentioned earlier, the landlord's policies enabled men to bring wives on to the estate from outside without paying a fee, making the marriage market even more competitive for women, who were required to pay a fee for marrying an outsider.[79] Only those women whose families could afford the quite substantial fee would have been able to choose a husband from outside Voshchazhnikovo.[80]

[78] Marital status for females is unambiguous in the documents: women are recorded as 'wives', 'spinsters', or 'widows'. There is therefore no danger that widows were unintentionally included in the sample.

[79] This is probably because Russian women traditionally joined their husbands' households upon marriage. When a female serf married someone from outside the estate, the landlord was effectively losing a 'soul', as well as taxes on the dowry she would take with her to her new home. On the other hand, the landlord gained when male serfs married non-estate females, since these women (with their dowries) came to live on the estates to which their husbands belonged.

[80] This fee, called *vyvodnie den'gi*, ranged from 50 to 250 roubles. The figures quoted by Bushnell for Orlov estates in the 1780s are significantly lower (15 roubles). Bushnell, 'Did serf owners?', pp. 424–5. It is possible that the Orlov figure is given in silver roubles and the Sheremetyev figure in *assignaty*; this would at least put the figures in roughly the same range. Of course, we must remember, as indicated in the Note at the beginning of this book, that the value of the paper rouble changed significantly over time.

Perhaps even more remarkable is how few men remained unmarried: virtually zero in most revision years. This is probably due, at least in part, to a marriage market which was extremely advantageous to males. Of course, one cannot rule out the possibility that the landlord's 'celibacy tax' provided a disincentive for remaining single, particularly if one had the opportunity to marry (the low sex ratio evidently made finding a spouse more difficult for women). According to the estate instructions, this tax was to be levied annually, on top of existing feudal and state obligations, on all presently unmarried persons between the ages of 20 and 40, including widows and widowers. They were required to pay an additional 2 to 6 roubles per year, starting at age 20, for each year they remained single.[81] Still, this tax cannot be the main explanation for universal marriage among men, since a significant number of women remained unmarried despite this policy. It seems plausible that conscription policies significantly affected male serfs' marriage decisions. In his instructions for conscription, Count Sheremetyev specifies that 'unmarried adult males' should be among the first considered when selecting recruits.[82] By getting married, men at Voshchazhnikovo may have been able to reduce their chances of being conscripted.

It is unlikely that the figures in Table 3.10 were mainly the result of geographical differences. It is true that a far smaller proportion of women remained unmarried on the Mishino and Petrovskoe estates, in the Central Black Earth Region, but the same is true for the Manuilovskoe estate in the Central Industrial Region. An 1851 listing for Manuilovskoe indicates that roughly 3 per cent of serf women aged 25–9 had never married; the corresponding figure for Voshchazhnikovo, in 1850, was 12 per cent. That demographic outcomes on three Gagarin family holdings were so similar, despite their different locations, appears to underscore the significance of local institutions and of serfdom in particular, as does the large difference between the Gagarin and Sheremetyev estates in the Central Industrial Region.

3.5   Headship

In rural Russia, married sons are widely believed to have remained in households headed by their fathers, assuming the role of head only upon their father's death. Thus Russian peasant households are said to have

---

[81] RGADA, f. 1287, op. 3, ed. khr. 555, l. 26 ('Instructions, 1796/1800').
[82] RGADA, f. 1287, op. 3, ed. khr. 677, ll. 4–5 ('Instructions and decrees, 1808').

been organised 'patriarchally', with headship, as a rule, assumed by the eldest adult male.[83] This is consistent with a joint-family pattern, where households are complex and marriage occurs early in the life cycle. As a result, the age at which headship is attained is usually higher than in simple-family household systems, and a substantial number of men never become heads of households, instead spending their entire lives in households headed by fathers, brothers, cousins, or uncles.[84]

It is difficult to investigate headship using soul revisions, which have a standard format: they always list the eldest male first, followed by the remaining males and then the females, noting how each person is related to the eldest male. Unfortunately, there is no way of knowing for sure whether the eldest male is in fact the head of household. In certain cases, such as when the eldest male is a young child, it is clear that he is not the head. In this analysis, we will assume that the eldest male was the household head, except where he was under 17 years of age, in which case it will be assumed that the eldest adult female (usually his mother) was the head.

The estate household registers are much more explicit than the soul revisions. They always list the head of household first, followed by the members of his or her immediate family, such as wife and children, and then other members of the household and how they are related to the head. The information in the household listings makes it clear that the eldest male was *not* always the head of household, since some household members are listed as 'father of head' or 'uncle of head'. This does not necessarily mean that the assumptions made about headship in the soul revisions have significantly distorted the findings; at worst, it suggests that the estimates of the ages at which males became household heads, as derived from the revisions, could be slightly inflated.

At what age did males attain headship in Voshchazhnikovo? The figures in Table 3.11 show the proportion of males in five age groups who were *not* heads of households in the soul revisions and estate household listings. The means suggest that only about half of all men became heads of household by their early thirties. The proportion of men who had not become heads of household by their late thirties drops to a little over one third, then to under a quarter by the time they have reached their forties. Again, while these findings may be broadly consistent with findings for other joint-household systems, they differ from those found for the Black Earth Region. On the Petrovskoe estate, over 90 per cent of males aged 25–9

---

[83] Haxthausen (e.g. *Studien*, vol. I, pp. 155–6) was particularly struck by what he saw as the 'patriarchal' nature of Russian peasant households.
[84] See Hajnal, 'Two kinds'.

Table 3.11. *Percentage of males in village of Voshchazhnikovo never having been heads of household, 1816–58*

Age categories	1816	1832[a]	1834	1838[a]	1850	1858	Mean
25–9	32.0	55.5	60.7	79.1	27.0	84.0	56.4
30–4	38.0	41.6	39.2	75.0	51.8	65.6	51.9
35–9	13.0	35.2	28.9	64.5	44.4	38.4	37.4
40–9	15.4	30.4	17.0	29.3	11.1	33.3	22.8
50–9	2.6	3.4	14.3	5.0	14.3	13.8	8.9

[a] Indicates estate household listing.
Sources: RGADA, f. 1287, op. 3, ed. khr. 1143 ('Inventories of households, 1832/8'), ed. khr. 2553 ('Soul revision, 1834'), ed. khr. 1941 ('Soul revision, 1850'); and GAYaO, f. 100, op. 8, d. 647 ('Soul revision, 1816'), and d. 2656 ('Soul revision, 1858').

had not yet attained headship. The figure drops to 76.9 per cent for men in their early thirties, then to 64.9 per cent for men in their late thirties – substantially higher than for the Voshchazhnikovo estate. In Petrovskoe, 34.2 per cent of men in their forties were not yet heads of household. Only for the age group 50–9 does the figure resemble that of Voshchazhnikovo (10.1 per cent for Petrovskoe, 8.9 for Voshchazhnikovo).[85]

In a patriarchal household formation system, such as that believed to have prevailed in pre-Emancipation rural Russia, one might expect to find a very low incidence of female headship. Widows and unmarried daughters would have been expected to spend their lives in the households of male relatives. This was not, however, the case in Voshchazhnikovo. In contrast to Mishino and Petrovskoe, where female solitaries and widow-headed households occurred quite infrequently,[86] female-headed households were relatively numerous on the Voshchazhnikovo estate. Figures calculated from the soul revisions show that female-headed households made up 17 per cent of all households in 1816, 16 per cent in 1834, 24 per cent in 1850, and 26 per cent in 1858.[87] Due to the lack of concrete headship data in the revisions, these figures include only those households for which there were no adult males recorded. Since it was possible for females to head households in which adult males *were* present, these must

[85] Hoch, *Serfdom and social control*, p. 87.
[86] Czap, 'The perennial multiple-family', pp. 12–13; Hoch, *Serfdom and social control*, pp. 80–1.
[87] These figures are significantly higher than those presented by Bohac for the Gagarin estate of Manuilovskoe, also in the Central Industrial Region. See Bohac, 'Widows and the Russian serf community'.

be regarded as minima. Even so, these figures are quite high – not only for patriarchal Russia, but by general European standards.[88]

The estate household listings, which provide higher-quality data on female headship, yield even more surprising figures. According to these documents, female-headed households made up 17 per cent of all households in 1832 and 45 per cent of all households in 1838. How can we explain such a significant increase in female headship in such a short period of time? In 1838, 83 of 184 households were female-headed households – 48 more than in 1832.[89] Of these 48 new female-headed households, 23 resulted from the death of the male head.[90] In twelve of these, the adult male members were listed as 'absent' in both listings, suggesting a change in recording practices between 1832 and 1838, with *de facto* female heads of household granted this status *de jure* in the later listing. Of the 48 households, 4 were new, having been established since the 1832 listing. And the remaining 9 female-headed households contained adult male members who were apparently deemed unworthy of headship by the estate authorities because they were drunks or otherwise dissolute.[91] We should be careful not to read too much into these findings. As we shall see in subsequent chapters, women at Voshchazhnikovo were marginalised and often denied full participation in village affairs and in the local economy. Nevertheless, it is remarkable that so many women in Voshchazhnikovo were heads of households – with *de jure* headship status, even when other adult males were present – and this must be taken into account in considering how the local economy functioned.

Overall, the findings for Voshchazhnikovo are not consistent with the notion of a uniformly 'Russian' household formation system, nor even a uniformly 'peasant' demographic culture. Instead, these data suggest substantial variation in household size and structure across space and time. Households at Voshchazhnikovo were smaller and less complex than on the Gagarin estates of Mishino and Petrovskoe in the Central Black Earth Region, but also smaller and less complex than at Manuilovskoe, a Gagarin estate in the Central Industrial Region. Marriage was somewhat later and a higher proportion of females never

---

[88] On female headship in Europe, see S. Ogilvie and J. Edwards, 'Women and the "second serfdom": evidence from Bohemia', *Journal of Economic History* 60 (2000), pp. 961–94.

[89] In 1832, 35 of 201 households were female-headed, and those households were still headed by females in 1838.

[90] It is possible that this period was one of extremely high male mortality, and that the rise in the proportion of female-headed households was at least partly due to excessive male deaths. A study of male mortality at Voshchazhnikovo is currently underway.

[91] All of this information comes from the household listings: RGADA, f. 1287, op. 3, ed. khr. 1143 ('Inventories of households, 1832/8').

married than on any of the Gagarin estates that have been analysed. And female-headed households were considerably more common in Voshchazhnikovo than on the Gagarin estates. The following sections consider some reasons for these differences.

3.6   The household economy

The joint-family household formation system is generally supposed to have been part of a larger family-oriented economic system. Joint households, it is argued, usually occur in the context of a Chayanovian peasant economy, where, due to the absence of markets in labour and land, the household is entirely dependent on its own members for production inputs.[92] In Russia, the repartitional land commune is thought to have provided an additional incentive for large, complex households, since communal land was supposed to have been distributed among member households in accordance with their labour capabilities and consumption needs. In other words, the more members a household had, the larger the share of the communal land it was likely to receive.[93]

According to Hoch, the economy of Petrovskoe was very much a traditional peasant economy in the Chayanovian sense. The large, complex households found on this estate were, he argues, consistent with this Chayanovian economic framework.[94] The economic environment around Voshchazhnikovo, however, seems to have borne little resemblance to the peasant economy described by Chayanov. As we will see in subsequent chapters, markets in land, labour, and credit existed in this region. There was remarkable specialisation in the economy, with many serfs producing non-agricultural goods for local markets. In the village of Voshchazhnikovo, very few serfs (between 5 and 10 per cent in the 1830s) lived from their communal allotments.[95] Many serf households in this village employed live-in servants and day labourers, especially during peak

---

[92] As discussed in Hajnal, 'Two kinds', pp. 475–6.

[93] See the discussion in R. Rudolph, 'Family structure and proto-industrialization in Russia', *Journal of Economic History*, 40 (1980), pp. 111–18. Also in Figes, *Natasha's dance*, p. 258. According to Figes, '[t]he peasantry's egalitarian customs gave them little incentive to produce anything other than babies. For the commune distributed land among the households according to the number of mouths to feed.'

[94] It must be noted that the documents for Petrovskoe provide little empirical evidence for the Chayanovian view. Hoch's discussion of the economic framework is based largely on secondary sources. See Hoch, *Serfdom and social control*, esp. chapters 1 and 3.

[95] Calculated from data in RGADA, f. 1287, op. 3, ed. khr. 1143 ('Inventories of households, 1832/8').

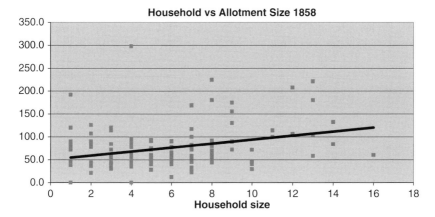

Figure 3.1 Household size versus allotment size, 1858

periods in the agricultural cycle. In fact, it was not uncommon in Voshchazhnikovo to find household heads sending their own sons out to work as live-in servants for merchants in the cities while hiring labourers to work their land at home.[96] Women, it seems, were also able to find non-agricultural wage work, often in textiles, or as servants or labourers.

The relationship between size of household and size of communal landholding in the village Voshchazhnikovo was positive, but weaker than the conventional view might predict. A correlation coefficient of 0.267 (significant at the .01 level) was derived using a value of household size calculated from the 1858 soul revision and a value of communal allotment size (area in sq. *sazhen'*) calculated from data provided in the 1858 descriptions of estates (the only source for household-level information on communal holdings at Voshchazhnikovo).[97] The haphazard nature of this relationship is highlighted in Figure 3.1: the data points are not clustered around the regression line, as we might expect if the relationship were a straightforward linear one. Instead, they appear more like a cloud, suggesting greater variance than the existing view might predict. Indeed, a closer look reveals numerous 'exceptions' to what we have come to regard as the general rule governing communal land allocation in Russia. There were households such as that of Vasily Slasnikov (three adult members), Fyodor Pugin (three adult members), and Mikhail Dolodanov (two adult members), which had very substantial communal

[96] *Ibid.* This will be discussed in greater detail in chapter 6.
[97] RGADA, f. 1287, op. 3, ed. khr. 2320 ('Descriptions of estates').

Table 3.12. *Ten largest households in Voshchazhnikovo, the number of adult males in each, and the size of each household's communal allotment, 1858*

Household	Total size	Adult males	Allotment size
Pugin	16	4	60.0
Achuev	14	5	84.0
Pugin	14	4	132.0
Dolodanov	13	6	180.0
Lavrent'ev	13	4	105.0
Shetov	13	5	221.0
Chernikhin	13	3	58.5
Komliakov	12	6	180.0
Titov	12	3	208.0
Chernikhin	11	2	100.0

Note: Total households = 160 in 1858. Allotment size was given in square *sazhen'*.
Source: RGADA, f. 1287, op. 3, ed. khr. 2320 ('Descriptions of estates, 1858'); and GAYaO, f. 100, op. 8, d. 2656 ('Soul revision, 1858').

allotments, and households such as that of Panteleimon Kriuchkov (five adult members), Vasily Achuev (eight adult members), and Dmitri Shetov (eleven adult members), which had much smaller communal allotments.[98] Tables 3.12, 3.13, and 3.14 offer additional detail. They show us the ten largest households, the number of adult males in each, and the sizes of their communal plots; the largest communal allotments by household; and the smallest allotments by household. Though just a sliver of the data set, these cases nevertheless cast considerable doubt on the idea that there was anything like a straightforward relationship between household size and size of communal holding on this estate.

In the conventional account, a similarly strong positive correlation is thought to have existed between wealth and household size, since larger households would have had more labour resources and would have been thus entitled to more land. On this view, land was always the main source of wealth in Russian peasant society. At Voshchazhnikovo, the correlation between wealth and size of communal holding was indeed positive. However, the relationship between wealth and allotment size was even weaker than that between household size and allotment size: 0.266.[99] This

[98] This information was obtained by linking data in the 1858 descriptions of estates with the 1858 soul revision (GAYaO, f. 100, op. 8, ed. khr. 2656).
[99] The calculated correlation coefficient was significant at the .01 level.

Table 3.13. *Top ten households in Voshchazhnikovo by communal allotment size, 1858*

Household	Total size	Adult males	Allotment size
Kriuchkova	4	2	298.0
Zemskov	8	3	225.0
Shetov	13	5	221.0
Titov	12	3	208.0
Popova	1	0	192.0
Dolodanov	13	6	180.0
Matal'ev	9	1	180.0
Pimenov	9	3	174.8
Kriuchkov	7	5	169.0
Yablokov	7	1	168.0

Note: See note to Table 3.12.
Source: RGADA, f. 1287, op. 3, ed. khr. 2320 ('Descriptions of estates, 1858'), and GAYaO, f. 100, op. 8, d. 2656 ('Soul revision, 1858').

Table 3.14. *Bottom ten households in Voshchazhnikovo by communal allotment size, 1858 (excluding solitary households)*

Household	Total size	Adult males	Allotment size
Aladin	6	4	12.0
Labutina	2	0	21.0
Kotal'zhkov	7	4	22.5
Toropikhin	5	1	27.9
Kriuchkov	10	3	29.4
Kotolazhnyi	7	4	29.4
Golovar'ev	3	1	30.0
Lodygina	3	1	31.5
Kovin	7	3	33.0
Komliakov	4	0[a]	35.0

[a] Household contained one 14-year old male
Note: See note to Table 3.12.
Sources: RGADA, f. 1287, op. 3, ed. khr. 2320 ('Descriptions of estate, 1858'), and GAYaO, f. 100, op. 8, d. 2656 ('Soul revision, 1858').

makes sense when we consider that very few of the better-off serf house-holds engaged in agriculture. In fact, none of the households in the top quartile for wealth (roughly thirty-five households) specialised in agriculture. The source of their wealth was not land, but trade, rural

Table 3.15. *Top ten households in Voshchazhnikovo by value of dwelling, 1858*

Household	Total size	Value of house (in roubles)	Allotment size
Slasnikov	3	1,600	120.0
Titov	12	1,500	208.0
Dolodanov	13	1,300	180.0
Pugin	5	1,200	93.5
Zhukov	9	1,000	89.7
Zemskov	8	1,000	225.0
Matal'ev	7	900	80.5
Popova	1	800	192.0
Dolodanov	4	700	84.0
Sedel'nikov	3	600	45.0
Kriuchkov	7	600	169.0

Note: See note to Table 3.12.
Source: RGADA, f. 1287, op. 3, ed. khr. 2320 ('Description of estates, 1858').

manufacturing, crafts, or migrant labour. And, as indicated in Table 3.15, some of the wealthiest households had large communal allotments, while others had much smaller plots. None of those with larger allotments specialised in agriculture: the Titov and Popov families, for instance, ran manufactories, and the Zemskov family was engaged in trade.[100] Furthermore, some wealthy households were large, while others were small. The relationship between the three variables is not as straightforward as the one predicted by the existing account.

It is not surprising that the correlation between wealth and size of communal allotment was positive (if weak), since on this estate there were feudal dues attached to communal allotments. But if a form of progressive taxation was at work here, why was the relationship not stronger? In other words, why did the wealthiest serfs not have the largest allotments and, thus, the largest tax obligations? One possible explanation, discussed in greater detail in chapter 4, is that wealthier serfs often had more power in the commune, which they could have used to shift the tax burden from themselves on to others. This does appear to have happened in some instances.[101]

[100] RGADA, f. 1287, op. 3, ed. khr. 1143 ('Inventories of households, 1832/8'), entries 49, 61, 191.
[101] The powers of communal elites are discussed in greater detail in T. K. Dennison and S. Ogilvie, 'Serfdom and social capital in Bohemia and Russia', *Economic History Review* 60 (3) (2007), pp. 513–44.

Voshchazhnikovo serfs also used an internal market to allocate communal land (and the obligations attached to it) amongst themselves. For instance, in July 1793, Voshchazhnikovo serf Mikhail Kolmykov paid the serf widow Vasilisa Dmitrieva 200 roubles for the communal land (*tiaglovaia zemlia*) that remained in her possession after the death of her husband.[102] In August of that same year, Voshchazhnikovo serf Vasily Voronov sold the communal land that remained after the death of his father to fellow Voshchazhnikovo serf Yegor Usachev for 80 roubles.[103] In 1832, the serf widow Matryona Zhilkova sold her communal allotment to fellow Voshchazhnikovo serf Il'ia Kalinin for 370 roubles.[104] Although it is not possible to determine how widespread the market in communal land was, the fact that it existed at all suggests that there were alternative ways of distributing obligations and resources among serf households on this estate.

These findings cast considerable doubt on the notion of a 'cyclical' household economy at Voshchazhnikovo. According to Chayanov, Russian peasant households became richer as they grew, since their labour resources were more abundant, as was, in a repartitional system, the amount of land allotted to them. As households progressed through the life cycle, it is argued, they eventually began to decrease in size through deaths and household divisions, and to shed labour and land. As a result, they became poorer. So the economic position of any given household depended on where it was in the life cycle, in this view; wealth, in other words, was 'cyclical'.[105]

This assumes, however, that peasants were not able to use markets to address imbalances in labour and land.[106] At Voshchazhnikovo, as we will see in subsequent chapters, there were labour markets, so serf households were not necessarily dependent on family labour. Moreover, land was not the only form of wealth in this society. As noted, the wealthiest serfs

---

[102] RGADA, f. 1287, op. 3, ed. khr. 612, l. 6 ('Serf contracts, 1793').   [103] *Ibid.*

[104] RGADA, f. 1287, op. 3, ed. khr. 1155, l. 18 ('Serf contracts, 1832'). It is interesting that these transactions appear to have been limited to Voshchazhnikovo serfs. This is almost certainly because the landlord forbade the sale of communal land to outsiders. Serfs did not own their allotments and were therefore technically forbidden to sell them. More will be said about this in chapter 5.

[105] See the discussion in Moon, *The Russian peasantry*, pp. 318–23.

[106] Chayanov admitted that land markets, where they existed, could have been used to address cyclical labour imbalances. He assumed this was irrelevant in Russia, though, since such adjustments were supposed to have been made through the repartitional commune. See Chayanov, *Theory of peasant economy*, pp. 68–9. For a discussion of the Chayanovian model in a non-Russian context, see R. M. Smith, 'Some issues concerning families and their property in rural England 1200–1800', in R. M. Smith (ed.), *Land, kinship, and lifecycle* (Cambridge, 1984), esp. pp. 6–31.

on the estate did not specialise in agriculture, but worked in trade, manufacturing, or as labourers in Moscow or St Petersburg.[107] The Chayanovian model assumes that accumulation of wealth within households was not possible. On this view, land and labour were the primary sources of wealth, and access to these changed as a household progressed through the lifecycle. Evidence presented in chapters 5–8 indicates that households at Voshchazhnikovo did accumulate wealth – often in the form of privately held land, buildings, and trade inventory – and that this wealth could be transferred from one generation to the next. Finally, the richest households at Voshchazhnikovo were not necessarily the largest nor those with the largest allotments. The families Slasnikov, Dolodanov, and Pugin, were, for instance, among the better-off serfs on the estate, though their households were relatively small (Table 3.15). And these wealthy households do not appear to have become poorer over time. The same names – Slasnikov, Dolodanov, Titov, and Yablokov – are found among the wealthiest serfs throughout the period under investigation.[108]

The repartitional commune, if it functioned at all, does not appear to have been a wealth-levelling mechanism on this estate. On the contrary, there was a substantial degree of socioeconomic stratification among households in the village of Voshchazhnikovo. The landlord and his central administration acknowledged this stratification in a formal wealth classification system. In 1796 Sheremetyev wrote, 'Let those serfs who have assets worth over 1,000 roubles be in the "first rank" (*pervostateinye*), while those with assets worth between 500 and 1,000 roubles will be in the "middle rank" (*srednostateinye*). In the "third" or "last rank" (*poslednostateinye*) should be those with assets under 500 roubles.'[109] Notes made by the bailiff on the economic position of each household indicate that, in 1832–8, roughly 30 per cent of all households were in the last rank, while

---

[107] Three of the twenty-two households that specialised in agriculture in 1832 were described as having been in 'good' financial shape. The rest were called 'poor'. Information about households' economic position is in RGADA, f. 1287, op. 3, ed. khr. 1143 ('Inventories of households, 1832/8').

[108] These names appear repeatedly under the list of 'first-rank serfs' (*pervostateinye krest'iane*) in attendance at communal meetings throughout the period. In addition, they come up frequently in contracts for credit and land transactions, petitions, and inventories of assets (carried out by estate officials).

[109] 'kto iz kapitala krest'ian sverkh tysiachi rubliov do neskol'ko tysiach imeniia i kapitalu imet, takovykh schitat' v pervoi stat'e ... vo vtoroi stat'e chislit' tekh, kto ot piati do tysiachi rubliov imet' kapitalu i imeniia ... v tretei stat'e chislit' tekh, kto menee piati sot imeniia imeet'', in RGADA, f. 1287, op. 3, ed. khr. 555, l. 49 ('Instructions, 1796/1800').

70 per cent were in either the first or middle rank.[110] As noted in chapter 2, this categorisation formed the basis of a system of progressive taxation.

There were undoubtedly parts of rural Russia where wealth was correlated with landholding, and, thus, in the context of a repartitional commune, with the life cycle. But it seems unlikely that the relationship between land, wealth, and household structure was always straightforward, even in broadly similar geographical contexts. On the Manuilovskoe estate (also in the Central Industrial Region), in contrast to Voshchazhnikovo, agriculture was the basis of the peasant economy, and land appears to have been an important correlate with wealth. However, despite the importance of land, wealth does not appear to have fluctuated in accordance with life cycle changes.[111] So, just as diversity in household size and structure undermines the notion of a Russian peasant household 'pattern', these same differences cast doubt on the idea of a universally 'peasant' model of economy in imperial Russia. It seems more likely that household patterns *and* economic conditions varied significantly across localities, in response to local institutional arrangements. In the period under examination here, serfdom – more specifically, the economic and social policies of the landlord and his investment in enforcement mechanisms for those policies – was one of the most important of these local institutions.

3.7   The role of serfdom

For a long time it was thought that Russian landlords had complete control over the personal lives of their serfs, with tales of landlords who rounded up unmarried serfs and forced them to marry appearing regularly in the literature.[112] When, upon closer examination, historians turned up very little empirical support for such practices, the trend began to move in the other direction, with many arguing that serfdom had little or no effect on serfs' demographic and other social behaviour.[113] Such inconsistency is at least partly due to the fact that serfdom and its effects can be quite

---

[110] Those in the last rank were described in the notes as 'poor'. However, it was impossible to determine which of those called 'good' were first-rank households and which were middle-rank households (some were called 'average' but not so many that 'average' could be used as a separate category). Chapter 8 attempts an estimate, using dwelling types and values as a proxy for socioeconomic status.

[111] Bohac, 'Family, property, and socioeconomic mobility', esp. chapter 7.

[112] As in V. A. Aleksandrov, *Sel'skaia obshchina*, pp. 303–13; a recent example of this view is in Figes, *Natasha's dance*, p. 246.

[113] See Bushnell, 'Did serf owners?'; A. Plakans and C. Weatherall, 'Family and economy on an early nineteenth-century Baltic serf estate', *Continuity and Change* 7 (2) (1992), pp. 199–223; Moon, *The Russian peasantry*, p. 168.

difficult to measure. It has been argued, for instance, that if we observe a particular estate rule to have been ignored by a substantial part of the population, we can assume that landlord regulation generally had little or no effect.[114] But in fact, landlords had their priorities, and some regulations were enforced more consistently than others. Enforcement can also vary over time, as we have seen, e.g. in response to events such as wars. Moreover, the effect of any given regulation will rarely be uniform over an entire population; an increase in the cost of a certain activity will, like any change in price, be responded to only at the margin, and the response may be slow if the activity is a well-established component of life in the community, requiring additional changes in behaviour as well. The general question of the role of serfdom in the local economy of Voshchazhnikovo will be addressed in chapter 9. Here, we turn to the possible effects of landlord policy on demographic behaviour.

The estate documents for Voshchazhnikovo show that the Count Sheremetyev did attempt to regulate the demographic behaviour of his serfs.[115] In a detailed set of instructions from the year 1796, he devoted four separate points to questions of marriage and household formation. The first of these attempted to regulate the marriage of female serfs to serfs from outside the estate, as discussed earlier in this chapter. It stated that serfs wishing to marry their daughters to non-estate grooms had to first petition the landlord for permission. If the request was granted, a one-time fee had to be paid before the marriage could take place: peasants of the 'first rank' were to pay 150 roubles, 'middling' peasants 100 roubles, and the poorer peasants 50 roubles.[116]

The second article concerned a tax levied on unmarried adults. It stated that any unmarried person (male or female, single or widowed) between the ages of 20 and 40 must pay an annual penalty, on top of their regular quitrent obligations, 'in order to compel them to marry'.[117] Unmarried serfs from the richer stratum were to pay 6 roubles annually, middling serfs were to pay 4, and poorer serfs had to pay 2 roubles per year.[118]

The third article stated that all households were to contain at least two males between the ages of 17 and 65. Households wishing to undertake a formal division had to ensure that each of the new, independent

[114] Bushnell, 'Did serf owners?'; Kolle, *Social change*, pp. 65–6.
[115] Similar instructions exist for the Sheremetyevs' Vykhino estate near Moscow and for Molodoi Tud in Tver' province. On Vykhino, see Avdeev, Blum, and Troitskaia, 'Peasant marriage', pp. 726–7; Molodoi Tud is discussed in Prokof'eva, *Krest'ianskaia obshchina*, pp. 154–6.
[116] RGADA, f. 1287, op. 3, ed. khr. 555, l. 49 ('Instructions, 1796/1800').
[117] RGADA, f. 1287, op. 3, ed. khr. 555, l. 26 ('Instructions, 1796/1800').   [118] *Ibid.*, l. 26.

households met this requirement. Any household that divided without permission, or without fulfilling the above criterion, was to be fined 3 silver roubles. Any household that could not afford to pay the fine would have its men conscripted to do hard labour.[119]

The fourth article concerned conscription, and was closely related to article three. It stated that all households had to be able to provide a recruit for the army when it was their turn in the queue (places in the conscription queue were assigned by lottery). If a household could not provide a recruit, it was to be fined the price of a recruit on the market – roughly 600 roubles at the time of this instruction.[120] Small households, the landlord noted, were to be subjected to great scrutiny in this matter.[121] These last two points indicate that Sheremetyev realised that recruitment policies provided an incentive for serfs to form smaller domestic units, since landlords were generally reluctant to send a household's only adult male to the army. To ensure serfs would adhere to his policy of two adult males per household, he demanded close scrutiny of household arrangements and implemented a system of penalties for noncompliance.

These four points were not minor considerations, especially for serfs in the lower and middle income ranges. A serf who wanted to save up for marriage and start his own household would have had to consider the mounting tax cost for every year he remained unmarried after his twentieth year. Then, in order to establish a separate household, he would have had to have had at least enough money to buy a recruit to send to the army or to pay the fine for not being able to provide one. That is, of course, if he could have obtained permission from the estate management to set up his own household, which was highly unlikely considering that any newly established household was required to contain two adult males. And if he established a separate household without estate permission, he faced yet another fine. In this way, it might have made more sense for a serf to marry relatively early, while still living in his parents' household, and to start a family, so that eventually he would have had the requisite number of males for a new household, as well as a bit of money put aside. Then later, in his thirties or forties, he might have been able to establish a new, independent household, provided, of course, he had not yet become head of the household he had grown up in.

Again, it is important to recognise that these regulations would not necessarily have affected all households in the same way. As already

---

[119] *Ibid.*, l. 24.
[120] RGADA, f. 1287, op. 3, ed. khr. 677, ll. 4–5 ('Instructions and decrees, 1808').
[121] *Ibid.*

noted, there was substantial socioeconomic stratification among the serfs at Voshchazhnikovo; some of the wealthier serfs on the estate declared taxable assets worth 10,000 to 20,000 roubles, while the poorest serfs had few assets and lived on 10 to 15 roubles per month.[122] Thus, some families may have been in an economic position to establish separate households despite the costs, while others would have found the fines imposed by the landlord prohibitive. We must also bear in mind that there were many other estate rules and regulations which were not directly concerned with household formation, but which nonetheless constrained serfs' economic and demographic decisions. Restrictions on geographical mobility, for instance, meant that a serf wishing to work outside the estate would have had to pay an annual passport fee.[123] In addition, he would have had to pay someone to work his communal lands in his absence, since the landlord fined serfs who left their communal allotments uncultivated.[124]

Considerations such as these would have affected the decisions serfs took about their livelihoods – decisions, which, in turn, influenced their demographic behaviour. So the effects of landlords' household formation policies on serf behaviour were not obvious or straightforward. That so many serfs do appear to have complied with estate regulations – one quarter to one third of all households were multiple-family ones, roughly one third contained two adult males, marriage for males was universal – suggests that they did have some effect. We cannot dismiss them because their effects were not uniformly distributed across the population.

The idea that household formation decisions were affected by landlords' policies is borne out in larger studies of household structure in the post-Emancipation period, such as that by Cathy Frierson on household divisions.[125] Frierson notes that *zemstvo* statistics for the end of the nineteenth century report a decline in average household size throughout the Central Industrial and Central Black Earth Regions. This is consistent with her finding that the number of serfs petitioning for household divisions increased steadily in the years after emancipation.[126] According to Frierson, these divisions resulted in a preponderance of nuclear-family households – a transformation that caused consternation among contemporary officials, who worried about the economic viability of such small units. As further evidence of this trend, Frierson refers to aggregate

[122] RGADA, f. 1287, op. 3, ed. khr. 1283 ('List of trading peasants and guilds, 1836'), and ed. khr. 1391 ('List of trading peasants and guilds, 1838').
[123] RGADA, f. 1287, op. 3, ed. khr. 555, l. 49 ('Instructions, 1796/1800').   [124] *Ibid.*, l. 24.
[125] C. Frierson, 'Razdel: the peasant family divided', in B. Farnsworth and L. Viola (eds.), *Russian peasant women* (Oxford, 1992), pp. 73–88.
[126] *Ibid.*, p. 75; see also Mironov, *Sotsial'naia istoriia*, vol. I, p. 231.

statistics which show that by 1884 some 52 per cent of Russian households had fewer than two male workers.[127]

The findings for Voshchazhnikovo cast doubt on the idea that household patterns in imperial Russia reflected certain uniform, underlying features of peasant behaviour. If there had been such underlying features, we would expect to find household patterns in Voshchazhnikovo similar to those found for estates in the Central Black Earth Region. Instead, we find a different pattern: smaller, less complex households, a higher age at first marriage, more solitaries, and a larger number of female-headed households. Household patterns, it seems, reflected rational responses to local constraints, and local constraints could vary even within a geographical region. Household patterns at the Gagarin estate of Manuilovskoe, located, like Voshchazhnikovo, in the Central Industrial Region, were similar to those on the Gagarin estates of Mishino and Petrovskoe in the Central Black Earth Region, suggesting that serfdom was not merely superstructure to an underlying demographic culture.

Serfdom not only provides a partial explanation for the structural differences in households observed between certain parts of Russia and western Europe. It also provides a way of accounting for at least some of the differences found within Russia itself. The specific local manifestations of serfdom in Russia were, in many respects, dependent on landlord-specific policies and regulations; not all landlords managed their estates in the same way. The large landlords had similar powers, and influenced social and economic life on their holdings as autonomously as the territorial princes in the pre-1800 Holy Roman Empire. We should therefore expect to see as much social and economic variation among Russian territories as we observe among German territories.

It was not only household patterns that were affected by serfdom. The economic characteristics of Voshchazhnikovo themselves were due at least in part to landlord-specific policies. As we will see in later chapters, a quasi-formal system of enforceable property rights based on rules set out by the estate management underpinned the existence of land, labour, and credit markets in this region. It is unclear just how much of this was due to landlord-specific policies and how much to regional trends, but this system appears to have been largely absent in the studies of the Gagarin family estates. The case of Manuilovskoe estate, again, suggests that such outcomes were more landlord-specific than region-specific. Manuilovskoe, like Voshchazhnikovo, was located in one of the central industrial provinces with clay-like soil and a short growing season. The two estates had, at least

---

[127] Frierson, 'Razdel', pp. 76–7.

superficially, economic similarities: serfs engaged in non-agricultural activities, paid at least some of their rents in cash, and migrated to other parts of Russia to find work. But there were also important differences. The Gagarins and their officials appear to have interfered more regularly (and more significantly) in local economic affairs than the Sheremetyevs. Moreover, Manuilovskoe seems to have lacked the sort of contract enforcement system that made extensive factor markets possible at Voshchazhnikovo. In imperial Russia, social structure may have been shaped more by the policies of the landlord than by the location of the estate.

4   The rural commune

4.1   What was the rural commune?

The rural commune is a central feature of the Russian Peasant Myth. According to Herzen, '[t]he Russian peasant [had] no real knowledge of any form of life but that of the village commune'.[1] It is thought to have been something quite unique, and to have paradoxically made the Russian peasantry both different from all others and the paradigmatic peasantry. The commune was, in the words of one scholar, 'a local authority, an economic entity, a collective landowner, a jury-like court and a policing organ, all in one'.[2] Russian communal practices, especially land repartitioning, are thought to have been more collectivist and egalitarian than those of other pre-modern village communities. Aleksandrov, perhaps the most widely respected Soviet scholar of the pre-Emancipation commune, maintains that 'the centuries-long history of the peasantry in Russia is unthinkable without an understanding of the essence of the rural commune'.[3]

But what sort of institution was this rural commune? In the historical literature, the term 'commune' often implies community in the sense of close-knit proximity, a dense social network, and a high degree of what is often called social capital.[4] Commune implies the very paradigm of the 'face-to-face society' we associate with the pre-modern world.[5] Thus Mironov describes the rural commune 'as a small social grouping, that is,

---

[1] Herzen, 'The Russian people and socialism', p. 183.
[2] T. Shanin, *Russia as a 'developing society'*, 2 vols. (London and New Haven, 1985–6), vol. I, p. 74.
[3] Aleksandrov, *Sel'skaia obshchina*, p. 3.
[4] There is, unfortunately, no straightforward way to define 'community'. See discussion in A. Macfarlane, *Reconstructing historical communities* (Cambridge, 1977), chapter 1; on 'commune vs community' in the Russian context, see R. Bartlett, 'Introduction', in R. Bartlett (ed.), *Land commune and peasant community in Russia: communal forms in imperial and early Soviet society* (London and New York, 1990), pp. 1–6.
[5] The phrase and the concept (though without reference to Russia) come from P. Laslett, 'The face to face society', in P. Laslett (ed.), *Philosophy, politics, and society*, First Series (Oxford, 1956), pp. 157–84.

a group based on personal contacts, where all the members [of the community] knew each other well'.[6] Such descriptions can be misleading, though, particularly where the pre-Emancipation commune is concerned. In fact, the literature on the pre-Emancipation commune focuses almost exclusively on the *estate commune*, a composite commune representing peasants from all villages on the estate. While there almost certainly were communes in Russia which coincided with a single village, we have very little evidence for them.[7] The data used by historians of the commune come primarily from the estate archives of Russia's largest landholding families and institutions (such as monasteries).[8] These estates were often quite large; they could easily have several thousand inhabitants. Many, like Voshchazhnikovo, consisted of twenty or thirty villages divided into a number of separate parishes. The estate commune was comprised of representatives of each village on the estate, often from widely different social groups. Under the guidance of estate officials, this grouping took decisions about the day-to-day management of the estate. Members of the estate commune did not necessarily live together in the same street, or see each other daily (villages on a single estate could be many miles apart), or even attend the same church.

This is not to say that the estate commune was in no sense a community in the way Mironov suggests. Its members did have common interests, they shared certain institutional constraints – mainly those imposed by serfdom – and there was certainly personal contact, especially on demesne estates where corvée labour was used. These are the features emphasised in more recent versions of the Peasant Myth, which see the pre-Emancipation commune as an autonomous peasant institution, impervious to outside influences. According to this view, landlords' attempts to interfere in the internal workings of peasant society invariably failed, resulting in the 'insignificance of the proprietor's imprint on the pattern of [peasant] life and work'.[9] While this view has its origins in the nineteenth century, a

---

[6] B. N. Mironov quoted in Burds, *Peasant dreams and market politics*, p. 9.

[7] D. Moon estimates that three-quarters of all communes in the eighteenth and nineteenth centuries coincided with a single village. Moon, *The Russian peasantry*, p. 201. Mironov cites similar figures in B. N. Mironov, 'Local government in Russia in the first half of the nineteenth century: provincial government and estate government', *Jahrbücher für Geschichte Osteuropas* 42 (1994), p. 170.

[8] Most of the widely cited studies of the pre-Emancipation commune (in both Russian and English) are based on evidence for *estate communes*, including: V. A. Aleksandrov, *Obychnoe pravo krepostnoi derevni Rossii, XVIII–nachalo XIX v.* (Moscow, 1984) and *Sel'skaia obshchina; N. A. Gorskaia, *Monastyrskie krest'iane tsentral'noi Rossii v XVII veke* (Moscow, 1977); Hoch, *Serfdom and social control*; Melton, 'Household economies and communal conflicts'; Prokof'eva, *Krest'ianskaia obshchina*; L. N. Vdovina, *Krest'ianskaia obshchina i monastyr v tsentral'noi Rossii v pervoi polovine XVIII v.* (Moscow, 1988).

[9] Field, *The end of serfdom*, p. 22, as quoted in chapter 1.

similar version was popular among Soviet historians, who argued that the commune represented rural class interests and provided a means for the expression of village solidarities, enabling serfs to rise up and assert their interests against feudal lords, capitalists, and other exploiters. Still another version of this view has become popular in recent years in connection with theories about social capital, the benefits thought to arise from membership in social networks. These theories view the benefits generated by *horizontal* networks such as communes – benefits in the form of shared norms, information, and collective action – as a check on the powers of *vertical*, or hierarchical, institutions such as, in this case, feudalism. It has been argued, for instance, that European societies with communes and 'communally managed natural resources' were better able to resist domination by feudal lords and eventually to abolish serfdom, unlike those without such institutions.[10]

Another view of the peasant commune, associated mainly with nineteenth-century *étatistes*, sees the institution as an artefact of feudalism. This view, the best-known version of which is usually attributed to B. N. Chicherin, one of the most prominent of the Russian liberal 'westernisers', rejects the notion of the commune as an organic, autonomous peasant institution dating from time immemorial, seeing it, and especially its land allocation functions, as resulting instead from specific state (and perhaps landlord) policies, particularly taxation policies in the sixteenth and seventeenth centuries.[11] Adherents of a more recent version of this view maintain that pre-Emancipation communes had very little autonomy, and served mainly as the instruments of feudal lords. According to this 'manorial dominance' approach, the commune was simply another feature of the feudal estate apparatus rather than a representation of peasants' collective interests.[12]

Over the years there have been attempts to reconcile or combine these two classic views. The best known of these, by Aleksandrov, holds that the

[10] R. Birner and H. Wittmer, 'Converting social capital into political capital: how do local communities gain political influence?', Paper presented at the Eighth Biennial Conference of the International Association for the Study of Common Property (2000), p. 1. For more on these views, see Dennison and Ogilvie, 'Serfdom and social capital', esp. pp. 514–15.

[11] Above all the policy of collective responsibility of the commune for rents and taxes; for a more detailed discussion see Aleksandrov, *Sel'skaia obshchina*, pp. 3–46; Goehrke, *Theorien*, pp. 37ff.; Gorskaia, *Russkaia feodal'naia derevnya v istoriografii XX veka* (Moscow, 2006), chapter five; Pushkarev, *Krest'ianskaia pozemel'no-peredel'naia obshchina*, esp. parts one and two. A useful summary of the debates over communal repartitioning can be found in J. Pallot and D. J. B. Shaw, *Landscape and settlement in Romanov Russia 1613–1917* (Oxford, 1990), pp. 136–9.

[12] Dennison and Ogilvie, 'Serfdom and social capital', pp. 517–18; Ogilvie, 'Communities and the second serfdom', pp. 72–5.

commune was actually both of these things; it was characterised by what Aleksandrov called 'dualism', meaning it served the interests of both peasants and landlords. It was able to function simultaneously as an integral part of the feudal administrative apparatus *and* in its traditional capacity as a form of peasant social organisation. Landlords were able to use the commune to secure feudal rents, while serfs used it to assert their collective interests against those of landlords.[13] Hoch has argued in a similar vein, maintaining that on the Petrovskoe estate, landlords' interests and those of the communal patriarchs coincided. Like the feudal authorities, the patriarchs were concerned about the economic viability of the estate, yet at the same time, 'they had the serfs' common well-being at heart'.[14]

In order to determine which of these three approaches fits best, we need to know more about what the pre-Emancipation rural commune did in specific localities, and how it interacted with other institutions. Existing studies tend either to focus on one particular aspect of the commune, such as land repartition, or to cover a whole range of commune-related issues across a large, geographical area (such as European Russia). The first kind of study is inadequate because communes had many interrelated functions. The second kind fails to consider variation in the social, economic, and political contexts in which communes were situated. In short, neither of these approaches tells us how the commune functioned as an institution in a particular local context. Mironov has summarised the problem thus: '[t]he literature on the repartitional commune is enormous: about three thousand books and articles . . . As a rule, however, scholars have limited their research to particular aspects of communal life, primarily economic and juridical dimensions, and have not examined the commune in all its important aspects as a total, internally coherent system.'[15]

The Voshchazhnikovo estate archive is in many ways ideal for a study of the commune in its local institutional context, since, in addition to the sources of information on serf economic and demographic behaviour discussed in previous chapters, it contains records from communal meetings for most of the period under investigation.[16] These *mirskie prigovory* (usually translated as 'communal resolutions') record the issues discussed at each communal meeting, the names of those present, the date on which the meeting was held, and the decisions taken. There are at least fifty sets of these *prigovory* for Voshchazhnikovo, beginning in the early eighteenth

---

[13] Aleskandrov, *Sel'skaia obshchina.*   [14] Hoch, *Serfdom and social control*, p. 158.

[15] Mironov, 'The peasant commune after the reforms of the 1860s', p. 33 (n. 4).

[16] It is difficult to find a locality for which there are good demographic sources as well as communal records. The Petrovskoe estate, studied by Steven Hoch, for instance, offers detailed household listings, but few communal records appear to have survived.

century and going through the first third of the nineteenth. Most of these are for the estate commune, though several sets of *prigovory* for individual village communes have survived (and will be discussed later).[17] The Voshchazhnikovo *prigovory* are quite extensive and address a wide range of issues. They are best used in conjunction with landlords' instructions, serf petitions, and correspondence between the estate administration and the landlord's headquarters in St Petersburg. When taken together, these documents provide a sense of the kinds of estate management issues that frequently arose at Voshchazhnikovo, and the different perspectives on them. They also provide valuable information about the institutional framework within which the commune functioned. In addition, the availability of demographic and economic data, to which one can link information in the resolutions, makes it possible to test theories about communal and estate authority against empirical evidence of serf behaviour.

Of course, some aspects of communal life probably escaped the official record. The *mirskie prigovory*, after all, cover only official meetings of the commune; i.e. those convened and run by communal officials and the estate administration. It is entirely possible that the commune occasionally held informal meetings to deal with issues unrelated to estate management, and that these meetings went unrecorded. Such meetings are never mentioned, even obliquely, in any of the surviving documents for Voshchazhnikovo. It is also possible – and quite likely – that decisions were occasionally taken by communal officials without calling a meeting of the commune. It should be noted, however, that the official responsibilities of the commune incorporated all of the most important aspects of economic, social, and demographic life on the estate. They included matters concerning land cultivation, trade, resource distribution, taxation, migration, marriage, conscription, welfare provision, inheritance, and social control. These issues are all addressed in the communal resolutions, as well as in petitions and official reports. It would seem, then, that the range of issues dealt with unofficially was probably fairly limited. In any case, this chapter will seek to exploit the available documents to broaden our understanding of how the commune functioned at the local level to the greatest extent possible. Section 4.2 addresses basic questions regarding the structure and responsibilities of the Voshchazhnikovo estate commune, particularly those activities which have been traditionally viewed as communal responsibilities: communal governance, land repartition, tax collection, village maintenance, welfare provision, conscription, conflict resolution, and social control. Where there are existing

---

[17] These few surviving records indicate that, on this estate, even decisions taken at the village level were written down.

theories about the role of the commune in these areas, they will be reviewed in the light of the Voshchazhnikovo evidence. Section 4.3 considers the commune in its institutional context, returning to more general theories about the nature of the commune as a peasant community and its relationship to the estate administration, as well as internal relationships among its own members.

4.2   The structure of the commune and its primary responsibilities

The main commune on the Voshchazhnikovo estate was the estate commune, which was a composite commune, consisting of representatives of each of the thirty estate villages. The estate commune, which generated most of the source material used in this chapter, was, in conjunction with the estate administration, responsible for the day-to-day management of the estate and the implementation of the landlord's policies. The estate commune had its own limited powers of taxation, and it kept its own accounts. Some of its specific remits included land repartition, tax collection, welfare provision, and conscription. In addition, the estate commune was responsible for the implementation of estate policies concerning agriculture, including the cultivation of communal arable land, the maintenance of estate granaries, and the management of non-arable land, such as pasture and forest. The estate commune worked with the estate administration in carrying out government edicts, including periodic soul revisions and land surveys. It served as the primary interface between the serf population and the landlord.

The estate commune at Voshchazhnikovo did not have regularly scheduled meetings; it appears, rather, to have convened whenever issues arose. Meeting frequency varied in any given calendar year from three or four times per week to only once per month. And while the estate commune technically comprised all (roughly 600) serf households on the estate, not all estate serfs – not even all adult men – regularly attended the communal meetings. The popular image of communal meetings as gatherings of the whole village, in New England town-hall style, bears little relation to what emerges from the Voshchazhnikovo records.[18] In most cases, villages would send only a few representatives.[19] There were, however,

---

[18] As so often in the literature on Russia, it was Haxthausen who put this image into circulation (*Studien*, vol. I, p. 104).

[19] Serfs in attendance were required to sign their names to communal resolutions, making it possible to determine roughly how many serfs were present at meetings. (Those who could not write had their names written in by the estate scribe.)

occasions when the estate administration insisted on having all household heads in attendance; for instance, when an important announcement concerning estate policies was to be made. Communal officials, elected by the serfs themselves, presided over the meetings, along with the landlord's bailiff (*prikazchik*). A scribe, usually one of the literate serfs from the estate, would record all decisions taken, and these would then be forwarded to the landlord's headquarters in St Petersburg for approval.

Beneath the estate-level commune were the individual village communes, one for each of the thirty villages on the Voshchazhnikovo estate. Each had its own communal officers, usually two or three elected representatives, who were responsible for implementing estate policies at the village level.[20] Village communes did not have the same powers as the estate commune. They could not make independent decisions about welfare provision or settle formal disputes, even among members of their own village.[21] They did not have powers of taxation and did not keep their own village accounts. The few surviving records for village communes suggest that they did occasionally meet separately in order to discuss issues specific to their particular locality.[22] However, there was little they could actually do without the approval of the larger commune and the estate administration. Village communes served mainly as liaison between the individual village communities and the larger estate commune, and were primarily responsible for enforcing the decisions of the estate commune at the village level.

The estate commune is the one that generated the *mirskie prigovory*, as well as the one that appears in documents generated by the landlord's officials, by local bureaucrats, and by serfs themselves (in petitions and wills). All references to 'the commune' hereafter should be understood to refer to the estate commune, and 'commune members' are members of the estate commune. The estate commune was responsible for implementing the landlord's instructions, and maintaining order on the estate. More specifically, the responsibilities of the estate commune can be classified roughly into eight categories, each of which will be separately addressed below.

---

[20] The estate commune often delegated responsibility for the implementation of its decisions to the individual villages. For example, in repartitioning communal lands, the estate commune would allocate land to each village, based on the number of taxable adults in each. The village communes were then in charge of distributing the land among their members.

[21] 'Formal disputes' are defined as those for which petitions were filed with the communal administration. It is possible – though no records exist – that village communes did deal with informal disputes between village members (see the discussion below).

[22] See, for instance, RGADA, f. 1287, op. 3, ed. khr. 565 ('Communal resolutions for the village Tomakovo, 1791').

Communal governance

One of the most widely held views of the commune, originating with the Peasant Myth, maintains that it was governed by its most senior male householders. According to this view, the 'elders' or 'patriarchs' were the most experienced members of the collective and therefore best suited to take decisions about communal welfare. By virtue of their age, the elders were familiar with all of the community's customs and traditions, enabling them to administer justice in accordance with received wisdom and communal precedent. Governing the commune was, in this view, a great honour, and the elders were viewed as having earned their position in society.[23]

The evidence for Voshchazhnikovo is not consistent with this view of communal governance. On this estate, the commune, supervised by the estate administration, held annual elections to choose officials, and these elected officials were responsible for managing all communal affairs. The elected officials usually included at least one of each of the following: *starosta* (elder), *vybornyi* (selectman), *zemskii* (clerk), *zborshchik* (tax collector), *prikhodo-raskhodchik* (accounts manager), *tserkovnyi starosta* (churchwarden), and *sotskii* (policeman). *Starosta*, *vybornyi*, and *zemskii* were probably full-time positions. These officials performed all the day-to-day administrative duties involved in running the estate, including presiding over communal meetings and corresponding regularly with officials in Count Sheremetyev's St Petersburg headquarters. The other communal officers were responsible only for a specific task, such as bookkeeping or tax collection.

The serfs elected to these positions were by no means chosen from among the eldest, most experienced men on the estate. In 1807, for instance, the two estate *zemskie*, Vasily Ivanov and Semyon Arnautov, were 28 and 31 years old respectively.[24] In 1821, the *vybornyi*, Vasily Blazhin, was 43; the *starosta*, Ivan Filiseyev, was 40; the *prikhodo-raskhodchik*, Ivan Dolodanov, was 30; and the *zborshchiki*, Ivan Kouzov, Matvei Deulin, and Yakov Rubezhev, were 55, 30, and 33 respectively.[25] In 1850, the *vybornyi*, Kozma Pavlov, was 33; the *starosta*, Ivan Antipin, was 26; the *zborshchiki*, Vasily Efremov, Mikhail Shaidakov, and Ivan Arnautov, were 38, 27, and 26 respectively.[26]

---

[23] This view is already high profile in Haxthausen, *Studien*; a more recent example is Shanin, *The awkward class*.

[24] RGADA, f. 1287, op. 3, ed. khr. 661, l. 11 ('Punishments meted out to serfs, 1807').

[25] RGADA, f. 1287, op. 3, ed. khr. 733, l. 3 ('On the election of estate officials, 1821').

[26] RGADA, f. 1287, op. 3, ed. khr. 1022, l. 3 ('On the election of estate officials, 1850').

That communal officials in Voshchazhnikovo were considerably younger than the traditional view would predict cannot be ascribed to underlying demographic features of the society. There were plenty of males over the age of 50 on the estate (roughly 15 per cent of the male population was over 50 years of age in each of the six nominal lists for Voshchazhnikovo between 1816 and 1858). In fact, many of the officials mentioned above came from households which contained other, more senior male members, such as fathers, brothers, or uncles. Seniority does not seem to have been a prerequisite for communal officeholding on this estate.

Of course, the election of communal officials was not unique to Voshchazhnikovo. Most communes are thought to have elected officials to perform the duties outlined above.[27] But the true rulers of the commune, it is argued, were in any case the patriarchs, who wielded their power unofficially.[28] According to this view, it would not matter that elected officials were younger men, since the real power was with the unofficial leaders. It seems unlikely, though, that older members of the Voshchazhnikovo community were playing an unofficial role in communal government – one not captured in the written records. The documents make clear the responsibilities of elected officials, which included the organisation and execution of land repartitions, the allocation and collection of taxes and dues, the distribution of poor relief, the maintenance of village lands and buildings, the settling of disputes, and the management of communal finances. Furthermore, as we shall see, elected officials do appear to have had a significant amount of power and influence. It is possible that the so-called patriarchs took part in the settling of informal disputes among commune members or dealing with social deviants, but there is no evidence of this. For even if unofficial actions themselves went unrecorded, one would expect to see references to them in the thousands of pages of petitions, depositions, resolutions, and reports, which touch on nearly every important aspect of serf life on this estate. That there are no such references does not enable us to rule out the possibility that senior members of the commune played an unofficial role in communal governance, but it does suggest that this role, if played, was a fairly marginal one.

It is also implied, in the conventional view, that governing the commune was a great honour. But at Voshchazhnikovo, as on other Sheremetyev estates, serfs did everything they could to avoid communal officeholding.[29]

---

[27] Aleksandrov, *Sel'skaia obshchina*, chapter 3; in the context of the estates of V. G. Orlov, pp. 145–8; Prokof'eva, *Krest'ianskaia obshchina*, pp. 31–5; Moon, *The Russian peasantry*, pp. 202–3.

[28] Mironov, 'Local government in Russia', pp. 173 –4.

[29] Prokof'eva, *Krest'ianskaia obshchina*, pp. 35–6.

The estate archive is full of petitions from serfs explaining why they could not possibly be expected to serve as commune elder, or tax collector, or bookkeeper. Some, like Yakov Rubezhev in 1821, argued that they could not afford to take so much time away from their livelihoods (officers were usually expected to serve one-year terms).[30] Others, like Matvei Deulin that same year, argued that they had to spend most of the year working outside the estate, making it impossible for them to perform official duties.[31] Still others, like Vasily Uliankov in 1847, insisted that poor health rendered them incapable of carrying out the tasks assigned to them.[32]

It was actually remarkably easy for an officer-elect in Voshchazhnikovo to avoid communal service. All he needed to do was hire another estate serf to do the job in his place. In most of the petitions concerning communal offices, serfs explained their reasons for not accepting the nomination and then noted that they had hired another estate serf to take up the position for them.[33] This was usually enough to satisfy the commune and the estate administration, whose main concern was getting the position filled as quickly as possible. Commune members themselves displayed little concern for the qualifications of their officers-elect. First, there is no mention of qualifications of any kind in any of the documents concerning elections. Second, in almost every recorded case of elections, the commune members at Voshchazhnikovo nominated serfs who were not present at the election meeting – i.e. those who could not protest against the nomination. It was then up to these 'elected' serfs to convince the estate administration that they should not be forced to take up the positions assigned to them. Finally, those who did volunteer to take on offices (usually in place of others) were always accepted. There is not a single instance of a serf being rejected for a communal office. It seems, then, that those who governed the commune at Voshchazhnikovo were neither elders nor democratically elected officials. They were not men who had somehow earned the respect of the community over the years. They had no particular qualifications other than that they were willing (perhaps for a price) to do the job.

But if these positions were so undesirable, why were any serfs willing to accept them? The sources indicate that these offices did confer considerable power and influence. This may not have outweighed the costs for serfs who engaged full time in trade, crafts, or migrant labour. But it may

---

[30] RGADA, f. 1287, op. 3, ed. khr. 733, l. 12 ('On the election of estate officials, 1821').

[31] Ibid., l. 13.

[32] RGADA, f. 1287, op. 3, ed. khr. 1745, l. 4 ('Petition regarding officeholding, 1847').

[33] All of those mentioned above, who claimed they could not serve as officials, eventually hired others to replace them.

have held some appeal for middling serfs, who were present on the estate year-round. Communal officers not only supervised the day-to-day affairs of the estate, they made important decisions about the allocation of resources and the distribution of obligations within the community. That communal officials wielded a certain power in these matters is supported by serf petitions, particularly those in which serfs complained about the abuse of this power. For example, in a petition from 1807, serfs complained that the then bailiff allowed his friends to under-report their earnings and exempt themselves from feudal taxes.[34] In an 1833 petition, serfs accused the former estate clerk and his well-off colleagues of collecting up to 2,000 roubles each year from estate villages and distributing them among themselves, with no accounts rendered to the community.[35] A serf from the village of Voshchazhnikovo petitioned in 1844 against communal officials, maintaining that they denied him access to communal land, having chosen instead to lease it to outsiders for lucrative sums.[36] These may be extreme examples of the abuse of power, but they nevertheless indicate that officials had the ability to allocate resources in a way that was beneficial to themselves and members of their social network. This is consistent with findings of other historians for Russian serf estates in this period.[37] At the same time these examples cast considerable doubt on the view that those who governed the commune used their authority in the best interests of the community.[38] Voshchazhnikovo serfs frequently complained that communal authorities acted primarily in their own interests, and at the expense of other peasants.

Land repartition

The Russian rural commune is perhaps best known for its land repartitioning practices. In the repartitional system, peasant holdings were periodically adjusted to reflect changes in the size of member households; households with new members received a larger portion of the communal land, while households which lost members had land taken away. This practice is thought to have operated as a collective risk-minimisation

---

[34] RGADA, f. 1287, op. 3, ed. khr. 668 ('Petition against Slasnikov, 1807').
[35] RGADA, f. 1287, op. 3, ed. khr. 2556, l. 33 ('Communal resolutions for 1833').
[36] RGADA, f. 1287, op. 3, ed. khr. 1635, l. 50 ('Communal resolutions for 1844').
[37] For instance, the Baki estate studied by Melton, as described in 'The magnate', and 'Household economies and communal conflicts', esp. pp. 570–2; the Koren estate, studied by Nosevich, in *Traditsionnaia*, pp. 202–9; and on Iusupov estates, as reported in Sivkov, *Ocherki po istorii krepostnogo khoziaistva*, pp. 208–10, and in A. Smith, 'Authority in a serf village: peasants, managers, and the role of writing in early nineteenth century Russia', *Journal of Social History* 43(1) (2009), pp. 157–73.
[38] Hoch, *Serfdom and social control*, p. 158.

strategy, which, in the absence of land, labour, and credit markets, could guarantee a minimum subsistence to member households by ensuring that all had access to land.[39] This guarantee is held to have been especially important in the context of *krugovaia poruka*, or 'collective responsibility' for taxes and dues. In accordance with *krugovaia poruka*, feudal and state obligations were not levied on individuals, but imposed on the commune as a whole, which then distributed the burden among individual households. If one household could not pay its share, the other member households were forced to make up the difference. According to this view, it was in everyone's interests to make sure each household could meet its obligations. Distributing communal land to members in roughly equal measure is thought to have been the best way of ensuring the viability of member households.

To what extent does this describe the situation at Voshchazhnikovo? It was mentioned in chapter 3 that the system of land repartition on this estate did not quite work in this way. As on other quitrent estates, the communal land distributed among commune members at Voshchazhnikovo had certain feudal obligations attached to it. Estate serfs were required by the landlord to take on this land and pay the dues attached to it.[40] Even those who did not engage in agriculture, such as migrant labourers and itinerant traders, were obligated to take on some share of the communal land. These families either hired labourers to work their communal allotments or they leased out the land to others (communal land was not allowed to go uncultivated).[41] Communal allotments could even be sold to other estate serfs, as we saw in chapter 3. Poor households were often deprived of an allotment, since they could not afford to pay feudal dues. Of the fifty-nine households in Voshchazhnikovon village described as poor in 1832, twenty-eight had no communal allotment and lived instead 'from their own labour'.[42] These findings imply that land repartition was not so much a way of distributing communal resources so that members could survive and meet their obligations as a form of (haphazardly) progressive taxation, or at least a way of distributing feudal obligations among households.

[39] As discussed earlier, the widely held Chayanovian view maintains that land, labour, and credit markets were rare in rural Russia, and that most peasants lived by working their communal plots with family labour.

[40] RGADA, f. 1287, op. 3, ed. khr. 555, l. 22 ('Instructions, 1796/1800').

[41] Only four of the thirty-eight households that held more than 2 *tiagly* of communal land in 1832 engaged in agriculture. The other thirty-four households either let their allotments to others or hired labourers to work them. Calculated from figures in RGADA, f. 1287, op. 3, ed. khr. 1143 ('Inventories of households, 1832/8').

[42] Calculated from figures in RGADA, f. 1287, op. 3, ed. khr. 1143 ('Inventories of households, 1832/8').

The existence of local factor markets further undermines the tradition-ally cited rationale for land repartition. Equal access to communal land was not the only way to ensure that households could survive and meet their tax obligations. Communal land, as mentioned above and as we will see in more detail in subsequent chapters, was not the primary means of subsistence on this estate. In fact, very few serfs actually lived from their communal holdings; not even 10 per cent of the Voshchazhnikovo population was reported as living from agriculture alone. Serfs in Voshchazhnikovo could earn a living in trade, crafts, rural industry, service, day labour, or migrant labour. They did not require access to land in order to be able to fulfil their quitrent obligations. Nor were they dependent on collectivist risk-minimisation strategies for economic survival. Individual strategies were feasible in a context of land, labour, and credit markets, in which Voshchazhnikovo serfs actively participated. Serfs could (and did) obtain land and labour through local markets, and they were able to save and borrow, thereby further reducing their dependence on communal resources.

If land repartition at Voshchazhnikovo was a risk-minimisation strat-egy, it was one imposed on serfs by higher authorities. Both government officials and landlords worried that serfs dependent on local markets for grain might be hard hit during a harvest failure. Furthermore, they real-ised that in such a situation they would be held responsible for making affordable food available to the serf population. As a result, a number of policies were introduced in an attempt to minimise the potential effects of famine. The central government passed a law in the nineteenth century that required estates to keep grain reserves, and all serfs were required to contribute some proportion of their harvest to these granaries.[43] As fur-ther insurance against hardship, the landlord insisted that all communal lands be cultivated.[44]

Finally, it is implied, in certain versions of the Peasant Myth, that periodic redistributions of land were in all serfs' interests, and were thus carried out in a broadly cooperative spirit.[45] But the evidence for Voshchazhnikovo shows that repartitions, not surprisingly, were far more likely to inspire conflict than consensus. In fact, conflict was such a common feature of the process that one of the land surveyors for the estate, in a letter to the Voshchazhnikovo estate administration in 1775, suggested that a formal procedure be established for dealing with

---

[43] See Moon, *The Russian peasantry*, pp. 94, 226; A. Lindenmeyer, *Poverty is not a vice: charity, society, and the state in imperial Russia* (Princeton, 1996), pp. 41–3.

[44] RGADA, f. 1287, op. 3, ed. khr. 555, l. 22 ('Instructions, 1796/1800').

[45] This seems to have originated with Haxthausen; see Haxthausen, *Studien*, vol. I, pp. 124–5.

disputes.[46] In his report, he notes that 'five disputes from the 1774 redistribution have not yet been resolved' and that 'the upcoming survey of serfs' additional holdings is sure to result in even more conflict'.[47] Most repartitions on the Voshchazhnikovo estate were partial repartitions: minor adjustments made annually in response to changes in households' abilities to pay feudal dues. Only rarely were surveyors called in from outside the estate; partial repartitions were usually carried out by communal officials, selected by the serfs themselves.[48] But even these partial repartitions could result in conflict. Serfs were very keen to ensure first that they were not being given too large a share of the feudal tax burden and second that the amount of land they received was commensurate with the amount in feudal dues they were required to pay. Disputes arose whenever serfs felt that these conditions had been violated.

In many repartition disputes on the Voshchazhnikovo estate, serfs complained that they were being forced to pay for more land than they had actually received. For instance, in 1825 serfs from the village of Kulelevo argued that on the basis of a repartition carried out in 1798 they were being required to pay feudal dues for 105 *desiatin* (approximately 283.5 acres) of communal land when they had only been given access to 94 *desiatiny* (approximately 253.8 acres). They demanded that they be allocated the additional 11 *desiatin* or that their feudal dues be reduced accordingly.[49] In other disputes, serfs argued that they were being asked to take on more of the tax burden than they could afford. In 1853, for example, serfs of the village Lykhino demanded that nineteen souls' worth of land in their possession be reallocated to another village, as they were not able to pay for it.[50] Still other disputes concerned the quality of land allotments. In 1724, serfs in the village of Musorovo complained that their allotments were of a poorer quality than those held by serfs in neighbouring villages, and argued that they were being forced to pay for land that was too far away for them to use.[51] Finally, there were serfs who complained about corruption in the system; in particular, the allocation of resources away from ordinary serfs and into the pockets of powerful officeholders. For instance, Pyotr Shepelev, of the village Dem'ian, petitioned against

[46] RGADA, f. 1287, op. 3, ed. khr. 323, ll. 8–9 ('Report to central administration reported in communal resolution, 1775').
[47] *Ibid.*, ll. 8–9.
[48] Surveyors were only brought in when a complete repartition was to be done. This seems to have happened only two or three times in Voshchazhnikovo during the period under investigation.
[49] RGADA, f. 1287, op. 3, ed. khr. 930, l. 2 ('Petition regarding land repartition, 1825').
[50] RGADA, f. 1287, op. 3, ed. khr. 2058, l. 1 ('Petition regarding land partition, 1853').
[51] As reported in Prokof'eva, *Krest'ianskaia obshchina*, pp. 69–70.

communal officials in 1844, claiming that he paid his *obrok* but received no allotment, because local officials were renting out communally held land for their own profit.[52]

In a sense, land repartition at Voshchazhnikovo was a form of redistribution, but it did not function in quite the way Haxthausen and Herzen and other proponents of the Peasant Myth imagined. Instead, it was a periodic redistribution of the tax burden among middling and prosperous households. The process was contentious, often resulting in conflicts which took years to resolve. But it seems one outcome could be relied on: the poorest households would remain without access to land.

Feudal obligations and taxation

There is very little concrete information in the existing literature on Russian peasant communes about the way the feudal tax system operated on individual estates. We know that *krugovaia poruka* (collective responsibility) was practised on many of the larger estates, and that the commune was generally responsible for distributing the burden among member households, as well as for the collection and delivery of feudal dues and state tax money.[53] But exactly what sort of dues and taxes were levied? And how did this system function in practice? Fortunately, the source materials for Voshchazhnikovo make it possible to address these questions, and to provide at least a first rough outline of how this system functioned.

According to the landlord's instructions for 1796, feudal dues (*obrok*) on the Voshchazhnikovo estate were set at 15 silver roubles per *tiaglo* of communal land per year.[54] Every household with at least one male between the ages of 17 and 65 was required to take on some of this land.[55] Households were then assessed according to the number of *tiagly* in their possession. The range was quite large; some households held only one half *tiaglo*, and while others held five or six *tiagol* and owed over 75 roubles per year in feudal dues.[56] On top of these dues, Sheremetyev levied an annual 'asset tax', whereby all serfs with combined assets valued at over 500 roubles were required to pay 0.5 per cent on each rouble over 500.[57]

---

[52] RGADA, f. 1287, op. 3, ed. khr. 1635, l. 50 ('Communal resolutions for 1844').

[53] Prokof'eva, *Krest'ianskaia obshchina*, pp. 147–51.

[54] RGADA, f. 1287, op. 3, ed. khr. 555, l. 22 ('Instructions, 1796/1800'). This does not seem to have changed over the nineteenth century. The same figure is given in the 1858 descriptions of estates in RGADA, f. 1287, op. 3, ed. khr. 2320 (1858), l. 12.

[55] *Ibid.*, l. 22.

[56] RGADA, f. 1287, op. 3, ed. khr. 1143 ('Inventories of households 1832/8').

[57] RGADA, f. 1287, op. 3, ed. khr. 555, l. 22 ('Instructions, 1796/1800'). As noted in chapter 2, assets were defined vaguely as 'capital and property' (*kapitaly i imeniia*) in the instructions.

Estate craftsmen were to pay an extra one rouble per year, in addition to their *obrok* payments.[58] There were also feudal dues in kind. Each serf household was required to provide some proportion of its grain harvest to the estate granary, to the landlord's households in Moscow and St Petersburg, as well as that on the estate, and finally to the estate stables (mainly oats). Finally, there were taxes levied on marriage and household formation, migration, land purchases, trade, and various other economic activities.[59] There was also an annual recruitment levy, discussed later in this chapter.

In addition to feudal dues, serf households paid state taxes and communal taxes. The state capitation tax – or soul tax – stood at roughly 86 silver kopecks per year for much of the nineteenth century.[60] It was levied on every male serf, regardless of age. In practice, however, it was not always distributed among households in accordance with the number of males in each. Instead, the total amount owed, based on the number of male serfs recorded in the last soul revision, was levied on the commune, who then distributed it in accordance with households' ability to pay.[61] A wealthy household with several daughters would, then, have subsidised a poor household with several sons.

Communal taxes, like feudal dues, were attached to landholdings. In 1825, the levy was 2 roubles 80 kopecks silver per *tiaglo* of land per household.[62] Data from the 1832 estate household listing suggests that households paid anywhere from 1.5 to 22 roubles per year, depending on the size of their communal holdings.[63] This money was used primarily to maintain the physical infrastructure of the estate and its parishes and to provide salaries for communal officials.

Collective responsibility (*krugovaia poruka*) was practised at Voshchazhnikovo, as on most Russian estates in this period. Taxes and dues were levied on the commune as lump sums, and the commune was responsible for distributing the burden among its members. So for 1,015 *tiagol* of land at 15 roubles per *tiaglo* per annum, the landlord expected to receive 15,225 roubles from the commune each year, leaving it to the serfs to decide how to divide up this sum. In fact, in one set of instructions, Sheremetyev explicitly stated that he was not interested in knowing how feudal dues were distributed among serfs; he was concerned only that he

[58] *Ibid.*
[59] All of these are set out in the 'Landlord's instructions'. RGADA, f. 1287, op. 3, ed. khr. 1305 ('Instructions, 1764'), and ed. khr. 555 ('Instructions, 1796/1800').
[60] Blum, *Lord and peasant*, p. 464.
[61] RGADA, f. 1287, op. 3, ed. khr. 555, l. 26 ('Instructions, 1796/1800').
[62] RGADA, f. 1287, op. 3, ed. khr. 944, l. 2 ('Communal account books, 1825').
[63] RGADA, f. 1287, op. 3, ed. khr. 1143 ('Inventories of households, 1832/8').

receive the total amount at his St Petersburg headquarters by the designated deadlines.[64] Taxes and dues were usually paid in three instalments: one in January, one in May, and one in September. The communal *zborshchiki* (tax collectors) were responsible for collecting the money, as well as in-kind grain payments, and making sure they were delivered promptly to Sheremetyev's headquarters.

Feudal dues had to be delivered three times per year to the St Petersburg headquarters (approximately 400 miles from the estate), while the soul tax money was delivered to state officials in the district capital of Rostov Velikii (about 20 miles from the estate). Grain payments often went to the Sheremetyevs' St Petersburg residence, but were occasionally delivered to the Sheremetyev household in Moscow (roughly 200 miles from the estate). For each of these deliveries, the commune hired a group of two or three estate serfs to make the journey. This was a serious assignment: those who accepted it were held accountable for the sums until they were signed for at their destination.

The estate *zborshchiki* kept annual account books in which they noted who had paid, how much had been paid, and whether the payment was on time. They also kept track of who was in arrears, how long it had been since they had last paid, and how much was outstanding. The entries are not always by household; communal officials seem to have kept track of who *within each household* paid dues and taxes. For instance, it is noted in several cases that one household member, such as the household head, had paid in full and on time, while another, such as his son, was in arrears.[65]

Unfortunately, there is no concrete information in the documents about the commune's way of compensating for those who could not pay their share on time. Information for other Sheremetyev estates suggests that the shortfall was usually divided among the economically viable households.[66] Interestingly, the number of Voshchazhnikovo serfs listed as being in arrears was never very large.[67] This is probably *not* because all serfs were well off in the eighteenth and nineteenth centuries; in fact, we know there were poor serfs on this estate (see the discussion of poor

---

[64] RGADA, f. 1287, op. 3, ed. 677, ll. 12–15 ('Instructions and decrees, 1808').

[65] This was the case with the sons of serf Fyodor Muravyov. Vasily was noted as having paid his dues on time, while Andrei, who resided in the same household, was said to have 'paid unreliably' due to his bad character. Similarly, in the Sopetov household, the head, Nikolai, was said to have paid slowly 'due to his tendency to drink', while the rest of the family 'paid on time'. In RGADA, f. 1287, op. 3, ed. khr. 1143, ll. 9, 68–9 ('Inventories of households, 1832/8').

[66] Prokof'eva, *Krest'ianskaia obshchina*, pp. 147–50.

[67] RGADA, f. 1287, op. 3, ed. khr. 2232 ('On serfs in arrears, 1855–60') and ed. khr. 1614 ('On the exile of serfs in arrears, 1843').

relief below). It may be that the existence of credit markets in this region took some pressure off the commune, by enabling serfs to borrow during difficult times. It is also possible, since many households had more than one wage-earner, that family members were pressured to compensate for brothers, sons, fathers, or uncles who did not pay, and only when this failed was the commune forced to contribute. In any case, it is clear that communal authorities and the estate administration did not look kindly on those who repeatedly failed to meet their obligations. Chronic offenders could be gaoled, conscripted, transferred to another estate, or even exiled.

One last point worth mentioning is that while the official documents, such as account books and estate reports, give the impression that tax collection was an orderly, well-regulated process, other sources indicate that there was ample scope for arbitrariness on the part of local officials. It seems unlikely, given how detailed the instructions were, that money collection was as complicated and haphazard as Melton describes for the Baki estate in Kostroma, where collections were sufficiently frequent and random that serfs rarely knew which instalment of which tax was being collected on a particular occasion.[68] Nonetheless, petitions from Voshchazhnikovo serfs to the landlord indicate that officers were able to take advantage of their taxation powers and their control of the communal purse. There was the example, mentioned earlier, of the estate clerk and his high-ranking colleagues, who were accused of collecting thousands of excess roubles from estate villages and dividing the surplus monies among themselves.[69] And, in another instance, the estate bailiff was accused, in 1835, of arbitrarily levying new taxes on serf households for his own profit.[70]

There is still much we do not know about taxation in this period. The records for Voshchazhnikovo offer an illuminating glimpse of the complex system that existed on Russian serf estates in this period. They also raise a number of important questions for future research. For instance, how did the commune convince (or coerce) its members to subsidise those who could not pay? Does a low level of arrears imply that communes were reasonably successful at this? How did the landlord ensure that the poll tax was paid in full? And how did the kinds of taxes and procedures for collection vary across estates? Unfortunately, the communal sources for Voshchazhnikovo are silent about these questions, but it is likely that other local estate records contain evidence that future local studies can use to shed light on them.

[68] Melton, 'Household economies and communal conflicts', pp. 571–2.
[69] RGADA, f. 1287, op. 3, ed. khr. 2556, l. 33 ('Communal resolutions for 1833').
[70] RGADA, f. 1287, op. 3, ed. khr. 1256 ('Petition against bailiff Tizengauzen, 1835').

Maintenance of village infrastructure

In most accounts of communal life in rural Russia, it is assumed that commune members were collectively responsible for the physical infrastructure of the estate and its composite villages. If a road or bridge needed to be repaired or a piece of land needed to be cleared, a group of volunteers was assembled to do the job.

Serfs at Voshchazhnikovo were collectively responsible for maintaining village infrastructure, but they rarely did the work voluntarily. Rather than coerce unwilling locals into providing labour for routine maintenance tasks, communal officials hired peasants – frequently from among estate serfs – to do these jobs, and paid them a wage from communal tax funds. Entries were made in the communal account books, noting the names of those hired, the type of job done, and the amount paid. For instance, in 1754, Kozma Pautov from the village of Dem'ian was paid 10 kopecks for cutting grass on the estate.[71] A Voshchazhnikovo serf, Grigory Abramov, was paid 50 kopecks for transporting building materials to Voshchazhnikovo from the village of Tomakovo.[72] Mikhail Andreev from the village Yurenino was paid 35 roubles 75 kopecks in 1824 for 'repairing the bridge over the river Keda'.[73] That same year, the serfs Mikhail Ivanov and Pyotr Abramov were paid 75 roubles each for digging drains along the Uglich road.[74] In 1837, Nikolai Povalikhin was hired to clean and paint part of a fence belonging to the estate, for payment of one rouble per *sazhen'* from communal funds.[75]

A few Voshchazhnikovo serfs worked full time carrying out routine tasks for the commune. The serf Ivan Buliaev, for instance, who was described in the 1832 household listing as 'very poor', earned his living from cleaning the ponds on the estate, for which the commune paid him a small stipend.[76] Another Voshchazhnikovo serf, Marko Melent'ev, was engaged by the commune as a driver (*iamshchik*) for the year 1844–5. The commune agreed to pay him an annual salary of 350 roubles for making regular trips to the cities of Yaroslavl', Rostov and Uglich.[77] The commune also engaged non-estate serfs for maintenance jobs. In 1824, a peasant glazier, Mikhail Petrov, from the village of Borisogleb, was brought in to replace glass windows in the estate management building and in the Sheremetyevs' manor house.[78]

---

[71] RGADA, f. 1287, op. 3, ed. khr. 189, l. 3 ('Communal account books, 1754').   [72] *Ibid.*
[73] RGADA, f. 1287, op. 3, ed. khr. 921, l. 25 ('Communal account books, 1824').
[74] *Ibid.*, l. 83.
[75] RGADA, f. 1287, op. 3, ed. khr. 1325, l. 37 ('Communal resolutions, 1837').
[76] RGADA, f. 1287, op. 3, ed. khr. 1143, l. 18 ('Inventories of households, 1832/8').
[77] RGADA, f. 1287, op. 3, ed. khr. 1635, l. 3 ('Communal resolutions, 1844').
[78] RGADA, f. 1287, op. 3, ed. khr. 921, l. 76 ('Communal account books, 1824').

Maintaining the local parish churches was another of the commune's responsibilities. The thirty villages on the estate were divided into six parishes: Voshchazhnikovo, Vioska, Semionovskoe, Nikola na Pen'e, Nikola na Beriozkakh, and Uslavtsevo. The estate commune was responsible for maintaining the church buildings in each of these parishes, and for providing salaries for the clergy, and the communal churchwarden. The serfs at Voshchazhnikovo, however, only very reluctantly provided financial support for their parish churches; in most cases they had to be forced to do so by the landlord. When the churches needed to be repaired (or in some cases rebuilt after fires or floods), serfs were ordered by Sheremetyev to provide the money from communal funds. When the widow of a priest requested poor relief or a pension, the landlord, again, forced the commune to comply. Hoch has reported similar findings for Petrovskoe. The church buildings on the Petrovskoe estate were described as dilapidated and in disrepair, with serfs unwilling to supply the funds needed to repair and maintain them. And Petrovskoe serfs frequently complained about the fees and fines extracted from them by parish priests.[79]

As noted in chapter 2, serfs at Voshchazhnikovo do not appear to have made voluntary donations to the church; the amounts collected by churches on their weekly collection plates were very small indeed. In 1764, the collection plate at the Voshchazhnikovo parish church (the largest on the estate) brought in only about 30 kopecks per week.[80] The amounts collected by the second-largest parish church on the estate, Semionovskoe, were equally small. According to account books for this parish, the total amount collected for the year 1793 was just over 9 roubles – less than 1 rouble per month.[81] This is rather surprising, given that these parishes had hundreds of parishioners, some of whom reported assets in the thousands of roubles. But, again, these findings are not inconsistent with those reported in other studies of Russian rural parishes in this period.[82] While an examination of religious attitudes is beyond the scope of this study, it could be argued that the marked unwillingness to provide voluntary support to the church and local clergy casts some doubt

---

[79] Hoch, *Serfdom and social control*, pp. 146–9. A similar account is given in Belliustin's nineteenth-century description of parish dynamics. Belliustin, *Description of the clergy*, esp. pp. 145–7.

[80] RGADA, f. 1287, op. 3, ed. khr. 294, ll. 1–2 ('Parish account books, 1764').

[81] RGADA, f. 1287, op. 3, ed. khr. 608 ('Parish account books, 1793').

[82] Similar findings are reported in Freeze, *The parish clergy*; and Hoch, *Serfdom and social control*. These are not consistent with the view held by, for instance, Haxthausen or Tolstoy, who portrayed the Russian peasant as deeply religious.

on the view that Russian peasants were especially devout adherents to the Orthodox faith.[83]

Welfare provision

The provision of poor relief has long been viewed as one of the most important functions of the Russian peasant commune.[84] 'In the Russian commune', wrote Haxthausen, 'there is an organic cohesion; a compact social strength inheres in them as nowhere else. This affords Russia the immeasurable advantage that to this date it has no proletariat, nor could a proletariat develop, as long as the communal organisation of society remains!'[85] This communal solidarity, he thought, was modelled on family solidarity, as the commune was a kind of extended family guided by the wisdom of its patriarchs. Russia, therefore, had no need of Saint-Simon or other western social prophets, as their utopia was already realised in rural Russia. Thanks to its communal institutions, Russia had been spared pauperisation and was therefore safe from the revolutionary movements threatening western Europe.[86]

Land repartition is generally considered the main form of communal welfare provision, since periodic reallocation is thought to have prevented or at least minimised socioeconomic stratification in peasant communities by providing all households with access to communal resources.[87] Elderly persons without family or those otherwise incapable of working communal land are supposed to have been provided with some form of assistance from the community. Again, it is often argued that it was in everyone's interests to keep all member households economically viable, so that each could pay its share of the collective tax burden.

The sources for Voshchazhnikovo paint a very different picture. We have already seen that the serf community on this estate was highly stratified, with some households claiming taxable assets of over 20,000 roubles, while others had few or no assets, and eked out a living on 50 roubles per year or less. Because there were feudal dues to be paid on each

---

[83] Michel Vovelle makes a strong case for regarding financial support as a proxy for religious attitudes in his *Piété baroque et déchristianisation en Provence au XVIIIe siècle: les attitudes devant la mort d'après les clauses des testaments* (Paris, 1973).

[84] Lindenmeyer, *Poverty is not a vice*, pp. 41–2; Aleksandrov, *Obychnoe pravo*, pp. 206–23; Moon, *The Russian peasantry*, pp. 225–6; J. M. Hartley, *A social history of the Russian empire 1650–1825* (London and New York, 1998), pp. 85–6.

[85] Haxthausen, *Studien*, vol. I, p. 129.

[86] *Ibid.*, vol. I, p. 156. Herzen shared this view, as evident in the essay, 'O sel'skoi obshchine v Rossii', pp. 508–9.

[87] Haxthausen, *Studien*, vol. I, pp. 129–30; Pallot, *Land reform*, p. 81.

piece of communal land, repartition did not function as a way of redistributing resources on this estate. If anything, the land repartition system reinforced existing disparities by distributing a larger portion of the communal land to the richer households on the estate, since those were able to pay for it.[88]

Nor was the commune especially forthcoming with assistance of any other kind. In many cases, it was the landlord's officials who forced the commune to provide relief for the indigent. In one particularly scathing letter to the Voshchazhnikovo estate administration in 1822, Sheremetyev observed that 'there are serfs on my estates who cannot work because they are too old, or blind, or otherwise infirm, and that these are living in abject poverty, often without homes or communal land, and with no way of supporting themselves'.[89] He then ordered the 'better-off peasants to provide these people with assistance, such that they will no longer feel compelled to beg from others'.[90] In another example, in 1844, a serf woman living in St Petersburg appealed to the commune for poor relief on the grounds that her husband was too ill to work and, without his earnings, they could no longer support their four young children.[91] The commune denied her request, arguing that she was capable of working to support her family, and suggesting that she return to the estate where she could find paid work.[92] The landlord's officials, however, overturned the decision of the commune, insisting that the family be provided with monetary assistance (10 roubles per month) until their eldest son reached the age of majority and could support the family with his own labour.[93]

Although the landlord was occasionally willing to step in and overrule the commune in its decision to withhold assistance from a petitioner, it would probably be a mistake to view such cases as evidence for 'paternalism' – the sense of moral obligation that landlords are widely believed to have felt toward their serfs. In fact, landlords had a strong incentive to ensure that their serfs were not reduced to begging in the streets. A state-level campaign against begging, which began in the eighteenth century under Peter I, held landlords responsible for their poorer serfs, and subjected them to ever-increasing fines for those caught begging.[94] It is

---

[88] It may therefore appear to have operated as a form of progressive taxation, at least as far as the distribution of dues was concerned. But the more prosperous serfs could invest more in their correspondingly larger parcels of land (e.g. farm them more intensively), rent them out, or sell them on the internal land market, so any redistributive effect would likely have been cancelled out. And those most in need of redistribution received no land whatsoever.

[89] RGADA, f. 1287, op. 3, ed. khr. 848, l. 2 ('On providing assistance to the poor, 1822').

[90] *Ibid.*   [91] RGADA, f. 1287, op. 3, ed. khr. 1635, l. 43 ('Communal resolutions, 1844').

[92] *Ibid.*, ll. 45–6.   [93] *Ibid.*, l. 48.   [94] See Lindenmeyer, *Poverty is not a vice*, chapter 2.

therefore not surprising that, in the examples above, the estate administration explicitly stated its concern about beggars. In the first case, the estate officials demanded that the poor be subsidised by better-off commune members 'so that they will no longer feel compelled to beg from others'.[95] In the second example, the petitioner is granted relief by the authorities but, as a condition, 'she is strictly forbidden to beg for alms'.[96]

The case for paternalism is further undermined by the number of cases in which the decision to deny relief funds to a petitioner was upheld by the landlords' officials. For example, an 1824 request for relief from a 24-year-old widow was denied by the commune on the grounds that she was young and able-bodied and capable of supporting herself. The estate administration supported this decision, stating that 'to judge by her youth, she is capable of earning a living by her own labour'.[97] In another case from the same year, the estate authorities upheld the decision to withhold relief from yet another serf widow, who they described as being 'prone to vagrancy', despite assistance granted to her in the past, and whose request was 'not worthy of respect'.[98]

While the commune very rarely granted requests for monetary assistance, it did occasionally offer some relief in the form of special land allotments (free of dues) or temporary exemption from feudal dues (*obrok*).[99] In 1804, for example, the recently widowed wife of Andrei Barsykov was granted a half-soul's worth of land free of feudal obligations.[100] In the same year, the serf Simion Vasiliev, who was unable to work 'due to his old age', was granted a quarter-soul's worth of land, free of dues.[101] In 1822, the commune refused the serf widow Vera Petrova's request for monetary assistance, offering instead 'one half-soul's worth of land, free of dues, on which [the family] ought to be able to get by'.[102] In 1844, the serf Aleksei Vasiliev was granted, 'for his extreme poverty, a half-soul's worth of land to support his family'.[103] That same year, the family of the deceased serf Ivan Malyshev was granted an exemption from the dues owed by him for the year 1843.[104] In 1849, the dues owed by the family of Avdotia

---

[95] RGADA, f. 1287, op. 3, ed. khr. 848, l. 2 ('On providing assistance to the poor, 1822').

[96] RGADA, f. 1287, op. 3, ed. khr. 1635, l. 49 ('Communal resolutions, 1844').

[97] RGADA, f. 1287, op. 3, ed. khr. 902, l. 18 ('Correspondence between central administration and Voshchazhnikovo estate authorities, 1824').

[98] *Ibid.*, l. 13.

[99] The commune at Petrovskoe provided similar forms of relief. Hoch, *Serfdom and social control*, pp. 138–9.

[100] RGADA, f. 1287, op. 3, ed. khr. 652, l. 69 ('Communal resolutions, 1804').   [101] *Ibid.*

[102] RGADA, f. 1287, op. 3, ed. khr. 844, l. 4 ('Petition for poor relief, 1822').

[103] RGADA, f. 1287, op. 3, ed. khr. 1635, l. 8 ('Communal resolutions, 1844').

[104] *Ibid.*, l. 1.

Chernikhina were reduced by half, as she was recently widowed and unable to meet all of her deceased husband's obligations.[105]

Still, the commune did not grant every request for dues waivers, either. The widow Avdotia Stulova, having apparently fallen behind in quitrent payments, petitioned the commune in 1849 to have 15 roubles in arrears waived, since her 'eldest son earned barely enough to cover his own dues, and the other one was still too young to work'.[106] The commune denied her request, stating that the money owed could be 'exacted from her children'.[107] In the same year, the serf Ivan Triapkin requested a temporary exemption from dues, since '[his] horse had died in July, followed by [his] cow in the autumn, and having to both replace his animals and pay dues would leave [him] in complete ruin'.[108] The commune rejected his petition, stating that 'such misfortunes happen to many, and, if we compensated everyone, it would be at the expense of those even poorer than Triapkin'.[109]

How did the commune at Voshchazhnikovo decide who was poor enough to qualify for relief? No clear answer to this question emerges from the documents; there do not seem to be any precise criteria by which the commune made decisions about welfare provision. Existing evidence suggests that those most likely to receive assistance were elderly people with no family and widows with young children. But even these criteria were not cast in stone. While the commune did, in several instances, grant relief (usually in the form of land allotments or dues exemptions) to widows with young children, there were also cases in which assistance to such women was denied. In one particularly illuminating case, the commune refused a widow's request for relief, noting that 'there are many poor widows with young children on this estate, who are in a similar position [as the petitioner], but manage to support their families with their own labour instead of demanding monetary handouts from the commune'.[110]

Nonetheless, three significant observations can be made on the basis of this evidence. First, the examples cited here make it clear that no one – neither the chronically poor nor those who found themselves temporarily impoverished – was guaranteed assistance from the serf community. Second, there does not seem to have been any explicit set of customs regarding welfare provision, which serfs would invoke when making requests for relief, or which could be invoked by the commune in its decision process. Phrases such as 'according to our tradition' or 'as custom dictates' do not appear in either the petitions from serfs or the

---

[105] RGADA, f. 1287, op. 3, ed. khr. 850, l. 3 ('Petition for poor relief, 1849').   [106] *Ibid.*
[107] *Ibid.*, l. 4.   [108] *Ibid.*, l. 12.   [109] *Ibid.*, l. 14.
[110] RGADA, f. 1287, op. 3, ed. khr. 1635, l. 46 ('Communal resolutions, 1844').

decisions (*prigovory*) handed down by the commune. Finally, every decision the commune made with respect to welfare provision had to be approved by the estate administration. The commune did not have the authority to act independently; its decisions could be, and occasionally were, overturned by the higher authorities.

Conscription

In addition to feudal obligations imposed by landlords, Russian serfs had two main obligations to the state: payment of the annual poll tax and provision of recruits for the tsar's army. Recruitment levies varied from year to year, ranging from 4 per every 1,000 male serfs in the 1820s[111] to 5–7 per 1,000 in the 1840s[112] and rising to over 30 per 1,000 during the Crimean War in the 1850s.[113] A variety of approaches to conscription has been reported for Russian peasant communes: some chose recruits by lottery, others used a queue, some delegated conscription decisions to individual households, others were more interventionist. Despite these differences, there are supposed to have been a few practices common to all communities. For instance, communes are thought to have used these annual levies to rid themselves of their economically weaker members – i.e. households which could not meet their obligations – and social deviants.[114] Serfs with reputations as troublemakers or drunks, or those in arrears in feudal dues, were in many cases among the first chosen. This practice is thought to have created an additional incentive to form large, multi-generational households, since the commune would have been more likely to target the smaller, economically weaker units first.[115] It is often argued that landlords rarely interfered in the selection process, instead allowing communal elders to take the decisions about whom to conscript.[116] Not surprisingly, most accounts indicate that conscription

---

[111] RGADA, f. 1287, op. 3, ed. khr. 991 ('State decree regarding conscription, 1827'), ed. khr. 1016 ('State decree regarding conscription, 1828').

[112] RGADA, f. 1287, op. 3, ed. khr. 1584 ('State decree regarding conscription, 1842'), ed. khr. 1684 ('State decree regarding conscription, 1845').

[113] This figure comes from Hoch, *Serfdom and social control*, p. 156. Unfortunately, no recruit figures are available for Voshchazhnikovo during the 1850s. There are no figures available for the early 1800s either, when the Napoleonic Wars would almost certainly have brought higher levies.

[114] Aleksandrov, *Sel'skaia obshchina*, pp. 273–87; Hoch, *Serfdom and social control*, p. 157; Prokof'eva, *Krest'ianskaia obshchina*, pp. 155–6.

[115] Aleksandrov, *Sel'skaia obshchina*, pp. 288–93; Prokof'eva, *Krest'ianskaia obshchina*, p. 155.

[116] Hartley, *A social history*, p. 85; Moon, *The Russian peasantry*, p. 209; Sivkov, *Ocherki po istorii krepostnogo khoziaistva*, p. 39. This was evidently not the case on the Gagarins' Manuilovskoe estate, where the estate administration, at least on certain occasions, supervised the process closely. See Bohac, 'The "mir"'.

was everywhere a contentious issue; the otherwise harmonious commune became a hotbed of conflict at the time of the annual draft.

On the Voshchazhnikovo estate, recruits were selected by the commune according to general guidelines set out by the Sheremetyevs in the estate 'instructions'. Unmarried males between the ages of 17 and 34 were to be carefully scrutinised. If they did not appear to be contributing to the household economy, instead 'leading dissolute lives' (*rasputnichat'*), then they should be considered 'unsound' (*neprochnyi*) and given to the army.[117] Additional recruits were to be chosen through an estate-wide lottery. In what was probably an attempt to protect smaller households from economic ruin, Sheremetyev instructed the commune to draw first from households having three or more males between the ages of 17 and 65, followed by those with two, and finally, as a last resort, from those with only one male of working age. Households with no males between the ages of 17 and 65 were excluded from the lottery.[118] As discussed in chapter 3, the Sheremetyevs were aware that this practice would give serfs an incentive to form small, nuclear-family households, rather than large, multi-generational ones, since recruits were to be taken first from the larger families. In order to prevent serf families from evading conscription by separating into smaller units, the landlord, as we have seen, devised strict rules concerning household division, enforced by a system of fines.

How was conscription actually carried out in practice on the Voshchazhnikovo estate? Evidence suggests that the commune did use conscription as a means of dealing with 'social deviants' and those Sheremetyev refers to as 'unsound' (*neprochnyi*) serfs. Among the examples in the estate records, there was the serf Leontei Aralov, 28, who was sent to the army in 1805 after leaving the estate without permission and allegedly robbing a Moscow merchant.[119] In the same year, Dmitri Kokin was accused of theft and drunkenness and sent to the army.[120] A year later the serf Yakov Kulikov, 30, was conscripted for 'living a dissolute life'.[121]

Additional recruits were chosen by lottery, in accordance with the landlord's instructions. It seems that estate officials had households draw lots, on the basis of which a conscription list was compiled. The households that drew numbers one, two, three, and four, for instance, would be called on to provide recruits for the current calendar year. Once they had fulfilled their obligation, these households would be removed from the list. The following year recruits would be taken from households

[117] RGADA, f. 1287, op. 3, ed. khr. 677, l. 8 ('Instructions and decrees, 1808').   [118] *Ibid.*
[119] RGADA, f. 1287, op. 3, ed. khr. 652, l. 116–17 ('Communal resolutions, 1804').
[120] *Ibid.*, l. 114.   [121] 'rasputnaia zhizn'', in *ibid.*, l. 115.

five, six, seven, and eight. This would continue until all those on the list had been called, at which point a new lottery was held.

The households called upon to provide recruits had several options. They could designate one of their own male members as a recruit and send him off to the army.[122] Or, if they had the financial resources, they could purchase a substitute recruit to send in the place of their male relative (these substitutes were usually non-estate peasants, who offered to go to the army in return for a payment). A third option was to purchase an exemption certificate from estate officials, who would then, with the money paid for the certificate, purchase a substitute recruit on the market.[123]

The conscription market was fairly well established and widely used among serfs on the Voshchazhnikovo estate, as well as on other Sheremetyev estates.[124] The overwhelming majority of households purchased substitute recruits or exemption certificates. Serfs paid anywhere from several hundred to several thousand roubles to avoid conscription. As a result, it was the poorer households – those who could not afford to buy substitutes – who bore the brunt of conscription. It was they who had little choice but to sacrifice a valuable male worker – at times the only male household member of working age. Poorer households were not necessarily 'targeted' by the Voshchazhnikovo commune for conscription, but they ended up carrying most of the burden all the same.

To say that the landlord and his officials did not interfere in recruitment decisions taken by the Voshchazhnikovo commune would be an exaggeration. Recruit selection appears to have been carried out in strict accordance with the landlord's instructions, and the names of those chosen had to be submitted to the estate administration for approval. While it is true that the commune had better access to information about the local population and the economic circumstances of estate households than did the landlord's officials in St Petersburg, the decision-making process was nonetheless closely monitored by the higher authorities.[125] In some cases, these authorities made the recruitment decisions. The serf Nikolai Chernikhin, for instance, was sent to the army in 1807, 'by the landlord's

---

[122] Complex negotiations were carried out within families over who would go to the army. In some cases, formal contracts were drawn up among brothers, in which compensation was promised to the one who agreed to be conscripted. A specific example of this can be found in RGADA, f. 1287, op. 3, ed. khr. 2317 ('Communal resolutions, 1858').

[123] References to the conscription market are scattered throughout the Voshchazhnikovo estate documents. For a summary and references to other Sheremetyev estates see Prokof'eva, *Krest'ianskaia obshchina*, pp. 153–5.

[124] RGADA, f. 1287, op. 3, ed. khr. 2312, l. 26 ('Instructions and decrees, 1857'). See also Prokof'eva, *Krest'ianskaia obshchina*, pp. 151–7; Shchepetov, *Krepostnoe pravo*, pp. 177–8.

[125] As at Manuilovskoe. Bohac, 'The "mir"'.

decree'.[126] Serfs who wished to purchase substitute recruits still had to petition the central authorities for permission. And exemption certificates could only be obtained through estate officials. Disputes over unfulfilled obligations or eligibility for conscription were referred for resolution to the local estate administration and, ultimately, the home office in St Petersburg. Furthermore, when communes wished to rid themselves of deviants or poorer members, they were careful to employ the language of the estate instructions to justify their decisions. The above-mentioned Yakov Kulikov was recruited for 'living a dissolute life', an offence explicitly cited in the instructions as grounds for conscription.[127] Similarly, the Malakhovo commune requested in 1825 that Ivan Sal'nikov be conscripted, because 'he manage[d] his household badly and ha[d] no way of providing for his family'.[128] Thus, conscription, like most communal responsibilities, was carried out by the Voshchazhnikovo commune in close cooperation with the landlord and his official representatives.

Conflict resolution

Dispute settlement is thought to have been another of the Russian commune's primary functions. Various forms of intra-communal and intra-familial conflict are supposed to have been resolved before the commune in accordance with customary law. Peasant communes, it is held, dispensed their own form of justice against those who, by stealing, disregarding communal regulations, or by failing to show respect to one's elders, violated collective norms. Disciplinary action was usually administered publicly and involved rituals – such as tarring and feathering – which were designed to humiliate the accused.[129] Such things may have occurred among the serfs at Voshchazhnikovo, but, unfortunately, there is no information in the estate documents about the role of communal justice and customary law in dealing with intra-communal conflict. On the other hand, the sources do provide a great deal of information concerning conflict resolution at the *estate* level. Estate records reveal that a formal process for settling disputes – a kind of *de facto* court system – had been

---

[126] 'po rezoliutsii ego Siiatel'stva', in RGADA, f. 1287, op. 3, ed. khr. 661, l. 10 ('Punishments meted out to serfs, 1807'). This is in contrast to the decisions made by communal resolution and approved by the higher authorities.

[127] RGADA, f. 1287, op. 3, ed. khr. 677, l. 8 ('Instructions and decrees 1808').

[128] 'po domashnemu ego ne radeniiu o krest'ianstve za neimenim khleba propityvaetsya emu s semeistvom ni chem', in RGADA, f. 1287, op. 3, ed. khr. 914, l. 1 ('petition from village Malakhovo residents against Sal'nikov, 1825').

[129] See discussions of customary law and peasant justice in S. Frank, *Crime, cultural conflict, and justice in rural Russia, 1856–1914* (Berkeley and Los Angeles, 1999), pp. 243–75; Moon, *The Russian peasantry*, pp. 227–8; Worobec, *Peasant Russia*, esp. chapters 2 and 5.

established on the estate as part of the Sheremetyev administrative apparatus, and that this process was employed to resolve a variety of intra-communal disputes.

The process usually began when a party to a dispute petitioned the estate authorities to hear his or her case. Others involved in the conflict were then invited by the authorities to submit (in writing) their versions of the case. Once all versions had been presented, the estate bailiff (*prikazchik*) would ask the commune to select several (usually three to five) 'honest men' from among its members to investigate the case. These men were to review the evidence and submit a recommendation to the authorities at the Sheremetyevs' central office in St Petersburg. Sometimes these arbiters took additional statements from witnesses or parties to the conflict. At the same time, the case was reviewed by the bailiff and the top communal officials (usually the *starosta*, the *vybornyi*, or both), who were also required to submit recommendations to St Petersburg. All cases involving property – such as inheritance disputes or credit disputes – required serfs to submit copies of official documents (contracts, wills, letters of credit, land surveys), along with their written statements, for the arbiters to review. Once the serfs' statements and the investigators' reports were received by the St Petersburg office, they were reviewed by the landlord's officials and a judgment was sent back to the estate. If a serf was unhappy with the decision, he could appeal directly to Sheremetyev, who would personally decide whether to uphold the decision or investigate the matter further.[130]

A wide variety of cases were resolved in this manner during the period under investigation. In 1795, for instance, Ivan Yablokov brought a case against his brother, Fyodor, for violating the inheritance agreement they had concluded before their father's death.[131] In 1820, Nikolai Sheshunov brought a case against Mikhail Kokin for publicly insulting him and making false accusations (such as calling him a 'swindler') in the presence of communal and estate officials.[132] In 1824, Grigory Sytinskii, who claimed to be 'old and in poor health' filed a petition against his son, who, living in St Petersburg, allegedly refused to pay his share of the household's tax burden and failed to provide for his elderly father, who was too old and sick to work.[133] That same year, Kozma Popov, Nikolai Yablokov, Kozma Moseevskii, Fyodor Krasavin, Vasily Ivanov, and Egor Shokhin collectively brought a case against the Baranov family over a piece

---

[130] RGADA, f. 1287, op. 3, ed. khr. 555, l. 53 ('Instructions, 1796/1800').
[131] RGADA, f. 1287, op. 3, ed. khr. 628 ('Petition regarding inheritance, 1795').
[132] RGADA, f. 1287, op. 3, ed. khr. 770 ('Petition regarding dispute, 1820').
[133] RGADA, f. 1287, op. 3, ed. khr. 912 ('Petition regarding household dispute, 1824').

of land worth 1,000 roubles, which each side claimed to own.[134] In 1828, Aleksandr Fedoseyev filed a petition against Ivan Chernikhin, who was, he claimed, 'interfering with his trade affairs'.[135] That same year, Ivan Kezin brought a case against his stepmother, over the property in her possession after his father's death.[136] In 1833, Vladimir Vasiliev, the parish priest from Uslavtsevo, along with the churchwarden, Yakim Mikhailov, filed a joint petition against Ivan Pugin, who had allegedly defaulted on a loan of 1,614 roubles, owed to the church of Uslavtsevo.[137]

That so many serfs were willing to submit to the formal procedures established by the estate, which required them to pay substantial fees,[138] suggests that this system was viewed as reasonably fair and impartial – or, at least, more impartial than the informal alternative, if there was one. And the wide range of disputes resolved in this fashion suggests that there was no obvious dividing line between those issues which should have come under the jurisdiction of customary law (communal justice) and those which would have been considered the affairs of the estate. Cases concerning inheritance, defamation, theft, land ownership, trade, debt recovery, and a variety of intra-familial conflicts were all heard at the estate level.[139]

This is consistent with recent findings for the post-Emancipation period, which demonstrate that Russian peasants, when they had the option, were keen to make use of more formal dispute resolution mechanisms.[140] It does not, of course, exclude the possibility that certain types of informal dispute, for which there are no written records, were settled communally, or that an informal system of communal justice functioned alongside the more formal estate-level system. Many disputes were probably resolved before they ever made it to St Petersburg. This is the case in most legal systems; going to court is a last resort. The complete absence of any reference to an informal system, though, suggests that, if it did exist, it had no official standing in the eyes of the commune or the estate administration,

---

[134] RGADA, f. 1287, op. 3, ed. khr. 886 ('Petition regarding property dispute, 1824').
[135] 'stesnenie ego v torgovle', in RGADA, f. 1287, op. 3, ed. khr. 994 ('Petition regarding property dispute, 1828').
[136] RGADA, f. 1287, op. 3, ed. khr. 993 ('Petition regarding inheritance, 1828').
[137] RGADA, f. 1287, op. 3, ed. khr. 1178 ('Petition regarding credit dispute, 1833').
[138] Serfs who wished to submit formal petitions had to pay to have several copies of the petition drawn up by estate scribes, as well as to have them registered with the estate administration. This will be discussed further in chapters 5–7.
[139] Criminal cases, such as those involving murder or theft from the landlord, would have been taken before higher authorities (district and provincial courts) rather than handled at the estate level.
[140] Jane Burbank has found that peasants made extensive use of township courts in the early twentieth century. Burbank, *Russian peasants go to court*.

and little weight in the eyes of Sheremetyev administrators. And the sheer numbers of cases brought to St Petersburg officials suggests that an informal system of justice, if it did exist, was used in only relatively marginal instances. But at this point we can only speculate about this, since the Voshchazhnikovo records give no indication whatever of the existence of a system of customary justice.

Social order and conformity

Conflict resolution shades gradually into the related but in some ways distinct functions of maintaining order, keeping the peace, and, as an incidental side-effect of communal enforcement, imposing conformity. As other historians have noticed, Russian landlords appear to have been interested in what is broadly called 'social control' only where it affected their own profits. This was the domain of public order in which the interests of landlords and those of the communal elite overlapped, as the former were concerned with maximising corvée labour or quitrent returns, while the latter wanted to ensure that their fellow villagers con- tributed as reliably as possible to the collective tax burden.[141] What one might call the 'moral' sphere, on the other hand – i.e. that concerned with the personal lives of individual serfs – does not appear to have been of great interest to the landlord. Instead, it is thought to have been moni- tored informally by the church, or by the commune, in accordance with peasant customary law.[142]

There were moral concerns, such as drunkenness, which were also considered economic issues: drunkenness was viewed not only as a sign of weak character, but also as a major cause of economic ruin. However, as we shall see, these 'grey areas' were relatively few on the Voshchazhnikovo estate. The examples of 'social control' which appear in the archival documents relate almost exclusively to behaviour which had fairly obvious economic implications; the moral dimension is curiously absent from the estate record.

At Voshchazhnikovo, three forms of coercion were brought to bear on serfs who did not comply with estate policies: fines, imprisonment, and corporal punishment. Fines were by far the most widespread sanction. Voshchazhnikovo serfs were fined for the unauthorised cutting of wood

---

[141] Hoch, *Serfdom and social control*, esp. pp. 91–132.

[142] Examples can be found in Frank, *Crime, cultural conflict, and justice*, pp. 243–75; Moon, *The Russian peasantry*, pp. 228–30; Worobec, *Peasant Russia*, pp. 140–2. Although some landlords apparently did take an interest in regulating the moral sphere. See, for instance, the example of F. V. Samarin, in Hartley, *A social history*, p. 86.

in estate forests (6–12 roubles).[143] They were fined for carrying out unauthorised household divisions (10 roubles).[144] Fines were levied on those who neglected to cultivate their communal allotments (25 roubles).[145] And those who were late with their *obrok* payments paid a fine in the form of an interest rate (3 kopecks per rouble per year).[146]

Imprisonment and corporal punishment appear to have been reserved for more serious infractions. A document detailing the punishments meted out to serfs during the year 1807 suggests that imprisonment and corporal punishment were used primarily on those whose behaviour was viewed as disruptive to the smooth functioning of the estate. Such behaviour included drunkenness, rowdiness, insubordination, and the use of violence against other commune members. Yakov Sheshunov, for instance, was imprisoned for three days for drunkenness.[147] Andrei Plotnikov was whipped with a birch rod for being drunk and disorderly.[148] Andrei Dolodanov was imprisoned for one day and whipped with a birch rod for hitting the selectman (*vybornyi*).[149] Ivan Trupov, who cursed the selectman and left the estate for twenty-two days without permission, was imprisoned for two days and whipped with a birch rod.[150] Yegor Kalinin, who got drunk and started a fistfight in the estate tavern, was imprisoned for one night and whipped.[151]

The same document (for the year 1807) suggests that officials used imprisonment and corporal punishment mainly when serfs failed to respond appropriately to fines for other offences. For instance, serfs Afanasii Botolov, Il'ia Tupytsin, Semyon Fyodorov, and Il'ia Ivanov were imprisoned for one night for not paying arrears in feudal dues.[152] Fyodor Leont'ev and Aleksei Labuzin were imprisoned for one night and whipped for not paying feudal dues.[153] Ivan Tryshin was imprisoned for one day in early November for failing to pay a fine of ten roubles.[154] At the end of November, when he still had not paid, he was imprisoned for two days and then released on the condition that he reappear on 1 December with the money owed.[155]

Other offences for which serfs were subjected to imprisonment or corporal punishment included theft and the breaking of contracts. In 1807, Arina Vasilieva was held for one night and whipped with the birch

---

[143] RGADA, f. 1287, op. 3, ed. khr. 934, ll. 3–4 ('On the unauthorised cutting of wood, 1825').

[144] RGADA, f. 1287, op. 3, ed. khr. 1766, l. 2 ('On unauthorised household divisions, 1847').

[145] RGADA, f. 1287, op. 3, ed. khr. 555, l. 24 ('Instructions, 1796/1800').   [146] *Ibid.*, l. 26.

[147] RGADA, f. 1287, op. 3, ed. khr. 661, l. 3 ('Punishments meted out to serfs, 1807').

[148] *Ibid.*   [149] *Ibid.*   [150] *Ibid.*, l. 4.   [151] *Ibid.*, l. 9.   [152] *Ibid.*, l. 8.

[153] *Ibid.*, l. 10.   [154] *Ibid.*, l. 9.   [155] *Ibid.*, l. 11.

rod for stealing 5 roubles.[156] In 1823, Ul'iana Pyriaeva was imprisoned for stealing property from the widow Nadezhda Shamina.[157] That same year, Semyon Vasiliev was whipped with the birch rod for stealing grain from other serfs.[158] Ivan Tryshin, who failed to repay a debt to a serf from Iukhot estate, was imprisoned for one night in 1807.[159] And Ivan Deulin was whipped with the birch rod in 1832 for failing to pay his servant.[160]

Whippings with a birch rod appear to have been the most commonly administered form of corporal punishment on the Voshchazhnikovo estate.[161] However, there are occasional references in the documents to other, more brutal measures. Sometimes a serf was made to sit for days in prison with an iron collar around his neck. Others were forced to spend long periods sitting (or standing) in a certain position without moving. One serf was whipped and then forced to clear out a nettle patch as his punishment.[162]

The disciplinary measures described here were all employed as a means of regulating serfs' economic behaviour. Offences such as drunkenness, violence, and insubordination were viewed as potential threats to the established order on the estate, and were punished severely. But what about serfs' 'moral' behaviour? Were serfs at Voshchazhnikovo punished for things such as fornication, adultery, or blasphemy? Interestingly, there are no references to any such offences in the documents. In much of pre-industrial Europe, the church would have been mainly responsible for, or at least heavily involved in, the regulation of peasants' moral conduct.[163] On the Voshchazhnikovo estate, the church appears to have taken no part in imposing conformity of this sort. Polygamy was the only 'moral' issue

---

[156] Ibid., l. 6.

[157] RGADA, f. 1287, op. 3, ed. khr. 898, l. 4 ('Punishments meted out to serfs, 1823').

[158] *Ibid.*

[159] RGADA, f. 1287, op. 3, ed. khr. 661, l. 11 ('Punishments meted out to serfs, 1807').

[160] RGADA, f. 1287, op. 3, ed. khr. 1325, l. 36 ('Punishments meted out to serfs, 1825').

[161] Voshchazhnikovo resembles Hoch's Petrovskoe estate in that corporal punishment was one of the standard disciplinary measures employed by authorities. However, corporal punishment does not seem to have been quite so widely applied on the Voshchazhnikovo estate as at Petrovskoe, and the range of offences for which it was employed appears to have been somewhat narrower.

[162] 'nakazen rozgami i vydiraniem krapivo', in RGADA, f. 1287, op. 3, ed. khr. 661, l. 4 ('Punishments meted out to serfs, 1807').

[163] On central Europe, see the discussion in S. Ogilvie, '"So that every subject knows how to behave": social disciplining in early modern Bohemia', *Comparative Studies of Society and History* 48 (1) (2006), pp. 38–78; on medieval England, see P. Schofield, *Peasant and community in medieval England 1200–1500* (London, 2003), esp. pp. 196–7; on France, see B. Gottlieb, ' The meaning of clandestine marriage', in R. Wheaton and T. Hareven (eds.), *Family and sexuality in French history* (Philadelphia, 1980), pp. 49–83; E. Le Roy Ladurie, *The peasants of Languedoc* (Champaign, IL, 1977), esp. pp. 170–1; P. Hoffman, *Church and community in the diocese of Lyon 1500–1789* (Yale, 1984), pp. 91–3.

with which the church courts seem to have been concerned, and, as far as one can tell, no Voshchazhnikovo serfs appear to have been accused of polygamy during this period. It is certainly possible that serfs' moral behaviour was regulated informally by the community, on the basis of customary law. But again, it is curious that among the thousands of petitions, reports, depositions, and various types of correspondence in the estate archive, there is not a single mention of such moral regulation.[164] This is again consistent with Hoch's findings for Petrovskoe, where 'there is no evidence that the bailiff, the central office, or even Prince Gagarin himself was at all concerned with the peasants' spiritual well-being, participation in religious rites, or church attendance'.[165] It may well be that moral transgressions, which were apparently of little interest to the central administrations of these estates, were translated into economic ones by those making complaints, in order to ensure that punishment by the landlord's officials would be forthcoming.

On the other hand, it is evident that communal involvement in the maintenance of public order and the punishment of small-time criminals also made the commune into a vehicle for imposing conformity. Serfs did monitor the behaviour of fellow serfs, and used the formal process established by the landlord to seek official sanctions against deviants. In 1825, for instance, a group of serfs from the village of Malakhovo filed a petition against their neighbour, Ivan Sal'nikov, whose behaviour they described as 'dissolute and disorderly'.[166] In the petition they listed Sal'nikov's offences, which included acting strangely, holding meetings with unfamiliar people late at night, leaving his grain unthreshed, and feeding unthreshed oats to his animals. Finally, they wrote that they suspected him of stealing from other serfs' granaries. Sal'nikov was promptly investigated by the estate authorities and sent to the army.[167] In another case, serfs from the village of Tomakovo filed a petition against the local miller who, they claimed, had been breaking estate rules by charging extremely high prices for milling services. In the course of the investigation it became clear that there had been a dispute between the miller and some of the petitioners over an unrelated issue, and that the villagers' charges against

---

[164] According to Behrisch, on questions of social and moral disciplining 'Russia has to be set apart from the counties of western Europe'. See L. Behrisch, 'Social discipline in early modern Russia, seventeenth to nineteenth centuries', in H. Schilling and L. Behrisch (eds.), *Institutionen, Instrumenten, und Akteure sozialer Kontrolle und Disziplinierung im frühneuzeitlichen Europa* (Frankfurt, 1999), pp. 356–7.

[165] Hoch, *Serfdom and social control*, p. 146.

[166] 'rasputnoe povedenie i neporiadki', in RGADA, f. 1287, op. 3, ed. khr. 941, l. 1 ('Petition against the serf Sal'nikov, 1825').

[167] *Ibid.*, ll. 1–2, 4.

the miller were unfounded.[168] In both of these cases, petitioners used formal complaints to the landlord as a means of imposing conformity on fellow villagers and sanctioning deviants. And in both cases, the complaints were couched in economic terms: in addition to odd behaviour, Sal'nikov was allegedly neglecting his grain and stealing from others; the miller from Tomakovo was allegedly charging unfair prices for his services. It appears that to impose communal norms on deviants, it was necessary to use a rationale that would pass muster with the estate administration. Again, we cannot rule out the possibility that informal means of social control were also employed; as these cases illustrate, serfs evidently kept close track of their neighbours' activities. But it is especially interesting that for a wide variety of offences Voshchazhnikovo serfs appear to have found it more effective to use formal estate channels to impose conformity on their neighbours.

4.3 The rural commune as an institution

Section 4.2 addressed the specific, concrete functions of the estate commune at Voshchazhnikovo in its major areas of responsibility. It is now time to return to the questions raised at the beginning of this chapter: What kind of institution was the rural commune? Was it an autonomous peasant collective, whose actions reflected the shared norms and interests of the serf community? Or was it merely an extension of the landlord's authority, part of an elaborate feudal apparatus?

The view of Haxthausen and Herzen, as well as later proponents of the Peasant Myth, is not well supported by the Voshchazhnikovo evidence. The documents suggest very little in the way of collective interests or village solidarity. Instead, they give the impression of internal conflict, with powerful members of the commune pursuing their own interests at the expense of their weaker neighbours. Most of the hundreds of disputes which came before estate officials concerned the allocation of communal resources. Disputes frequently involved complaints about the expropriation and misallocation of those resources, and about the allocation of state and feudal tax burdens among commune members. There are only three instances, across a period covering more than one hundred years, of collective petitions to the landlord from 'the serfs of Voshchazhnikovo'. All other petitions were filed by serfs against other serfs (examples of which were presented in the sections above), indicating that intracommunal conflict was far more prevalent in this society than village

---

[168] RGADA, f. 1287, op. 3, ed. khr. 1325 ('Communal resolutions, 1837').

solidarity. These findings are consistent with those of more recent studies by Bohac, Melton, and others, which have emphasised conflict over harmony in Russian peasant communes.[169] It must also be noted that, contrary to some widely held views about the Russian rural commune, the Voshchazhnikovo estate commune had almost no autonomy to act – in these matters or any others – without at least the approval, and often the explicit guidance and outright prodding, of the estate management.[170] It is usually impossible to identify actions of the commune in complete isolation from the oversight or at least involvement of the estate management representing the interests of the landlord.

This does not mean, however, that the commune at Voshchazhnikovo should be seen as nothing but an instrument of the estate management. It is true that the commune operated within a framework whose parameters were largely defined by estate authorities, but this does not mean either that the commune itself had no bargaining power against the landlord or that its members did not try to use it to further their own interests. Although the Sheremetyevs had the power to overrule communal decisions, they did not regularly use it. They relied on the cooperation of the commune for the day-to-day management of the estate and, ultimately, to secure their feudal rents. This in turn gave the commune leverage, and enabled its members to assert their interests, at least in cases where the costs to the landlord were relatively low. Compromises were made on both sides. The commune, for instance, at the landlord's insistence, occasionally agreed to provide relief to the poor,[171] and the Sheremetyevs, at the commune's insistence, occasionally agreed to reduce the fees for marrying non-estate serfs.[172]

This is not entirely consistent with the concept of 'dualism' put forward by Aleksandrov, which assumes that there were distinct and opposed landlord interests and serf interests, and supposes that the commune was able to mediate successfully between them. According to Aleksandrov, the commune was able to function both as an extension of the feudal apparatus *and* as a peasant interest group. But the evidence from Voshchazhnikovo clearly shows that the interests of these two groups were often diametrically opposed, and could only be traded off at each others' expense, even in the

[169] Bohac, 'The "mir"'; Melton, 'The magnate' and 'Household economies'. These and others are discussed in D. Moon, 'Reassessing Russian serfdom', *European History Quarterly* 26(4) (1996), pp. 511–12.

[170] It has been hypothesised that communes on *obrok* estates enjoyed much greater autonomy than those on corvée labour estates. See Melton, 'Household economies', p. 564; Mironov, 'Local government in Russia', p. 195.

[171] As in RGADA, f. 1287, op. 3, ed. khr. 1635, ll. 45–6 ('Communal resolutions, 1844').

[172] RGADA, f. 1287, op. 3, ed. khr. 555, ll. 49–50 ('Instructions, 1796/1800').

restricted range of matters that came before the commune. In such cases (when, for instance, serfs were forced by landlords to provide funds for the church or poor relief, or where serfs were in conflict with each other), the 'dualist' approach offers no guidance, has no predictive power, and fails to capture the trade-off between landlord and peasant interests which Marx had portrayed so vividly.

There is a way, though, in which a dualistic view does come closest to an accurate depiction of the situation at Voshchazhnikovo. The landlord did try to use the commune to serve his interests, as did the peasants. However, the commune was not dualistic in Aleksandrov's sense of being able to serve both sets of interests, but rather in the sense that, as Hoch has suggested, it was often in the interests of the powerful serfs to cooperate with estate authorities.[173] The commune at Voshchazhnikovo, like any commune on any estate, was part of a larger economic and institutional context that shaped the particular equilibrium that local peasant–landlord relations had settled into. The quasi-formal legal system on the Sheremetyev estates, discussed in greater detail in subsequent chapters, provided formal channels for solving disputes, established property rights, and made it possible to engage in a wide spectrum of economic transactions, including land purchases and sales, the hiring of labour, and money lending. The more prosperous serfs who dominated the Voshchazhnikovo commune were dependent on these institutional arrangements for their wealth and power.[174] Moreover, they were dependent on the landlord himself, and his estate management, for favours and patronage. This did not mean that their interests necessarily *coincided* with those of the landlord, but it was very much in their interests to collaborate with their powerful patron. It was Count Sheremetyev himself, after all, who granted local monopoly rights to mills and fisheries, and who had the power to procure commercial privileges for his trading peasants. By cooperating with the landlord and his officials, the local elite attempted to secure access to such rights and privileges.[175] Yet they also sought to limit the costs to themselves of such cooperation. As illustrated by examples given earlier, this often meant using their power to allocate feudal burdens away from themselves and members of their families and social networks to other members of the commune. Similarly, they often managed to allocate a larger share of communal resources to themselves and

[173] Hoch, *Serfdom and social control*, esp. chapter 3.

[174] The dominant serfs on the estate were not necessarily the communal officers, though, as noted earlier, they were often able to use their power and wealth to persuade communal officers to act in their interests.

[175] Such cooperation between feudal authorities and communal oligarchs is explored in greater detail in Dennison and Ogilvie, 'Serfdom and social capital'.

their closest associates. These serfs were neither agents of the landlord nor champions of communal interests. They used the manorial framework, adopting its formal language and procedures, to maintain and improve their own positions in the community.

There were certain institutional features at Voshchazhnikovo which served to some extent as checks on the power of serf oligarchs. Because the estate had no particular specialism – i.e. it was neither a predominantly agricultural estate nor a proto-industrial estate – there was no dominant interest group. Serfs were engaged in a wide variety of economic activities, whose special interests only occasionally intersected. At times, this occupational diversity brought members of the elite into conflict with one another, preventing them from forming a united front against the less powerful. Perhaps most important was that the Sheremetyevs' St Petersburg officials made clear, in several cases, that they were not unwilling to rule against powerful serfs when provided with evidence of misconduct.[176] Were it not for this demonstrated willingness to intervene, the local oligarchy might have behaved in ways even more corrupt than those described in the surviving petitions and reports.

On other Russian estates under different landlords, the balance of interests was different. For instance, where peasants' interests coincided more closely with each other, and the landlord had less clout than a Sheremetyev, the corporative interests of the controlling faction of peasants might hold the balance against a relatively weak landlord, and the estate would be run largely for the benefit of that faction. This seems to have been the case on the Baki estate, studied by Melton, where a few rich serf families – those in charge of the estate's main industries – were able, through patronage networks, to control the commune (and the estate manager), forcing it to take decisions which served their own interests, often at the expense of landlord interests.[177] In still another equilibrium, where peasants had neither unified interests nor much bargaining power at all, we might find a balance of power just as lopsided on the landlord's side. In short, the extent to which landlords and communal oligarchies were able to pursue their respective interests depended on the larger institutional framework of the estate. There is no simple formula to predict what the equilibrium would be across the board;

[176] As in the case brought by serfs against the bailiff, described in RGADA, f. 1287, op. 3, ed. khr. 1256 ('Petition against bailiff Tizengauzen, 1835') .

[177] Melton, 'Household economies and communal conflicts'. Similar examples are given by C. Leonard, 'Landlords and the "Mir"', in R. Bartlett (ed.), *Land commune and peasant community in Russia: communal forms in imperial and early Soviet society* (London and New York, 1990), pp. 134–5.

it would be different in each locality depending on the specific balance of power among the contending parties.

Despite broad similarities across estates in its official functions, the Russian commune was not a monolithic institution. It was neither an appendage of the estate apparatus nor a peasant interest group. On each particular estate, the commune reflected the particular balance of social and economic forces (local and global) operating in that particular situation. Like many institutions, it merely expressed the underlying configuration of the parties and forces it mediated. On smaller estates with a weak or absentee landlord, where peasant interests were largely aligned, it is entirely possible that the Russian commune was quite similar, in many respects, to a German *Gemeinde*. But this does not seem to have been the rule, and outcomes like those at Petrovskoe, where landlord interests appear to have dominated, or at Voshchazhnikovo, where the interests of the landlord and the widely divergent interests of the richer serfs resulted in a somewhat less coercive configuration, appear to have been fairly common.

5   Land and property markets

If one had to choose a single characteristic that is most widely believed
to have distinguished the Russian peasantry from others, it would be
communal land tenure. Land in rural Russia is thought to have been
held mainly by village communes, rather than by individuals through
leases and private purchases, and allocated among member households
according to their labour capabilities and consumption needs, with periodic adjustments made in response to demographic change.[1] The private
ownership of land by peasants, where it has been observed, is often
assumed to have been a largely peripheral phenomenon, relevant only to
the wealthiest peasant farmers.[2]

The widespread practice of communal land tenure is supposed to have
resulted in an 'underdeveloped sense of private property' among Russian
peasants.[3] The Russian peasantry, it has been argued, 'was oblivious to
the Western (ultimately Roman) concept of property in land'.[4] Herzen
himself wrote of '[t]he Russian peasant who has ... a strong aversion to
every form of landed property'.[5] More recent expression is given to this

---

[1]   This view of rural Russia has become widespread in the literature on peasant societies. See,
for instance, A. Macfarlane, *The origins of English individualism: the family, property, and
social transition* (Oxford, 1978), chapter 1, and, more recently, J. Whittle, *The development of
agrarian capitalism: land and labour in Norfolk, 1440–1580* (Oxford, 2000), pp. 92–7.
[2]   In his 1982 doctoral thesis, R. Bohac describes the large amount of land held privately by
Manuilovskoe serfs as a 'feature of the estate economy rarely found in the non-black earth
region, or in the rest of Russia'. See Bohac, 'Family, property and socio-economic
mobility', p. 10. In fact, Soviet historians have long acknowledged the existence of private
property among serfs, though they generally assume that it was limited to the wealthy elite.
See, for instance, Fyodorov, *Pomeshchech'i krest'iane*, pp. 32–42; Prokof'eva, *Krest'ianskaia
obshchina*, pp. 102–10; Rubinshtein, *Sel'skoe khoziaistvo*, pp. 38–48.
[3]   Steven Hoch, for instance, notes the 'weak sense of property in Russian peasant society'.
Hoch, 'The serf economy', p. 314. Christine Worobec similarly refers to the 'weak understanding of private property' among Russian peasants. Worobec, *Peasant Russia*, p. 28.
[4]   Field, *The end of serfdom*, p. 58. According to Field, the Russian peasantry's inability to
grasp the concept of private property was 'the greatest single obstacle to emancipation'
(p. 58).
[5]   A. Herzen, 'The Russian people and socialism: an open letter to Jules Michelet' (1851),
reprinted 1979 (Oxford), p. 180.

view by Richard Pipes who argues, in his book *Property and freedom*, that many of Russia's current economic problems can be attributed to the weak development of property institutions in the pre-Soviet period. Pipes refers to imperial Russia's 'antiproprietary culture', a culture he sees very much rooted in the peasant mentality, since 'to the peasant land was not a commodity but rather the material basis of life'.[6] This view harks back to Chayanov, who maintained that peasants were incapable of calculating factor costs, since the peasant farm was not a capitalist enterprise but a household's primary means of subsistence.[7]

Because this has been the dominant paradigm among historians of the peasantry for so long, substantial empirical evidence to the contrary has gone largely unexamined. References to private property, especially land purchased and held in individual tenure, can be found in a number of Soviet studies of the serf economy, including the well-known publications of Fyodorov and Rubinshtein.[8] In a 1930s book devoted to this subject, V. N. Kashin presented a wide range of archival evidence for private land purchases by serfs on a wide variety of estates throughout much of European Russia.[9] According to Kashin, the archival record clearly demonstrates that '[o]n different estates, in different provinces, under different manorial regimes, serfs obtained, bequeathed, sold, and otherwise disposed of their own immoveable property'.[10]

But how was this possible in the context of serfdom? These studies are all rich in empirical accounts of private landholding, but none adequately addresses this question. This chapter attempts to shed some light on the issue, with an examination of property rights and property transactions among serfs at the local level.

As discussed in chapters 3 and 4, Voshchazhnikovo serfs did hold land in communal tenure. This was feudal land, owned by the Sheremetyev family, and allocated to the estate serfs in return for regular quitrent payments. Because there were feudal dues attached to communal allotments, the commune preferred to allocate land to households with adequate financial resources, regardless of their labour capabilities. As shown in chapter 3, there was at best a very weak correlation between size of household and size of communal allotment on this estate. We noted

[6] R. Pipes, *Property and freedom* (New York, 1999), p. 204.
[7] Chayanov, *Theory of peasant economy*, pp. 1–7.
[8] Fyodorov, *Pomeshchich'i krest'iane*, pp. 32–41; idem, 'Zemlevladenie krepostnykh krest'ian v Rossii po materialam tsentral'no-promyshlennykh gubernii', *Vestnik moskovskogo universiteta* 1 (1969), pp. 47–66; Rubinshtein, *Sel'skoe khoziaistvo*, pp. 43–4; V. I. Semevskii, *Krest'iane v tsarstvovanie imp. Ekateriny II*, 2 vols. (St Petersburg, 1888–1901), vol. I, pp. 338–9.
[9] V. N. Kashin, *Krepostnye krest'iane-zemlevladel'tsy* (Moscow, 1935), esp. pp. 12–28.
[10] *Ibid.*, p. 16.

that there were households containing two or three adult members which had larger communal allotments than those with seven and eight adults. Furthermore, poor households were often entirely deprived of communal land, because they could not pay the feudal dues. Of the fifty-nine households described as 'poor' in 1832, more than half (thirty-one) had no communal allotment.[11] Some households, such as that of Matvei Malinnikov, were even described explicitly as 'too poor to engage in agriculture'.[12] Such findings undermine the widely accepted explanation for the supposed absence of land markets – i.e that periodic repartition worked to balance land–labour ratios. The repartitional commune at Voshchazhnikovo did not bring these ratios into balance, nor did it provide all member households with access to land.

5.1   Property transactions

It is clear from the Voshchazhnikovo source materials that these serfs, like those studied by Kashin and others, did possess private landholdings. In a book of landlord's instructions from 1796, Count Sheremetyev reported that the land for this estate totalled '12,030 *desiatin* (approx. 32,480 acres), not including those lands purchased by serfs themselves, and in their possession, for which no payments are made into my treasury'.[13] A set of contracts dated 1759 details sales of land by neighbouring landlords to Voshchazhnikovo serfs, with prices paid ranging from 20 to 1,700 roubles.[14] Additional contracts from the early to mid-nineteenth century record land transactions among the serfs themselves. In 1831, the serf Martin Bauman sold a piece of privately held land to the serf Ivan Arnautov for 175 roubles.[15] Similarly, in 1840, the Voshchazhnikovo serf Filip Malyshev sold for 100 roubles to his fellow serf Filip Shagan the piece of land he had purchased from Egor Dolodanov in 1820.[16] In 1837, Voshchazhnikovo serf Grigory Bulygin purchased 19 *desiatin* from a noble landowner, Natal'ia Shchupinskaia, at 30 roubles per *desiatina*.[17]

---

[11] Calculated from figures in RGADA, f. 1287, op. 3, ed. khr. 1143 ('Inventories of households, 1832/8').

[12] 'po krainei ikh bednosti zemlopashestvom ne zanimaiut'sa', in *ibid.*, l. 67.

[13] RGADA, f. 1287, op. 3, ed. khr. 555, l. 21 ('Instructions, 1796/1800'). 'No payments made into my treasury' refers explicitly to annual *obrok* payments. This has been interpreted by some historians to mean that private landholdings were entirely exempt from feudal levies (see, for instance, Fyodorov, 'Zemlevladenie', pp. 63–4). But, as we will see shortly, this was not the case.

[14] RGADA, f. 1287, op. 3, ed. khr. 229 ('Land transaction contracts, 1759').

[15] RGADA, f. 1287, op. 3, ed. khr. 1108 ('Serf contracts, 1831').

[16] RGADA, f. 1287, op. 3, ed. khr. 1523 ('Serf contracts, 1840').

[17] RGADA, f. 1287, op. 3, ed. khr. 1336, l. 1 ('Serf contracts, 1837').

References to private ownership of land appear throughout the documents, in a variety of contexts. One finds, for instance, serfs using private landholdings as collateral for loans. In 1832, Ivan Stulov borrowed 600 paper roubles from Filip Petrov, offering as collateral 'a piece of land owned by me'.[18] Other references are found in serfs' wills, such as that of Nikolai Yablokov, who bequeathed to his eldest son in 1787 the 'lands purchased by me in different districts [of Yaroslavl' Province]'.[19] The privately purchased lands inherited by serfs' children were in many cases sold or used as loan collateral. In 1832, the serf Leontei Matal'ev sold the land he had inherited from his uncle to Grigory Kovin for 900 paper roubles.[20] Likewise, Dmitri Yablokov borrowed 356 silver roubles from fellow serf Aleskei Titov in 1831, offering as collateral a piece of land he had inherited in Uglich district.[21]

How can we be sure these lands were privately owned by individuals and not communal allotments? Voshchazhnikovo serfs were careful to distinguish between communal lands and their own privately held lands. In referring to private holdings, they used expressions such as 'the land purchased by me',[22] 'land in my permanent possession',[23] or 'land belonging to me'.[24] Communal holdings, on the other hand, were called 'tiaglovye zemli' – the lands to which feudal dues were attached. These usually included the land on which a serf's house was situated, as well as the serf's garden plot (ogorodnaia zemlia). Private holdings were further distinguished by their location; they were seldom to be found on or near the estate itself. In referring to their private holdings, serfs nearly always mentioned their location. Finally, most references to private landholdings occur in the context of sales or credit contracts. As serfs were technically forbidden by the landlord to sell or mortgage their communal lands, the land used in these ways could only, in theory, have been privately held land.[25]

We can conclude, then, that serfs in Voshchazhnikovo did hold land privately, in addition to their communal allotments. But how much land

---

[18] RGADA, f. 1287, op. 3, ed. khr. 1155, l. 2 ('Serf contracts, 1832').
[19] RGADA, f. 1287, op. 3, ed. khr. 620, l. 4 ('Petition regarding property dispute, 1787').
[20] RGADA, f. 1287, op. 3, ed. khr. 1155, l. 1 ('Serf contracts, 1832').
[21] RGADA, f. 1287, op. 3, ed. khr. 1108 ('Serf contracts, 1831').
[22] 'zemlia kuplennaia mnoi'.
[23] 'v moem postoiannom vladenii' or 'v moem vechnom vladenii'.
[24] 'zemlia prinadlezhit mne' is somewhat more ambiguous, since communal allotments did, in a sense, belong to serfs. However, when referring to communal lands, serfs almost always used the terms 'tiaglovaia zemlia' or 'ogorodnaia zemlia'.
[25] This was not always the case in practice, but, fortunately, serfs were careful to distinguish their communal holdings from private ones in contracts, as seen in RGADA, f. 1287, op. 3, ed. khr. 1108, 1155 ('Serf contracts, 1831 and 1832').

was privately owned? Who owned it? And where was it located? These questions are more difficult to answer, especially for the earlier part of the period under discussion. Though the sources provide numerous references to the private landholdings of individual serfs, they offer very little quantitative data on private ownership in general. The most comprehensive information can be found in an estate report from 1858.[26] The aggregate figures recorded in this document suggest that private ownership was more than a peripheral phenomenon among Voshchazhnikovo serfs. According to the report, some 9176 *desiatin* (approx. 24,775 acres) were communal lands, for which the serfs were required to pay feudal dues, while the 'lands purchased by the serfs themselves', for which no feudal dues were paid to the landlord, totalled 5,646 *desiatin*.[27] Total serf holdings would thus equal 14,822 *desiatiny* of which some 38 per cent consisted in privately held land.

To which serfs did these private holdings belong? It is difficult to say with certainty, since none of the existing documents provides a comprehensive list of holdings for each household. There is, however, enough information available to enable us to address two existing theories.

The first of these maintains that private holdings were held primarily by the wealthy peasants, who sought to expand their agricultural enterprises or rural industries, usually at the expense of the poorer serfs. According to this view, the rich serfs would buy up the land of the poor serfs and then employ the poor as labourers.[28] This does not seem to have been the case on the Voshchazhnikovo estate. While there were serfs who specialised in agriculture, rural industry or both, these were not the only ones investing in private landholdings. The owners of private holdings were a diverse group, many of whom were themselves engaged in wage labour, often as servants or day labourers. They were not necessarily the richest serfs on the estate. For instance, the serf Grigory Kovin, who purchased 900 roubles' worth of land in 1832, worked as a live-in servant. Egor Dolodanov, who had several private holdings, worked as a servant in St Petersburg. The sisters Natal'ia and Anna Zhukova, who made their living working for others on the estate, purchased land worth 6,000 roubles

---

[26] RGADA, f. 1287, op. 3, ed. khr. 2320 ('Descriptions of estates, 1858').

[27] 'sverkh togo ... pustoshiam 5646 desiatin 1528 sazhen' kuplennye samimi krest'ianami', in RGADA, f. 1287, op.3, ed. khr. 2320, ll. 10–11 ('Descriptions of estates, 1858'). The lands purchased by serfs are described as 'lands for which no payments are made into [the landlord's] treasury' ('zemli za kotorye platezhu nikakogo v kaznu moiu nyet') in RGADA, f. 1287, op. 3, ed. khr. 555, l. 21 ('Instructions, 1796/1800').

[28] See Fyodorov, *Pomeshchich'i krest'iane*, pp. 32–46; Rubinshtein, *Sel'skoe khoziaistvo*, p. 43. Kashin extensively discussed the role of wealthy serfs in rural land markets. *Krepostnye krest'iane-zemlevladel'tsy*, pp. 77–103.

in Uglich district.[29] Ivan Trykin, whose household was described as 'poor', was reported to have 'a private holding, the income from which provides for his family and enables him to pay feudal dues'.[30] Cases such as these indicate that access to local land markets was not limited to a small number of wealthy households.

The second theory maintains that private holdings were obtained by serfs in an attempt to supplement inadequate communal allotments.[31] Population growth, according to this view, meant that communal holdings became progressively smaller, making it more and more difficult for serfs to support their families with them. Serfs were thus forced to buy land on the market to supplement their allotments. While this may have been the case on some estates in this region, the description does not fit Voshchazhnikovo. As indicated in earlier chapters, very few serfs on this estate lived from the cultivation of their communal lands. In fact, many of those who invested in private landholdings let their communal allotments to others. Aleksei Tupytsin, who held land privately, leased his communal land to other serfs and supported his household with his earnings from trade.[32] Similarly, Aleksandr Liapin, who also held land privately, practised trade in St Petersburg and let his communal allotment to other serfs.[33] Ivan Yablokov also let his communal land to others, earning an income instead from 'live-in service and rents on privately purchased land'.[34] Considering that these serfs did not even cultivate the allotments for which they paid feudal dues, it seems unlikely that the land they purchased on the market was used for subsistence agriculture.

The location of serfs' privately purchased land casts further doubt on the 'subsistence' theory. Privately held land was usually located too far away from the estate to be cultivated by serfs themselves; some private holdings were in entirely different parts of the province. According to the 1858 report, only about 500 *desiatin* of private land were located in the same district as the estate itself (Rostov district), while 4,850 *desiatin* were

---

[29] This information was obtained by linking the contract records (RGADA, f. 1287, op. 3, ed. khr. 1108 (1831) and 1155 (1832)) with data from the inventories of households for the village of Voshchazhnikovo (RGADA, f. 1287, op. 3, ed. khr. 1143 ('Inventories of households, 1832/8')).

[30] 'imeia pokupnyi na imia Ego Siiatel'stva pustoshi s koikh dokhody poluchaemy na prodovol'stvie semeistva i platit' podatei', in RGADA, f. 1287, op. 3, ed. khr. 1143, l. 53 ('Inventories of households, 1832/8').

[31] Fyodorov, *Pomeshchich'i krest'iane*, pp. 32–42.

[32] RGADA, f. 1287, op. 3, ed. khr. 1143, ll. 46–7 ('Inventories of households, 1832/8').

[33] *Ibid.*, ll. 31–2.

[34] 'propitanie ot prozhivanii u khoziaev v usluzhenii . . . i pustoshei kuplennye na imia ego Siiatel'stva' in *ibid.*, l. 20.

located in Uglich district, more than 30 miles from the estate.[35] Given their location, it seems likely that serfs' private holdings were used primarily as a form of savings, investment, and loan collateral, rather than as a means of subsistence.

It is not clear from the documents why so much of this privately purchased land was held so far from the estate. That so many serfs owned land in Uglich district could be related to the fact that Iukhot, another Sheremetyev estate, was located in this region. Perhaps existing social networks – in particular, connections with other Sheremetyev serfs in Yaroslavl' province – provided Voshchazhnikovo serfs with knowledge about and access to land markets in far-off districts. This is the view of Kashin, who also observed serfs with private holdings in places beyond their home districts and provinces.[36] The pattern observed here may have resulted to some extent from a Sheremetyev policy (discussed below) requiring that serfs who wished to sell private holdings offer them to other Sheremetyev serfs before seeking buyers from outside.

Another possibility is that Voshchazhnikovo serfs preferred land in Uglich district, because it was of higher quality than land in other parts of Yaroslavl' and thus easier to rent to others. Details from rental agreements on lands owned by the Voshchazhnikovo serf Ivan Yablokov suggest that this could have been the case. Yablokov held a number of private holdings in various districts, including Uglich. According to the contracts, which date from 1793, the rents he received on the Uglich lands were considerably higher than those on holdings in other parts of the province. For instance, three pieces of land held by Yablokov in Borisogleb district were let for 4 roubles per year; another piece in the same district was let for 10 roubles per year.[37] A piece of land held in Rostov district (where the Voshchazhnikovo estate was located) was let for four years for a total of 16 roubles 60 kopecks, or 4 roubles 15 kopecks per year.[38] Another holding in Rostov district was let for 4 roubles per year.[39] Yablokov's holdings in Uglich district, on the other hand, seem to have been significantly more valuable. One of these was let for 17 roubles per year, while two others were let for 25 roubles per year each.[40] It is unlikely that these

---

[35] RGADA, f. 1287, op. 3, ed. khr. 2320, ll. 76–7 ('Descriptions of estates, 1858').

[36] Kashin, *Krepostnye krest'iane-zemlevladel'tsy*, pp. 17–18. Kashin took this view even further, arguing that serfs were constrained in their land purchases by an institutional framework which made it impossible for them to transact with anyone except other serfs. The Sheremetyev framework was indeed constraining, but, as we will see below and in subsequent chapters, it did allow market transactions across socio-legal boundaries. Voshchazhnikovo serfs could (and did) engage in a variety of market transactions with free persons.

[37] RGADA, f. 1287, op. 3, ed. khr. 612, ll. 3, 5, 6 ('Serf contracts, 1793').

[38] *Ibid.*, l. 3.   [39] *Ibid.*, l. 3.   [40] *Ibid.*, ll. 3, 6, 7.

differences in rents were related to the amount of land being let in each case, since the holdings, as described in the contracts, appear to have been roughly the same size.[41] It may have been that, due to the quality of the land or the size of the population, the demand for land in this part of the province was greater than that in other areas. Unfortunately, none of the surviving sources sheds any light on these questions. The only thing we can say with some certainty is that this pattern was not unique to Voshchazhnikovo. Kashin has noted similar findings for serfs on a number of landlords' estates in different parts of European Russia: serfs in Riazan province held land in Vladimir province; serfs in Moscow province purchased land in Riazan province; and a number of serfs owned land in their home provinces but in districts other than their own.[42]

Another interesting aspect of these rental transactions concerns the form of rent payment for landholdings. Although each of the contracts cited above involved a fixed money rent, not all of Yablokov's tenants paid their rents purely in cash. Several of the contracts describe mixed-rent arrangements. For instance, Yablokov let one piece of land on a year-long lease to Dmitri Savyolev, an estate serf from the village of Ketskovo, for 'four roubles and one day of ploughing'.[43] In another example, Yablokov let a piece of land (*odna tret'ia chast'*) to estate serf Mikhail Stulov, from the village of Beriozy chto na Pen'e, for 'two roubles per year plus four days of ploughing'.[44] Such agreements contradict the Chayanovian assumption that peasants were unable to calculate factor costs, because they did not view land and labour as commodities. In these examples, Voshchazhnikovo serfs assigned a cash value to the land and labour they agreed to exchange.

In addition to land, serfs owned houses and other buildings, including threshing barns (*ovinniki*), bathhouses or saunas (*bani*), icehouses (*ledniki*), sheds (*sarai*), and stalls on the local market square (*lavki*), which they also frequently bought and sold. In 1831 the serf widow Afimya Pugina sold the house she had inherited from her husband to the Voshchazhnikovo serf Aleksei Titov for 800 roubles.[45] During that same year Ivan Kalinin sold his stall (*lavka*) on the market square to Mikhail Dolodanov for 50 roubles.[46] In 1832, Andre Beliaev sold his stall on the market square

[41] Each contract involved *odna tret'ia chast'*, literally 'one-third portion'. This, like so many of the measures in the documents, seems to have been a matter of convention; precise dimensions, even in *sazhen'*, are rarely given. These exact words are used in each of the contracts cited in this context.

[42] Kashin, *Krepostnye krest'iane-zemlevladel'tsy*, pp. 17–18.

[43] 'otdal ... pustosh' ... na odin god tsenoiu po chetyre rubli za god raboty plugom odin den'', in RGADA, f. 1287, op. 3, ed. khr. 612, l. 5 ('Serf contracts, 1793').

[44] 'otdal ... na god tsenoiu za dva rubli raboty chetyre dni na pluge', in *ibid.*, l. 8.

[45] RGADA, f. 1287, op. 3, ed. khr. 1108, entry no. 11 ('Serf contracts, 1831').

[46] *Ibid.*, entry no. 8.

to Ivan Matal'ev for 60 roubles.[47] In 1840, Arina Zanaimaia, from the village of Kanditovo, sold her wooden house to Ignatei Gavrilov, from the village of Uslavtsevo, for 60 roubles.[48]

Houses and other buildings were also used by serfs as loan collateral. In 1831, Aleksandr Pyriaev from the village of Voshchazhnikovo offered his house as collateral when he borrowed 500 roubles from Praskov'ia Kalinina.[49] In 1832, Pyriaev was sent to the army before paying off the debt and the house was formally repossessed by Kalinina. She then sold it to her fellow serf Marfa Baramokhina for 1,000 roubles.[50] Such transactions were usually confined to estate serfs, since outsiders had to have special permission from the landlord to take up residence in one of the estate villages (if granted, outsiders would then be required to pay an annual residence fee to the landlord).[51] Moreover, serfs were technically forbidden to sell or mortgage the land on which these buildings stood, since it was communal land or, in other words, estate land, over which they had no rights of ownership.[52] While Voshchazhnikovo serfs frequently did sell their communal allotments, as shown in chapter 3, it is significant that the recorded transactions involving these *tiaglovye zemli* involved only local serfs, as it suggests that the rule against sales to outsiders was consistently enforced or, at least, that such transfers were unenforceable and, consequently, less attractive to outside buyers.

Rental agreements, on the other hand, do not seem to have been confined to estate serfs, presumably since they did not involve a transfer of title. Some serfs were probably able to satisfy their feudal obligations with payments received from renters and, so long as the dues were paid and the land was cultivated, the landlord did not object. According to the inventories of households for 1832, roughly 30 per cent of serf households in the village of Voshchazhnikovo leased out their allotments to others.[53] Communal land was also let collectively by village communes.

---

[47] RGADA, f. 1287, op. 3, ed. khr. 1155, entry no. 6 ('Serf contracts, 1832').
[48] RGADA, f. 1287, op. 3, ed. khr. 1523, entry no. 15 ('Serf contracts, 1840').
[49] RGADA, f. 1287, op. 3, ed. khr. 1108, entry no. 4 ('Serf contracts, 1831').
[50] RGADA, f. 1287, op. 3, ed. khr. 1155, entry no. 12 ('Serf contracts, 1832').
[51] RGADA, f. 1287, op. 3, ed. khr. 555, l. 21 ('Instructions, 1796/1800'). An example of the way this restriction worked in practice can be observed in RGADA, f. 1287, op. 3, ed. khr. 1385 ('Petition from merchant Sheshunov, 1838'), where, in 1838, the merchant Afinogen Sheshunov requested permission to reside in the village of Voshchazhnikovo in return for an annual payment of 100 roubles.
[52] RGADA, f. 1287, op. 3, ed. khr. 867, l.1 ('Instruction on the sale and mortgage of communal lands, 1821–2').
[53] Of the 172 households recorded as having communal allotments in 1832, 49 let their communal land to other peasants. This is noted in the documents as 'zemliu otdaiut drugim krest'ianam iz platy'. Data provided in RGADA, f. 1287, op. 3, ed. khr. 1143 ('Inventories of households, 1832/8').

The communal meeting minutes for 1844, for instance, record that the village authorities in the estate settlement of Dem'ian were letting communal land to serfs from a neighbouring estate.[54]

Voshchazhnikovo serfs were also active in the market as renters of land. The land they rented seems to have been used primarily to cultivate flax, the main cash crop in central Russia.[55] Most of those who engaged in flax cultivation did so as a by-employment. For instance, Grigory Achuev and Andrei Sytinskii grew flax on rented land but worked mainly as live-in servants.[56] Ivan Slasnikov and Mikhail Zhelvakov, who also rented land for flax cultivation, earned their primary living as communal officials.[57] Aleksandr Sedel'nikov practised trade in St Petersburg, while his wife cultivated flax on rented land.[58] Notes made by the estate bailiff on the economic circumstances of those households renting land for flax cultivation ranged from 'good' to 'average' to 'poor', suggesting that renters at Voshchazhnikovo came from all socioeconomic strata.

Nor did those who rented land and those who leased it to others form distinct groups. Of the fourteen households in the village of Voshchazhnikovo that cultivated flax on rented land in 1832, six simultaneously let their communal land to others.[59] This is perhaps not so surprising if one considers that the three-field rotation system imposed considerable constraints on the crops that could be grown on serfs' communal lands. Compulsory crop-sequencing probably made it impossible for serfs to use their allotments for the cultivation of flax.[60] In addition, serfs were obligated to pay feudal dues in cash and kind for the use of communal land. Since there is nothing in the documents to suggest that rented land was of poorer quality or further from the estate than communal land, it seems plausible that these constraints raised the relative costs of cultivating communal land over rented land. And, if the marginal return to flax cultivation was higher than that to grain cultivation, it would have made sense for serfs to allocate their time and labour resources to flax.

Still, it is worth noting that eight of the fourteen households recorded as having rented land for the cultivation of flax were described as 'poor' by

[54] RGADA, f. 1287, op. 3, ed. khr. 1635, l. 50 ('Communal resolutions, 1844').
[55] Smith, *Peasant farming*, pp. 39–40; Hoch, *Serfdom and social control*, p. 37; Melton, 'Serfdom and the peasant economy in Russia: 1780–1861', unpublished Ph.D. thesis (Columbia University, 1984), pp. 147–86.
[56] RGADA, f. 1287, op. 3, ed. khr. 1143, ll. 10, 31 ('Inventories of households, 1832/8').
[57] *Ibid.*, ll. 43, 55–6.   [58] *Ibid.*, ll. 46–7.   [59] *Ibid.*, ll. 10, 21–2, 35–6, 43, 45, 46–7.
[60] For an overview of the three-field system in the Russian context, see Moon, *The Russian peasantry*, pp. 122–6. On the constraints of two- and three-field systems, see S. Ogilvie, 'The European economy in the eighteenth century', in T. C. W. Blanning (ed.), *The eighteenth century: Europe 1688–1815* (Oxford, 2000), pp. 103–4.

estate officials.[61] Of these, three had no communal land, another three had communal land but let it to others, and one cultivated both communal land and rented land. It was not clear whether the eighth household held communal land. The conventional view of the peasant economy maintains that poor households were the least likely to engage in markets, since those living closest to subsistence level are supposed to have been the most risk-averse.[62] Furthermore, the decision to shift from subsistence production to cash cropping is thought to have been an especially risky one. According to Scott, '[a] successful subsistence crop more or less guarantees the family food supply, while the value of a nonedible cash crop depends on its market price and on the price of consumer necessities. Quite apart from the frequently higher costs of growing and harvesting cash crops, a bumper cash crop does not, by itself, assure a family's food supply.'[63] That there were some poor serfs at Voshchazhnikovo who chose to cultivate a cash crop on rented land instead of sowing grain on a communal allotment suggests that even poor peasants were willing to take risks and engage in markets if their expected return from that particular use of their labour exceeded that from other possible uses of it. Such behaviour casts further doubt on the 'moral economy' view of the Russian peasantry.

Rental markets for other forms of real property also existed at Voshchazhnikovo. According to an estate report from 1837, the Voshchazhnikovo serf Ivan Matal'ev let his stall on the market square to Yakov Andreyev, a non-estate peasant, for 17 roubles per year.[64] Vasily Ivanov let his stall to a state peasant, Nikolai Shipinskii, for 15 roubles per year.[65] A Rostov merchant, Abram Fyodorov, rented a stall from Andrian Dolodanov for 40 roubles per year.[66] The non-estate peasants Luka and Semyon Ivanov paid 10 roubles each to Voshchazhnikovo estate serfs Fyodor Kotkhov (from the village of Uslavtsevo) and Grigorii Kliapyshev (from the village of Kanditovo) for the use of their blacksmith shops for the summer months.[67] Dmitri Titov let the wooden house he built near his threshing floor to non-estate craftsmen for 30 roubles per year.[68] In 1831, the serf Ivan Stulov (from the estate village of Vioska) agreed to let

---

[61] RGADA, f. 1287, op. 3, ed. khr. 1143, ll. 7, 17, 30–1, 35–6, 45, 49, 50 ('Inventories of households, 1832/8').

[62] According to Scott, peasants avoid risk for 'fear of food shortages'. He argues that they prefer traditional practices that provide them with a minimum subsistence to risky innovations – especially market transactions – that are fraught with uncertainty. In Scott, *The moral economy*, pp. 2–3.

[63] *Ibid.*, p. 20.

[64] RGADA, f. 1287, op. 3, ed. khr. 1345, entry no. 1 ('Report on serfs' buildings, 1837').

[65] *Ibid.*, entry no. 2.   [66] *Ibid.*, entry no. 3.   [67] *Ibid.*, entry no. 5.   [68] *Ibid.*, entry no. 5.

his privately purchased meadowland to estate serf Filip Petrov (from the village of Semionovskoe) for eight years in return for a payment of 60 paper roubles.[69]

5.2   Serfs' rights to property

Such significant participation in land and property markets implies the existence of a system of enforceable property rights. But how could Russian serfs, who were themselves considered the property of their lords, exercise ownership rights over property? It is especially remarkable that so many Voshchazhnikovo serfs held privately purchased land, since Russian serfs were actually prohibited by law from purchasing land in their own names until 1848.[70] While some historians, as noted earlier, have acknowledged a certain degree of private land ownership among Russian serfs before this date, none has adequately addressed the question of how such a system might actually have worked in practice, given the legal environment. The notion of an institutional framework supporting private ownership of land among peasants would appear incompatible with serfdom in Russia, where landlords are thought to have exercised far greater power over their serfs than their English or European counterparts of an earlier period. It seems improbable that property institutions could develop in a society where people had so few formal rights. After all, any land a Russian serf did hold privately would, in theory, have been vulnerable to arbitrary confiscation by landlords or other persons against whom there was no legal recourse.[71] The absence of any reliable contract enforcement mechanism should have resulted in a strong disincentive for private investment in land.

Interestingly, the evidence for Voshchazhnikovo suggests that it was possible for a quasi-formal system of enforceable property rights to develop, despite the legal constraints imposed by serfdom. In order to circumvent these legal barriers, the Sheremetyevs, like some other landholders, allowed serfs to purchase land in the landlord's name. When a serf wished to make a land purchase he was issued with a formal document, in which the landlord gave his serf a binding but narrowly defined power of attorney (*doverennost'*) to negotiate a transaction and sign a contract in his name. In this *doverennost'*, the landlord renounced all subsequent rights to the land

---

[69] RGADA, f. 1287, op. 3, ed. khr. 1108, entry no. 3 ('Serf contracts, 1831').
[70] O. Crisp, 'Peasant land tenure and civil rights implications before 1906', in O. Crisp and L. Edmondson (eds.), *Civil rights in imperial Russia* (Oxford, 1989), p. 37.
[71] These are the aspects emphasised in most studies. See, for instance, Fyodorov, 'Zemlevladenie', pp. 64–5.

and swore not to 'challenge or interfere with' the transaction in future.[72] The landlord's signature to these documents was witnessed by a third party and notarised, and then the sale contract between landlord and seller was registered with the provincial courts. Once the transaction had taken place, the serf had six months to register his purchase with the estate administration.[73] Upon registration, the landlord's central administration issued a formal certificate of title to the serf as proof of ownership. Copies of this certificate were kept by the local estate administration and the landlord's officials in St Petersburg, in case a dispute should arise at a later date.[74] A serf was also required to produce this certificate should he desire to sell his land.[75] This certificate of title was especially important to serfs who pledged privately purchased land as collateral for loans, as discussed in chapter 7.

While some historians have acknowledged the existence of private land purchases among serfs, they have omitted mention of the extent to which serfs' rights of ownership were upheld by estate officials. Instead, they have emphasised landlords' ability to confiscate the private holdings of their serfs.[76] According to this view, the threat of arbitrary confiscation made investment in land far too risky for most serfs.

The Voshchazhnikovo estate records, on the contrary, indicate that rights to property were taken very seriously by Sheremetyev officials. There was a firmly established procedure, similar to that described in chapter 4, for dealing with disputes over ownership of land. Parties to a dispute set out their respective positions in formal petitions to the landlord. In an attempt to make as fair a decision as possible, the estate administration and the commune together selected four or five 'honest men' to investigate the matter. At the same time, the estate bailiff was required to present his version of the conflict, as was an independent investigator, usually someone from outside the estate hired by the central administration. After examining the evidence presented by each of the appointed investigators, officials in the landlord's home office handed down a

---

[72] 'sporit' i prikosnovat' ne budu', in RGADA, f. 1287, op. 3, ed. khr. 1336, l. 7 ('Petition regarding land purchase, 1837').

[73] The instructions for Voshchazhnikovo state that the landlord had the right to confiscate all privately purchased lands that were not formally registered within the six-month period. RGADA, f. 1287, op. 3, ed. khr. 555, l. 23 ('Instructions, 1796/1800').

[74] This description of the land-purchase process is derived from the petitions and contracts in the Voshchazhnikovo estate archive. Some examples include: RGADA, f. 1287, op. 3, ed. khr. 1492 ('Petition regarding land purchase, 1840'), ed. khr. 1336 ('Petition regarding land purchase, 1837'), ed. khr. 652, l. 23 (land transaction discussed in 'Communal resolutions, 1804').

[75] The sale of land was carried out in a similar fashion, with the serf negotiating the sale in the landlord's name.

[76] For instance in Blum, *Lord and peasant*, pp. 434–5; Fyodorov, 'Zemlevladenie', pp. 64–5.

decision.[77] The surviving documents suggest that the central administration did try to reach an impartial judgment, based strictly on the available evidence. Recorded decisions do not seem to have favoured any particular group of serfs during any period covered by this study. The administration was, for instance, quite capable of ruling against communal officials or other prominent members of the village when presented with evidence of their culpability. In one illuminating example, communal officers at Voshchazhnikovo were found guilty of confiscating and selling the land of a serf widow. Officials in the central office were able to confirm that the land in question did belong to the plaintiff, and they then ordered local officers to buy it back for her.[78] Further examples of property rights being upheld are found in disputes over credit agreements. For instance, in 1830 Andrei Sytinskii of the village of Voshchazhikovo was compelled to relinquish a private landholding he had pledged as collateral to Vasily Kriuchkov, when he defaulted on the loan of 1200 roubles Kriuchkov had made to him several years earlier.[79] And in 1839 the house that Kozmin Moiseyevskii sold on credit to a neighbouring serf, Grigory Achuev, was returned to Moiseyevskii after Achuev failed to come up with the payment by the agreed date.[80]

Notable for its absence is any effort by the estate administration to use such conflicts or grey areas to gain control of the disputed land for the landlord. It is possible that there was an effective awareness, at least in the Sheremetyev administration and perhaps in those of certain other wealthy landlords, that any hint of such behaviour would jeopardise the whole system of property-holding and credit relations on which the estate economy was based. The size and scope of markets in property (and credit, as we shall see in chapter 7), as well as the smoothness and predictability with which they functioned, offer further indications that property rights were consistently enforced. References to private property and property rights occur in a variety of contexts, in different documents, throughout the period under discussion, conveying the impression that a system of enforceable property rights was widely seen as fundamental to the local serf economy.

It was not only serfs who benefited from this system. At Voshchazhnikovo, serfs' private landholdings may have been exempt from annual quitrent

---

[77] Examples of this process at work can be found in RGADA, f. 1287, op. 3, ed. khr. 2518 ('Petition regarding property dispute, 1791'), ed. khr. 2317 (property dispute discussed in 'Communal resolutions, 1858').

[78] This case is detailed in RGADA, f. 1287, op. 3, ed. khr. 745 ('Petition regarding property dispute, 1820').

[79] RGADA, f. 1287, op. 3, ed. khr. 1108, l. 2 (contract number 2) (contracts for 1831).

[80] RGADA, f. 1287, op. 3, ed. khr. 1523 (contract 8) (contracts for 1840).

levies, but they were not entirely free of feudal levies. The Sheremetyevs imposed fees at every stage of the property-transaction process. Serfs paid to file a formal petition requesting a purchase or sale contract from the landlord. If the landlord agreed to the request (as was usually the case), the serf was charged a fee (in the range of 10–12 roubles) for the contract itself.[81] Serfs paid another fee to the estate to have the new title registered. In addition to these fees, the Sheremetyevs collected taxes on income from land and property transactions. Serfs who purchased land and property were required to pay the landlord a tax worth 10 per cent of the purchase price.[82] Serfs who sold privately held land or property had to pay the landlord 5 per cent of the sale price.[83] Those who held land and property privately were also required to pay the landlord an annual 'asset' tax. According to this arrangement, serfs who possessed taxable assets (such as land, buildings, or trade inventory) were required to make a yearly payment to the landlord worth 0.5 per cent of the total value of their assets.[84] Because serfs could only make land purchases in the landlord's name, it would have been very difficult for them to hide their purchases to avoid paying the asset tax on land. The same would have been true for any privately held property that had been transferred by contract, since all contracts were approved by and registered with the estate administration. The only way serfs could avoid paying these taxes was to transfer property via informal agreement (i.e. without a written contract). This, however, would have been much riskier, since the parties to the agreement – especially the buyer – would have had limited legal recourse in case of dispute, and the value of the property for resale or as collateral would have been greatly reduced. That so many property transactions at Voshchazhnikovo were conducted formally, with written contracts, indicates that serfs were willing to bear the tax costs in exchange for a greater degree of security in their rights to property.

The documents for Voshchazhnikovo suggest that the activities discussed here were at the very least a regional phenomenon. Records of land transactions show serfs purchasing land from and selling land to landlords and serfs in various parts of the province.[85] This is consistent

---

[81] References to such figures can be found in RGADA, f. 1287, op. 3, ed. khr. 1492 ('Petition regarding land purchase, 1840'), ed. khr. 1336 ('Petition regarding land purchase, 1837').
[82] RGADA, f. 1287, op. 3, ed. khr. 525, l. 1 ('Communal resolutions, 1787').
[83] RGADA, f. 1287, op. 3, ed. khr. 1155, l. 9 ('Serf contracts, 1832').
[84] RGADA, f. 1287, op. 3, ed. khr. 555, l. 22, point 6 ('Instructions, 1796/1800').
[85] Some examples include RGADA, f. 1287, op. 3, ed. khr. 229 and 460 (a total of fifteen contracts for land purchases from various landlords in different parts of Yaroslavl' province in 1759 and 1783), ed. khr. 303 (purchase contract for land in neighbouring district, 1770) and 357 (several purchase contracts for land in Rostov and Uglich districts in 1777).

with other studies of the Russian serf economy – such as those by Fyodorov, Indova, and Rubinshtein – which have also described land transactions among serfs in this period. It thus seems likely that serfs throughout Yaroslavl' province, perhaps even throughout the Central Industrial Region, and possibly even in other parts of Russia, actively participated in land and property markets.[86]

While the evidence presented here indicates that property institutions in Russia – at least in this part of Russia – were much better developed than has generally been assumed, this system also had its limitations. For instance, serfs who purchased land in the landlord's name had to secure permission from him before they could sell this land, particularly if they wished to sell it to someone from outside the estate. Records in the Voshchazhnikovo archive suggest that permission was often granted, but only when no estate serfs were willing to buy the land.[87] Moreover, the system of property rights and contract enforcement outlined here was still largely *informal*. Serfs had no legal recourse against their landlords. Unlike serfs in medieval England or in parts of eastern Europe under the second serfdom, Russian serfs could not seek justice beyond the boundaries of their home estates.[88] In this sense, serfs were, at least in theory, vulnerable to arbitrary decisions on the part of landlords. While there are very few examples of confiscation or other arbitrary violations of property rights in the Voshchazhnikovo archive, the fact that these remained a theoretical possibility probably imposed a higher degree of uncertainty than there would have been under a more comprehensive system of property rights anchored in a formal legal system.[89] The implications of

---

[86] Bohac found that serfs on the Gagarin estate of Manuilovskoe in the Central Industrial Region also had substantial private holdings. In Bohac, 'Family, property, and socio-economic mobility', p. 10. See also the discussion of land markets in Fyodorov, *Pomeshchich'i krest'iane*, pp. 32–42; Indova, *Krepostnoe khoziaistvo*, pp. 102–5; Kashin, *Krespostnye krest'iane-zemlevladel'tsy*, esp. pp. 38–76; Rubinshtein, *Sel'skoe khoziaistvo*, pp. 38–48; Semevskii, *Krest'iane*, pp. 325–59.

[87] RGADA, f. 1287, op. 3, ed. khr. 1438 ('Petition regarding property dispute, 1839'). There appears to have been a formal right of first refusal. A more detailed discussion can be found in Dennison and Ogilvie, 'Serfdom and social capital', pp. 529–34.

[88] On extra-manorial justice in medieval England, see Briggs, 'Rural credit', esp. p. 555; for a Prussian example, see Hagen, *Ordinary Prussians*, esp. pp. 575–7.

[89] Several examples of expropriation of serf property, including one involving the Sheremetyevs, are described in Blum, *Lord and peasant*, pp. 434–5. Fyodorov similarly illustrates the weakness of serfs' rights to property with examples of expropriation. He cites a case in which one of the Sheremetyevs reportedly confiscated the private landholdings of serfs in order to compensate for arrears in feudal quitrent payments. Fyodorov, 'Zemlevladenie', p. 62. N. M. Druzhinin, similarly, focuses on the expropriation of serfs, particularly during the transition to free status in the 1860s in *Voprosy sotsial'no-ekonomicheskoi istorii i istochnikovedeniia perioda feodalizma v Rossii* (Moscow, 1961), pp. 177–8.

this informal institutional framework will be discussed in greater detail in chapter 9.

Nonetheless, the property rights framework at Voshchazhnikovo (and possibly throughout European Russia) does seem to have provided a functioning institutional basis for a local economy that generated a remarkable degree of wealth for both serfs and landlords. It is particularly remarkable that this institutional basis could fulfil that function without being integrated into, or even consistent with, imperial legislation governing serf property rights. This demonstrates that consulting only the laws will tell us very little about the character of Russian serfdom. In its actual effect, the over-arching framework of serfdom was evidently far from homogeneous across Russia. Instead, this loose framework appears to have made imperial Russia a hothouse of institutional diversity, where local experiments in institutional evolution could luxuriate quite independently of the supposedly uniform rules governing local behaviour.

6   Labour markets

The preceding chapters have shown that the commune, and especially communal land, played a very different role in Voshchazhnikovo from the classic Chayanovian role assigned it in the Peasant Myth. Some scholars would argue that a Chayanovian peasant economy might still obtain in such an environment, since Chayanov's theory was, at least in some instances, compatible with the existence of rural land markets.[1] Labour markets, however, are more difficult to reconcile with a Chayanovian economic framework. Chayanov himself maintained that 'on the family farm which has no recourse to hired labour, the labour force pool, its composition, and degree of labour activity are entirely determined by family composition and size'.[2]

This is thought to have been especially true for Russia, where communal land tenure and repartitioning practices are thought to have substituted for markets in labour. As one historian has noted, 'instead of family members moving in and out of the household through wage labour, sharecropping, tenancy, apprenticeship, or service in the attempt to adjust to changes in household composition and status, it was the land that moved around'.[3] According to this view, the labour force in rural Russia was determined by family size, and communal land allotments were adjusted in accordance.

The evidence presented in this chapter shows that serfs were not only involved in local land markets, they were also active participants in labour markets. Voshchazhnikovo serfs, all of whom belonged to repartitional communes, not only worked as labourers themselves, but hired labour as well, often to perform their seigneurial obligations, so as to allocate their own time to more profitable uses. Serfs hired labourers from other parts of the province (and from other provinces), and worked for wages themselves in other parts of the Central Industrial Region, and even as

---

[1] For a discussion of these ideas in the context of medieval peasant societies, see Smith, 'Some issues', esp. pp. 10–12.
[2] Chayanov, *Theory of peasant economy*, p. 53.   [3] Hoch, 'The serf economy', p. 314.

far away as Helsinki, Riga, and Odessa. Moreover, the evidence for Voshchazhnikovo indicates that serfs were not simply taking advantage of existing labour market opportunities in the Central Industrial Region. The institutional framework established by the Sheremetyevs actually created labour market opportunities – for their own serfs and for other peasants in the region.

This chapter draws primarily on evidence from the inventories of households (*podvornye opisi*) for the village of Voshchazhnikovo, described in detail in chapter 3, and the eleven surviving passport lists for the estate, in which the names of incoming and outgoing labourers were recorded. In addition to information on the sex, age, and marital status of household members, the inventories of households provide notes on each household's primary occupation, its major sources of income, and its economic viability, including any arrears in feudal dues. These notes are especially useful when used in conjunction with the Sheremetyevs' own wealth classification system for serf households, as outlined in chapters 2 and 3. While much useful information on labour market activity is provided, these household listings are not exhaustive; they mainly report occupations for heads of households, thus women's work is mentioned only when the household head was female. Information on occupations of children – even adult offspring – is provided occasionally, but not systematically. Despite these shortcomings, however, the information recorded is quite detailed and, as we shall see, reveals much about rural labour markets in this region.

The estate passport lists, discussed in greater detail below, were essentially registers of non-estate peasants permitted to work as servants or labourers on the Voshchazhnikovo estate and Voshchazhnikovo serfs granted permission to work off the estate. Passport lists for incoming labourers survive for the years 1746, 1762, 1820, and 1825. For outgoing labourers they exist for 1760, 1762, 1825, 1832, 1834, 1859, and 1860. The information recorded on incoming servants and labourers is much more detailed than that provided for Voshchazhnikovo serfs going elsewhere. In addition to the labourer's name, age, sex, and marital status, the compilers often recorded information on the labourer's village of origin, the Voshchazhnikovo household employing him or her, the length of the contract, and occasionally even the nature of the labour. This makes it possible to say a bit more about who these people were, what they did, and how far they travelled to find work.

6.1   Labour on the Voshchazhnikovo estate

As noted previously, Voshchazhnikovo serfs engaged in a wide variety of economic activities, including wage labour. There were serfs who earned

Table 6.1. *Summary of household labour activity, village of Voshchazhnikovo, 1832*[a]

	Number of households (201 total)	Percentage
Earnings from agriculture alone	22	11
Earnings from day labour	32	16
Earnings from rural service[b]	28	14
Contain migrant labourers	74	37
Contain craftsmen	11	5
Hire agricultural labour[c]	26 (see note below)	29
Engage in trade or manufacturing	41	20

[a] Many households fell into more than one category.
[b] These are households whose own members worked as rural servants, not households which employed servants. The difficulties associated with counting households employing servants are discussed below.
[c] This percentage was derived using the total number of households engaged in agriculture (90) as the denominator rather than the total number of households in the village (201), since only those who practised agriculture would have been in the market for agricultural labourers.
Source: RGADA, f. 1287, op. 3, ed. khr. 1143 ('Inventories of households, 1832/8').

their living labouring for others on the estate or on nearby estates, and serf households that hired labourers to work communal land, to work in manufactories, to tend livestock, and to perform various services. Table 6.1 provides a rough indication of labour market activity among households in the main settlement on the estate as recorded in the 1832 household listing.

The household listings tell us mainly which serfs in the village of Voshchazhnikovo themselves worked as labourers. Except in the case of agricultural labour, the inventories tell us nothing about labourers employed by Voshchazhnikovo residents. This problem will be discussed in greater detail in the following sections. For now, though, we should note that these data almost certainly underestimate the amount of labour market activity in this area. We should also bear in mind that households which neither hired labour nor contained members working as labourers were not always self-sufficient. There were lively land and credit markets around Voshchazhnikovo, and serfs who 'lived from agriculture alone' also bought, sold, or rented land. In addition, there were serfs who lived from trade, selling a range of wares from agricultural produce to manufactured goods. Finally, most Voshchazhnikovo households fit into more than one of the categories set out in Table 6.1, while some – such as that of Pelageia Kokina, who earned a living teaching local children to read,[4] or that of Mikhail Zhelvakov, who earned a salary as an estate officer[5] – fit into none.

As indicated in Table 6.1, 32 of 201 households (16 per cent) had members who worked as day labourers, while 28 (14 per cent) had members who worked as live-in labourers (or servants in husbandry, about whom more will be said shortly). Furthermore, 26 of the 90 households (about 29 per cent) that engaged in agriculture in this period hired labourers to work their communal allotments. There were also rural markets in non-agricultural labour. For instance, as mentioned in an earlier chapter, there were seven small serf-owned manufactories on the estate – two leather manufactories, one brickworks, one candle works, two paper manufactories, and two distilleries – and all of these employed labourers.[6]

Many households on the estate both simultaneously bought and sold labour. A fairly typical example was the household of the Uliankov brothers, Vasily and Mikhail, who themselves worked as servants in St Petersburg while hired labourers cultivated their communal plot at home.[7] Similarly, Ivan Kopev hired labourers to sow his lands while he worked as a servant in Kronstadt.[8] And the Chernikhin brothers, who owned the candle works on the estate, hired others to operate it while they, like the Uliankovs, worked as servants in St Petersburg.[9] In all, 149 of 201 households in this village were explicitly recorded as having bought or sold labour (or both) in 1832.

There is a certain ambiguity related to the remaining 52 households, especially where the occupations of female members were concerned. For instance, Semyon Sedel'nikov, 65, was recorded in the 1832 listing as earning a living from agriculture. No additional occupations were recorded for his household, whose other members included Sedel'nikov's second wife, his daughter, and his daughter-in-law – all of whom could have been working for wages.[10] A similar example is the household of 38-year-old Nikolai Sopetov, which was recorded in 1832 as earning a living from agriculture. But the list does not make clear whether agriculture was in fact the primary occupation of Sopetov's mother (age 59) and wife (age 36) as well.[11] This suggests that the number of Voshchazhnikovo

---

[4] RGADA, f. 1287, op. 3, ed. khr. 1143, entry 128 ('Inventories of households, 1832/8').
[5] *Ibid.*, entry 118.
[6] RGADA, f. 1287, op. 3, ed. khr. 1119 ('Report on estate manufactories'). Serf-owned industries were not uncommon on Russian estates. Some serfs even managed to turn these into large and profitable enterprises. Blum, *Lord and peasant*, pp. 472–3; Gorshkov, 'Serfs on the move', p. 648; Melton, 'Proto-industrialization', pp. 73–81. In the context of the Sheremetyev estates, see Gestwa, *Proto-Industrialisierung*. It is not clear from the sources just how many hired labourers worked at Voshchazhnikovo manufactories.
[7] RGADA, f. 1287, op. 3, ed. khr. 1143, entry 144 ('Inventories of households, 1832/8').
[8] *Ibid.*, entry 198.   [9] *Ibid.*, entry 10.   [10] *Ibid.*, entry 189.   [11] *Ibid.*, entry 22.

households explicitly described as participating in labour markets should be treated as the lower bound for this village.

Migrant labour

In the literature on the Russian serf economy, most references to labour markets concern migrant labour in the Central Industrial Region. It is usually noted that the soil was poorer and the growing season shorter in this area than in the Black Earth Region to the south, and thus fewer estates specialised in agriculture. As a result, many landlords in this region demanded feudal dues in cash or kind rather than labour for the demesne, thereby freeing their serfs to sell their labour in nearby towns and cities.

The data for Voshchazhnikovo are in certain ways consistent with this view. As noted earlier, with some exceptions (building and road main-tenance, for instance) feudal dues were indeed paid in cash and kind on this estate, and very few serfs lived solely from agriculture. In 1832, only 22 of the 201 households in the village of Voshchazhnikovo (roughly 11 per cent) were reported as having income from agriculture alone.[12] Moreover, 74 of those 201 (about 37 per cent) had at least one member working as a migrant labourer in an urban area when the 1832 inventory was drawn up.[13] Passport registers indicate that between the years 1762 and 1859, anywhere from 10 to 40 per cent of the adult male population in Voshchazhnikovo worked as migrant labourers in towns and cities.[14] Like many migrants from Yaroslavl', these serfs engaged in a wide range of economic activities. There were traders, such as Kozma Moseyevskii and his sons, Vasily and Aleksandr, who 'made their living trading in Moscow'.[15] There were servants, such as Boris Smirnov, who 'earned a living in service in Vyborg'.[16] There were also craftsmen, such as Fyodor Golovarev, who worked in St Petersburg as a milliner, and Dmitrii Shumilov, who worked there as a tailor.[17] The majority of Voshchazhnikovo migrants were in middling or better-off socioeconomic strata, similar to those described by Bohac for neighbouring Tver' province.[18] On the other hand, nearly all of those who worked outside the estate did so year-round (*postoianno*, or

---

[12] *Ibid.* This was fairly typical for estates in the Central Industrial Region. On proto-industrial estates, the proportion was often even smaller. See, for instance, Gestwa, *Proto-Industrialisierung*, esp. pp. 258–9; Melton, 'Proto-industrialization,' pp. 76, 87.

[13] *Ibid.*

[14] RGADA, f. 1287, op. 3, ed. khr. 272, 958, 1158, 1246, 2390 ('Passport lists, 1762, 1825, 1832, 1834, 1859/60').

[15] RGADA, f. 1287, op. 3, ed. khr. 1143, entry 65 ('Inventories of households, 1832/8').

[16] *Ibid.*, entry 18.   [17] *Ibid.*, entries 5 and 202.

[18] Bohac, 'Agricultural structure'. Only five Voshchazhnikovo households with migrants were described as 'poor'.

'permanently', as noted in the inventories of households), returning to Voshchazhnikovo only very occasionally, if at all.[19] They did not, as some historians have suggested, rely on other household members, such as wives and children, to work their communal allotments in their absence.[20] Instead, they hired labourers and servants for this purpose.

Day labourers

Roughly 16 per cent of households in Voshchazhnikovo village contained members who in 1832 were reported as earning a living 'from their own labour' (*ot svoego truda*) or 'from working for others' (*ot raboty dlia drugikh krest'ian*). It is not always clear from the sources what these labourers did or who employed them. Sometimes the entries are quite specific, such as that for Mikhail Pugin, who 'received a small salary for work as a labourer at the estate paper manufactory'.[21] In most other instances, though, they are vague. Ivan Pyriaev and his sister Aleksandra were said only to have earned their living 'working for other serfs'.[22] The widow Aleksandra Smirnova 'lived from her own labour'.[23] Similarly, Egor Kezin and his two half-sisters, Matryona and Anna, 'earned a living from their own labour'.[24]

We have more specific information about the socioeconomic strata from which these labourers came. Some historians have maintained that serf labourers were mainly poor landless serfs, who worked for their better-off neighbours.[25] While it is true that day labourers at Voshchazhnikovo

---

[19] For example, the Baramokhin household was noted as living year-round in Kronstadt, where the household head worked in service. Similarly, the Murav'ev household lived year-round in Moscow. RGADA, f. 1287, op. 3, ed. khr. 1143, entries 121 and 181 ('Inventories of households, 1832/8'). It was necessary to have estate permission (and a travel pass) to remain away for so long. Many serfs managed this by sending money back to their families or neighbours each year for *obrok* payments and passport renewal fees.

[20] V. A. Fyodorov emphasises the importance of migrants' parents, wives, and children in 'Naemnyi trud v zemledelii nakanune krest'ianskoi reform 1861 g. (po materialam tsentral'no-promyshlennykh gubernii)', *Vestnik moskovskogo universiteta* 3 (1968), p. 93. Moon suggests wage labour was a response to rural 'underemployment' in *The Russian peasantry*, p. 144. At Voshchazhnikovo a maximum of twelve households containing migrants relied on family labour to cultivate their allotments. Four were explicitly noted as doing so, while eight cases were ambiguous. The remaining households either hired labourers or let their land to others.

[21] 'rabotaet na bumazhnei fabrike iz nebol'shoi platy', in RGADA, f. 1287, op. 3, ed. khr. 1143, entry 193 ('Inventories of households, 1832/8').

[22] 'propitanie imeet ot prislugi u raznykh krest'ian', in *ibid.*, entry 20.

[23] 'propityvaet'sia ot svoikh trudov', in *ibid.*, entry 72.

[24] 'propityvaet'sia svoimi trudiami', in *ibid.*, entry 136.

[25] See discussion in Fyodorov, 'Naemnyi trud', pp. 91–2; *idem*, *Pomeshchich'i krest'iane*, pp. 78–9; Moon, *The Russian peasantry*, p. 149.

often came from poorer households, only about half of labouring house-holds (15 of 32) were landless. The other 17 had access to communal land, though very few of them actually cultivated it. Instead, they let it out to other serfs, or hired other labourers to cultivate it for them.[26] The widow Anna Kouzova, for example, and her two daughters-in-law let their communal allotment to others and worked as labourers.[27] Fyokla Kuvaeva hired labourers to cultivate her household's communal allotment, while her grandsons worked elsewhere as servants and she worked on the estate as a day labourer.[28]

But not all labouring households were poor; according to the household listings, roughly a quarter were of the middling sort. As noted earlier, the inventories of households include notes on households' economic activities and their economic viability. Thus we know that the household of the widow Avdotia Balateva and her two adult daughters, all of whom 'lived from their own labour', was a financially stable one of average means.[29] Similarly, Nikolai and Pelageia Kouzov, a couple in their 60s, were said to be financially secure and living 'on previous earnings' from labour.[30] Natalia Mukova and her daughter, both of whom worked as labourers, paid all their feudal obligations on time and maintained a communal allotment and two-storey house in Voshchazhnikovo village.[31]

The number of Voshchazhnikovo households containing day labourers might seem rather small at first glance. But the data for Voshchazhnikovo shed light on only one small part of the market in day labour in this area. The household listings, as mentioned above, were concerned primarily with the occupations and incomes of serfs resident in the village of Voshchazhnikovo. They tell us who in the village worked as day labourers, but they do not tell us much about who hired day labourers, unless that hired labour was being used to cultivate communal allotments. (The land-lord's officials closely monitored the cultivation of communal land, as discussed in greater detail below.) Other households may well have been employing labourers to tend livestock or perform other household tasks, such as washing, fetching water, or tending garden plots. And there is no reason to assume *a priori* that the day labourers employed were from the village of Voshchazhnikovo. There were, after all, twenty-nine other settlements on the estate – settlements for which, unfortunately, no house-hold listings have survived. Moreover, it is entirely possible that serf

---

[26] Such arrangements were not uncommon where labour market imperfections (such as serfdom) existed. E. Sadoulet, A. de Janvry, and C. Benjamin, 'Household behaviour with imperfect labor markets', *Industrial Relations* 37(1) (1998), pp. 85–108.
[27] RGADA, f. 1287, op. 3, ed. khr. 1143, entry 196 ('Inventories of households, 1832/8').
[28] *Ibid.*, entry 146 (1832).   [29] 'ot svoikh trudov', in *ibid.*, entry 81.
[30] 'ot prezhneiu nazhitku', in *ibid.*, entry 132.   [31] *Ibid.*, entry 48.

households hired day labourers from outside the estate, and that these transactions went unrecorded. The Voshchazhnikovo estate covered a substantial geographical area, and some villages were closer to settlements outside estate boundaries than they were to other estate villages. For instance, the non-estate village of Nikifortsevo was closer to the village of Voshchazhnikovo than all but 2 of the other 29 estate villages. Day labourers might have come in to work from such neighbouring settlements, and there would have been no reason for officials to record the presence of such people in the inventories of household or passport lists, since they would not actually have been resident on the estate.

To complicate matters, it was not only individual households that engaged day labourers, but communes as well, using communal funds. The communal resolutions (*mirskie prigovory*) of the Voshchazhnikovo estate commune contain scattered references to the hiring of labourers. These workers were usually hired to perform the routine tasks assigned as corvée labour. Most of these tasks involved maintenance of estate infrastructure. For instance, a resolution from 1785 allocates communal funds to the hiring of labourers to help build a new road and church in the village of Voshchazhnikovo.[32] Resolutions from 1837 mention the hiring of labourers to repair a shed,[33] to paint estate structures,[34] and to clean roads.[35] A resolution from 1844 talks of hiring a serf, Marko Melent'ev, to provide transport between the estate and the Sheremetyevs' Moscow headquarters.[36] Again, we only have access to documents for the estate commune (not the village communes) and only for select years, though it is clear that annual records were kept. But these examples suggest that communes regularly employed labourers – from either inside or outside the estate – to fulfil certain feudal obligations.

Servants in husbandry

In addition to day labourers, Voshchazhnikovo serfs employed servants. These were not domestic servants, as a rule, but what the English historiography terms servants in husbandry – i.e. agricultural labourers who were hired on long-term contracts, usually several months to one year, and who lived in their employers' households.[37] Service is often viewed as an institution unique to northwest Europe; some historians have even

---

[32] RGADA, f. 1287, op. 3, ed. khr. 496, l. 3 ('Communal resolutions, 1804').
[33] RGADA, f. 1287, op. 3, ed. khr. 1325, l. 31 ('Communal resolutions, 1837').
[34] *Ibid.*, l. 37.   [35] *Ibid.*, l. 43.
[36] RGADA, f. 1287, op. 3, ed. khr. 1635, l. 3 ('Communal resolutions, 1844').
[37] For a detailed account of service in an early modern English context, see A. Kussmaul, *Servants in husbandry in early modern England* (Cambridge, 1981).

argued that it played an important role in early industrialisation by encouraging labour mobility and keeping population in check through later marriage, since young people in these societies usually worked as servants for some years to save money for marriage.[38] It has even been suggested that the institution of service was indicative of a 'fundamentally different economic behaviour' on the part of northwest Europeans, as compared to that of east Europeans, who are supposed to have relied primarily on family to meet their labour demands.[39]

It has long been assumed, therefore, that live-in agricultural servants did not exist in Russia.[40] The two best-known studies of Russian peasant households appear to support this widely held view. Czap, in his work on household structure on the Mishino estate, a Gagarin-family holding in the Central Black Earth Region, noted that peasant households 'were almost exclusively kin-based'.[41] And Hoch in his work on the Petrovskoe estate, another Gagarin family holding in the same region, remarks that 'the practice of taking in domestic servants, apprentices, or lodgers simply did not exist'.[42] Czap and Hoch based their claims on findings from the state soul revisions and the inventories of households (*podvornye opisi*) carried out by estate officials. The problem, as noted in chapter 3, is that soul revisions and inventories of households were not census documents but tax registers. They did not record the names of those who were actually resident at the time of a particular count, but rather those who owed taxes and dues in a particular place.[43] Peasants were therefore recorded as members of households in their home settlements, where they paid taxes, and not in the places where they were living when the registers were drawn up.[44] In other words, these listings excluded live-in labourers and other resident non-kin by definition. It only becomes clear that such people did exist when one looks at other estate documents – in particular, the estate passport lists.

---

[38] Hajnal, 'Two kinds', pp. 470–6; P. Laslett, 'The European family and early industrialization', in J. Baechler, J. Hall, and M. Mann (eds.), *Europe and the rise of capitalism* (Oxford, 1988), esp. pp. 237–9. For a more recent articulation, see T. de Moor and J.-L. van Zanden, 'Girl power: the European marriage pattern and labour markets in the North Sea region in the late medieval and early modern period', *Economic History Review* 63 (2010), pp. 1–33.

[39] Hajnal, 'Two kinds', pp. 475–6.

[40] *Ibid.*, pp. 473–4. See also Czap, 'The perennial multiple-family', p. 7; Hoch, *Serfdom and social control*, p. 77.

[41] Czap, 'The perennial multiple-family household', p. 7.

[42] Hoch, *Serfdom and social control*, p. 77.

[43] Though it was often noted in the household listings for Voshchazhnikovo when serfs were absent.

[44] RGADA, f. 1287, op. 3, ed. khr. 555, l. 22 ('Instructions, 1796/1800').

Russian serfs who left their landlords' estates for any reason were required by imperial law to carry an internal passport.[45] Historians have used information from these passport lists to study migration to urban areas in the nineteenth century.[46] But lists of in-migrants into Russian estates have not been given nearly so much attention. When a serf took up residence in another place – in a town or on another estate – his passport information was registered by local authorities there.[47] These passport registration lists, where they have survived, can be used to find out about workers invisible in other sources such as soul revisions and inventories of households. In particular, they show that there were indeed live-in labourers and servants in rural Russia.

Voshchazhnikovo officials kept annual passport registration lists, though, as noted earlier, only a few of these have survived. In most cases, these lists included copies of serfs' passport letters, along with notes about the location on the estate of the migrant in question and the serfs for whom they were working. The passport letters usually took a form similar to the following example:

1746 yr. May 5th, the serf Pyotr Stepanov, from the village Bezmetsov, on the estate of retired lieutenant Andrei Ivanov Saltykov in Rostov district, Vedenskii stan', was granted permission to earn a living within 30 versts of the estate and to remain there until 1st Nov 1746. If he should return after this date, he will be fined in accordance with estate regulations.[48]

Once the letter was copied out for the registration list, a Voshchazhnikovo estate official noted where on the estate this serf was working. In this case, he noted that 'Pyotr Stepanov is located in the village of Kanditovo, where he lives as a labourer in the household of the serf Vasily Mikhailov.'[49]

The passport lists thus provide information on the sex, estate of origin, length of contract, and occasionally even the marital status and place of employment for outside workers resident at Voshchazhnikovo. While some of these in-migrants were described in the documents as 'living with

[45] A more detailed discussion of the passport system in imperial Russia can be found in D. Moon, 'Peasant migration, the abolition of serfdom, and the internal passport system in Russia, c. 1800–1914', in D. Eltis (ed.), *Coerced and free migration: global perspectives* (Palo Alto, 2002); V. G. Chernukha, 'Pasport v Rossiiskoi imperii: nabliudeniia nad zakonodatel'stvom', *Istoricheskie zapiski* 122 (2001), pp. 91–131.

[46] Examples include Burds, *Peasant dreams*; Fyodorov, *Pomeshchich'i krest'iane* (chapter 4); Moon, 'Peasant migration'.

[47] This process is described in Chernukha, 'Pasport', pp. 99–100.

[48] Condensed version of entry no. 2 in RGADA, f. 1287, op. 3, ed. khr. 131, l. 2 ('Passport lists, 1746').

[49] '[Pyotr Stepanov] nakhodit'sa v derevne Kanditove u krest'ianina Vasiliia Mikhailova v rabotnikakh'. Example in *ibid.*, l. 2, entry 4.

[name of employer] as a *labourer* (*zhivet u nego v rabotnikakh*),[50] others were recorded as 'living with [name of employer] *in service*' (*zhivet u nego v usluzhenii*).[51] These terms seem to have been used interchangeably in the Voshchazhnikovo documents. Because we know so little about what these people were doing, it is difficult to say whether the terms 'servant' and 'labourer' implied different types of work or different types of employment relationship. We do know that the terms were not gender-specific, since they were used to describe both male and female in-migrants. During the year 1746–7, Arina Kozmina, an unmarried serf woman from the estate of Afanasii Alabiev, was described as a 'labourer' in the household of Voshchazhnikovo serf Fyodor Kokin.[52] The serf Pyotr Ivanov, who worked in the household of Voshchazhnikovo serf Aleksei Nabilkin, was also described as a 'labourer'.[53] Similarly, in 1832, the serf widow Matryona Kuverina and the serf Ilya Lodygin were said to have earned their respective livings 'in service' for others.[54] We do know that some of the people recorded in these lists were doing agricultural work,[55] that they were hired for relatively long periods of time (on contracts of three to twelve months), and that they lived with their employers – the three main characteristics of servants in pre-industrial Europe. Therefore they will be referred to as 'servants' in this chapter. While it may be too early to say much about service as an institution in the Russian context, it is still worth identifying the servants at Voshchazhnikovo as a specific type of hired labour, if only to provide a finer-grained picture of the rural labour market while keeping the wider European context in mind.

Table 6.2 sets out some general features of service at Voshchazhnikovo. The data presented in this table indicate that servants on the Voshchazhnikovo estate were quite different from those found in early modern England and northwest Europe. For one thing, there appears to have been far fewer of them. The total number of registered servants

---

[50] As in the case of Vasily Derofeyev, who was said to have been 'residing in the village of Voshchazhnikovo as a labourer for the serf Vasily Konoplev' ('on nakhodit'sa v sele Voshchazhnikove u krest'ianina Vasilia Konopleva v rabotnikakh'). In RGADA, f. 1287, op. 3, ed. khr. 776, l. 1 ('Passport lists, 1820').

[51] As in the case of Ivan Ekimov, who was said to be living in the village of Lykhino as a servant for the serf Mikhail Gavrilov ('on nakhodit'sa v derevne Lykhino u Mikhaila Gavrilova v usluzhenii'). In RGADA, f. 1287, op. 3, ed. khr. 271 ('Passport lists, 1762').

[52] 'ona u Fyodora Kokina v rabotnitsakh', in RGADA, f. 1287, op. 3, ed. khr. 131, l. 8 ('Passport lists, 1746').

[53] 'on u Alekseia Nabilkina v rabotnikakh', in *ibid.*, l. 4.

[54] 'propitanie ot prozhivaniia u drugikh v usluzhenii', in RGADA, f. 1287, op. 3, ed. khr. 1143, l. 35–7 ('Inventories of households 1832/8').

[55] Those listed as 'herdsmen' were clearly engaged in agricultural work. Also, there are references in other documents to serfs hiring live-in employees to 'work their communal lands' ('otrabotyvat' tiaglovye zemli').

Table 6.2. *Servants working on the Voshchazhnikovo estate, 1746–1825*

	1746	1762	1820	1825
Total number	31	71	72	72
Males	18	60	67	70
Married	—	—	—	43
Unmarried	—	—	—	11
Unknown	—	—	—	16
Females	13	11	5	2
Married	0	4	1	1
Widowed	1	0	0	1
Single	12	7	3	0
Unknown	0	0	1	0
Herdsmen (males)	5	45	26	10
From different district	0	0	62	67
From different province	0	0	—	5
1-year contracts	1	2	—	—
6–11-month contracts	15	27	—	—
3–5-month contracts	12	35	—	—
Unknown length	3	7	—	—
Pre-arranged	7	27	—	—
Working in Voshchazhnikovo	0	0	18	21
Working in smaller villages	28	64	54	51
Unknown location	3	7	0	0

Sources: RGADA, f. 1287, op. 3, ed. khr. 131 ('Passport lists, 1746'), ed. khr. 271 ('Passport lists, 1762'), ed. khr. 776 ('Passport lists, 1820'), ed. khr. 958 ('Passport lists, 1825').

was fairly low – only 2 to 3 per cent of the population. In early modern England, servants comprised at least 10 per cent of the rural population, and for other parts of northwestern Europe the figure was 6–8 per cent.[56]

However, several things must be taken into account when analysing these data. First, the population figures for Voshchazhnikovo cited earlier in this chapter (roughly 3,500 serfs in 1858) are *de jure* figures; they have been calculated from the soul revisions and household listings, which were tax registers not census documents.[57] Not all of these people were actually present on the estate. Passport lists for out-migrating serfs suggest that more than 10 per cent of the recorded estate population was absent at

---

[56] Kussmaul, *Servants in husbandry*; Ogilvie, *A bitter living*, p. 110; Laslett, 'Introduction', pp. 82–3.
[57] As discussed in chapter 3, the inventories of households, unlike the soul revisions, often noted which serfs were permanently absent from the estate – i.e. the migrants who lived year-round in Moscow or St Petersburg. However, they did not record in-migrants and did not always note temporary absences.

any given time in the eighteenth and nineteenth centuries.[58] For the male population, this proportion was even higher, since the large majority of migrant labourers from Voshchazhnikovo were men. Figures for the village of Voshchazhnikovo in 1834 (the only year for which we have both a soul revision and a list of migrants) show that 20 per cent of males over age 14 were living off the estate.[59] Using population data for estate males for 1858[60] and migration data for 1859,[61] we arrive at a similar figure for the estate population: 18 per cent of males over 14 years of age were absent. If the proportion absent was similar for the earlier part of the nineteenth century (and the 1834 figures for Voshchazhnikovo suggest that it was), the 60–70 male in-migrants who were working as servants on the estate in the 1820s would have comprised some 6–7 per cent of the adult male population – a figure not far from those observed in early modern north-west Europe.

Second, there are reasons to think that these passport lists are fragmentary. Other documents contain references to serfs hiring servants and labourers from outside the estate and these outsiders do *not* appear in the passport lists. For instance, a report on estate manufactories notes that the serf Fyodor Pugin hired eighteen employees each year, between 1812 and 1840, to work in his paper manufactory. These labourers were said to have come from the Voshchazhnikovo estate and from Uglich district.[62] But none of the people recorded in the passport lists for 1820 and 1825 was noted as working for Pugin.[63] Similarly, the paper manufactory operated by the serf Dmitri Slasnikov in the 1820s was said to have hired thirty

---

[58] RGADA, f. 1287, op. 3, ed. khr. 262, 272, 957, 1246 ('Passport lists', 1760, 1762, 1825, 1834).

[59] This figure was obtained by linking data from the 1834 soul revision (RGADA, f. 1287, op. 3, ed. khr. 2553, 1834) with the list of passports issued to Voshchazhnikovo estate serfs in 1834 (RGADA, f. 1287, op. 3, ed. khr. 1246, 1834).

[60] Because the 1858 population figures were not broken down by age, we must assume that the age structure of the total male population on the estate was similar to that in the village of Voshchazhnikovo, where roughly 30 per cent of males were under age 14 in 1858. Using this baseline figure, we get 1,216 estate males over age 14. Total population figures for 1858 are from RGADA, f. 1287, op. 3, ed. khr. 2320 ('Descriptions of estates, 1858'). The figures for Voshchazhnikovo are from the 1858 soul revision, GAYaO, f. 100, op. 8, d. 2656, 1858.

[61] According to the passport lists, a total of 257 passports were issued to estate serfs in 1859. If we assume that 15 per cent of these were issued to women, we get a total of 218 passports issued to estate males. (It is worth bearing in mind that 15 per cent is probably an overestimate, as the largest figure on record for female passports at Voshchazhnikovo is 12 per cent in 1834.) See figures in RGADA, f. 1287, op. 3, ed. khr. 2390 ('Passport lists, 1859–60') and 1246 ('Passport lists, 1834').

[62] RGADA, f. 1287, op. 3, ed. khr. 1119, ll. 4–5 ('Report on estate manufactories').

[63] RGADA, f. 1287, op. 3, ed. khr. 776, 958 ('Passport lists', 1820 and 1825).

labourers each year from among Rostov craftsmen, Uglich *meshchanstvo*,[64] and other paper-manufacturing settlements.[65] But, as with Pugin, none of those in the 1820 or 1825 lists was noted as working for Slasnikov.[66] That such people should have been registered is clear from the source materials. The landlord's instructions explicitly state that serfs were permitted to hire servants and labourers from outside the estate, but that these employees had to have official passports that could be registered with the estate administration.[67] A fine of 10 kopecks per day was set for any serf caught employing unregistered outsiders.[68]

It is not apparent, then, why those working for Pugin and Slasnikov were not included in the passport lists. They were clearly outsiders and they were hired for relatively long periods of time, some on monthly contracts, others on annual ones.[69] Many of them came from distant parts of Yaroslavl' province (such as Uglich district), so they would certainly have been resident on the Voshchazhnikovo estate. It is possible that separate lists were kept for those who came into Voshchazhnikovo to work in local manufactories, but that none of these has survived. It is also possible that owners of manufactories were somehow able to get around the registration requirement (for instance, by bribing officials). In any case, it seems safe to assume that the passport registers described in Table 6.2 are not comprehensive lists of all outsiders working on the Voshchazhnikovo estate.

The findings reported in Table 6.2 indicate that most servants working on the Voshchazhnikovo estate were married males.[70] In this respect Voshchazhnikovo servants more closely resembled those found in southern European societies than those found in northwest Europe. In early modern England and northwest Europe, where multi-generational households were rare, service provided young men and women with the opportunity to earn money for marriage and the establishment of new,

---

[64] The term *meshchanstvo* is difficult to translate into English. It simultaneously implies a very specific legal status – an urban estate, comprised of artisans and petty traders – and a somewhat vague socioeconomic category along the lines of *petit bourgeois*.

[65] RGADA, f. 1287, op. 3, ed. khr. 1119, ll. 3–4 ('Report on estate manufactories').

[66] RGADA, f. 1287, op. 3, ed. khr. 776, 958 ('Passport lists', 1820 and 1825).

[67] RGADA, f. 1287, op. 3, ed. khr. 555, l. 22 ('Instructions, 1796/1800'). This rule was probably designed to discourage the hiring of fugitive serfs, for whom the landlord would have been ultimately held legally accountable.

[68] RGADA, f. 1287, op. 3, ed. khr. 2212, l. 1 ('On the hiring of labourers with passports (no date)'). It is not clear how systematically this was enforced.

[69] RGADA, f. 1287, op. 3, ed. khr. 1119, ll. 3–5 ('Report on estate manufactories').

[70] Because marital status was not systematically recorded in the earlier lists, figures were not included in the table. It seems likely, however, that most servants in these lists were married. Unmarried men in these lists were usually referred to as *kholostiak*, or 'bachelor'. If we assume that those *not* referred to as bachelors were in fact married, then the proportion married can be put at roughly 80 per cent in each of the earlier lists.

independent nuclear-family households. In these societies, service was a 'life-cycle' phenomenon, or, in other words, an occupation associated with a particular period in people's lives – in this case, the phase before marriage. Very few servants in these societies remained servants after they had married. In joint-household societies, like those in imperial Russia, where married sons often remained in their parents' houses, service was not related to any particular phase in the life cycle. Men and women of all ages and marital statuses worked as servants, many for their entire lives. Servants in these societies are often called 'lifetime' servants.[71] The figures in Table 6.2 suggest that the servants working at Voshchazhnikovo were lifetime rather than life-cycle servants. Because landlords' policies on marriage and household formation made it very difficult for serfs to establish separate, independent households at marriage, service did not – could not – play the same role in this society that it did in early modern northwest Europe. At Voshchazhnikovo, those who worked as servants often continued working as servants after they had married.

Married servants from outside Voshchazhnikovo did not usually bring their families with them. In fact, only one servant in these lists was noted as having come to the estate with his family. A passport was issued to Ivan Nikiforev, a serf of the Novodevichy monastery in Lekino, 'with his wife and children'.[72] He had been hired by the Tomakovo miller, Pytor Timofeyev, and he and his family lived at the mill.[73] The notes on him do not make clear whether any other members of the family were working as servants for the miller. And none of the other entries for married servants mentions families. Most married servants, it seems, came to work at Voshchazhnikovo by themselves, and returned to their families once their passports expired.

It is remarkable that so many servants on the Voshchazhnikovo estate were male. This is very different from the pattern found in northwest Europe, where sex ratios among servants were more balanced.[74] At Voshchazhnikovo the proportion of female servants recorded for 1746 was substantially larger than for any of the subsequent lists. If this trend turned out to be empirically robust, and could be substantiated with other data, or observed on other estates or in other regions, it would suggest that

---

[71] See discussion in Hajnal, 'Two kinds', pp. 470–3.

[72] 'otpushchen toi votchiny ... Ivan Nikiforov ... s zhenoiu i s det'mi svoimi', in RGADA, f. 1287, op. 3, ed. khr. 271, l. 20 ('Passport lists, 1762').

[73] Ibid., l. 21.

[74] For England, see Kussmaul, *Servants in husbandry*, p. 4; Ogilvie, *A bitter living*, p. 110. Servants were predominantly male in some parts of southern Europe. See Kertzer and Hogan, *Family, political economy, and demographic change*, p. 108.

sex ratios among some subpopulation of servants in early eighteenth-century Russia more closely resembled those in northwest Europe than they did in the period after 1762. But this cannot be asserted with confidence on the basis of only four surviving lists.

There are two possible explanations for the preponderance of males in the servant population. First, the demand for male servants may have been greater than that for females, given the low sex ratio on this estate. Households made up primarily of females may have imported male servants to help them cultivate their communal land. To test this theory, we would need to know the sex composition of households that hired male servants. Unfortunately, the majority of servants in these lists were located in the smaller villages on the estate and household information for these villages is not currently available; so we will have to regard this as an open question.[75]

The second possible explanation relates to restrictions on the mobility of serf females. While there are no indications in the documents of an *explicit* policy to limit migration by females, certain references imply that serf women were, nonetheless, more constrained in this respect than men.[76] For example, a landlord's decree about the use of hired labour on the Voshchazhnikovo estate states that those wishing to take a female servant into their homes must first get permission from the administration, and even then 'only women who will conduct themselves honourably' should be taken in.[77] Such stipulations were probably motivated by concern about the sexual behaviour of unmarried females, who, should they fall pregnant, were likely to require financial support.[78] This might also explain why, as we will see, very few passports were granted to young, unmarried females from Voshchazhnikovo; most women who left the estate were married or widowed. It may be that estate policies limiting the mobility of women were more strictly enforced in the nineteenth century and, as a result, the number of unmarried females working as

---

[75] Many of the soul revisions for the smaller villages at Voshchazhnikovo have been damaged, and will have to be restored before they can be used by researchers.

[76] That the behaviour of women was more closely monitored than that of men is a well-documented feature of traditional society. See the discussion in Ogilvie, *A bitter living*, although in this society it did not prevent female servants from migrating. In the Russian literature, see the essays in Clements, Engel, and Worobec (eds.), *Russia's women*; and in B. Farnsworth and L. Viola (eds.), *Russian peasant women* (Oxford, 1992); also in Worobec, 'Victims or actors?'

[77] 'puskat' tol'ko tekh, kotorye po povedeniiu budut zasluzhennymi', in RGADA, f. 1287, op. 3, ed. khr. 2212 ('On the hiring of labourers with passports (no date)').

[78] Leslie Page Moch notes that illegitimate pregnancy was a concern with regard to female migrants in France. See Page Moch, *Moving Europeans*, pp. 90–3. Similar concerns were reportedly expressed by authorities on the Sheremetyevs' Vykhino estate. See Avdeev, Blum, and Troitskaia, 'Peasant marriage', p. 727.

servants on the Voshchazhnikovo estate declined. It seems plausible that both of these features – restrictions on the movements of women and an increased demand for male labour – might have been responsible for the changing sex ratios reported in Table 6.2.

Since 'herding' was actually given as an occupation in the passport lists (it was, in fact, the *only* occupation specifically mentioned for in-migrants), we do have a rough estimate of the number of servants working on the estate as herdsmen. There is, however, some ambiguity regarding herdsmen in the documents. In certain cases, it is clear that individual serfs employed servants to work for them tending livestock. For example, there was Pyotr Kostrov from the village of Zadubrov'e, whose household hired two servants and a herdsman in 1825.[79] Another example is the serf Aleksei Gavrilov, from the village of Vioska, who hired Pyotr Dementiev to work for him as a herdsman in 1746.[80] These entries make clear that the herdsmen were resident in the households of their employers.[81] In other cases, though, the notes are more ambiguous, stating only that 'Yevsevii Yermolayev is located in the village of Strelki as a herdsman'.[82] Such entries provide no information about the employers or living arrangements of herdsmen, raising the possibility that they were hired collectively by a village commune rather than as servants for a particular household. Collective hires seem plausible in this context; a household would need to have fairly substantial livestock holdings to require its own herdsman. Since this question cannot be answered with the information available, we should at least allow for the possibility that the total number of household servants in these lists could be slightly inflated (especially for the years 1762 and 1820, when the number of herdsmen was particularly large), since some of those working as herdsmen may have been village employees rather than household servants.

Where did servants come from? How far did they travel in order to work on the Voshchazhnikovo estate? All servants recorded in the passport lists for 1746 and 1762 came from estates in Rostov district, where the Voshchazhnikovo estate itself was located. A substantial number of these (20–30 per cent) came from the estate of the Borisogleb monastery, some 6 to 10 miles from the Voshchazhnikovo estate. Others came from estates of smaller landlords in the district, mostly within 20 miles of Voshchazhnikovo.[83]

[79] RGADA, f. 1287, op. 3, ed. khr. 958, l. 4 ('Passport lists, 1825').

[80] RGADA, f. 1287, op. 3, ed. khr. 131, ll. 3–4 ('Passport lists, 1746').

[81] 'on nakhodit'sa *u Petra Kostrova* v pastukhakh' or '*u Alekseia Gavrilova* v pastukhakh'.

[82] 'Yevsevii Yermolayev v derevni Strelki v pastukhakh', in RGADA, f. 1287, op. 3, ed. khr. 271, ll. 4–5 ('Passport lists, 1762').

[83] Many serf passports for 1746 and 1762 explicitly state that serfs were not to venture further than '30 versts' (just over 30 kilometres) from their estates of origin.

By 1820 the situation had changed considerably. Only ten servants in the 1820 list came from Rostov district, and in 1825 there were none. The servants in these lists came from entirely different parts of Yaroslavl' province, some of which – Rybinsk, Kamensk, and Poshekhon'e districts – were located more than 60 miles from Voshchazhnikovo. In a few cases, servants came from entirely different provinces. Among those recorded for 1825 are three servants from Moscow province and two from Vladimir province, at least 60 miles from Voshchazhnikovo.[84] These were substantial distances to travel for seasonal work, especially considering that the estate was located some distance away from the major roads in this region.[85]

What lay behind such a significant change in the structure of the rural labour market between 1760 and 1820? Is it possible that the surviving registers reflect legal or administrative changes at the state level, such as those permitting serfs to travel short distances without official passports?[86] This is unlikely, since the landlord still required, even after reforms in the early eighteenth century, that all servants and labourers resident at Voshchazhnikovo, no matter where they came from, be registered with the estate management.[87] (Estate officials were not merely fulfilling a state obligation by registering passports; they were also keeping track of the economic activities of their own serfs as well as those of outsiders resident on the estate). Nor is there anything in the Voshchazhnikovo archive that indicates any sort of change in local hiring policies during this period.

The most likely explanation is that more and more people in this region were migrating to cities and towns as servants and labourers, making it more difficult for those who stayed behind to attract labour from the local area. Fyodorov, in his work on serfs in the Central Industrial Region, advances a similar argument, noting that as migrant labour became more attractive to Yaroslavl' serfs, hired labourers had to be recruited from more agricultural provinces such as Tver' and Vladimir.[88] According to Fyodorov, the situation was especially acute in Rostov district, since the Rostov garden farmers (*ogorodnichiki*) in the nineteenth century were increasingly taking their commercial gardening expertise to cities and towns,

---

[84] RGADA, f. 1287, op. 3, ed. khr. 958, ll. 2, 4, 8 ('Passport lists, 1825').

[85] The main road to Moscow (from the city Yaroslavl') was located roughly 20 miles from the estate. The road to the west, which ran between Rostov and Uglich was about 7 miles from the estate. These distances were reported in RGADA, f. 1287, op. 3, ed. khr. 2320, ll. 14–15 ('Descriptions of estates, 1858').

[86] See the discussion in Moon, 'Peasant migration', esp. pp. 326–8.

[87] RGADA, f. 1287, op. 3, ed. khr. 555, l. 22 ('Instructions, 1796/1800'). These instructions were issued in the period 1789–1807, well after the decrees on mobility issued in the early eighteenth century (1719, 1722, and 1724).

[88] Fyodorov, *Pomeshchich'i krest'iane*, pp. 77–8.

along with labourers from their home district.[89] These developments may have forced Voshchazhnikovo serfs to begin importing labourers from further away. Ideally, one would test this hypothesis using regional wage data for agricultural and migrant labourers. Unfortunately, there are very little wage data in the Voshchazhnikovo archive, nor in existing studies for other localities, which might shed light on this finding. More empirical work on Russian rural labour markets will need to be done before this question can be answered.

While a few of the servants working at Voshchazhnikovo had one-year contracts, the majority of service contracts were seasonal. They usually began in May or June and ran through October or November. The shortest ones ran just for the summer, from June through September. Length of contract was not recorded at all in 1820 and not systematically in 1825, so no numbers have been presented in the table. However, to judge by those entries which did include dates, the pattern was similar to that in earlier years.[90] This is different from the pattern observed in early modern England and northwest Europe, where the majority of servants were hired on annual contracts.[91] The seasonal pattern of service found for Voshchazhnikovo may have been due to the severity of the Russian winter, which limited the amount of agricultural work available for full-time employees during the coldest months. It seems unlikely, for instance, that herdsmen would have been needed year round, given that animals were usually kept inside until late April or early May. This might explain why contracts for herdsmen at Voshchazhnikovo tended to run from May to November. Those Voshchazhnikovo serfs who did hire servants on year-long contracts, such as Pyotr Timofeyev, the miller in the village of Tomakovo, were probably able to provide them with some form of non-agricultural work in the winter months.[92]

One interesting detail not mentioned in Table 6.2 concerns the socio-legal categories (legal estates, or *soslovii*) to which servants belonged. While most of those who came in to work as servants were agricultural serfs (*krepostnye krest'iane*), there are occasional references to servants from other socio-legal groups. In 1746, Vasily Alekseyev, a 'deacon of An'frevo parish', worked as a herdsman for the serf Aleksei Klianyshev

---

[89] Fyodorov, 'Vozniknovenie', pp. 54–5.
[90] Of the 24 contracts with definite dates in the 1825 list, 19 were seasonal. RGADA, f. 1287, op. 3, ed. khr. 958 ('Passport lists, 1825').
[91] While there were servants in early modern England who worked on seasonal contracts, annual contracts were more typical. See Kussmaul, *Servants in husbandry*, pp. 51–5.
[92] In 1762, Pyotr Timofeyev, the Tomakovo miller, hired Ivan Nikiforov as a servant for one year. RGADA, f. 1287, op. 3, ed. khr. 271, ll. 20–1 ('Passport lists, 1762').

in Kanditovo.[93] In 1762, the 'household serf' Nikita Stepanov worked as a shepherd in the village of Lykhino.[94] And in 1825, the serf Fyodor Krasavin, of the village of Sytino, hired the 'free agricultural peasant' Vasily Ivanov as a servant.[95] Although such entries occur fairly infrequently (most servants were agricultural serfs), that they do occur suggests that Russian rural labour markets extended across socio-legal as well as geographical boundaries.

In most cases, the passport letters issued to serfs were quite formulaic, granting them permission to seek employment 'within Rostov district' or 'within 20 miles of their estate of origin' or 'in the place of his/her choice'.[96] But some of the letters were much more specific, implying that contracts had been pre-arranged. Instead of simply granting a serf permission 'to seek employment in Rostov district', a pre-arranged contract would state, for instance, that 'Ivan Genat'ev [was] granted leave to work as a labourer for the serf Mikhail Fyodorov, in the village of Musorovo, on the Voshchazhnikovo estate of Count Pyotr Borisovich Sheremetyev.'[97] More than one third of the contracts in the 1762 list were pre-arranged. It could be that some of these servants came back to work for the same employers every year. It is also possible that servants heard about employment opportunities through kin or other social contacts and were able to secure positions for themselves in advance. There are no references in the documents to 'hiring fairs' of the sort described for early modern England,[98] though that does not mean such things did not exist. As we will see in chapter 8, there were a number of markets and fairs in the Central Industrial Region, and it is possible that those seeking employment in service used these events to arrange service contracts.

The last panel of Table 6.2 shows the number of servants working in the main village of Voshchazhnikovo and the number working in the twenty-nine smaller villages on the estate. The proportions noted in the later two lists (1820 and 1825) reflect the population distribution on the estate fairly accurately. Roughly one third of Voshchazhnikovo serfs lived in the village of Voshchazhnikovo; it therefore seems reasonable that about one third of incoming servants should have been located there. It is

[93] 'tserkovnyi prichetnik sela An'freva', in RGADA, f. 1287, op. 3, ed. khr. 131, l. 5 ('Passport lists, 1746').
[94] 'dvorovoi chelovek' in RGADA, f. 1287, op. 3, ed. khr. 271, l. 10 ('Passport lists, 1762').
[95] 'svobodnyi khlebopashets', in RGADA, f. 1287, op. 3, ed. khr. 958, l. 8 ('Passport lists, 1825').
[96] 'v rostovskom uezde' or 'ne dalee ot tridtsati verst' or 'gde on/a zakhochet zhit''. See letters in RGADA, f. 1287, op. 3, ed. khr. 131, 271 ('Passport lists, 1746, 1762').
[97] RGADA, f. 1287, op. 3, ed. khr. 271, l. 11 ('Passport lists, 1762').
[98] Kussmaul, *Servants in husbandry*, pp. 58–61.

surprising, though, that none of the servants in the 1746 and 1762 lists was recorded as resident in the village of Voshchazhnikovo. Perhaps during these years Voshchazhnikovo serfs were able to meet their labour needs through local labour markets. Because it was the main settlement on the estate, Voshchazhnikovo was probably able to attract servants and labourers from the smaller estate villages. These would not appear in the lists, since they would not have needed passports. Again, we must bear in mind that hiring servants from outside was only one of several options for Voshchazhnikovo employers. The figures in Table 6.2 do not by any means provide a complete picture of labour market activity on the estate.

Purchased labour

A third, if somewhat less frequent, option for serfs was to purchase serf labour. In other words, there were serfs at Voshchazhnikovo who were themselves owners of serfs. Strange as it may sound, this practice was not so unusual on the estates of wealthier Russian landlords, especially among better-off serfs.[99] The process was similar to that described for land and property purchases, in that a serf would petition the estate administration for a contract enabling him to purchase a serf for his household in the landlord's name. So, for instance, in 1839 Fyodor Egorov, from the village of Fedos'ina, petitioned the administration for 'permission to buy a person to work his communal lands'.[100] Grigory Pavlov, from the village of Vioski, requested permission to purchase a serf labourer in 1840.[101] And Sidor Shavin, from the village of Voshchazhnikovo, requested permission to buy a labourer to help him work his communal lands, since his sons, who worked full time as craftsmen, did not reside on the estate.[102] It is impossible to say how representative these households were, since the Voshchahzhnikovo documents do not tell us how many serf households owned serfs over the period under investigation. The only information we have comes from petitions such as these, and from the lists of 'purchased labourers' which appear at the end of the soul revisions. (These serfs were not listed as members of the households in which they resided, making it difficult to determine precisely who on the estate owned serfs.)

---

[99] Blum, *Lord and peasant*, pp. 361, 425–7. The Sheremetyev holdings (though not Voshchazhnikovo) are mentioned explicitly as estates where this practice is known to have occurred.

[100] 'razreshchenie na pokupku cheloveka dlia obrabatyvaniia tiaglovoi moei zemli', in RGADA, f. 1287, op. 3, ed. khr. 1434 ('Petition regarding labourer purchase, 1839').

[101] RGADA, f. 1287, op. 3. ed. khr. 1492 ('Petition regarding land purchase, 1840').

[102] RGADA, f. 1287, op. 3, ed. khr. 1563, l. 3 ('Petition regarding land purchase, 1840').

It is unlikely that purchased labour was used to the same extent as hired labour, since a household probably needed to be reasonably well off in order to purchase a serf. One not only needed the money to pay for the serf, one also had to feed, clothe, and house this person while he worked as a labourer. That said, it was not only the wealthiest serfs at Voshchazhnikovo who owned serfs. In 1839, the brothers Aleksei and Yakov Shalkov, who belonged to the second, or middle, rank of serfs on the estate, petitioned the Count Sheremetyev for permission to 'purchase a person' to work their communal allotment.[103] The above-mentioned Sidor Shavin, who made a similar request in 1840, was also described as being of the middling stratum.[104]

Why would serfs at Voshchazhnikovo incur the costs of serf ownership when it was possible to hire labour? The main reason was probably conscription. Unlike a hired servant, a serf labourer could be sent to the army in place of a family member, should a household's number come up in the conscription lottery.[105] The documents indicate that many Voshchazhnikovo serfs who purchased serf labourers had precisely this in mind. Vasily Kotkov, for instance, purchased a serf labourer in 1844, 'intending, after some time, to send him to the army for [his] family'.[106] The 1816 soul revision for Voshchazhnikovo village lists fifteen such 'serf labourers', thirteen of whom had been sent to the army within three years of purchase.[107] The 1834 revision counts four such persons, all of whom were eventually conscripted.[108] Unfortunately, the documents offer no prices related to these purchases. In fact, the purchase of substitute military recruits was a fairly widespread phenomenon in pre-Emancipation Russia.[109] What is interesting about this practice at Voshchazhnikovo is that serfs were explicitly using these substitutes to meet their labour demands before sending them to the army.

---

[103] 'kupit' cheloveka', in RGADA, f. 1287, op. 3 ed. khr. 1435 ('Petition from Shalkov brothers, 1839'). The Shalkovs were classified as 'second rank' according to the wealth classification scheme designed by the Sheremetyevs and outlined above.

[104] RGADA, f. 1287, op. 3, ed. khr. 1563, l. 3 ('Petition regarding land purchase, 1840').

[105] Estates were obligated to provide serf recruits for the army, as discussed in chapter 4.

[106] 'imeem … my nakupnogo na imia Ego Siiatel'stva grafa cheloveka … koego po vyder-zhaniiu godichnago vremeni namereny zdat' za semeistvo v rekruty', in RGADA, f. 1287, op. 3, ed. khr. 1635, l. 60 ('Communal resolutions, 1844').

[107] GAYaO, f. 100, op. 8, d. 647 ('Soul revision, 1816').

[108] RGADA, f. 1287, op. 3, ed. khr. 2553 ('Soul revision, 1834'). It is interesting that the number of purchased labourers drops off so steeply between the 1816 and 1834 revisions. This may be some indication that the purchase of serf labourers was more common at times when conscription levies were high.

[109] This practice was common, for instance, on the Gagarins' Manuilovskoe estate, studied by Bohac. Bohac, 'The "mir"', esp. pp. 657–8. See also the discussion in Moon, *The Russian peasantry*, pp. 209–10.

Voshchazhnikovo serfs had a number of ways at their disposal, then, to meet their labour demands; hiring outsiders as live-in servants was only one of them. And, while the available data do not indicate the relative prevalence of each form of hired labour, they do suggest that a substantial number of estate serfs employed hired labourers. The inventories of households for the village of Voshchazhnikovo tell us that in 1832 some 20 per cent of serf households used hired labour to cultivate their land.[110] The local manufactories in this village also employed labourers.[111] And, although no inventories have survived for the other twenty-nine villages on the estate, references in other source materials (such as passport lists and petitions) indicate that households in these settlements also hired servants and purchased serf labourers. There were also two distilleries, a second paper factory, a textile manufactory, and at least one mill in the villages, all of which were noted in the documents as using hired labour.[112]

6.2   Outmigration

This chapter has so far been focused on the demand for hired labour on the Voshchazhnikovo estate. But what about the supply of labour on the estate? As discussed earlier in this chapter, some serfs from Voshchazhnikovo were recorded as earning their livings as servants or labourers. Most of these were resident on the Voshchazhnikovo estate, working for other Voshchazhnikovo serfs. But there were also Voshchazhnikovo serfs who left the estate to engage in wage labour in other localities. These serfs, like those who came into Voshchazhnikovo, were required to obtain passports from the estate authorities before they could leave. The officials kept annual lists recording the names of those who left the estate. These lists do not provide nearly as much information as those compiled for incoming servants. In most cases they note only the serf's name, village of residence, destination, and length of stay. A departing serf was often required to have a sponsor from the estate population – that is, some person, usually another serf, who would vouch for the migrant and guarantee his or her eventual return. The first names and patronymics of sponsors are provided in some of the lists, but surnames appear only rarely, ruling out any sort of record linkage.

---

[110] 36 of 175 households. These figures were derived from data in the inventories of households, RGADA, f. 1287, op. 3, ed. khr. 1143 ('Inventories of households, 1832/8').

[111] RGADA, f. 1287, op. 3, ed. khr. 1119, ll. 1–4 ('Report on estate manufactories').

[112] Information on the distilleries and the paper factory is in *ibid.*; the textile manufactory is discussed in Shchepetov, *Iz zhizni krepostnykh*, pp. 17–18; hired servants for the mill are mentioned in RGADA, f. 1287, op. 271, l. 20 ('Passport lists, 1762').

Table 6.3. *Total number of passports issued to Voshchazhnikovo estate serfs and proportion issued to serfs from the village of Voshchazhnikovo, 1760–1860*

	1760	1762	1825	1832	1834	1859	1860
Total passports	221	240	310	344	258	257	278
Voshchazhnikovo (N)	—	44	104	103	94	78	—
Voshchazhnikovo (%)	—	18.3	33.5	29.9	36.4	30.4	—

Sources: RGADA, f. 1287, op. 3, ed. khr. 262 ('Passport lists, 1760'), ed. khr. 272 ('Passport lists, 1762'), ed. khr. 957 ('Passport lists, 1825'), ed. khr. 1158 ('Passport lists, 1832'), ed. khr. 1246 ('Passport lists, 1834'), and ed. khr. 2390 ('Passport lists, 1859–60').

Lists for the years 1760, 1762, 1825, 1832, 1834, 1859, and 1860 have survived. The total number of passports issued to estate serfs is given for each of these years, while five of the seven lists also show how many passports were issued to serfs from the village of Voshchazhnikovo as opposed to those from smaller villages on the estate. A summary appears in Table 6.3.

The passport data indicate that the Voshchazhnikovo estate exported more labour than it imported. More than three times as many serfs left Voshchazhnikovo in 1762 as came in to work on the estate from outside; in 1825, there were more than four times as many serfs going out as there were coming in. In most years (except 1762), roughly one third of those who left were from the village of Voshchazhnikovo, proportionate to that village's share of the estate population.

Most serfs who left Voshchazhnikovo apparently went to cities rather than neighbouring estates to find work. The language used in passport letters suggests that Voshchazhnikovo serfs were given more freedom of movement than the serfs who came into the estate as servants. For instance, where most of the in-migrants at Voshchazhnikovo had been granted permission to 'earn a living within 30 versts' of their estates of origin, Voshchazhnikovo serfs were granted permission to 'earn a living in various cities'.[113] Occasionally, serfs were granted passports for travel to one particular city. Cities mentioned in passport lists include Moscow, St Petersburg, Kronshtat, Rostov Velikii, Yaroslavl', Vyborg, Narva, Helsinki, Riga, and Odessa. There are very few references in the passport lists to rural destinations. In 1762, two serfs were granted permission to

[113] 'otpushchen dlia prokormleniia v raznye goroda'. See letters in RGADA, f. 1287, op. 3, ed. khr. 262 ('Passport lists, 1760') and 272 ('Passport lists, 1762').

seek employment 'within 30 versts' of the Voshchazhnikovo estate.[114] In 1834, two serfs were granted permission to work on Iukhot estate, a Sheremetyev estate in the Uglich district of Yaroslavl' province. That same year, another serf was permitted to seek employment on the Sheremetyevs' Ivanovo estate in Vladimir province.[115] All other entries in the lists suggest urban destinations.

Why did so many serfs from Voshchazhnikovo go to work in cities instead of working as servants or labourers on other estates? Like migrants from other societies, Russian peasants are thought to have used social networks to help them find work in faraway destinations. A number of historians who have written about migration to cities in nineteenth-century Russia have stressed the importance of *zemliachestvo*, the bond that is supposed to have existed among peasant migrants from the same region.[116] Social networks based on *zemliachestvo* are thought to have underpinned chain migration in this period, resulting in certain forms of regional specialisation in nineteenth-century Russian cities. For instance, serfs from a particular district in Tver' province who found work as builders in St Petersburg, told others, upon returning to their villages, about the availability of work in the building industry, and the wages they might earn. These serf migrants might even offer to secure employment for friends and relatives who wished to work in St Petersburg. These new recruits told their friends and relatives, and so on. Before long, this particular district became known for its migrant builders. In this way, networks based on *zemliachestvo* are thought to have helped serfs from particular regions to secure employment in advance, or, at the very least, to have reduced the information costs involved in finding work in a faraway place.[117]

Most discussions of *zemliachestvo* networks and chain migration focus on regional networks at the provincial or district level. The documents for Voshchazhnikovo suggest that even smaller geographical entities, such as the estate, may have fostered networks which serfs used to secure outside

---

[114] RGADA, f. 1287, op. 3, ed. khr. 272, ll. 1, 15 ('Passport lists, 1762').

[115] RGADA, f. 1287, op. 3, ed. khr. 1246, entry ('Passport lists, 1834').

[116] See discussions in R. E. Johnson, *Peasant and proletarian* (New Brunswick, NJ, 1979); E. Ekonomakis, *From peasant to Petersburger* (London and New York, 1998); Morrison, 'Trading peasants'; Engel, *Between the fields and the city*; Burds, *Peasant dreams*.

[117] Similar forms of chain migration have been observed in other societies. See, for instance, the discussion of migrants to early twentieth-century Paris in P. E. Ogden and S. W. C. Winchester, 'The residential segregation of provincial migrants in Paris in 1911', *Transactions of the Institute of British Geographers* 65 (July 1975), pp. 29–44, esp. pp. 33–4. On nineteenth-century Germany, see S. Wegge, 'Chain migration and information networks: evidence from nineteenth-century Hesse-Cassel', *Journal of Economic History* 58 (4) (1998), pp. 957–86.

employment. Although serfs from Voshchazhnikovo were not known for any particular specialism, those who worked as craftsmen, servants, or apprentices in cities may have been able, through their urban networks, to secure city jobs for friends and relatives from the estate. While there are no explicit references in the sources to this type of *zemliachestvo*, there are sporadic references to urban networks comprised of Voshchazhnikovo serfs.[118] It is possible that other Sheremetyev estate archives contain more comprehensive information about migrant serfs, which could shed additional light on urban networks and the role they played in helping other estate serfs to obtain work, housing, credit, or poor relief in urban areas.

Similar networks may also have helped serfs to find jobs in rural areas. The passport lists for in-migrants working at Voshchazhnikovo indicate clusters of estates in Rostov district from which servants and labourers came. For instance, in the 1746 list, 9 servants came from the estate of the Borisogleb monastery and another 5 from the estate of Ivan Ryboltovskii.[119] In 1762, 15 servants came from the estate of the Borisogleb monastery, 4 from the estate of Aleksei Naumov, and another 4 from the estate of Semyon Saltykov. The estate of Prince Pyotr Shekhovskii and that of Yakov Korobovskii also sent several servants to Voshchazhnikovo that year.[120] This regional 'clustering' phenomenon was even more pronounced in the 1820 list, where roughly half of the servants working at Voshchazhnikovo (39 of 72) were said to have come from the estate of the Marschallin Mar'ia Zherebtsova in Kaminskii district.[121] A more detailed study of rural labour markets might consider the extent to which local and regional networks influenced the structure of the hiring market. Why, for instance, did so many serfs come to Voshchazhnikovo from Kaminskii district in the nineteenth century? Why were there no servants from this area in the eighteenth century? While these questions are beyond the scope of the present study, the documents for Voshchazhnikovo indicate that there are sources available which could be used to explore these issues in greater detail.

Most serfs who left the estate, like most of those who came in as servants, were male. In 1760, only one woman was granted permission to work off the estate; in 1762, there were three women on the list. These

---

[118] In response to a request for poor relief from a Voshchazhnikovo serf living in St Petersburg, the commune demanded that the petitioner seek assistance from the Voshchazhnikovo community in St Petersburg rather than from those living on the estate. In RGADA, f. 1287, op. 3, ed. khr. 1635, ll. 45–6 ('Communal resolutions, 1844').

[119] RGADA, f. 1287, op. 3, ed. khr. 131 ('Passport lists, 1746').

[120] RGADA, f. 1287, op. 3, ed. khr. 271 ('Passport lists, 1762').

[121] RGADA, f. 1287, op. 3, ed. khr. 776 ('Passport lists, 1820').

Table 6.4. *Number of female passport recipients from the village of Voshchazhnikovo, and their marital status, 1825–59*

	1825	1832	1834	1859
Total passports	104	106	94	78
Females	17	20	14	15
Married	7	8	5	5
Widowed	7	4	5	5
Single	0	4	4	3
Unknown	3	4	0	2

Sources: RGADA, f. 1287, op. 3, ed. khr. 957 ('Passport lists, 1825'), ed. khr. 1158 ('Passport lists, 1832'), ed. khr. 1246 ('Passport lists, 1834'), and ed. khr. 2390 ('Passport lists, 1859–60').

figures seem to have increased somewhat in the nineteenth century, though the figures provided for the later period are only for the village of Voshchazhnikovo rather than the whole estate. The 1860 list, unfortunately, provides no information about the sex of migrants. The data from the four later lists are summarised in Table 6.4.

According to these data, most of the women who left the estate were either married or widowed. The few single women given permission to leave the estate in 1834 were either travelling with family members or intending to join family members at their destination. For example, Matryona and Aleksandra Balisheva, two of the unmarried women on the list, were travelling with their widowed mother, Avdot'ia Balisheva, to St Petersburg.[122] Another single woman, Aleksandra Pavlova, was travelling to St Petersburg to join her brothers, who worked there.[123] There is somewhat less information available about the unmarried females in the 1832 and 1859 lists. Linking passport data with information in the soul revisions makes it possible to establish ages for some of the single women who left the estate during these years. Anna Zhukova, an unmarried female who travelled to St Petersburg in 1832 with her mother, the widowed Mar'ia Zhukova, was 46 years old. Praskov'ia Deulina, another unmarried female who went to St Petersburg that year, was 69 years old.[124] Alimpiada Pugina, an unmarried woman who was granted a

[122] RGADA, f. 1287, op. 3, ed. khr. 1246, entries 164, 165, 166 ('Passport lists, 1834').

[123] *Ibid.*, entry 182. This information was obtained by linking the passport lists with the inventories of households, RGADA, f. 1287, op. 3, ed. khr. 1143, l. In the inventory for 1832, it is noted that Aleksandra Pavlova's brothers (her parents had died) were living permanently in St Petersburg.

[124] Ages were obtained by linking RGADA, f. 1287, op. 3, ed. khr. 1158, ll. 6, 8 ('Passport lists, 1832') with RGADA, f. 1287, op. 3, ed. khr. 1143 ('Inventories of households, 1832').

passport in 1859, was 38 years old. Another single woman travelling in 1859, Elizaveta Chernikhina, was 34 years old.[125] Again, though there are no explicit references in the documents to limitations on the mobility of female serfs, the passport lists for out-migrants suggest that women – especially young and unmarried women – were more constrained in their movements than men.[126] Furthermore, it seems likely that these constraints were imposed by landlords rather than peasants' own social norms, since, as several recent studies have established, Russian peasant women began moving into cities in large numbers after serfdom was abolished in 1861.[127]

The only other piece of information given in these lists is the length of time for which the passports were valid. This information is provided most systematically in the lists for 1825, 1832, and 1834. Most passports in these lists were granted for either one year or one month. While some passports were issued for 'half a year' or '20 days' or 'two months', this was apparently less common. In 1825, 80 of 104 passports issued to serfs in Voshchazhnikovo village were valid for one year. This figure declined somewhat in subsequent years. In 1832, 54 of 106 passports were for one year, 32 were issued for one month, and 6 were issued 'without any time limits'. The remaining 14 passports specify no time limit. In 1834, 55 of 94 passports were issued for one year, while the remaining 39 were for one month. The decline in the number of year-long passports does not necessarily imply that fewer serfs were absent from the estate for long periods of time during the 1830s. It was possible for Voshchazhnikovo serfs to obtain more than one month-long pass during the course of the year. In some of the lists, certain names indeed come up several times. A one-month passport was issued to Mikhail Dolodanov in January of 1832, and then again in August of the same year. Andrei Murav'ev received a one-month passport in February 1832, and another in April.[128] Ivan Fedoseyev received one-month passports in January and July of 1834. One-month passports were issued to Aleksei Titov in January and May of that same year.[129] Similarly, Aleksandra Rukovishnikova received a one-month passport in May of 1859 and another in December.[130]

[125] Ages were obtained by linking RGADA, f. 1287, op. 3, ed. khr. 2390, ll. 12, 23 ('Passport lists, 1859'), with GAYaO, f. 100, op. 8, d. 2656 ('Soul revision, 1858').

[126] The findings for Voshchazhnikovo are consistent with those of other studies of serf migration in this period. Fyodorov, *Pomeshchich'i krest'iane*, pp. 209–10; Gorshkov, 'Serfs on the move', pp. 642–3.

[127] See, for instance, Engel, *Between the fields and the city*; Burds, *Peasant dreams*; R. Glickman, *Russian factory women: workplace and society, 1880–1914* (Berkeley and Los Angeles, 1984).

[128] RGADA, f. 1287, op. 3, ed. khr. 1158 ('Passport lists, 1832').

[129] RGADA, f. 1287, op. 3, ed. khr. 1246 ('Passport lists, 1834').

[130] RGADA, f. 1287, op. 3, ed. khr. 2390 ('Passport lists, 1859').

There is thus abundant evidence of serf participation in labour markets on the Voshchazhnikovo estate. Unfortunately, there is little information about the wages of these labourers. Wage data are difficult to find for any pre-industrial society; given the fragmentary nature of the archival documents, it is not surprising they do not exist for Voshchazhnikovo. All we have are sporadic references to earnings in a few of the documents generated by the estate administration. The landlords' instructions for 1796, for instance, note that unmarried females must also pay *obrok* since 'it is well known that women in these parts can earn 15 to 25 roubles per year' in textile production.[131] The 1858 descriptions of estates states that agricultural labourers were paid 16 silver roubles per *desiatina* of rye cultivated, 10 silver roubles per *desiatina* of barley, and 10 silver roubles per *desiatina* of hay.[132] This tells us very little, though, since we have no idea how many *desiatiny* the average labourer worked per season. The descriptions of estate manufactories are similarly vague. The paper manufactory run by Dmitri Slasnikov was reported to have spent a total of 1,200 roubles per year on hired labour. But officials said very little about how this was broken down, noting only that there were roughly thirty employees, some of them possibly not full time.[133] The documents also mention payments to serf labourers for specific jobs, such as the 100 roubles per year paid to the serf Ivan Buliakov for keeping the roads clean, or the 1 rouble per *sazhen'* paid to Nikolai Povalikhin for painting estate buildings.[134] While these examples are valuable, they tell us little about the actual earnings of wage labourers, since we have virtually no information about how much time people spent working and how many different jobs they did.

Rural labour markets are often viewed as a way for households to compensate for cyclical imbalances in labour. When children were too young to contribute labour, households could hire servants. A household containing 'surplus' labour could sell that labour on the market. The evidence for Voshchazhnikovo suggests that some households may have been using labour markets in this way. For instance, Vasily Konopliev, age 44, and his wife Avdot'ia, age 38, lived alone and hired labourers to work their communal land.[135] Yegor Dolodanov and his wife, who were both in their thirties and had only one young daughter, also hired labourers to work their allotment.[136] Similarly, Andrei Pugin and his wife, whose only son was just 6 years old, used hired labour to work their land.[137]

[131] RGADA, f. 1287, op. 3, ed. khr. 555, l. 26 ('Instructions, 1796/1800').
[132] RGADA, f. 1287, op. 3, ed. khr. 2320, point 9 ('Descriptions of estates, 1858').
[133] RGADA, f. 1287, op. 3, ed. khr. 1119 ('Report on estate manufactories').
[134] RGADA, f. 1287, op. 3, ed. khr. 1325, ll. 43 and 37 ('Communal resolutions, 1837').
[135] RGADA, f. 1287, op. 3, ed. khr. 1143, l. 30 ('Inventories of households, 1832/8').
[136] *Ibid.*, l. 41.   [137] *Ibid.*, l. 73.

In other cases, though, the use of labour markets involved more complex economic calculations. Of the thirty-six households that hired labour to work their communal lands, thirty-one contained men who were themselves engaged in full-time wage labour. This was not the sort of 'like for like' exchange found in early modern northwest Europe, where households sent young adults out to work as servants and hired servants of their own to replace them. The men in these households at Voshchazhnikovo were not working as agricultural labourers, but as traders, servants, apprentices to craftsmen and merchants in cities, or operators of local manufactories. Aleksandr and Ivan Aladin, for instance, worked as servants in St Petersburg while hired labourers worked their household's communal holding.[138] Egor and Nikolai Golovar'ev also worked as servants in St Petersburg and hired labourers to cultivate their communal allotment.[139] Aleksei Titov and his sons operated a leather manufactory behind their house, and used hired labour to work their land.[140] In this way, local labour markets enabled serfs to allocate their own time and labour to occupations they thought would bring them the highest returns. A significant number of households at Voshchazhnikovo perceived that they were better off meeting their feudal obligations through the use of hired labour than cultivating their communal allotments themselves and forgoing (higher) earnings in other occupations. Local labour markets made such trade-offs possible. In addition, they offered poorer serfs who could not afford to take on a communal allotment the possibility of earning a living.

6.3   Labour markets and the role of institutions

The extent to which Russian peasants participated in labour markets in this period is often thought to have been determined mainly by geography. It is widely held that wage labour was more prevalent in the Central Industrial Region than in the southern Central Black Earth Region, and that this was due to the adverse ecological conditions that are supposed to have made agriculture less profitable in the northern provinces. According to this view, peasants took advantage of proximity to towns and cities, engaging seasonally in crafts, trade, and rural industry to supplement their earnings, since the short growing season and infertile soil made it impossible to live from agriculture alone. Implicit in this view is the assumption that labour markets were already established in the Central Industrial Region, and that serfs were merely exploiting these exogenous opportunities.

---

[138] *Ibid.*, l. 42.   [139] *Ibid.*, ll. 62–3.   [140] *Ibid.*, ll. 72–3.

The case of Voshchazhnikovo, however, highlights the impact of local institutions on labour markets, casting doubt on purely geographical, or ecological, explanations for economic variation. It is true that the Sheremetyevs allowed their serfs to engage in markets, perhaps even to a greater extent than other landlords. They allowed their serfs to work as migrant labourers in towns and cities throughout European Russia, and permitted them to hire labourers to work their communal allotments or, as discussed in chapter 4, to perform their labour obligations. But landlords like the Sheremetyevs did more than simply allow their serfs to take advantage of existing wage labour opportunities. They influenced the shape of local markets by, for instance, permitting their serfs to establish manufacturing and retail enterprises of various sorts, for which hired labour was required. In other words, serfs on the Voshchazhnikovo estate were not simply exploiting existing labour markets. Their tanneries and brick manufactories and paper mills were contributing to these markets by creating a demand for wage labour.

The Sheremetyevs not only shaped markets by permitting serfs to engage in them, they also shaped them by constraining that participation, from which they also benefited. The landlords affected the price of labour by levying fees on travel permits for migrant labourers, collecting annual taxes from craftsmen and owners of rural industries, and imposing registration costs on those who hired labourers. They insisted that those who engaged full time in wage work should still cultivate their communal allotments, which created a local market for agricultural labour. The most restrictive policies were those concerning female labour force participation. Women were rarely allowed to leave the estate, as we have seen, and serfs wishing to hire female labourers, especially on long-term contracts, required special permission. Women were permitted to engage in wage work locally, but estate restrictions constrained their choices and probably depressed their wages by denying them access to outside options.

This is not to suggest that geography played no role at all. The transition from labour to cash rents in this region does seem to indicate that landlords perceived that agriculture was not the highest-return employment for serf labour. But geography can hardly be the whole story when it was, after all, possible to make agriculture quite profitable in this ecologically unpromising region. Around Rostov there was a thriving commercial gardening industry, which expanded significantly over the course of the nineteenth century as towns expanded and urban demand for produce increased.[141] Agrarian *Intensitätsinseln* existed around

---

[141] Fyodorov, 'Vozniknovenie'.

Moscow and St Petersburg just as they did around early modern central and western European cities.[142] Although grain yields were modest at best, grain prices remained low, as we will see in chapter 8, suggesting that grain was in plentiful supply. This, too, may have been an artefact of institutional arrangements, as the Sheremetyevs – and probably other landlords in the region – required their serfs to cultivate communal allotments even when returns to serf labour were clearly higher in other occupations. Thus the evidence for Voshchazhnikovo strongly suggests that the evolution of institutions, and the incentive structures they established, contributed more to economic outcomes in imperial Russia than can be accounted for by geographical constraints.

---

[142] V. A. Fyodorov, 'Torgovoe zemledelie krest'ian Moskovskoi gubernii v pervoi polovine XIX v.', *Vestnik moskovskogo universiteta* 8 (2003), pp. 93–105; also in Morrison, '*Trading peasants*', pp. 231–4. For Europe, see J. de Vries, *The economy of Europe in an age of crisis 1600–1750* (Cambridge, 1976), esp. p. 34.

7   Credit and savings

The administrative framework that evolved under the Sheremetyevs not only allowed serfs to participate in markets in land and labour, it also enabled them to engage in credit transactions and accumulate savings. Credit markets have at least three important functions: for lenders, they provide opportunities for preserving the value of their savings; for borrowers, they afford a means for smoothing consumption over time, on the one hand, and they supply capital for investment, on the other. Credit markets enable lenders to put unused surpluses to work, while enabling borrowers to consume or invest now and pay later.[1] Until recently, these functions were considered to be of importance only in economically advanced societies of the past century or two.[2] We now know, however, that credit markets are of equal, if not even greater, importance in developing societies.[3]

Rural credit markets in Russia have received even less attention than markets in land and labour.[4] This may be at \least partly due to the paucity of sources; references to credit transactions are not always readily apparent in the archival records for Russian estates.[5] But the neglect of rural

---

[1] 'The avenue of borrowing allows risk-averse households to smooth their consumption across time and contingencies. In short, the possibility of smoothing consumption through borrowing allows households to engage in high-risk activities with large expected returns.' In P. Dasgupta, *An inquiry into well-being and destitution* (Oxford, 1993), p. 252.

[2] See the discussion in P. T. Hoffman, G. Postel-Vinay, and J.-L. Rosenthal, 'Information and economic history: how the credit market in old regime Paris forces us to rethink the transition to capitalism', *American Historical Review* 104 (1) (1999), esp. pp. 69–75.

[3] A. Gill, *Rural credit markets: financial sector reforms and the informal lenders* (New Delhi, 2000), esp. chapters 1 and 2. See also World Bank, *World development report 1989: financial systems and development* (Oxford, 1989), pp. 25–40.

[4] Tarlovskaia notes that credit was critical to the pre-industrial Russian economy and points out that, despite its importance, 'not a single pre-revolutionary study is devoted to the question of money lending . . . and in the Soviet historiography there is only one article devoted entirely to this issue'. In V. R. Tarlovskaia, 'Rostovshchicheskie operatsii moskovskikh kuptsov i torgovykh krest'ian v nachale XVIII v.', *Vestnik moskovskogo universiteta ser. istoriia* 3 (1977), pp. 44–5.

[5] A system of written credit contracts is useful, as is a formal system of dispute resolution (which generated written records), since many credit transactions only become visible once they have broken down. Voshchazhnikovo had both of these, but, as we will see, significant challenges still exist due to the number and quality of surviving records.

credit markets is reinforced by the prevailing view of Russian peasants as dependent on communal institutions for insurance and welfare provision. Through its land-repartitioning activities, the commune is supposed to have guaranteed a minimum level of subsistence to its member households. Households in temporary financial straits were supposed to have been provided for by the commune through communal grain reserves, money, and even voluntary labour services (whereby wealthier households, for instance, assisted their poorer neighbours with the cultivation of their communal allotments).[6] This is consistent with the 'moral economy' view of peasant society, which maintains that peasants preferred collectivist risk-minimisation strategies – such as the repartitioning of communally held land – to the riskier individualistic strategies offered by land, labour, and credit markets. According to this view, peasants were reluctant to engage in any types of markets and did so only when desperate.[7]

Credit markets have no role in the original Chayanovian theory of the peasant economy. While Chayanov admitted that the demographic constraints on the peasant household economy might be loosened where land markets existed, he assumed that credit, like hired labour, was not available to peasants. In both the moral economy view and the original Chayanovian theory, peasants are assumed to have 'culturally defined income targets' centred on subsistence. Peasants, according to this view, were less interested in material wealth than in maximising leisure and status.[8] Credit, in such cases, would not have been required to smooth consumption, since consumption patterns were fairly uniform and limited to subsistence requirements. Any household unable to meet its subsistence needs, by this argument, would have received assistance from the community. Nor would there have been opportunities for investment, since a subsistence-oriented economy would not have generated adequate surpluses. In Russia, as Hoch has argued, 'the practice of land redistribution, and the egalitarian distribution of wealth that resulted, limited the accumulation of reserves and provided a substantial disincentive for

---

[6] Moon, *The Russian peasantry*, pp. 226–7; Worobec, *Peasant Russia*, pp. 23–4.

[7] This was clearly not the case in western European peasant societies, where, as research has shown, credit markets were widespread well before industrialisation. C. Briggs, *Credit and village society in fourteenth-century England* (Oxford, 2009); Sreenivasan, *The peasants of Ottobeuren*, esp. chapter 4; J.-L. Rosenthal, 'Rural credit markets and aggregate shocks: the experience of Nuits St. Georges, 1756–1776', *Journal of Economy History* 54 (1994), pp. 288–306.

[8] See, for instance, the discussion in B. N. Mironov, 'Work and rest in the peasant economy of European Russia in the 19th and early 20th centuries', in I. Blanchard (ed.), *Labour and leisure in historical perspective: thirteenth to the twentieth centuries* (Stuttgart, 1994), pp. 55–64, esp. p. 63.

capital investment'.[9] Since there was always the chance that some portion of a household's arable land would be taken away after some time and given to another household, serfs were reluctant to make long-term investments.

We have already seen that the commune at Voshchazhnikovo did not operate in such a way as to distribute available resources equally among member households. On this estate, land was allocated mainly to those who could pay for it, rather than those who needed it, as shown by the number of middling and prosperous households who leased out their communal lands to others and engaged exclusively in non-agricultural activities. Furthermore, the commune was reluctant to provide relief for the poor, and often needed to be forced to do so by seigneurial officials. Conditions at Voshchazhnikovo, then, do not meet the Chayanovian conditions for the absence of a demand for credit. So it should not surprise us to find that there was not only a demand but also a supply, and that, along with land and labour markets, credit markets were fairly well established in the period covered by this study.

7.1   Credit transactions

The evidence for credit markets at Voshchazhnikovo is scattered and incomplete, unfortunately, making any kind of rigorous quantitative analysis unfeasible. Much of the evidence presented here is qualitative, and serves mainly to establish that credit markets did exist in this region, and that they were fairly well institutionalised. One of the main sources of information about credit is the formal loan contracts concluded by serfs and recorded in annual registers kept by the estate administration. However, only 33 credit contracts have survived, and these date from scattered years: 1793 (7 contracts), 1826 (5 contracts), 1831 (6 contracts), 1832 (10 contracts), and 1840 (5 contracts).[10] Furthermore, the surviving sets are clearly incomplete. The registers either break off at some point in the middle of the year (1840, for instance, is incomplete after the first entry in June), or contain missing pages throughout, with some even breaking off in the middle of an entry. Such deficiencies in the surviving archival records make it impossible to speculate about the average annual number of credit contracts registered with the authorities, let alone about the total volume of credit transactions in this community.

---

[9] Hoch, 'The serf economy', p. 316.
[10] RGADA, f. 1287, op. 3, ed. khr. 612 (1793), ed. khr. 977 (1826), ed. khr. 1108 (1831), ed. khr. 1155 (1832), ed. khr. 1523 (1840).

Table 7.1. *Number of surviving contracts by size of loan,*
1793–1840[a]

Loan amount	N	%
< 100 roubles	3	9
100 to 199	10	30
200 to 299	7	21
300 to 399	3	9
400 to 499	2	6
≥ 500	6[b]	19
Not given	2	6
Total	33	100

[a] Only five sets of contracts survived for this period.
[b] 2 of these loans were > 1,000 roubles.
Sources: RGADA, f. 1287, op. 3, ed. khr. 612 ('Serf contracts, 1793'), ed. khr.
977 ('Serf contracts, 1826'), ed. khr. 1108 ('Serf contracts, 1831'), ed. khr.
1155 ('Serf contracts, 1832'), ed. khr. 1523 ('Serf contracts, 1840').

We do have additional evidence for credit transactions, though, such as the eighty-eight petitions regarding disputes over credit that have survived over the period 1790–1840. Of course, these disputed transactions represent only a small proportion of total borrowing, since most agreements probably did not break down and only a small proportion of those that did would have made it to the landlord's Petersburg office. References to credit transactions also appear in other sources such as household inventories, probate inventories, and estate correspondence.[11] Moreover, as we will see, it seems likely that there were informal credit arrangements among serfs for which no estate records were kept.

The surviving credit contracts for Voshchazhnikovo were formal agreements between serfs, which, like contracts for land and property purchases, were registered with the landlord's central administration. They covered a variety of transaction types – including cash loans and mortgages – involving sums ranging from 25 to 1,500 roubles. Table 7.1 provides a breakdown of the surviving contracts by size of loan. Most loans in these surviving contracts were fairly substantial, with over 60 per

[11] For example, in an 1836 inventory of a serf woman's possessions, drawn up in the context of a dispute over dowry, a piece of jewelry is said to have been put up as collateral for a loan. The loan is not recorded in any of the surviving credit documents. Similarly, in estate correspondence from 1846, there is a reference to a loan made by the serf Kriuchkov to the serf Pyotr Chernikhin, but there is no record of this loan in the surviving contracts and petitions. RGADA, f. 1287, op. 3, ed. khr. 1713, l. 43 ('Correspondence between St Petersburg office and estate officials, 1846').

cent larger than 200 roubles. To place these sums in perspective, an annual income of 200 roubles put a serf squarely in the middling stratum on this estate. The under-representation of small loans may have been related to the costs of registration, to be discussed shortly.

The credit contracts were characterised by a considerable degree of variation. Contracts for the year 1793, for instance, tell us that the Voshchazhnikovo serf Ivan Yablokov borrowed 200 roubles from Kozma Smirnov, to be paid back within five months with 10 per cent interest.[12] That same year, the serf Ivan Borisov, from the village of Malakhovo, borrowed 400 roubles from the serf widow Avdot'ia Sakharova (no terms specified).[13] In 1831 the Voshchazhnikovo serf Grigory Sytinskii borrowed 1,200 roubles from Vasily Kriuchkov, to be paid back at 150 roubles per year (no interest rate specified).[14] That same year, Ivan Arnautov purchased a piece of privately held land from the serf Martin Bauman for 175 roubles, paying 25 roubles up front and agreeing to pay the remaining 150 to Bauman at an annual interest rate of 5 per cent (no time period specified).[15] In 1832 Mikhail Stulov borrowed 600 roubles from Semyon Dolodanov to be repaid 'with interest'.[16] We even find formal contracts for smaller loans, such as the loan of 25 roubles made by Matvei Usachev to Boris Pavlov in 1831.[17]

Additional information about credit transactions can be derived from the numerous petitions to estate authorities. Of the 221 surviving petitions in the Voshchazhnikovo archive concerning disputes among serfs, 88 (roughly 40 per cent) were disputes over credit transactions.[18] In a petition from 1822, for instance, Dmitri Kalmykov and Stepan Sedel'nikov asked estate officials to force Dmitri Malyshev to pay back the 1,100 roubles they had lent him a year earlier.[19] In 1824, Timofei Savinkov, from the Sheremetyev estate of Iukhot, filed a petition demanding that the 550 roubles he had lent to the recently deceased Voshchazhnikovo serf Denis Aralov be paid back with interest by Denis's brother Vasily.[20] A

[12] RGADA, f. 1287, op. 3, ed. khr. 612, l. 1 ('Serf contracts, 1793').   [13] *Ibid.*, l. 9.
[14] RGADA, f. 1287, op. 3, ed. khr. 1108, entry no. 2 ('Serf contracts, 1831').
[15] *Ibid.*, entry 5.
[16] 's protsentami' in RGADA, f. 1287, op. 3, ed. khr. 1155 ('Serf contracts, 1832').
[17] RGADA, f. 1287, op. 3, ed. khr. 1108, entry 9 ('Serf contracts, 1831').
[18] The remaining 133 petitions involved disputes over inheritance, conscription practices, property transactions, and defamation. The total number of petitions in the archive is much greater than 221 (roughly 1,500), but only 221 deal explicitly with disputes. The others are mostly concerned with requests for permission to engage in various activities including the purchase of land or labourers, marriage, the setting up of an independent household, and the cutting of wood in the estate forests.
[19] RGADA, f. 1287, op. 3, ed. khr. 843 ('Petition regarding credit dispute, 1822').
[20] RGADA, f. 1287, op. 3, ed. khr. 911 ('Correspondence between St Petersburg administration and estate officials, 1824').

petition was filed in 1833 by the Uslavtsevo parish priest, Vladimir Vasiliev, requesting that the Voshchazhnikovo serf Ivan Pugin be made to repay the 1,614 roubles he owed to the church.[21] Mikhail Shkolnov petitioned the estate administration in 1835 to assist him in collecting a debt of 225 roubles from Grigory Kovin.[22]

7.2   Enforcement

The formalisation of credit agreements concluded by Voshchazhnikovo serfs involved a process similar to that for land transactions. A formal contract was drawn up, usually by an estate scribe. Once it had been signed by all parties to the agreement, it was notarised and registered with the provincial notarial office or the district court, as well as with the Sheremetyevs' central authorities.[23] And, as was the case with land transactions, fees were levied at each stage of the process: for drawing up a formal contract, for registering the contract with the central authorities, for obtaining copies of the contract in the case of a dispute, and even for registering the dispute itself. Each stage of the process required that a serf pay a price ranging from 50 kopecks to several roubles.[24]

At first glance such prices may not appear especially onerous, but they may have deterred poorer serfs who would have borrowed and lent smaller sums. Such fees would have discouraged the registration of small loans of only 10 roubles or so. This may to some extent explain why the loans formalised with registered contracts were fairly substantial, with fewer than 10 per cent being lower than 100 roubles. This explanation is lent further support by one of the few surviving probate inventories for Voshchazhnikovo, that for Kozma Popov, who left debts totalling over 9,000 roubles. Popov was not a poor serf. But the inventory of his debts is interesting nonetheless, since it provides details of formal loan contracts for substantial sums, as well as several 'loans made without a contract', ranging in size from 7 to 47 roubles.[25] That formal contracts existed for all

---

[21] RGADA, f. 1287, op. 3, ed. khr. 1178 ('Petition regarding credit dispute, 1833').

[22] RGADA, f. 1287, op. 3, ed. khr. 1227 ('Petition regarding credit dispute, 1835').

[23] The procedure for registering formal contracts changed frequently over the eighteenth century. For details, see the discussion in G. D. Kapustina, 'Zapisnye knigi Moskovskoi Krepostnoi Kontory kak istoricheskii istochnik pervaia chetvert' XVIII v.', in *Problemy istochnikovedeniia*, vol. VII (Moscow, 1959), pp. 216–73.

[24] This is an estimated range based on the prices noted on various documents (contracts, petitions, certificates). The prices do not appear to have been related to the sizes of loans; unfortunately, there is no document in the Voshchazhnikovo archive which explicitly outlines the system of fees for these services.

[25] RGADA, f. 1287, op. 3, ed. khr. 1133, l. 33 ('Petition regarding credit, 1832'). All creditors for small sums appear to have been local Voshchazhnikovo serfs.

the larger sums (ranging roughly from 100 to 1,200 roubles) might be interpreted as evidence that smaller loans were not worth formalising.

The credit transactions that appear in the Voshchazhnikovo sources are not unlike those described in the few existing studies of credit in this region in earlier periods. Evidence from registers (*zapisnye knigi*) kept in a Moscow notarial office (*moskovskaia krepostnaia kontora*) in the early eighteenth century indicates that merchants and trading peasants frequently formalised their credit transactions.[26] Borrowers and lenders from as far away as Nizhnyi Novgorod, Vologda, and Tambov registered their contracts in Moscow.[27] It was apparently quite straightforward to register a written contract, even for peasants. The difficulties, especially for serfs, concerned the enforcement of these agreements. The use of civil courts was restricted, as landlords had nearly complete jurisdiction over their serfs. As a result, landlord policy played a significant role in contract enforcement. On the Sheremetyev estates, credit agreements were enforced in much the same way as land and property transactions.

When a credit agreement was violated, the plaintiff petitioned the estate authorities, who then appointed investigators to examine the case. Copies of credit contracts were reviewed, and each person involved was given the opportunity to present his or her version of events. In some instances, the authorities would offer serfs the opportunity to meet with estate officials to work out an amicable solution to the disagreement. This was the case in the above-mentioned dispute between the serfs Timofei Savinkov and Vasily Aralov, who were called before estate officials to 'settle their dispute voluntarily'.[28] They did so, and the terms of the new agreement were recorded by the estate authorities, who promised to take action in the event of a subsequent breach of contract.[29] In other cases, estate authorities intervened directly to enforce the terms of a contract, sometimes going so far as to order the sale of a serf's property to satisfy his creditors. Voshchazhnikovo serfs who were found to have violated the terms of credit contracts could even be imprisoned or subjected to corporal punishment.[30]

---

[26] Tarlovskaia, 'Rostovshchicheskie operatsii'. A more detailed discussion of the *zapisnye knigi* is in Kapustina, 'Zapisnye knigi', pp. 216–73.

[27] Tarlovskaia, 'Rostovshchicheskie operatsii', p. 49.

[28] 'predostavit'' im raschest'sa dobrovol'no v protsentnykh den'gakh', in RGADA, f. 1287, op. 3, ed. khr. 911, l. 4 ('Correspondence between St Petersburg administration and estate officials, 1824').

[29] 'esli sego neispolniat'' to mozhet Savinkov iavit'sa v voshchazhnikovskoe votchinoe pravlenie, poruchiv onomu [protsentnye den'gi] rasschitat'', in *ibid.*, l. 4.

[30] As in the case of Ivan Tryshin, who, as noted in chapter 4, was imprisoned for failure to repay a debt to a serf from the Sheremetyevs' Iukhot estate. RGADA, f. 1287, op. 3, ed. khr. 661, l. 11 ('Punishments meted out to serfs, 1807').

There was also an established procedure for dealing with the creditors of serfs who died without paying their debts. Announcements were made at communal meetings and notices were placed in local and regional papers, asking creditors of the deceased to make themselves known to the estate administration, and to provide evidence for the debt, preferably in the form of a written contract.[31] The administration would then oversee payment of the debts. Where there were heirs, this process was usually fraught with acrimony. The sons of the deceased serf Nikolai Yablokov, for instance, resisted the estate administration's order that they pay off their father's debts – totalling over 3,000 roubles – with their inheritance.[32] When a serf died without heirs, his or her property was usually auctioned off in order to pay outstanding debts.[33]

That contracts were regularly enforced by estate authorities does not mean that credit transactions were without risk. For one thing, the juridical process was a lengthy one. The administration required time to carry out a thorough investigation. Before taking a decision, officials collected information about the petitioners, appointed investigators, and reviewed reports and depositions. Sometimes there were several rounds of inquiries and depositions. All rulings on credit cases were handed down by the central administration in St Petersburg, so documents had to travel between the estate and St Petersburg, a distance of 500 miles. In some cases it took well over a year for the authorities to rule on a credit case.[34] This gave indebted serfs ample time to hide or sell off their assets. The petition filed by Dmitri Kalmykov and Stepan Sedel'nikov, creditors of Dmitri Malyshev, suggests that this did occasionally happen. In their petition, the creditors complained that Malyshev, knowing that his business was in trouble and that he could not pay the 9,000 roubles he owed (including 1,100 to them), had taken advantage of the slow pace of the juridical proceedings by 'selling his trade inventory and marrying off his

---

[31] One of the creditors of serf Anna Shatilova sent copies of credit contracts to the estate management in response to an announcement he had seen in *Moskovskie Vedomosti* in May 1819. RGADA, f. 1287, op. 3, ed. khr. 729, l. 1 ('Petition regarding credit, 1819').

[32] RGADA, f. 1287, op. 3, ed. khr. 629 ('Petition regarding credit, 1795'). This document suggests that the legal battle between Yablokov's creditors and his heirs went on for over four years. It seems that the heirs were obligated to pay the debts in the end.

[33] Examples of such cases can be found in RGADA, f. 1287, op. 3, ed. khr. 629, 706, 729, 1133 (all are credit-related petitions).

[34] Sometimes it took the authorities several years to make a decision. The petition filed by Pyotr Saburov in 1818 regarding the 550 roubles owed him by Semyon Kolmykov was only finally resolved in 1820 (RGADA, f. 1287, op. 3, ed. khr. 706 ('Petition regarding credit, 1820')). A petition made in 1845 by Semyon Dolodanov, regarding a loan made to Vasily and Dmitri Dolodanov, was still under investigation in 1847 (RGADA, f. 1287, op. 3, ed. khr. 1764 ('Petition regarding credit, 1847')). See also the reference to the Yablokov case in n. 32 above.

son'.[35] The petitioners asked the officials to conduct an investigation immediately and, if necessary, to order the sale of Malyshev's personal belongings in order to meet his obligations.[36]

It was also possible for a serf to die without heirs and without enough in assets to cover outstanding debts. This is what happened in the case of Kozma Popov, who died in 1832 with outstanding debts worth 9,242 roubles 20 kopecks.[37] The estate administration sold his property, but was only able to raise 2,008 roubles 23 kopecks. So, in the end, each of Popov's twenty-six creditors received only 21.5 kopecks on the rouble.[38]

In most credit transactions the degree of risk was probably reflected in the interest rate, in conjunction with the form of collateral. Interest rates are not always mentioned in credit contracts; some contracts simply refer to 'interest payments' without any mention of a rate, while others make no mention of interest whatever. However, contracts that do contain explicit information on rates give the impression that they varied widely, apparently reflecting different levels of risk. The lowest rate mentioned in the credit contracts is 5 per cent, paid by the serf Martin Bauman on the 150 roubles advanced to him by Ivan Arnautov in 1831.[39] Several contracts mention rates of 10 per cent. Nikolai Yablokov, for instance, who borrowed 300 roubles from Kozma Smirnov in 1793, agreed to repay this sum within five months at 10 per cent.[40] In the same set of contracts there is a reference to a loan of unknown size made by Vasily Mikhailov, from the village of Uslavtsevo, that was to be repaid at 10 per cent.[41] In 1782, the serf Semyon Barin borrowed 900 roubles from Nikolai Yablokov to be repaid at 12 per cent.[42] The highest rate mentioned in the Voshchazhnikovo documents is 30 per cent, to be paid by Anna Shatilova on the 200 roubles she borrowed from the Ivanovo serf Ivan Kuvaev in 1818.[43] Shatilova had also borrowed over 700 roubles from the Ivanovo serf Afanasii Burymin at the same rate.[44]

---

[35] 'vospol'zovavshis' medlennostiu proizvodstva dela, uspel ves imeiushchiis'a u nego tovar rasprodat' i zhenit' syna svoego', in RGADA, f. 1287, op. 3, ed. khr. 843, l. 3 ('Petition regarding credit dispute, 1822').

[36] *Ibid.*, ll. 3–4.

[37] RGADA, f. 1287, op. 3, ed. khr. 1133, l. 1 ('Petition regarding credit, 1832').

[38] *Ibid.*, ll. 32–3.

[39] RGADA, f. 1287, op. 3, ed. khr. 1108, entry 5 ('Serf contracts, 1831').

[40] RGADA, f. 1287, op. 3, ed. khr. 612, l. 11 ('Serf contracts, 1793').   [41] *Ibid.*, l. 13.

[42] RGADA, f. 1287, op. 3, ed. khr. 588, l. 1 ('Petition regarding credit, 1792').

[43] RGADA, f. 1287, op. 3, ed. khr. 729, l. 25 ('Petition regarding credit, 1819').

[44] *Ibid.*, l. 25. It is not clear whether being female made Shatilova 'high risk', since there are no other female borrowers in the surviving documents with whom she might be compared. It is possible that the high rate of interest set by Kuvaev and Burymin was related to

Forms of collateral also varied across transactions. Privately held land was the most common form of collateral. In 1793, Ivan Yablokov borrowed 300 roubles from Kozma Alekseyev, offering as collateral a piece of privately held land in Uglich district.[45] Mikhail Stulov, who borrowed 600 roubles from Semyon Dolodanov in 1832, also offered a private holding as collateral.[46] Similarly, Mikhail Stepanov, who borrowed 435 roubles from Vasily Kriuchkov in 1840, put up an inherited private landholding as collateral.[47] Other forms of collateral included privately held buildings, trade inventory, and even grain. In 1831, Aleksandr Pyriaev borrowed over 500 roubles from Praskov'ia Kalinina, offering his house as collateral.[48] Ivan Pugin, whose family ran one of the estate paper manufactories, put up 50 *pood* (about 800 kilograms) of his inventory of white paper against a loan made to him by Aleksei Shalkov in 1832.[49] Aleksandr Dolodanov borrowed 110 roubles from Pyotr Dolodanov in 1832, offering as collateral the rye he had stored in the granary of Vasily Slasnikov.[50]

Collateral could be and occasionally was seized by authorities when debts were not repaid. The house put up by Aleksandr Pyriaev against the 500 roubles he borrowed from Praskov'ia Kalinina was repossessed when Pyraiev defaulted on the loan.[51] The privately held land put up by Dmitri Yablokov against the loan made to him by Aleksei Titov in 1830 was transferred to Titov in 1831 when Yablokov failed to meet the terms of their contract.[52]

Interest rates and collateral are not always mentioned in the Voshchazhnikovo credit contracts, which makes them hard to analyse systematically. While there are contracts in which both interest and collateral are mentioned, these are rare. Instead, we find contracts that refer only to interest (though they do not always specify the rate), contracts that mention only collateral, and still others which make no mention of either. It is unclear whether those not specifying terms of repayment were also unsecured. Interest payments might have been made in kind,[53] and the terms agreed to informally. This is often called 'hidden interest', and it has

---

the fact that Shatilova already had a number of outstanding debts. It would appear from the available range of credit-related documents that the likelihood of the same – very high – interest rate being charged coincidentally to the same person is very small.

[45] RGADA, f. 1287, op. 3, ed. khr. 612, l. 9 ('Serf contracts, 1793').
[46] RGADA, f. 1287, op. 3, ed. khr. 1155, l. 3 ('Serf contracts, 1832').
[47] RGADA, f. 1287, op. 3, ed. khr. 1523, entry 4 ('Serf contracts, 1840').
[48] RGADA, f. 1287, op. 3, ed. khr. 1108, entry 4 ('Serf contracts, 1831').
[49] RGADA, f. 1287, op. 3, ed. khr. 1155, l. 1 ('Serf contracts, 1832').
[50] *Ibid.*, l. 16.   [51] *Ibid.*, ll. 8–9.
[52] RGADA, f. 1287, op. 3, ed. khr. 1108, entries 9 and 10 ('Serf contracts, 1831').
[53] As in the examples quoted in the land market section above, where serfs pledged their labour services as payment for rented land.

been noted for a number of modern-day developing economies.[54] On the other hand, it seems odd that serfs would go to the trouble of formalising their contracts, without formalising the terms of repayment. It is possible that in some cases interest was simply included in the amount to be repaid. In a number of contracts for Voshchazhnikovo, the amount to be repaid is not a round figure, such as 200 roubles or 350 roubles, but a very specific amount, such as the '261 roubles' borrowed by Ivan Stulov[55] or the '356 roubles' borrowed by Dmitri Yablokov.[56] Similarly, Afanasii Burymin lent '747 roubles 20 kopecks' to Anna Shatilova in 1818.[57] Pyotr and Dmitri Dolodanov were to pay back the loan of '1,512 roubles' made to them by Anna Kalmykova in 1826.[58] And in a contract from 1832 it was noted that Mikhail Shetov owed '168 roubles 20 kopecks' to Vasily Slasnikov.[59] While it is possible that borrowers in these cases asked their creditors for very specific sums, it seems more likely that a fixed amount in interest was included in the figures reported in the contracts – especially since none of them mentions interest in any other form. But this is something we cannot determine with any degree of certainty, given the lack of uniformity in the contracts.

It does seem that the system of contract enforcement and intermediation in place on this estate substantially reduced the amount of risk involved in money lending, since the numerous credit transactions of Voshchazhnikovo serfs transcended social and geographical boundaries. Many of the examples mentioned above were taken from contracts in which both the lender and borrower were local serfs. But Voshchazhnikovo serfs also borrowed from serfs from other estates, merchants, and even landlords. In 1793, Ivan Borisov of Malakhovo (on the Voshchazhnikovo estate) borrowed 400 roubles from Avdot'ia Mikhailova, a serf widow from an estate belonging to Vladimir Orlov (in Yaroslavl' province).[60] Anna Shatilova borrowed nearly 1,000 roubles from serfs on the Sheremetyev estate of Ivanovo in Vladimir Province.[61] Denis Aralov borrowed 550 roubles in 1805 from Timofei Savinkov, a serf on the Sheremetyev estate of Iukhot, in Uglich district (Yaroslavl' province).[62] Kozma Popov borrowed 1,200 roubles in 1826 from the 'monastery serf'

[54] See discussion in D. Ray, *Development economics* (Princeton, 1998), pp. 563–4.
[55] RGADA, f. 1287, op. 3, ed. khr. 977, l. 2 ('Serf contracts, 1826').
[56] RGADA, f. 1287, op. 3, ed. khr. 1108, entry 10 ('Serf contracts, 1831').
[57] RGADA, f. 1287, op. 3, ed. khr. 729, l. 25 ('Petition regarding credit, 1819').
[58] RGADA, f. 1287, op. 3, ed. khr. 977, l. 5 ('Serf contracts, 1826').
[59] RGADA, f. 1287, op. 3, ed. khr. 1155, l. 11 ('Serf contracts, 1832').
[60] RGADA, f. 1287, op. 3, ed. khr. 612, l. 2 ('Serf contracts, 1793').
[61] RGADA, f. 1287, op. 3, ed. khr. 729, l. 25 ('Petition regarding credit, 1819').
[62] RGADA, f. 1287, op. 3, ed. khr. 911, l. 1 ('Correspondence between central administration and estate officials, 1824').

Lev Sakharov, as well as 340 roubles in 1827 from a serf in Rybinsk district (Yaroslavl' province).[63]

Voshchazhnikovo serfs also engaged in credit contracts with freemen, though this was apparently forbidden by law.[64] The Marquis de Custine, on his famous tour of Russia in 1839, noted with great surprise that although 'the law forbids the serf to ask, or the freeman to grant him, a credit of more than five roubles . . . they deal with some of these people, on the strength of their word only, for sums ranging from two to five hundred thousand francs; and the dates for payment are very distant'.[65] The information provided in the two most detailed probate inventories in the Voshchazhnikovo archive is consistent with Custine's observation. Anna Shatilova and Kozma Popov – both serfs from the village of Voshchazhnikovo – died before paying their debts, leaving the estate administration to sell off their property in order to satisfy creditors. But, before doing so, estate officials made detailed lists of the debts outstanding in each case.

Shatilova, who seems to have earned a living selling headscarves and other small cloth items at periodic markets, borrowed mostly from merchants. In 1819, when the inventory was carried out, she owed the Moscow merchant Mikhail Sheblyov 600 roubles; the Moscow merchant Stepan Karetnikov 419 roubles 75 kopecks; the Moscow merchant Ivan Miasnikov 219 roubles; the Yaroslavl' merchant Ivan Kiselyov 255 roubles 50 kopecks; and the Rostov merchant Semyon Shmagin 1039 roubles.[66] She had also borrowed 400 roubles from a priest in the city of Rostov.[67]

Similarly, a number of free individuals appear among the creditors of Kozma Popov. A Moscow merchant, Andrei Zabrodin, had lent Popov 3,000 roubles in 1827, and a merchant from Pereslavl', Ivan Zubkov, lent Popov 1,500 roubles in 1828.[68] Another Pereslavl' merchant, Dmitri Pichushkin, lent 1,840 roubles to Popov.[69] In addition, Popov owed the Countess Ushakova, who had an estate in Rybinsk district, 201 roubles.[70] Credit transactions at Voshchazhnikovo, then, were not confined to estate

[63] 'monastyrskii krest'ian', in RGADA, f. 1287, op. 3, ed. khr. 1133, l. 4 ('Petition regarding credit, 1832').

[64] The registers from the Moscow notarial office in the early eighteenth century also recorded credit transactions between serfs and people of other (free) legal estates. Tarlovskaia, 'Rostovshchicheskie operatsii', pp. 48–50.

[65] A. de Custine, *Letters from Russia* (repr. New York, 2002), pp. 562–3. According to one source, 1 franc was worth 1.1 roubles in 1839. A. Artynov, *Vospominaniia krest'ianina sela Ugodich, Iaroslavskoi gubernii Rostovskago uezda* (ed. A. A. Titov) (Moscow, 1883), p. 117.

[66] RGADA, f. 1287, op. 3, ed. khr. 729, ll. 1–7, 17 ('Petition regarding credit, 1819').

[67] Ibid., ll. 18, 25.

[68] RGADA, f. 1287, op. 3, ed. khr. 1133, ll. 32–3 ('Petition regarding credit, 1832').

[69] *Ibid.*   [70] 'Grafina Ushakova', in *ibid.*, l. 4.

serfs. These inventories suggest that credit networks in this region may have been very extensive indeed.[71]

It is ironic that the most compelling evidence for the importance of the Sheremetyevs' system of contract enforcement is also an indication of its shortcomings. Non-serf parties to these credit transactions were all lenders. Free persons were willing to extend credit to Voshchazhnikovo serfs because they knew they could use the contract enforcement services of the Sheremetyevs to recover the sums. For this same reason, Voshchazhnikovo serfs lent to other Sheremetyev serfs, but not, it seems, to free persons (or even to other landlords' serfs). This is unsurprising since the lender assumes the risk in credit transactions. Because Russian serfs had no legal rights beyond their estates, a serf would have been unable to bring a civil law suit against a free person who had defaulted on a loan. The enforcement services the Sheremetyevs provided applied only to their own serfs. They could force their own serfs to adhere to contracts, but not free persons. And here we see one of the main drawbacks of this quasi-formal institutional arrangement. In addition to the administrative costs and lengthy decision times, there were considerable limits to transactions, particularly lending, beyond the boundaries of the Sheremetyev holdings. Consequently, serious capital investment would have been constrained by the credit available among the serf population of the estate – a potentially serious brake on investment and growth.

7.3   The local context

How much overlap was there between borrowers and lenders on this estate? Because the credit data for Voshchazhnikovo are so fragmented, it is not possible to say for sure. Probate inventories were not carried out as a matter of course, but only in the event of a dispute or, as we have seen, when a serf died before paying off debts. The wills regularly drawn up by serfs did not include detailed inventories and made no mention of debts. In two surviving documents, the same serf is both borrower and lender. Nikolai Yablokov petitioned the estate administration in 1792 over the 900 roubles he had lent to Semyon Barin, who also appears as a lender in a contract from 1826.[72] And, according to the contracts for 1832, Mikhail Stulov, from the village of Vioska, borrowed 600 roubles from one serf,

---

[71] In his study of the Manuilovskoe estate in Tver' province, Bohac notes that 'money lending was an activity of pivotal importance for the estate's economy'. In Bohac, 'Family, property, and socioeconomic mobility', p. 64.

[72] RGADA, f. 1287, op. 3, ed. khr. 588, l. 1 ('Petition regarding credit, 1792'), and ed. khr. 612, l. 9 ('Serf contracts, 1793').

then, later that year, lent 350 to another.[73] These transactions indicate that it was *possible* for the same serf to be both borrower and lender and that it did occasionally happen. They do not, however, tell us how widespread this phenomenon was among Voshchazhnikovo serfs. It seems inherently likely that it was common, especially among the better-off serfs, who may have wanted to maintain the value of their savings, but did not want to concentrate their risks.[74]

What did serfs at Voshchazhnikovo use credit for? In the traditional view of the peasant economy, it is argued that, since credit was not available, peasant households were unable to undertake the investment required for agricultural or industrial development.[75] We have seen that credit was available to Voshchazhnikovo serfs. Although the documents tell us very little about the uses to which borrowed money was put, the few references we do have suggest that some serfs did use credit to make investments. Of thirty-three surviving contracts, fourteen provide some information about the ways in which borrowed money was used: three were for land purchases, three were for house purchases, five were for purchases of land or buildings, two were for substitute conscript purchases, and one was for a draught animal purchase. In 1831, for instance, Ivan Arnautov bought a piece of privately held land worth 175 roubles, on credit, at a 5 per cent annual interest rate.[76] In January 1832, Grigory Kovin bought a house and a piece of land from Leontei Matal'ev for 900 roubles, also on credit, to be paid for by 30 September of the same year.[77] In 1826, Mikhail Shetov used credit to purchase a horse worth 60 roubles from Ivan Briukhanov.[78] At least some of the debts incurred by Anna Shatilova seem to have been related to the purchase of commercial inventory – the headscarves and cloths that she sold at local and regional markets.[79] The use of credit to purchase trade inventory was apparently not unusual. A trading peasant from Moscow province noted in 1704 that 'without loans . . . it would be impossible to operate a trading enterprise'.[80] Access to credit markets meant that serfs were not necessarily at the mercy

---

[73] RGADA, f. 1287, op. 3, ed. khr. 1155, ll. 2–3 ('Serf contracts, 1832').
[74] It was not uncommon in other pre-industrial societies. See the discussion in Briggs, *Credit and village society*, esp. pp. 130–5; C. Muldrew, *The economy of obligation: the culture of credit and social relations in early modern England* (New York and Basingstoke, 1998).
[75] T. Shanin, 'The nature and logic of the peasant economy', *Journal of Peasant Studies* 1 (1973), p. 71.
[76] RGADA, f. 1287, op. 3, ed. khr. 1108, entry 5 ('Serf contracts, 1831').
[77] RGADA, f. 1287, op. 3, ed. khr. 1155, l. 1 ('Serf contracts, 1832').
[78] RGADA, f. 1287, op. 3, ed. khr. 977, l. 3 ('Serf contracts, 1826').
[79] RGADA, f. 1287, op. 3, ed. khr. 729, l. 4 ('Petition regarding credit, 1819').
[80] Tarlovskaia, 'Rostovshchicheskie operatsii', p. 50.

of nature, demographic cycles, or bad luck; they could borrow to invest in future productive capacities.

For lenders, credit markets offered a way of diversifying their savings. It may have been a higher-risk form of savings than investments in land or property, but, given the interest rates, it also may have yielded higher returns. Peasant savings are not often considered in more traditional views of peasant economy; it is assumed that surpluses are rare, and that when they do occur, they are either redistributed among the poorer members of the community or confiscated by landlords or states.[81] The Chayanovian formulation of this theory sees peasants as incapable of making the necessary calculations that would enable them to save for the future.

References from a variety of estate documents indicate that serfs at Voshchazhnikovo were not only capable of making these calculations, but were capable of sufficiently long-term thinking to consider lifetime income, i.e. saving for retirement.[82] For example, Dmitri Slasnikov and his wife, both in their early 60s, were recorded in the 1838 inventory of households, as 'living from previously accumulated earnings'.[83] The same was reported for Nikolai Kouzov, age 70, and his wife Pelageia, age 54.[84] In 1857, the serf widow Maria Lobanova asked to withdraw the interest on two state treasury notes she had purchased in 1855 for her children.[85] State treasury notes appear to have been a popular form of saving among serfs. So popular, indeed, that the Sheremetyev administration made formal provision for it in a kind of estate 'bank' or depository. Ivan Semyonov deposited a treasury note for 300 roubles in this bank in 1844.[86] In 1853, the unmarried serf woman Praskov'ia Kalinina deposited a treasury note for 150 roubles.[87] Fyodor Pugin deposited a bond for 200 roubles in 1855.[88]

It was not only the rich serfs at Voshchazhnikovo who saved. Nikolai Kouzov, who, with his wife, lived from savings, had worked as a labourer.[89] Dmitri Slasnikov, recorded as living on savings in 1838, had

---

[81] Shanin, 'The nature and logic', p. 71.

[82] This is consistent with evidence from modern developing societies, which indicates that even the poorest peasants are capable of making the calculations necessary in order to save for the future. See the discussion in Dasgupta, *An inquiry*, pp. 221–56.

[83] 'propityvaet'sa ot svoego prezhnogo nazhitku', in RGADA, f. 1287, op. 3, ed. khr. 1143, l. 55 ('Inventories of households, 1832/8').

[84] 'propityvaet'sa ot prezhnogo nazhitku', in *ibid.*, l. 47.

[85] RGADA, f. 1287, op. 3, ed. khr. 2280, l. 2 ('Petition regarding savings, 1857').

[86] RGADA, f. 1287, op. 3, ed. khr. 2241, l. 1 ('Record of sums belonging to serfs').

[87] *Ibid.*

[88] *Ibid.*, l. 2. References to these bonds raise many interesting questions about the estate's role as bank or intermediary. Unfortunately, the Voshchazhnikovo documents shed no light on how this system functioned.

[89] RGADA, f. 1287, op. 3, ed. khr. 1143, l. 47 ('Inventories of households, 1832/8').

earned his money by working as the Voshchazhnikovo church elder for twelve years.[90] Maria Lobanova, who petitioned in 1857 to withdraw the interest on her treasury note, was a widow with two young children, and was reported by officials as being in financial straits, hence her request to withdraw funds.[91]

There were several serf women among the lenders at Voshchazhnikovo. Female lenders appear in eleven of the thirty-three credit contracts and in two credit-related petitions. Some of these cases are particularly interesting as they indicate that unmarried women possessed and were able to exert control over their own resources, even when they resided in households headed by men.[92] For instance, the unmarried serf woman Anna Shikhina, who lived in her father's household, along with her two brothers, made a loan of 500 roubles in 1827.[93] That same year, the widow Mar'ia Zhukova, who lived in a household headed by her adult son, made a loan of 1,000 roubles.[94]

Most of the female lenders at Voshchazhnikovo appear, however, to have been widowed heads of households. It has been argued that wealthy widows were often important sources of credit in pre-industrial western European societies.[95] Since many of the widows at Voshchazhnikovo who lent money were from the smaller villages for which we have no economic data, quantitative parameters cannot be given.[96] But in the few instances where we can match widowed female lenders to economic or occupational data, they were not particularly well off. The widows Katerina and Praskov'ia Kalinina, who made loans of 100 and 1,000 roubles respectively, were described as earning a living trading light goods from a stall on the market square for 'insubstantial sums of money'. Their business was

---

[90] *Ibid.*, l. 55.

[91] RGADA, f. 1287, op. 3, ed. khr. 2280, l. 4 ('Petition regarding savings, 1857').

[92] This is consistent with the observation that peasant women in Russia, unlike those in parts of western Europe, were permitted to retain control over their dowries and other forms of moveable property. See, for instance, Worobec, *Peasant Russia*, pp. 62–70. For comparisons with other societies, see Briggs, *Credit and village society*, pp. 112–16; S. Ogilvie, *A bitter living*, esp. pp. 186–8.

[93] This information was obtained by linking credit contracts (RGADA, f. 1287, op. 3, ed. khr. 1133, l. 32 ('Petition regarding credit, 1832')) with nominal lists (GAYaO, f. 100, op. 8, d. 647, household no. 66 (1816)).

[94] *Ibid.*, l. 32.

[95] B. A. Holderness, 'Widows in pre-industrial society: an essay upon their economic functions', in R. M. Smith (ed.), *Land, kinship and lifecycle* (Cambridge, 1984), pp. 435–42. More recent studies of the role of widows in money lending have cast doubt on this view. See, for instance, Briggs, *Credit and village society*, pp. 112–16. Also in C. M. Frances, 'Networks of the life course: a case study of Cheshire, 1570–1700', unpublished Ph.D. thesis (Cambridge, 2000), pp. 152–96.

[96] Only three of ten widows mentioned in the Voshchazhnikovo contracts could be linked to a household listing.

described as being 'in a poor state'.[97] And the widow Katerina Tupytsina, who also lent money, was said to have 'lived from her own labour'.[98] It is possible that other widows who lent money were better off than the Kalinina sisters or Tupytsina, but, given how limited women's economic opportunities were in this society, it seems unlikely that they would have been especially wealthy.

Credit markets are not always viewed by historians as a positive feature of pre-industrial society. Some have argued that credit markets, where they existed, benefited the richer peasants in the society at the expense of the poor.[99] According to this view, the poor peasants became dependent on the rich, who exploited them by charging exorbitant interest on loans.[100] There is not enough information in the Voshchazhnikovo documents to address this question systematically. What we do know, though, suggests that this view is oversimplified. Rich serfs at Voshchazhnikovo may have been lending to poorer serfs, but they were borrowing money from them (and each other) as well. Some of the serfs who appear repeatedly as borrowers in credit contracts – such as the Yablokovs, Dolodanovs, and Titovs – were from households in the top income bracket at Voshchazhnikovo (the *pervostateinye krest'iane*, or peasants of the 'first rank'). These richer serfs were not the only ones who borrowed money, but their names do appear more frequently than others in credit contracts. For example, members of the Yablokov family – Nikolai and his three adult sons – appear as borrowers in at least fifteen of the transactions described in surviving contracts and petitions.[101] Furthermore, these richer serfs were the ones borrowing from 'poor' widows such as Katerina Kalinina and Katerina Tupytsina. It seems plausible that these serfs had greater access to credit because they were viewed as good risks by

---

[97] Katerina Kalinina appears as a lender in RGADA, f. 1287, op. 3, ed. khr. 1133 ('Petition regarding credit, 1832'), and Praskov'ia appears in RGADA, f. 1287, op. 3, ed. khr. 1108, entry 4 ('Serf contracts, 1831'). Their business affairs are described in RGADA, f. 1287, op. 3, ed. khr. 1391, l. 4 ('List of trading peasants and guilds, 1838').

[98] A reference to money lent by Katerina Tupytsina appears in RGADA, f. 1287, op. 3, ed. khr. 1713, l. 43 ('Correspondence between the St Petersburg administrative office and estate officials, 1846'). Her economic affairs are described in RGADA, f. 1287, op. 3, ed. khr. 1143, l. 47 ('Inventory of households, 1832/8').

[99] Development economists argue that, on the contrary, the benefits of credit are much greater than the potential costs, especially to members of poor societies. See Dasgupta, *An inquiry*, pp. 221–56; Ray, *Development economics*, pp. 529–86; World Bank, *World Bank development report 1989*, pp. 25–40.

[100] Fyodorov outlines this view in *Pomeshchich'i krest'iane*, esp. pp. 174–6. See also Shanin, 'The nature and logic', p. 75.

[101] RGADA, f. 1287, op. 3, ed. khr. 612 ('Serf contracts, 1793'), ed. khr. 629 ('Petition regarding credit, 1795'), ed. khr. 977 ('Serf contracts, 1826'), ed. khr. 1108 ('Serf contracts, 1831').

lenders. They had houses and manufactories worth substantial sums, they owned land privately, and they often had trade inventory and other capital reserves they could use to secure loans made to them. Poor serfs, on the other hand, who had no collateral, had fewer credit opportunities, and were thus forced to rely on small, informal loans from close friends and family members or on the generosity of others.

The system of property rights and contract enforcement under the Sheremetyevs had many drawbacks. Most of these derived from its lack of integration into any larger legal framework, as discussed in chapter 9 below. But one advantage of the system may have been the extent to which it enabled serfs of all strata to diversify their economic survival strategies. Those who had been able to accumulate wealth were better able to preserve it and make it available for investment by themselves and others. Those who were less well off had additional opportunities to save for old age and infirmity. Voshchazhnikovo serfs could, perhaps to a greater degree than on other Russian landlords' estates, assemble a portfolio of different survival strategies – labouring locally, emigration, agriculture, employing others, entrepreneurship, investment in land, lending, and borrowing – which suited their individual situations, preferences, abilities, and time constraints. In other words, the local institutional framework provided a flexibility that seems to have made Voshchazhnikovo serfs better off than those on many other Russian estates.

8   Retail markets and consumption

The preceding chapters have shown that Voshchazhnikovo serfs were integrated into a larger market economy in a number of ways. They bought and sold labour and land and engaged in credit transactions across established socio-legal categories and geographical boundaries. But what about their consumption, and the retail markets for consumer goods? What goods did people in the countryside buy and what levels of material culture characterised the standard of living on this estate?

Discussions of the living standards of Russian peasants in this period have tended to focus mainly on food. Cross-sectional studies of grain and meat consumption are used to estimate the caloric intake of the 'average peasant' in various parts of the Russian empire, and those who consumed the most meat and dairy products are assumed to have had the highest standard of living.[1] While better-off peasants may have consumed more meat on average than poorer peasants, this is none-theless a very crude measure, which obscures important differences in consumption.

For one thing, it is based on the assumption that food was the only thing peasants consumed. According to this view, the Russian country-side was a largely natural economy, in which the little money in circu-lation was used to pay rents to landlords and purchase food for the household. Since peasants had no contact with wider markets that could have made consumer goods available, they faced tightly constrained decisions about how to allocate their cash resources. But suppose for a moment that one or two consumer goods were introduced into such a society. What would happen? A peasant might decide, for instance, to spend a bit less on beef in order to be able to buy some tea or vodka or a new hat. Would this indicate a decline in her standard of living? An analysis that measured standard of living solely by food consumption might well reach this conclusion. It is thus difficult to evaluate the

---

[1] See discussion in Moon, *The Russian peasantry*, esp. pp. 282–98; and in Hoch, *Serfdom and social control*, pp. 28–49.

significance of food choices without some knowledge of the full consumption bundle in the society.[2]

Another popular measure of peasant well-being – arrears in quitrent obligations – is flawed in much the same way: it assumes that if peasants had money, they would spend it first on their *obrok* payments. Serfs in arrears in their feudal obligations must, it is assumed, have been in financial straits.[3] As we shall see shortly, this was not necessarily the case. There were other things, in addition to rents and food, that Voshchazhnikovo serfs could, and did, spend their money on.[4]

The documents for Voshchazhnikovo do not, as noted earlier, provide the sort of wage and price data required for even a rudimentary examination of living standards. They do, however, provide rich qualitative evidence concerning local markets and material life on the Voshchazhnikovo estate, which greatly broadens our understanding of the consumption behaviour of Russian serfs. The estate archive shows that serfs bought and sold food and a wide array of other household items, and that a consumer culture was taking hold in at least some parts of the Russian countryside well before 1861.

8.1   Local trade

Voshchazhnikovo serfs did not need to travel far to sell their goods and services and purchase items they required, since there was a weekly market on the estate grounds. This market was held every Friday on the market square (*torgovaia ploshchad'*) in the village of Voshchazhnikovo. In addition to providing trading serfs with an opportunity to sell their wares, the weekly market offered the Sheremetyevs additional revenues. Rights

---

[2] An interesting and informative account of the complexities of food consumption in the context of public eating establishments can be found in A. Smith, 'Eating out in imperial Russia: class, nationality, and dining before the Great Reforms', *Slavic Review* 65 (2006), pp. 747–68.

[3] Bohac, 'Family, property, and socioeconomic mobility', pp. 77–82. There has been some debate over the extent to which data on arrears in the post-Emancipation period accurately reflect peasants' living standards. See the discussion in Moon, *The Russian peasantry*, pp. 285–6.

[4] A few historians, such as Steven Hoch and Ian Blanchard, have argued that Russian peasants enjoyed a higher standard of living than is often assumed, but this view is not generally acknowledged in the wider historical literature on the peasantry. See S. L. Hoch, 'On good numbers and bad: Malthus, population trends and peasant standard of living in late imperial Russia', *Slavic Review* 53 (1994), pp. 41–75; I. Blanchard, *Russia's 'age of silver': precious-metal production and economic growth in the eighteenth century* (London and New York, 1989), esp. chapter 5. Travellers to Russia, including Haxthausen himself, frequently remarked on the high standard of living of peasants, especially with reference to the grain wage (as discussed below). *Studien*, vol. I, p. 119.

to the market square were usually auctioned off by the landlord to one or two serfs for a period of several years at a time. In 1820, the rights were purchased by the serf Aleksei Averin, from the village of Uslavtsevo, for two years at 650 roubles per year.[5] In 1822, Averin purchased the rights for two more years, this time for 800 roubles per year.[6] In 1837, the rights were sold for 600 roubles annually, this time to the Voshchazhnikovo serfs Gerasim Ivanov and Ivan Sergeev.[7] Serfs who purchased the rights to the market square then sold trading licences to those who wished to set up stalls on the square.

These trading stalls (*lavki*) were not makeshift devices, set up opportunistically by serfs when they had something to sell; they were more like small shops. They were considered a form of real estate by serfs who owned them and, as shown in chapter 5, they could be bought and sold and even used as loan collateral. Serfs who owned stalls were required to pay an annual fee to the landlord as rent for the land on which these stalls were built, in addition to the fee paid to the leaseholder for the right to trade.[8] A list for 1820 shows that there were forty-three stalls on the market square, for which local serfs paid annual rents ranging from 3 to 11 roubles to the landlord. There was also a small hostel, which offered food and drinks to those visiting the market. The hostel was also run by a Voshchazhnikovo serf, Aleksandr Fedoseyev, who paid 30 roubles annually in rent to the landlord. According to the list, the landlord received a total of 302 roubles in rents from local stallholders, in addition to the 650 roubles paid by the above-mentioned Aleksei Averin for the rights to the square.[9] With monopoly rights to the square, Averin could sell trading privileges to outsiders as well as local traders, which presumably justified the investment of 650 roubles.

In 1820, the forty-three stalls on the market square were rented by thirty-nine different serfs – a few stallholders held more than one. Ivan Chernikhin, for example, held two stalls, for which he paid a combined rent of 13 roubles per year. Semyon Rybkin also held two stalls, for which he paid a total of 10 roubles per year in rent. Dmitri Slasnikov held three stalls, and paid 21 roubles in rent.[10] It was not possible to

---

[5] RGADA, f. 1287, op. 3, ed. khr. 864, l. 4 ('On the letting of the market square, 1820').

[6] *Ibid.*, l. 1.

[7] RGADA, f. 1287, op. 3, ed. khr. 1325, ll. 32–3 ('Communal resolutions, 1837').

[8] This is very similar to the system of periodic markets in medieval England. Here, too, the rents that landlords collected from stallholders corresponded to the size of the stall. See R. M. Smith, 'A periodic market and its impact on a manorial community: Botesdale, Suffolk, and the manor of Redgrave, 1280–1300', in Z. Razi and R. Smith (eds.), *Medieval society and the manor court* (Oxford, 1996), pp. 450–81.

[9] RGADA, f. 1287, op. 3, ed. khr. 739, ll. 1–2 ('Monies collected from stallholders, 1820').

[10] All of these figures are in *ibid.*, ll. 1–2.

determine the socioeconomic characteristics of these trading serfs, since the only list of stallholders we have is for 1820 and the most detailed socioeconomic information on the serf population only dates from the 1830s. It is worth pointing out, though, that the surnames associated with the wealthier serfs on the estate – Dolodanov, Titov, Chernikhin, Slasnikov, Yablokov – all appear, among others, on the list of stallholders. Furthermore, only two of the forty-three stallholders were women. While this does not necessarily mean that only the better-off serfs could hold stalls, it does suggest that it may have been considerably more difficult for poorer serfs to obtain the necessary capital to open a stall on the market square.[11]

In addition to the Friday market, at least some everyday trade was conducted in Voshchazhnikovo village. Some of this trade took place on the grounds of the Voshchazhnikovo parish church. In 1844, for instance, the 'everyday trade' of the Voshchazhnikovo serfs Dmitri Baramokhin, Vasily Zemskov, and Sergei Slasnikov involved the operation of a hostel on the church grounds, where they also sold a number of small goods.[12] The petty trader Mikhail Bacharnikov, during this same year, ran a similar business in the same spot.[13] Other documents in the archive suggest that the church, like the landlord, collected rents from those who conducted trade on its grounds. In 1792, for example, eighty-nine serfs were recorded as having paid for the right to trade on the church grounds. The rents paid ranged from 5 kopecks to 3 roubles.[14] It is difficult to compare these rents with those paid by stallholders on the market square in 1820, since the lists are for different years. Moreover, we do not have information about serfs' earnings from these stalls, the volume of their trade, or the prices of their wares. It may be significant that the church records, unlike those for the market square, do not mention trading stalls. While some of those who traded on church grounds, such as those mentioned above, clearly *did* have proper shops, it is possible that others, such as those who paid 5 or 10 kopecks per year, simply paid for the right to sell goods on church property. They may have come each day to sell apples or cabbages from a sack. On the other hand, only seven of the eighty-nine serfs paying rent to the church were female. If trading on church grounds had in fact been substantially less costly than setting up

---

[11] It would not be unusual to find that wealthier serfs were better represented among stallholders. See the discussion in Smith, 'A periodic market', pp. 471–3.

[12] 'kazhdodnevnaia torgovlia', in RGADA, f. 1287, op. 3, ed. khr. 1643, l. 1 ('Petition regarding trade dispute, 1844').

[13] *Ibid.*, ll. 1–2. Bacharnikov was not a serf, but a member of one of the urban estates (*meshchanstvo*) in a nearby town.

[14] RGADA, f. 1287, op. 3, ed. khr. 575 ('Monies collected from stallholders, 1792').

a stall on the market square, we might expect to find a larger number of female traders. It is not clear from the documents whether those who held stalls on the church square were also required to pay a fee to the landlord. Nor is it clear whether the church auctioned off the rights to its market square in the same way that the estate did. If so, the costs of trading to serfs could have been significantly higher than suggested by the figures in the 1792 account books.

It was not only local serfs who engaged in trade on the market square and on the church grounds. The documents indicate that traders, enserfed and free, came from other parts of the province – and, perhaps even the region – to trade on the estate. The above-mentioned Bacharnikov, a member of the local *meshchanstvo* in nearby Kolomenskoe, had a stall on the church grounds. In 1837, a Rostov merchant, Abram Fyodorov, rented a stall on the market square from the serf Andrian Dolodanov.[15] Similarly, the 'non-local peasant', Yakov Andreyev, rented a stall on the market square that same year.[16] In a report from 1858, estate officials noted 'that there are weekly Friday bazaars in Voshchazhnikovo, to which come traders from nearby towns and districts'.[17] Local serfs, such as Aleksandr Fedoseyev and Ivan Chernikhin, operated small hostels, where they sold food and tea to 'those passing through on market days'.[18]

What sorts of goods were on offer at the local market in Voshchazhnikovo? In 1831, the local government administration for Rostov district sent out a list of 'basic provisions' (*povsednevnye pripasy* or *nazhiznennye pripasy*) sold at local markets, and requested officials on manorial estates to provide them with price information for the goods listed.[19] The information provided for the Voshchazhnikovo estate is shown in Table 8.1.

Beer, wine, and spirits were included on the list, but without prices, since these could be purchased only at the estate tavern, whose proprietor held monopoly rights over the sale of these items.[20] Non-food items for sale at the market (listed without prices) included linen cloth, needles,

[15] RGADA, f. 1287, op. 3, ed. khr. 1345, entry no. 1 ('Report on serfs' buildings, 1837').

[16] 'postoronnyi krest'ian' ('foreign peasant'), in *ibid.*, entry 3.

[17] 'v Voshchazhnikove no piatnich'nym dniam byvaiut ezhenedel'nye bazary, na kotorye s'ezzhaiuts'a iz blizhaishikh gorodov i uezdov onye torgovtsy', in RGADA, f. 1287, op. 3, ed. khr. 2320, point 17 ('Descriptions of estates, 1858').

[18] These 'kharchevny' operated 'vo vremya piatnichnykh torgovykh dnei i proizvodit'sa dlia priezzhikh raznykh liudei prodazha chaju i raznykh s'estnykh pripasov', in RGADA, f. 1287, op. 3, ed. khr. 994, l. 20 ('Petition regarding property dispute, 1828').

[19] RGADA, f. 1287, op. 3, ed. khr. 1070, ll. 57–60 ('Instructions from Rostov district, 1831').

[20] RGADA, f. 1287, op. 3, ed. khr. 994, l. 20 ('Petition regarding property dispute, 1828'). Monopoly privileges will be discussed in chapter 9.

Table 8.1. *Goods for sale at the Voshchazhnikovo market, c. 1831*

Basic provisions sold locally	Highest price in roubles	Average price in roubles
Beef, per *pood*	6.00	5.50
Salt, per *pood*	2.40	2.30
Green onions, per *chetverik*	0.80	0.60
Oat flour, per *pood*	1.40	1.20
Hops, per *pood*	12.00	11.00
Butter, per *pood*	16.00	15.00
Eggs, per 100	2.00	1.80
White sugar, per *funt'*	1.50	1.00
Hemp straw, per *chetverik*	3.50	2.50
Rye flour, per *pood*	1.50	1.30
Candles, per *pood*	13.00	12.50
Hemp oil, per *pood*	10.00	9.50
Oats, per *chetvert'*	6.50	6.00
Hay, per *pood*	1.00	0.80

Note: metric equivalents of these measures can be found in the Glossary.
Source: RGADA, f. 1287, op. 3, ed. khr. 1070, ll. 57–8 ('Instructions from Rostov district, 1831').

thread/yarn, tobacco, quills, and ink. Additional items on the list included cabbages, apples, cranberries, plums, carrots, horseradish, barley, mustard, yeast, mint, milk, honey, starch, lard, rapeseed oil, and vinegar, but none of these was regularly available at the Voshchazhnikovo market. The final item noted under 'basic provisions' was coffins, which were sold at Voshchazhnikovo for between 2 and 2.5 roubles per unit. While we should probably refrain from drawing any hasty conclusions about mortality on the basis of this entry, it is nonetheless interesting that coffins were regarded as basic provisions by those who compiled the lists.

It was also possible to buy grain in bulk at the Voshchazhnikovo market. According to the 1831 list, one *chetvert'* of rye (roughly 130 kilogrammes) sold for 13 roubles, while a *chetvert'* of oats sold for 6 roubles 50 kopecks (wheat and barley were not sold in bulk at Voshchazhnikovo).[21] The limited information we have about serfs' wages suggests that these prices were remarkably low.[22] Estate officers in the 1840s earned between 250

---

[21] *Ibid.*, l. 57.
[22] They are, however, consistent with prices recorded elsewhere. See, for instance, Blanchard, *Russia's 'age of silver'*, p. 239; R. Hellie, *The economy and material culture of Russia, 1600–1725* (Chicago, 1999), pp. 12–30; B. N. Mironov, *Khlebnye tseny v Rossii za dva stoletiia XVIII–XIX vv.* (Leningrad, 1985), pp. 68–9.

and 700 paper roubles per year.[23] In 1844 a serf was hired by the estate
to work as a coachman (*iamshchik*) for 350 paper roubles per year.[24]
Nikolai Chernikhin, who worked as a servant in St Petersburg in 1846,
claimed to have earned a salary of 500 paper roubles per year.[25] Figures
for the late eighteenth century indicate that average annual per capita
grain consumption in Russia stood at approximately 1.1 *chetvert'*.[26] At
Voshchazhnikovo prices, this would mean an expenditure of about 14.3
roubles on grain per person per year. Even allowing for fluctuations in
the value of the paper rouble in this period, grain at these prices would
have been affordable to all but the very poorest on this estate.[27] This is
consistent with Haxthausen's observation that 'a weaver earns enough
here that for her daily wage she can buy nearly a whole *Scheffel* of grain;
in Bielefeld, in Westphalia, she could barely make enough to buy a tenth
of that!'[28]

The Friday market at Voshchazhnikovo was part of a larger network of
periodic markets and annual fairs in the region.[29] These included weekly
rural markets, of the Voshchazhnikovo sort, as well as urban markets, such
as those located in the cities of Rostov and Yaroslavl'. The annual Rostov
fair, which lasted for three weeks and attracted merchants from all over
the Russian empire (and even beyond) was attended regularly by
Voshchazhnikovo serfs.[30] According to descriptive surveys of Yaroslavl'
province for the late eighteenth century, there were over sixty smaller
annual fairs, held in villages throughout the province.[31] The largest of
these took place in the settlement of Velikoe, also located in Rostov
district, some 30 miles east of Voshchazhnikovo. The fair at Velikoe lasted
for a week and attracted traders – merchants and peasants – from all over
the Central Industrial Region.[32]

In addition to the fairs in Yaroslavl', there was the annual Makarev fair
(*makar'evskaia yarmarka*), by far the largest in imperial Russia and,
according to some contemporary observers, one of the largest in the

---

[23] RGADA, f. 1287, op. 3, ed. khr. 1635, ll. 4–6, 10 ('Communal resolutions, 1844').
[24] *Ibid.*, l. 3.
[25] RGADA, f. 1287, op. 3, ed. khr. 1713, l. 43 ('Correspondence between St Petersburg
  officials and Voshchazhnikovo estate officials, 1846').
[26] Blanchard, *Russia's 'age of silver'*, p. 239.
[27] Low grain prices in this region can perhaps account for Sheremetyev's assertion that
  unmarried women living alone at Voshchazhnikovo were well off enough to make *obrok*
  payments.
[28] Haxthausen, *Studien*, vol. I, p. 119.
[29] Morrison, 'Trading peasants', pp. 278–81. For an interesting discussion of regional
  markets in the eighteenth and nineteenth centuries and the extent to which they comprised a 'national market', see B. N. Mironov, *Vnutrennyi rynok Rossii vo vtoroi polovine
  XVIII–pervoi polovine XIX v.* (Leningrad, 1981).
[30] Morrison, 'Trading peasants', pp. 271–2.   [31] *Ibid.*, p. 278.   [32] *Ibid.*

world.[33] It was held for six weeks every summer in Nizhnyi Novgorod, on the banks of the Volga and Oka rivers, about 200 miles southeast of Voshchazhnikovo. Merchants and peddlers from all parts of the Russian empire, as well as from places as far away as England, Germany, France, Greece, Finland, Persia, and Mongolia, travelled to the fair at Nizhnyi to deal in a wide array of goods, ranging from iron, potash, and timber, to furs, precious stones, and tea.[34]

Estate documents such as passport lists, credit contracts, and inventories of manufactories indicate that Voshchazhnikovo serfs frequently travelled to regional markets, as well as annual fairs to trade their wares. For example, Aleksei Titov, who ran a leather manufactory on the estate, purchased his raw materials and sold finished products both locally and 'at the Rostov fair'.[35] The paper manufactory run by Dmitri Slasnikov obtained raw materials 'at the Rostov fair and at markets in Kostroma province' and sold finished products 'at the Rostov and Makarev fairs'.[36] Selivan Terpigorev, who operated a distillery on the estate, sold his wares 'at the Rostov fair and at various markets in Yaroslavl' province'.[37] In 1762, the serfs Fyodor Dmitriev, Andrei Alekseyev, and Fyodor Nikitin obtained one-month passports for travel 'to the Makarev fair'.[38] An 1834 list shows that one-month passports were granted to serfs Pyotr Nikolayev Fedoseyev, Ivan Petrov Fedoseyev, and Mikhail Dolodanov (among others) for travel to the Makarev fair.[39] In a petition to the estate administration, one of the creditors of the deceased serf widow Anna Shatilova claimed that he had sold her 419 roubles' worth of goods on credit at the Makarev fair in 1817.[40]

8.2   Consumption

In so far as a 'consumer culture' existed in rural Russia, it is thought to have emerged in the post-Emancipation period, with increased exposure to urban tastes and norms. According to this view, the abolition of serfdom marked the beginning of a pronounced transition from rural self-sufficiency to market consumption.[41] Even then, the vast majority of Russian peasants are thought to have remained outside this market

---

[33] De Custine, *Letters*, p. 547.

[34] See de Custine's fascinating account of his visit to the Makarev fair in *Letters*, pp. 545–67.

[35] RGADA, f. 1287, op. 3, ed. khr. 1119, l. 2 ('Report on estate manufactories').

[36] *Ibid.*, ll. 3–4.   [37] *Ibid.*, ll. 5–6.

[38] RGADA, f. 1287, op. 3, ed. khr. 272, l. 15 ('Passport lists for 1762').

[39] RGADA, f. 1287, op. 3, ed. khr. 1246, entries 193, 194, 196 ('Passport lists for 1834').

[40] RGADA, f. 1287, op. 3, ed. khr. 729, l. 1 ('Petition regarding credit, 1819').

[41] Burds, *Peasant dreams*, chapter 6, esp. pp. 43–5.

culture, spending their limited cash earnings on only 'the traditional staple of salt and such items as tea, matches, and kerosene, which by the end of the nineteenth century had become necessities'.[42]

Is the evidence for Voshchazhnikovo consistent with this view? It is difficult to analyse consumption among the serfs on this estate in any systematic way, because so few of the documents that describe serfs' possessions – such as wills, marriage contracts, and probate inventories – have survived for Voshchazhnikovo. What we have are only tantalising glimpses of the serfs' material culture through remarks made in passing in petitions to the landlord or the occasional dowry or probate inventory. While this is not enough to tell us how representative these examples were, it does tell us what was *possible* in this society in the late eighteenth and early nineteenth centuries. And, interestingly, the kinds of consumer goods reportedly available in the Central Industrial Region in the post-Emancipation period – clothing, jewelry, foodstuffs, household items, building materials – are the very same kinds that appear in Voshchazhnikovo documents from the early nineteenth century.[43]

Two of the more interesting documents for Voshchazhnikovo include an 1837 inventory of the personal possessions of Avdot'ia and Aleksandr Yefremov, a serf couple of middling status, and an 1820 inventory of the dowry of Praskov'ia Pugina, a serf woman who married into a household of the middle stratum (no information is given about the household she grew up in). Avdot'ia and Aleksandr Yefremov died in quick succession, Avdot'ia in 1836 and Aleksandr in 1837, leaving behind several young children.[44] After their deaths, the estate authorities carried out an inventory of their belongings, probably in order to divide them among the children. No household furnishings, livestock, or farm equipment were included in the inventories; only personal possessions were listed. Aleksandr Yefremov's possessions were fairly modest, and included a pair of trousers, two waistcoats, two shawls, one headscarf, two patterned frocks, two fur coats, one silver ring, a mirror, and several icons made of silver and copper.[45] The list for his wife, Avdot'ia, was considerably longer. Her possessions included five dresses of different colours, three bonnets (one of which was described as 'Levantine'), a red shawl with a fringe, three French headscarves (pink, blue, and black), one green neckscarf, two nightshirts with calico sleeves, four plain nightshirts (two with sleeves, two without), two plain coats (one with a sable collar), two

[42] Worobec, *Peasant Russia*, p. 34.
[43] On the post-Emancipation period, see Burds, *Peasant dreams*, chapter 6.
[44] RGADA, f. 1287, op. 3, ed. khr. 1325, ll. 2, 3, 5, 10 ('Communal resolutions, 1837').
[45] *Ibid.*, l. 5.

rabbit fur coats, two shearling coats (one with sable trim, the other with rabbit trim), a fur collar, and winter stockings. In addition, she owned seven pairs of earrings of various sorts, four rings set with different kinds of stones, four rings of silver and gold, a silver cross on a silver and gold chain (to be worn around the neck), and a pearl necklace (which, interestingly, was said to have been 'with Pyotr Dolodanov as collateral for a cash loan').[46] A number of household items were listed as Avdot'ia Yefremova's personal possessions; many of them may have been part of her dowry. The list included three tablecloths, three sheets, one napkin, one cotton blanket, one woollen blanket, one feather bed, five feather pillows, five pillowcases (one white, four patterned), one towel trimmed with lace and ribbon, six patterned towels, eight plain towels, one pair of green curtains, one copper samovar, and one icon.[47]

The inventory of Praskov'ia Pugina's dowry was included with a petition she sent to the estate administration in 1820, in which she accused her father-in-law, Andrei Yegorov Pugin, of confiscating items belonging to her, valued at 4,293 roubles.[48] Pugina's dowry contained articles of clothing similar to Avdot'ia Yefremova's, including a dozen headscarves of French silk valued at 120 roubles, three pairs of silk stockings valued at 30 roubles total, a sable muff worth 60 roubles, and a beaver hat worth 50 roubles. She also owned a pearl necklace, valued at 1,100 roubles, as well as seven pairs of earrings with assorted precious stones valued at 105 roubles in total, and five rings worth 123 roubles (total). The household items listed were also similar to those described in the inventory of Avdot'ia Yefremova's belongings, though there were some additional luxury items, such as a silver goblet that weighed roughly one pound and was valued at 96 roubles. Pugina also owned a silver coffee pot worth 192 roubles, and a 40-piece silver tea service valued at 450 roubles.[49]

Again, it is not possible at this point to assess how representative these inventories are, since they are so far the only examples available for Voshchazhnikovo. But in the absence of any other information about serf consumption, there is no reason to assume *a priori* that these glimpses of serf consumption were unrepresentative. These two particular inventories seem to have survived by chance; there is no reason to think that there were not many others like them.[50] We know that the Yefremovs were

[46] 'nakhodit'sa u Petra Dolodanova v zaloge', in *ibid.*, l. 2. As noted in chapter 7, this loan does not appear in any of the surviving credit-related contracts or petitions.
[47] All of these items appear in *ibid.*, ll. 2–3, 10.
[48] RGADA, f. 1287, op. 3, ed. khr. 766 ('Petition regarding property dispute, 1820').
[49] All of these items appear in *ibid.*, ll. 3–4.
[50] A broader selection of such documents may exist for another Sheremetyev estate, and these might be used to carry out a more systematic study of serfs' consumption.

not among the wealthiest serfs on the estate. They lived in a wooden house with a wooden roof, which, as we shall see, was a typical dwelling for a family of the middling stratum.[51] They were young – Avdot'ia was 26 when she died, and Aleksandr was 28[52] – so they had not had a great deal of time to accumulate wealth. According to the 1832 household listing, they and their children shared a living space with Aleksandr's aunt and uncle, and Aleksandr worked as a servant in St Petersburg.[53] Praskov'ia Pugina could not be linked to her parents' household, since the inventory gave no indication of her surname prior to marrying Ivan Pugin. The family she married into, though, was like that of the Yefremovs. They, too, lived in a wooden house with a wooden roof, and their primary income was from their work as servants.[54] Unless Praskov'ia Pugina married into a household of a lower status than her household of origin, she and Avdot'ia Yefremova were of roughly the same socioeconomic background. They were definitely not poor, but they were also not among the serfs of the wealthiest stratum.[55] Thus even middling serfs at Voshchazhnikovo in the 1820s and 1830s were apparently able to possess scarves of French silk, considerable amounts of jewelry and clothing, and certain luxury household items. This suggests that the consumer culture associated with the late nineteenth century existed, at least in some rural areas, well before Emancipation.

The most comprehensive data available on consumption habits at Voshchazhnikovo consist of descriptions of serfs' houses. Despite the Sheremetyevs' attempts to 'prevent extravagance in serfs' buildings', serfs at Voshchazhnikovo continued to invest in improvements to their houses and farm buildings.[56] While about a quarter of the houses on the estate were traditional peasant huts (*izby*), made of wood with thatched roofs, there was a great deal of variation in the other three-quarters of serf dwellings. Among the more spectacular examples of extravagance was the

---

[51] RGADA, f. 1287, op. 3, ed. khr. 1143, l. 75 ('Inventories of households, 1832/8').

[52] Ages based on data in the 1834 revision, RGADA, f. 1287, op. 3, ed. khr. 2553, household no. 188.

[53] RGADA, f. 1287, op. 3, ed. khr. 1143, l. 75 ('Inventories of households, 1832/8').

[54] *Ibid.*, ll. 73–4.

[55] By 1838 Praskov'ia Pugina was widowed, and had separated from her deceased husband's family. She lived with her adult children (one son and one daughter) and their household was described as 'poor'. In *ibid.*, l. 65.

[56] RGADA, f. 1287, op. 3, ed. khr. 1598, l. 1 ('On serfs' houses, 1843'). It is not clear how the landlord intended to prevent serfs from building extravagant houses. It seems more likely that he realised that he could not in fact prevent it, so he thought he might as well impose a fine or tax on those serfs who did it. This would explain why he was so keen to know which of his serfs had *already* built exceptionally large and luxurious houses on the estate.

house of Vasily Slasnikov, a two-storey stone house, which was plastered and painted and 'furnished in the merchant's style'.[57] The house had ten windows facing out to the front, and six more on the side. In the back was another stone building from which Slasnikov operated his candle manufactory.[58] The house of Vasily and Dmitri Dolodanov was similarly luxurious. The Dolodanovs also had a two-storey stone house, with separate living areas for the two families. Like the Slasnikovs, the Dolodanovs had their house painted and plastered, with merchant-style furnishings. The house had eighteen windows in front.[59] The two-storey house of Grigory Zhukov was more modest. Only the foundation was stone (the upper part was made of wood), there were six windows facing the front, and no extravagant (*izlishnye* – literally 'superfluous') furnishings.[60] The house of Ivan Yablokov was one storey, with the front part built of stone while the back was made of wood. There were six windows in front, and no plasterwork. It was described by officials as being 'in the manner of a typical peasant house'.[61] Similarly, the one-storey brick house of serf Flegont Krasavin in the village of Sytino was described as being 'of the simple peasant sort'.[62]

The differences in dwelling types were perhaps the most obvious manifestation of socioeconomic stratification on this estate. Of the 184 households listed as resident in the village of Voshchazhnikovo in 1838, 34 were recorded as occupying houses made of stone with wooden roof tiles; 108 households lived in wooden houses with wooden roof tiles; and 42 had wooden houses with roofs of thatched straw.[63] Moreover, there is a very strong correlation between the economic position of the household (as defined by estate officials in the inventories of households) and the type of dwelling. Of the 34 households with stone dwellings, 3 were described as 'average', while the remaining 31 were recorded as 'good'. Of the 109 with wooden houses and wooden roofs, 27 were called 'poor', 15 were 'average', and the remaining 67 were 'good'. Those who lived in wooden houses with roofs of thatched straw were predominantly poor. Of these, 2 were called 'good' (one of these had two houses on the estate), 3 were called 'average', and 37 were 'poor', with 4 described as 'extremely

---

[57] 'dvukh-etazhnoi, vykrashen … otshtukaturen … mebliroven kupechiskom vkusom', in *ibid.*, entry 2.
[58] *Ibid.*, entry 2.   [59] *Ibid.*, entry 4.   [60] *Ibid.*, entry 13.
[61] 'po manere obyknovennykh krest'ianskikh domov', in *ibid.*, entry 9.   [62] *Ibid.*, entry 16.
[63] This information is in RGADA, f. 1287, op. 3, ed. khr. 1143 ('Inventories of households, 1832/8'). For each household, a brief description of its dwelling is provided. A typical example might read: 'wooden house with wooden roof shingles, 3 × 7 *sazhen* in area, bathhouse and threshing barn in back', or 'stone house, 2 storeys, wooden shingles, 8 × 15 *sazhen* in area, no additional buildings'.

poor'.[64] If we use dwelling type as a proxy for income group, we find that roughly 19 per cent of households were in the well-off first rank (*pervaia stat'ia*), 58 per cent were middling (*srednaia stat'ia*), and 23 per cent were poor (*poslednaia stat'ia*).

A broad array of consumer goods, it seems, was available at Voshchazhnikovo, including clothing, jewelry, and household furnishings. But were these goods available only to the few who had resources left after paying taxes and dues? Not necessarily. Some Voshchazhnikovo serfs bought things for themselves *instead* of paying their taxes. In a decree from 1843, the Count Sheremetyev noted that it had come to his attention that serfs who were in arrears in their quitrent payments also had 'several changes of the best sort of clothes'.[65] In future, he said, serfs in arrears, and their wives and children, must be prohibited from having more than two changes of clothes. If serfs in arrears were caught with *more* than two changes of clothes – or with luxury items such as silk scarves – then these garments were to be 'confiscated and sold and the money put toward their dues payments'.[66] That Voshchazhnikovo serfs were buying consumer goods instead of paying their feudal obligations, and that this was explicitly acknowledged by the landlord further undermines the idea that peasants on this estate were in some way 'subsistence-oriented'.

This decree also shows that figures on arrears in taxes and feudal dues are not wholly reliable as indicators of serfs' standards of living. We cannot always be sure that those who were in arrears were *unable* to pay their taxes and dues. Even some relatively poor serfs, who were able to make a plausible case for delaying tax payments, evidently harboured a desire to buy consumer goods, and did not see why that desire should be subordinated to the landlord's claims on their available funds. Of course, much better data about incomes and consumption habits would be needed to reach any definitive conclusions about standards of living under serfdom. But in the meantime we should bear in mind that serfs in some parts of rural Russia did not 'raise or make most of what they had';[67] rather, they spent their discretionary income, and sometimes even more, on a wide variety of consumer goods.

---

[64] The economic position of each household is described in the inventories of households (*ibid.*). The most common terms used are 'good' (*khorosho*), 'average' (*sredstvenno*), and 'poor' (*bedno*). Occasionally households are said to be in extreme straits (*v krainou bednosti*) or in very good shape (*pokhval'no* or 'laudable').

[65] 'tem iz nikh, kto neplatit v svoe vremia podatei, vospretit' imet' kak na sebye, tak na zhenakh i detiakh plat'ia luchshikh sortov po neskol'ku peremen', in RGADA, f. 1287, op. 3, ed. khr. 1615, l. 1 ('Decree prohibiting serfs in arrears from having the best sorts of clothing, 1843').

[66] 'takovye u [neplatil'shchikov] otbirat' i prodat' s torgu dlia otchistki nedoimok', in *ibid.*, l. 1.

[67] Hellie, *Economy*, p. 645.

While these glimpses of consumption in a rural community can tell us little about Russia as a whole, they do suggest that ordinary Russian serfs knew a great deal more about what the larger world had to offer than they are usually given credit for. Knowledge of new consumption patterns had clearly penetrated deep into the countryside, far from Moscow or St Petersburg. And in this respect, it seems unlikely that Sheremetyev serfs, for all the differences in their institutional structure, were atypical. It has been suggested that the industrial revolution in northwest Europe was pre-dated by an 'industrious' revolution, involving a change in the time-allocation decisions of households, whereby their members allocated more time to wage work in order to take advantage of new possibilities for market consumption.[68] The evidence presented here suggests that by the early nineteenth century the serf population in some parts of Russia was poised for just the sort of major shift in time allocation and market consumption that had characterised the industrious revolution in northwest Europe a century or so earlier. Although more research is needed to establish the extent of such economic behaviour in rural Russia, its existence in at least one region raises the question whether Russia as a whole might not have become more prosperous by the early twentieth century if the Emancipation Act of 1861 had taken a different form.

---

[68] J. de Vries, *The industrious revolution: consumer behaviour and the household economy 1650–present* (Cambridge, 2008).

9 The institutional framework of Russian serfdom

This book began with the question of how to explain why Russia was (and perhaps is) so different from 'the west'. Three different approaches to this question were discussed, of which one, the cultural approach, has attracted by far the greatest following over the century and a half or so since this question began to occupy the minds of Russian, and eventually western, intellectuals. In subsequent chapters the preponderance of the evidence reviewed has favoured the institutional over the cultural approach. However, when one thinks of the institutional structure of rural Russia in this period, the first thing that comes to mind is something called 'serfdom'. Yet serfdom has played a seemingly peripheral role in the discussion of peasant society in these pages. What exactly was its relevance – if any – to the local economy we have been discussing?

9.1   Russian serfdom

It hardly needs to be repeated, after everything that has been said, that the rural society depicted in this study comes across as a much more open, dynamic society than that usually portrayed in the literature on Russian peasants. The rural inhabitants of Yaroslavl' province do not appear to have been 'subsistence-oriented', as the Peasant Myth maintains, or reluctant to engage in market transactions. Serfs at Voshchazhnikovo engaged in land, labour, and credit transactions with each other, with serfs from other estates, with free peasants and merchants from different parts of the Central Industrial Region, and even with members of the landholding class. They were integrated into a wider regional economy through these commercial ties, as well as through trade, migrant labour, and local fairs and markets, where people from other parts of the region (and even other regions) met to exchange goods and services. Some Voshchazhnikovo peasants managed to accumulate considerable wealth, despite their status as serfs.[1] A few of these

---

[1] RGADA, f. 1287, op. 3, ed. khr. 1283 ('Report on trading serfs and their guild associations, 1836'), and ed. khr. 1391 ('List of trading peasants and guilds, 1838').

even purchased their freedom and became members of the merchant class.[2]

How are we to understand serfdom in the light of this evidence? As noted earlier, some historians have argued that the effects of serfdom on peasant societies were minimal. Is that the lesson of the last seven chapters of this book? Many Voshchazhnikovo serfs were, after all, able to get around the landlord's rules and regulations. If a serf could pay for a passport, he was usually granted permission to travel. If he could pay the fine, he could risk establishing a separate household without estate permission or hiring an unregistered outsider to work his land. If he could pay the tax, he could marry his daughter to a non-estate serf. If he had the resources, a serf could hire labourers to cultivate his communal allotment, while he himself engaged in trade or worked as a migrant labourer in one of the cities. Serfdom, it might seem, was not nearly so restrictive as it has been traditionally portrayed.

Or is the story told here compatible, rather, with the view of Gerschenkron and others, that serfdom, despite its flexibility, inhibited economic growth, and contributed to Russia's 'backwardness' compared to western Europe?[3] According to this view, serfdom kept Russian peasants poor through burdensome taxes in cash, labour, or kind, restrictions on mobility, and various forms of coercion. In addition, the lack of clearly defined property rights for peasants – and the communal repartition system, in particular – is thought to have stifled innovation in agriculture, which, in turn, inhibited Russian industrialisation.[4]

The answer to this question is not as straightforward as either alternative would appear to suggest. One problem is that 'serfdom' evidently had no uniform meaning across Russia. Though anchored in certain legislative formulations, such as the Muscovite Law Code (*Ulozhenie*) of 1649, these were only loose constraints which did not impose much positive content on the form serfdom took in different localities.[5]

---

[2] According to the soul revisions, five serf households purchased their freedom and joined the merchantry between 1834 and 1850, and another four between 1850 and 1858. Calculated from RGADA, f. 1287, op. 3, ed. khr. 1941 ('Soul revision, 1850') and GAYaO, f. 100, op. 8, d. 2656 ('Soul revision, 1858').

[3] Gerschenkron maintained that '[t]he main reason for the abysmal economic backwardness of Russia was the preservation of serfdom until the emancipation of 1861', in Gerschenkron, *Economic backwardness*, p. 17.

[4] *Ibid.*, pp. 17–21. See also O. Crisp, *Studies in the Russian economy before 1914* (London and Basingstoke, 1976), pp. 70–2.

[5] The sections of the Muscovite Law Code (*Ulozhenie*) of 1649 which are now viewed as the legal foundations of Russian serfdom were concerned primarily with (the prohibition of) peasant mobility and procedures for dealing with fugitive serfs. See the discussion in R. Bartlett, 'Serfdom and state power in imperial Russia', *European History Quarterly* 33 (2003), pp. 29–64 esp. pp. 30–1.

Imperial law largely left it to landlords to run their estates as they saw fit. This loose legislative cloak gave rise to a vast heterogeneity of different local and landlord-specific forms by the early nineteenth century. In any particular local context, what serfdom amounted to was the policy of the landlord, both its explicit official framework and its actual day-to-day, year-to-year implementation.

These gaps in the legal framework meant that it was possible for serf-dom, as it existed at Voshchazhnikovo, to have certain positive aspects for estate inhabitants. Most of these resulted from the reasonably well-developed and quasi-formal legal and administrative framework developed by the Sheremetyevs to oversee their many scattered holdings. We have seen some specific aspects of this system in the preceding chapters. The framework itself had two main parts: first, a legislative component, a written set of rules and regulations (*instriuktsii* or 'instructions'), accord-ing to which all estates were to be governed; and second, an enforcement mechanism, the central authority (*domovaia konsulariia*) to which all bailiffs and stewards and elected officials were accountable. The so-called instructions were usually quite detailed; one surviving set for the Voshchazhnikovo estate, from the year 1764, contained ninety-five sepa-rate points.[6] The instructions covered many different aspects of estate life, as indicated previously. They addressed questions of taxation and feudal obligations and how these were to be assessed and collected, rights of access to communal resources (such as meadows and forests), estate administrative procedures (how bailiffs' reports should be written and what sorts of records should be kept), policies concerning the building of houses, barns, and other structures on the estate, and guidelines for hiring outsiders as servants and labourers and for renting property to outsiders. In addition, they set out the penalties (fines and other punish-ments) to be imposed on serfs who broke these rules. These rules and regulations were regularly updated through additional decrees (*prikazy*), issued from the landlord's central office. Complete, updated sets of instructions seem to have been issued periodically, though only those for the years 1764 and 1796 have survived for Voshchazhnikovo.

It should be noted that there was no one set of instructions by which all Sheremetyev estates were governed. Serfs on Sheremetyev estates in the southern agricultural zone, for instance, owed different types of feudal obligations to those in the quitrent areas; these would have been specified in the 'instructions' for estates in this region. On the other hand, there do not seem to have been separate sets of rules and regulations for each

---

[6] RGADA, f. 1287, op. 3, ed. khr. 1305 ('Instructions, 1764').

estate. The 1764 instructions for Voshchazhnikovo are, for example, also addressed to the officials for the Iukhotskaia votchina, the other Sheremetyev estate in Yaroslavl' province.[7] It seems likely that the 'instructions' – at least the parts that set out obligations and fines – were tailored to the specific socioeconomic structure of the different estates (both Voshchazhnikovo and Iukhotskoye were quitrent estates without any particular economic specialisation). The administrative procedures set out by the instructions were probably fairly uniform, though. One indication of this can be found in the lists of documents in the Sheremetyev family archive: all of the family's holdings appear to have generated similar kinds of records.[8]

It was the central administrative office in St Petersburg that provided the Sheremetyevs' legal and administrative framework with some degree of uniformity and consistency. Officials in the central office were in constant contact with estate managers and other officials from each of the Sheremetyev holdings.[9] The Voshchazhnikovo records make clear, as indicated in chapter 4, that all decisions taken at the local level required authorisation from the central office. Furthermore, the Voshchazhnikovo archive reveals that reports on serfs' economic activities and other aspects of daily life on the estate were sent regularly to officials in St Petersburg. Local officials also consulted with the central office on any issues not covered by the instructions. In one such case, a Voshchazhnikovo serf who had purchased an exemption from military service wanted to sell his exemption certificate to another serf. Estate officials wrote to St Petersburg to ask for advice, since there was no provision for such a transaction in the written regulations. The central office decided that the transaction ought to be permitted, since similar transactions took place on other Sheremetyev estates.[10] This is one of the more explicit references to a sort of precedent system, and it implies that the central office at least made an attempt to apply a reasonably consistent set of principles to all estates. They evidently tried to avoid arbitrarily forbidding serfs on one estate to engage in transactions permitted to serfs on other holdings.

The main advantage to the serfs of this legal and administrative system is that it provided a relatively explicit and stable framework within which they could take decisions about their daily lives, especially those decisions

---

[7] *Ibid.*, l. 22.   [8] RGADA, f. 1287, op. 3, 4, 5, and 6 in particular.
[9] It is not clear from the Voshchazhnikovo documents how many officials worked in the St Petersburg home office, but it may be possible to investigate this question later, using other files in the Sheremetyev archive.
[10] RGADA, f. 1287, op. 3, ed. khr. 2312, l. 26 ('Instructions and decrees, 1857').

that had implications, and carried commitments, for future periods. The basic rules governing social and economic life on the estate were clearly spelled out, as were the consequences of breaking those rules. Procedures for the administration of justice were also made explicit, so that serfs had some idea how the legal system functioned and to whom they should turn in the event of a dispute or other grievance.[11] Furthermore, the rules were enforced by a relatively impartial central authority, staffed by officials whose interests were not necessarily aligned with those of the dominant interest groups in the localities. It was this relative transparency and impartiality – relative because, as we will see shortly, the Sheremetyev system was still, in a larger sense, an extralegal one – that made it possible for serfs on this estate to engage in land, labour, and credit markets, and to save and invest their earnings, to the extent observed in previous chapters.

The Sheremetyevs' administrative framework had three specific positive effects on social and economic life at Voshchazhnikovo. First, it enabled serfs to overcome legal obstacles to participation in land, property, and credit markets, by allowing serfs to purchase and hold land in the name of the landlord.[12] Russian serfs were not permitted by state law to hold land in their own names until 1848.[13] By providing a framework within which serfs could own property despite the legal constraints imposed by the state, the Sheremetyevs made it possible for Voshchazhnikovo serfs to pursue more diverse intertemporal resource allocation and risk-minimisation strategies. As we saw in chapter 7, privately held property provided serfs with a form of savings, as well as greater access to rural credit markets, since land and other forms of real estate could be used as loan collateral. The availability of such options meant that Voshchazhnikovo serfs were not forced to rely on the collectivist risk-minimisation strategies offered by communal land tenure and the periodic redistribution of arable.

A second, equally important, aspect of the Sheremetyevs' centralised legal system was the contract enforcement component, which greatly reduced the risk involved in market transactions. Although land was officially purchased in the landlord's name, it was formally acknowledged

---

[11] It must be noted that it is not clear from the sources *how* these regulations, procedures, and penalties were made known to the serf population. All one sees in the surviving documents is that serfs followed the procedures as spelled out and referred to them in their various petitions and depositions.

[12] As noted in chapter 5, the Sheremetyevs were not the only landlords who permitted serfs to purchase land in their names. Bohac's work on the Manuilovskoe estate indicates that the Gagarin family also had such a system in place. See Bohac, 'Family, property, and socioeconomic mobility', p. 10.

[13] Crisp, 'Peasant land tenure', p. 37.

by the landlord and his officials as the private property of the purchaser; the landlord himself signed away his rights to this land in the contract he issued to a serf at the time of purchase.[14] Serfs kept copies of the purchase contracts and certificates of title as did the estate administration, so that they could be produced in the event of a dispute. We saw in chapters 5 and 7 that the central office had formal procedures in place to deal with disputes over property and credit. Officials in St Petersburg could force the return of unlawfully confiscated property, as they did in the case of the serf widow Fedos'ia Mishutina, who had her land unlawfully expropriated and sold by communal officials in 1820.[15] Similarly, in the case of credit contracts, the landlord's officials were willing, if necessary, to force the debtor to sell property to ensure that credit obligations were met, or to arrange property auctions if the debtor refused or was deceased.

Finally, the centralised administrative framework provided serfs with access to legal recourse beyond the local community. If a serf felt that he was unlikely to receive a fair hearing by the commune (either the estate commune or the local village commune), he could take his case to the landlord's officials in St Petersburg. This policy was made explicit in a decree from 1789, in which P. N. Sheremetyev wrote that 'all of [his] serfs should be at liberty to bring their concerns directly to [him]'.[16] This option, as discussed in chapter 4, would have been especially important to those who wished to bring cases against more powerful members of the community. In the absence of recourse to a higher authority, serfs may have been less inclined to bring petitions against communal officers or members of other dominant groups. Communal officials, after all, usually presided over communal gatherings, and they would have been very unlikely to rule against themselves or their colleagues. Similarly, members of other powerful groups – such as the very wealthy serfs – may have been able to influence legislation and local decision making in their favour. So serfs could not always rely on the bailiff to mediate, since, although he was, in theory, an outsider who reported to the landlord, he lived and worked on the estate and was therefore at least partially integrated into the local community, and subject to pressure from local elites.

Officials in St Petersburg were less beholden to powerful local interest groups. They lived far from the estate and depended almost entirely on the

---

[14] For an example of *doverennost'*, see RGADA, f. 1287, op. 3, ed. khr. 1563, l. 8 ('Petition regarding land purchase, 1840').

[15] RGADA, f. 1287, op. 3, ed. khr. 745 ('Petition regarding property dispute, 1820').

[16] 'chtob vse iz krest'ian moikh komu nadobnost' nastoiat' budet imeli svobodu prikhodit' priamo ko mne so svoimi nuzhdami kak o tom v povelenii moem ot 20-go aprel'ia 1789 goda predpisano bylo', in RGADA, f. 1287, op. 3, ed. khr. 555, l. 2 (letter written in 1790, included with 'Instructions, 1796/1800').

landlord's patronage. Thus the central office seems to have been viewed by serfs as a more impartial dispenser of justice than the local commune. This view was reinforced when officials in St Petersburg showed that they were willing to rule against local elites when provided with evidence of wrongdoing.[17] Even bailiffs – the landlord's own officials – were not immune; serfs at Voshchazhnikovo brought cases against bailiffs on at least two occasions (against the bailiff Slasnikov in 1807 and against the bailiff Tizengauzen in 1835), one of which (serfs versus Slasnikov) resulted in the bailiff's dismissal.[18] Allowing serfs to appeal directly to St Petersburg may have helped the landlord to constrain the power of local officials.

It was not only petitions against local authorities, though, that were sent to the landlord's officials. Serfs at Voshchazhnikovo addressed the central office with a large variety of requests and complaints. As noted in chapter 4, petitions concerning disputes among serfs over property transactions, inheritance, communal repartitions, as well as petitions for poor relief, were sent from Voshchazhnikovo to St Petersburg. Serfs even went to the landlord with cases involving defamation and other assaults on their 'honour'.[19] Nearly half of the documents in the Voshchazhnikovo archive are petitions from serfs to the St Petersburg office (there are at least 1,000 petitions in the archive for the period 1800–50). That so many serfs petitioned the central office with such a wide range of complaints suggests that there was a strong demand for an extra-local judicial system.[20] And, while this system may have been particularly valuable to marginalised groups who had little clout in the community, serfs from all socioeconomic strata apparently made use of it.

This semi-formal system of property rights and contract enforcement, administered by a non-local judiciary, significantly reduced the amount of risk involved in property and credit market transactions, and enabled a surprisingly large number of serfs at Voshchazhnikovo (and, it seems, on

---

[17] As in the above-mentioned case of the widow Fedos'ia Mishutina, who took her case against the communal elite to the landlord's officials and received a ruling in her favour. See RGADA, f. 1287, op. 3, ed. khr. 745 ('Petition regarding property dispute, 1820'), and references in ed. khr. 770, l. 5 ('Petition regarding dispute, 1820').

[18] Details of these cases can be found in RGADA, f. 1287, op. 3, ed. khr. 668 ('Petition against Slasnikov, 1807'), and ed. khr. 1256 ('Petition against bailiff Tizengauzen, 1835').

[19] As in RGADA, f. 1287, op. 3, ed. khr. 770 ('Petition regarding dispute, 1820'), in which Nikolai Sheshunov brought a case against Mikhail Kokin for calling him a 'swindler'; or RGADA, f. 1287, op. 3, ed. khr. 768 ('Petition regarding dispute, 1820'), in which Pyotr Dolodanov brought a case against Pyotr Shishkin for cursing at him and calling him a thief.

[20] This is consistent with Burbank's findings for the post-Emancipation period, as discussed in *Russian peasants go to court*.

Sheremetyev estates more generally) to achieve a considerable degree of wealth.[21] What we must bear in mind, though, when thinking about the effects of serfdom in Russia more generally, is that not all Russian land-lords ran their estates like the Sheremetyev family. While many of the other large landholding families also used centralised administrative systems to oversee their holdings, we currently know very little about the way these functioned at the local level. Scattered evidence from the Gagarin family estates suggests that this family's approach was considerably less flexible than that of the Sheremetyevs; Hoch, Czap, and Bohac, in their studies of Gagarin estates, describe a more rigid system of social control, a low tolerance for commercial activities, and a greater likelihood of arbitrary confiscation of property than observed at Voshchazhnikovo.[22] And serfs on those estates appear to have been considerably poorer than those at Voshchazhnikovo.[23] However, these studies did not focus on landlord policy, and thus the evidence related to it is only fragmentary.

Landlords on smaller estates, like the one memorably described by Goncharov in his novel *Oblomov*, would have been even less like the Sheremetyevs. This class of landlord, which was of course much more numerous than the landholders of Sheremetyev dimensions, did not have the resources required to establish such an elaborate management system. Many of those who lived in the city, like Oblomov himself, would probably have been forced to rely on an at best sporadically monitored bailiff or on communal officials to manage their estates. And those who did live on their estates are not likely to have done much better. (Portrayals of gentry landholders by writers such as Turgenev and Tolstoy, themselves land-lords, reinforce this impression.) But since these small landlords did not generate as many records as the large landholders, we know very little about the way their estates were run.

If the Sheremetyev approach to estate management was so successful at raising revenues, it would be reasonable to wonder why it was not adopted

---

[21] As shown in chapter 8, some 70 per cent of serfs at Voshchazhnikovo were in either the first or second rank, possessing taxable assets worth at least 500 roubles. The estates of Iukhotskoe, Ivanovo, Pavlovo, and Molodoi Tud appear to have been similar in economic and social structure to Voshchazhnikovo. See Shchepetov, *Krepostnoe pravo*; Gestwa, *Proto-industrialisierung*; Prokof'eva, *Krest'ianskaia obshchina*.

[22] Hoch, *Serfdom and social control*; Bohac, 'Family, property, and socioeconomic mobility', esp. pp. 48–59 on 'forced migration'; also in Bohac, 'Agricultural structure', pp. 376–80. Czap discusses the Gagarin officials' coercive approaches to serf marriage in 'A large family', pp. 120–1.

[23] This is not to say that they were poor. Hoch has emphasised that serfs at Petrovskoe had a varied diet and substantial livestock holdings (*Serfdom and social control*, pp. 21, 47–8). But they do seem to have been poorer than Voshchazhnikovo serfs. Their dwellings were smaller and more primitive and, according to Hoch, they remained vulnerable to famine-induced mortality crises in the nineteenth century.

by all Russian landlords. In considering this question, two points must be made. First, it seems unlikely, from available sources, that the Sheremetyevs themselves could have predicted the outcomes described here when they designed their estate administrative system. The archival record suggests that some of the critical factors – for instance, contract enforcement and extra-local dispute mediation – evolved gradually over the period under consideration. For instance, petitions to the landlord over property and credit disputes and references to formal credit contracts seem to have increased substantially from the late eighteenth century. This pattern might be random; these are simply the documents that survived to the present day. But it could also be that a system originally designed to enable serfs to engage in land and property transactions (in the name of the landlord), a system in operation at Voshchazhnikovo from at least the 1730s, was gradually applied to other transactions over time, as the Sheremetyevs and the serf elite realised they could benefit from them. The use of formal notarial documents to record transactions and the enforcement of these agreements by the central administrative office may have been, over time, applied to credit transactions and then eventually to contracts of other kinds. At this point we can only speculate, but, in the absence of convincing evidence to the contrary, it seems a reasonable hypothesis.[24]

The second point to consider is that not all Russian landlords faced the same constraints. As mentioned above, a centralised system like the Sheremetyevs' would have been expensive to implement and administer, which probably explains why only the very wealthiest landlords had them.[25] Employing staff to handle all the petitions from serfs (Voshchazhnikovo was only one of dozens of Sheremetyev estates) – to investigate their complaints, undertake depositions, to enforce decisions – would have surely added enormously to management costs. It is possible that the Gagarin family, or the Orlovs or Demidovs, were not willing or able to make this sort of investment. They may have had greater debts to service than the Sheremetyev family, or more lavish parties to throw, or entrepreneurial endeavours to finance. As a result, their time horizons were shorter: they sought to squeeze as much revenue as possible from their serfs each year, rather than invest in a costly management system which would only pay off over a longer period. Smaller landlords, of the sort described above, would

---

[24] It is possible that the Sheremetyevs' voluminous correspondence, with other landlords and with their own administrative officials, might offer clues about their intentions.

[25] It is true that these landlords also had more estates to administer. But there were also smaller landlords with several holdings or absentee landlords who did not use the same kind of centralised apparatus. See, for instance, Melton's study of the Lieven family serfs ('The magnate').

almost certainly have lacked the resources to create such a system, with many of them heavily in debt by the nineteenth century. Once again, this is hardly more than a suggestive hypothesis for future research.

This does not make the Sheremetyevs highly exceptional or the Voshchazhnikovo estate unrepresentative. The Voshchazhnikovo archive indicates that serfs from other estates in the region were engaged in the same kinds of economic activities as those from Voshchazhnikovo. As we have seen, Sheremetyev serfs engaged in property, labour, and credit transactions with serfs, and non-serfs, from various parts of Yaroslavl' province and beyond. Even Gagarin family serfs, according to Bohac, engaged in private land purchases in their landlord's name, as did serfs of other wealthy landholding families.[26] In the present state of our knowledge, the best guess would have to be that Russian serfdom was a loose framework in which a wide continuum of different forms of estate governance (i.e. of landlord policy) could be implemented. In economic terms, the Russian empire was as much a 'composite state'[27] as the Holy Roman Empire, if not even more so, with greater power in the hands of landlords to shape the institutional framework (central European princes appear to have been much more constrained by local corporate groups and their traditional rights and privileges).[28] Thus the spectrum of observed institutional frameworks may have been even wider in Russia than in central Europe. Near one end of this spectrum would be landlords who, like the Sheremetyevs, maintained a kind of stable – though informal – framework of property rights and the rule of law. The Gagarins would seem, from the little we know, to have been nearer the other, more arbitrary end of this continuum, though perhaps closer to the Sheremetyev end than the thousands of small landholders like Oblomov, whose serfs were very likely ruled by strong local communities or the arbitrary whim of their local serf elite (like the serfs at Baki, described by Melton) or of the small landlord himself, without recourse to any external jurisdiction.

9.2   Obstacles to growth

Even on the relatively well-managed estates of the Sheremetyev family, serfdom had its negative aspects. The main problem was that the policies

---

[26] *Ibid.*, p. 10. Kashin, *Krepostnye krest'iane-zemlevladel'tsy*, pp. 10–27.

[27] As described by H. G. Koenigsberger in 'The crisis of the seventeenth century: a farewell?', in *idem, Politics and virtuosi: essays in early modern history* (London, 1986), pp. 149–68.

[28] A general overview of the institutional framework in early modern German central Europe can be found in S. Ogilvie, 'The state in Germany: a non-Prussian view', in J. Brewer and E. Hellmuth (eds.), *Rethinking Leviathan: the eighteenth-century state in Britain and Germany* (Oxford, 1999), pp. 167–202.

of Russian landlords were not integrated into a larger legal framework; they were what Hernando de Soto has called 'extralegal social conventions'.[29] In other words, there was no larger body of law, issuing from a central authority, in which the Sheremetyevs' policies were embedded. In medieval England, as in parts of central Europe during the second serfdom, the manor was part of a set of interlocking institutions. Since serfs in these regions were not only the subjects of their lords, but also of the crown, they could appeal beyond their landlords' jurisdictions to the Royal Courts or, in the case of the German lands, to the emperor himself.[30] Russian serfs, on the other hand, were considered the subjects – the *property*, in fact – of their lords, and, consequently, had far fewer rights before the crown. This absence of a larger legal framework had two important implications. First, it meant that Russian serfs were not able to challenge more restrictive and coercive estate policies; the Russian state was evidently reluctant to interfere in the affairs of landlords.[31] Second, because serfs had no legal rights, the more beneficial estate policies – such as those granting property rights to serfs – were not recognised outside the landlord's own jurisdiction. It is in this sense that landlords' policies were 'extralegal'.

That serfs' rights to property were not embedded in any larger legal context meant that property and credit transactions – no matter how sophisticated the informal legal system – were always fraught with risk. If the landlord had arbitrarily decided to confiscate the wealth of his serfs, there was nothing they could have done about it, since their rights to property were not recognised by any higher legal authority. This implied a considerable degree of uncertainty, given that policies could change from one generation of landlords to the next. Boris Petrovich Sheremetyev may have honoured serfs' rights to property, but how could his serfs be sure that his son Pyotr Borisovich would do the same? That so many Voshchazhnikovo serfs engaged in land, labour, and credit markets suggests that they considered the risks involved to be relatively low. Nevertheless, these transactions were considerably riskier than they would have been if carried out within a formal legal framework.

And while it is true that a surprising number of Voshchazhnikovo serfs did manage to prosper within the informal system that evolved under the Sheremetyevs, their extralegal activities were carried out at a considerable cost. For one thing, significant amounts of time, effort, and money were

---

[29] H. de Soto, *The mystery of capital* (London, 2000), especially chapter 6.
[30] Briggs, 'Rural credit', pp. 39–54. See Ogilvie, 'The state in Germany', pp. 200–1; Hagen, *Ordinary Prussians*, pp. 541–59.
[31] Bartlett, 'Serfdom', pp. 30–3.

devoted to devising ways to get around arbitrary constraints. Some of these were estate regulations, such as the obligation that serfs cultivate their communal lands, even when the returns to their time were higher in other occupations. Thus Voshchazhnikovo serfs who wanted to work as traders or servants in cities were, as we saw in chapter 6, forced to pay others to cultivate their lands in their absence. There were also state-level regulations, such as that which forbade serfs to purchase or hold land in their own names. On the Sheremetyev estates, a system was developed to help serfs overcome this legal obstacle. But at what cost? A serf who bought land in the lord's name had to pay the landlord 10 per cent of the purchase price, in addition to the annual 1 per cent asset tax. There were also assorted fees involved in the purchase process, including the one levied by the landlord for the 'power of attorney' document, as well as those related to the drawing up of contracts, and the registration and formalisation of the sale.

These are examples of the more explicit costs imposed by this particular institutional framework. But there were other, less obvious costs associated with serfdom. Because they lacked formal legal rights, serfs were often forced to develop complex informal strategies to circumvent institutional restrictions. One such strategy involved the use of what anthropologists have called 'many-stranded relationships' or what are known to sociologists and other social scientists as 'social networks'.[32] With this strategy, serfs used their personal relationships – members of their extended kin groups, neighbours, fellow craftsmen – to obtain goods and services that were inaccessible through more direct channels. This practice is known to Russians as *blat*, and is often associated with the Soviet era.[33] In fact, it has a much longer history in Russia. Although serfs may not have called it *blat* (this word does not appear in the Voshchazhnikovo records), the documents suggest that the strategy itself was familiar to them. Friends in high places do seem to have helped

---

[32] On many-stranded relationships see S. Popkin, *The rational peasant: the political economy of rural society in Vietnam* (Berkeley and Los Angeles, 1979); Scott, *The moral economy*; Wolf, *Peasants*, pp. 84–9. 'Social networks' are discussed in J. S. Coleman, *Foundations of social theory* (Cambridge, MA, 1990), pp. 318–20; and in R. D. Putnam, *Making democracy work: civic traditions in modern Italy* (Princeton, 1993). With reference to serfdom, see Dennison and Ogilvie, 'Serfdom and social capital'.

[33] For an illuminating analysis of *blat* in the Soviet era, see A. V. Ledeneva, *Russia's economy of favours: blat, networking and informal exchange* (Cambridge, 1998). An economic analysis of this phenomenon can be found in G. Grossman, 'Informal personal incomes and outlays of the Soviet Union population', in A. Portes, M. Castells, and L. Benton (eds.), *The informal economy* (Baltimore, 1989), pp. 150–70. On post-Soviet Russia, see R. Rose, 'Getting things done in an antimodern society: social capital networks in Russia', in P. Dasgupta and I. Seregeldin (eds.), *Social capital: a multifaceted perspective* (Washington, 1999), pp. 147–71.

Voshchazhnikovo serfs to get around various rules and regulations. In a petition from 1807, several serfs complained that communal officials were allowing their friends (*tovarishchi*) to break estate rules. Aleksei Chernikhin, an associate of the estate elder and owner of a four-year lease on the estate fisheries, was, for instance, permitted by the elder to break the rules against overfishing in estate ponds.[34] Similarly, as friends of the elder, Kozma and Nikolai Popov were permitted, contrary to estate regulations, to run their leather manufactory on threshing ground. The same Aleksei Chernikhin was allowed to thwart the rules on building by putting his brick manufactory on arable land.[35]

Wealthy serfs were evidently able to use their money and their contacts to broaden their social networks. They could persuade others to do favours for them, because they were in a position to reciprocate in some way. Some Voshchazhnikovo serfs attempted to expand their social networks through marriage.[36] There is some indication in the documents of inter-marriage among the richer serfs on the estate. For example, a petition from 1847 suggests that the son of one of the wealthy Voshchazhnikovo families (Dmitri Dolodanov) was married to the daughter of another wealthy serf family (Katerina Titova).[37] Even more interesting are the lengths to which poorer serfs would go to marry their children to members of a higher legal estate (*soslovie*). As we saw in chapter 3, the Sheremetyevs charged the families of serf women substantial fees for marrying their daughters to outsiders. The documents for Voshchazhnikovo suggest that some poorer families were willing to pay these fees in order to marry their daughters to merchants or members of the petite bourgeoisie. The family of Matryona Efremova, for example, who were in the 'last rank' (*poslednaia stat'ia* – the lowest income bracket), agreed in 1832 to pay the landlord a fee of 100 roubles, so that Matryona could marry the merchant Abrokov.[38] Similarly, in 1833, the family of Elizaveta Slasnikova, also in the 'last rank', agreed to pay the fee of 100 roubles, so that Elizaveta could be married to Nikolai Aristarkhov, a *meshchanin* from Uglich.[39] That same year, Pytor Shepelyev, a serf of the 'last rank' from the village of Dem'ian, paid the landlord 100 roubles for permission to marry his daughter Aksin'ia to Fyodor Andreyev, the son of

---

[34] RGADA, f. 1287, op. 3, ed. khr. 668, ll. 4–5 ('Petition against the estate bailiff, Slasnikov, 1807').

[35] *Ibid.*

[36] See the discussion in Morrison, '*Trading peasants*', pp. 351–66.

[37] The petitioner refers to Aleksei Titov as Dolodanov's father-in-law. In RGADA, f. 1287, op. 3, ed. khr. 1764, l. 3 ('Petition regarding credit, 1847').

[38] RGADA, f. 1287, op. 3, ed. khr. 1124, l. 41 ('Petitions regarding marriage, 1832').

[39] RGADA, f. 1287, op. 3, ed. khr. 1181, l. 46 ('Petitions regarding marriage, 1833').

a merchant (*kupecheskoi syn*).[40] That poorer families were willing to pay substantial fees to marry their daughters to members of other (higher) social groups suggests that they expected to benefit later from the alliance.[41]

In addition to social networks or *blat*, serfs used bribery to get around rules and regulations. Since bribery is by definition an extralegal activity, one often only learns of its existence through oblique references in scattered sources. The Voshchazhnikovo documents are exceptional in that they contain, surprisingly, a number of direct references to bribery.[42] Most references to bribes – *vziatki* as well as more euphemistic versions, such as money or goods offered *v pochest'* or 'in tribute' – occur quite often in the communal resolutions (*mirskie prigovory*). In the communal resolutions for 1750, for instance, serfs agreed to deliver a petition (*proshchenie*) to the estate manager (*upravitel'*) along with a 'bribe of 3 roubles'.[43] The resolutions for 1754 indicate that, along with their quitrent payments, Voshchazhnikovo serfs sent bribes in the form of pork and beef to officials in St Petersburg.[44] An even more substantial offering appears in the resolutions for 1763, where serfs agreed to pay a bribe of 100 roubles to the bailiff Ivan Zhenalov.[45] Unfortunately, none of these entries tells us what the serfs expected in return for these bribes. An entry for 1791 is a bit more specific, recording that serfs agreed to send the selectman Grigory Zhukov to Yaroslavl' 'to bribe whomever necessary, with money from our communal funds, in order that Voshchazhnikovo serfs will not have to help with the paving and building of bridges in Borisogleb district'.[46] The use of bribery seems to have been so widespread at Voshchazhnikovo that serfs even made official entries for bribe money in the communal account books. According to account books from 1750, 15 kopecks were used to

---

[40] *Ibid.*, l. 15.

[41] It is, of course, possible that the grooms themselves were paying the exit fees for poorer serf families. But this is not incompatible with the hypothesis that greater benefits accrued from such alliances.

[42] They are exceptional when compared to documents for non-Russian societies. Work by other historians of Russia suggests that direct references to bribes were not unusual on the estates of the larger landholders.

[43] 'podat' upravitel'iam Grigoriiu Voroblyovskomu i Fyodoru Kliucharevu v pochest' 3 rub', in RGADA, f. 1287, op. 3, ed. khr. 141, l. 8 ('Communal resolutions, 1750').

[44] 'pri posylke obrochnykh deneg poslat' v Moskvu … ego vysokografskogo Siiatel'stva upravitil'em v pochest' na miaso svinye i korov'e', in RGADA, f. 1287, op. 3, ed. khr. 174, l. 2 ('Communal resolutions, 1754').

[45] 'prikashchiku Ivanu Zhenalovu podnest' pochest' sto rublyov', in RGADA, f. 1287, op. 3, ed. khr. 275, ll. 9–10 ('Communal resolutions, 1763').

[46] 'delat' komu sleduet pochtenie iz mirskou nashei summy s tem chtob izbavit'sa ot moshcheniia i postroiki Borisoglebskikh mostov', in RGADA, f. 1287, op. 3, ed. khr. 2518, l. 5 ('Communal resolutions, 1791').

purchase 250 eggs, which were sent to an estate official as a bribe.[47] An account book from 1754 records that 2 roubles 20 kopecks were paid to the estate elders for delivering a bribe in the form of grain to the Rostov district governor.[48] Another serf was paid 37 kopecks for delivering 250 eggs to the estate bailiff as a bribe.[49] Several entries in the account book for the year 1787 concern 'gifts' that were offered to local officials. 'In honour of the New Year', serfs sent the Rostov district governor a fatted hog and 1 rouble 10 kopecks, along with 5 kopecks for each of his deputies. The same was sent to the two district surveyors, as well as to the district registrar, whose deputies also received 3 kopecks each.[50]

Bribery was not condoned by the Sheremetyevs; on the contrary, they seem to have tried unsuccessfully to stop it. In 1764, P. B. Sheremetyev acknowledged that large sums were being recorded in communal account books as *pochesti* (bribes). He demanded that his serfs stop using bribery; instead, they were to appeal to him when they encountered institutional obstacles.[51] Sheremetyev threatened to introduce a fine for the use of bribes, but, as the above examples indicate, the practice continued, as did the formal account entries. In 1800 another decree was issued, in which the count admitted that bribery was still a problem on his estates, and that, to his dismay, a large number of the bribes (*vziatki*) were paid to his own officials (the account books of the Ivanovo estate for the year 1800 revealed 1,185 roubles spent on bribes paid to local estate managers).[52] This time, instead of threatening the serfs, Sheremetyev announced that he would be increasing the salaries of all his employees, so that they would no longer feel the need to accept bribes from serfs.[53] While this attempt was admirable, it is unlikely that it actually changed anything. Bribery was not unique to the area around Voshchazhnikovo; it was systemic in Russia.[54]

This is the basic problem we began with, that the Sheremetyev legal system, however well it worked locally, was still extralegal. As a result, there were too many 'grey' areas in the *actual* legal framework – especially where serfs were concerned – that local officials (both government officials and estate officials) could exploit to their own advantage. Apparently, the Orlov family likewise grappled with the sort of corruption described above

---

[47] RGADA, f. 1287, op. 3, ed. khr. 141, l. 10 ('Communal resolutions, 1750').
[48] RGADA, f. 1287, op. 3, ed. khr. 189, l. 4 ('Communal account books, 1754').
[49] *Ibid.*, l. 4.
[50] RGADA, f. 1287, op. 3, ed. khr. 530, l. 3 ('Communal account books, 1787').
[51] RGADA, f. 1287, op. 3, ed. khr. 1305, l. 19 ('Instructions, 1764').
[52] RGADA, f. 1287, op. 3, ed. khr. 555, ll. 56–8 ('Instructions, 1796/1800').
[53] *Ibid.*, ll. 57–8.
[54] Even the church was not immune. See the discussion in Freeze, *The parish clergy*, pp. 55–9.

on their estates.[55] Hoch notes that bribery and corruption were also widespread on the Gagarin's Petrovskoe estate.[56] And Melton has reported similar findings for the Baki estate in Kostroma province.[57]

At Voshchazhnikovo, it was the poor and other marginalised groups (such as unmarried females) who were especially disadvantaged by these aspects of the institutional framework of 'serfdom'. The monopoly privileges granted by the landlord and by the state to local corporate groups imposed significant costs on poorer serfs, by denying them access to low-investment ways of earning a living. For instance, instead of common rights of access to estate fisheries, the landlord granted monopoly rights to these resources, so that those who wished to fish were obligated to pay a fee to the local leaseholder. Similarly, monopoly rights to the market square were auctioned off to local serfs, and those who wished to trade there had to pay fees to both the leaseholder *and* the landlord. The state granted monopoly privileges to merchant guilds, who regularly demanded that all serfs who engaged in trade be made to purchase guild licences.[58] Because the guilds had the support of the state, Sheremetyev could not protect his serfs against their demands. It was especially difficult for poorer serfs to get around arbitrary rules and regulations, since they could not afford to pay bribes and were often without *blat* or influential social contacts. Furthermore, 'serfdom', as portrayed here, exacerbated communal conflict and stratification, since the absence of formal legal rights meant that serfs were dependent on landlord patronage for access to markets and local resources. In particular, the granting of monopoly privileges to certain groups and individuals facilitated the emergence of communal oligarchies and the kinds of social networks described above, whose members had a strong interest in cooperating with estate authorities.[59] These powerful serfs, as we saw in chapter 4, were often in a position to direct communal resources toward themselves and away from their fellow villagers.

The landlord's taxation policies made it very difficult for those at the bottom – in the so-called 'last rank' – to improve their situation. Those who could not afford to pay the feudal dues on land were not eligible for communal allotments. At the same time, earnings from non-agricultural

[55] Aleksandrov, *Sel'skaia obshchina*, pp. 147–8.   [56] Hoch, *Serfdom and slavery*, pp. 142–6.

[57] Melton, 'Household economies and communal conflicts', pp. 572–7.

[58] RGADA, f. 1287, op. 3, ed. khr. 1283 ('Report on trading serfs and their guild associations, 1836'), and ed. khr. 1391 ('List of trading peasants and guilds, 1838'). Conflicts between merchant guilds and peasant traders in this period are discussed in Morrison, '*Trading peasants*', pp. 238–40.

[59] This particular artefact of serfdom is described in greater detail in Dennison and Ogilvie, 'Serfdom and social capital'.

activities, such as crafts and trade, were taxed.[60] As noted in chapter 3, unmarried persons between the ages of 20 and 40 (including those who had been widowed) were liable for an additional tax – the annual 'celibacy tax', which was to be paid 'on top of existing quitrent obligations'.[61] This tax was particularly burdensome for unmarried females, who, unlike males, were seldom permitted to seek work outside the estate. The land-lord did not consider this grounds for exemption, though, since, in the local textile industry 'a woman could earn 15 to 25 roubles per year' and could therefore meet her tax obligations.[62]

But serfdom at Voshchazhnikovo was not only harmful to the poor. This system also imposed costs on those serfs who could afford to pay feudal rents and bribes, in that they were forced to channel considerable resources in money, effort, and time into unproductive avenues.[63] Resources allocated to building social networks and bribing local officials could not be invested in local manufactories or agricultural improve-ments. In addition, the ruthless profit-skimming activities of landlords and the bribe or payoff demands of other corporate groups (such as local officials and merchant guilds) made property rights less secure. The pattern appears to have been a typical one in traditional societies: where a surplus was generated, it was confiscated by someone in authority, usually the landlord or the state.[64]

It is widely believed that serfs on quitrent estates were relatively free from interfering landlords. According to this view, landlords on corvée labour estates were more likely to regulate their serfs' activities, because they needed the serfs to work their demesne land. On quitrent estates,

---

[60] RGADA, f. 1287, op. 3, ed. khr. 555, ll. 22–3 ('Instructions, 1796/1800').

[61] '[den'gi] ... brat' sverkh obyknovenago obroka', in *ibid.*, l. 26.

[62] 'vsiakaia zhenshchina ... mozhet priobresti ot 15 rub. do 25 rub. v god', in *ibid.*, l. 26. As noted in chapter 3, the poorest unmarried serfs had to pay 2 roubles per year for each year they remained unmarried (until age 40), the better off were required to pay 6 roubles per year, and those in the middle (*srednaia stat'ia*) had to pay 4 roubles per year.

[63] This is a well-known feature of informal economies, including those in modern societies. See discussions in W. Easterly, *The elusive quest for growth: economists' adventures and misadventures in the tropics* (Cambridge, MA, 2002), pp. 241–52; J. Blanes Jiménez, 'Cocaine, informality, and the urban economy in La Paz, Bolivia', in A. Portes, M. Castells, and L. Benton (eds.), *The informal economy* (Baltimore, 1989), pp. 135–49; M. Lanzetta de Pardo, G. Murillo Castano, and A. Triana Soto, 'The articulation of formal and informal sectors in the economy of Bogotá, Colombia', in A. Portes, M. Castells, and L. Benton (eds.), *The informal economy* (Baltimore, 1989), pp. 95–110; H. de Soto, *The other path: the invisible revolution in the third world* (New York, 1989), esp. chapter 5; V. Tanzi, 'Corruption: arm's length relationships and markets', in G. Fiorentini and S. Peltzman (eds.), *The economics of organised crime* (Cambridge, 1995), pp. 161–80.

[64] This pattern and its impact on economic growth in early modern Europe is outlined by Ogilvie in 'The European economy'.

where there was no demesne, serfs are supposed to have had more autonomy. So long as serfs on these estates paid their feudal dues, it is argued, landlords did not intervene in their affairs.[65] The evidence for Voshchazhnikovo suggests this difference is exaggerated. We saw in chapter 3 that the Sheremetyevs, like landlords of corvée labour estates,[66] did try to regulate their serfs' demographic behaviour. And in chapter 4 we saw that the Voshchazhnikovo estate commune was rarely allowed to take decisions without consulting the landlord's officials in St Petersburg. Moreover, the evidence presented in chapters 5–8 shows that the landlord and his officials interfered significantly in the serf economy. While it is true that there was no demesne land at Voshchazhnikovo, serfs were still required to take on and cultivate communal land. Serfs who preferred to allocate their resources to non-agricultural activities were therefore obligated to hire labourers to cultivate these communal allotments. In addition to the feudal dues attached to communal land, serfs owed some proportion of their yields to the landlord: oats for the estate stables, wheat and rye for the lord's household, and some proportion of each for the estate granary.

Serfs at Voshchazhnikovo may have been somewhat freer to engage in non-agricultural activities than serfs on corvée estates, but these freedoms always had a price. Those who engaged in crafts, trade, or manufacturing were required to pay a yearly tax of between 1 and 10 silver roubles. Serfs who sought work off the estate were required to pay for permission and for a passport. And those who managed to accumulate assets worth more than 500 roubles were required to pay an annual asset tax of 0.5 per cent on each rouble over 500. Various punishments were meted out to serfs who failed to fulfil their obligations. Fines were prescribed for a number of infractions, including the failure to cultivate communal land, leaving the estate without a passport, and travelling with an expired passport. Serfs who did not pay their feudal dues on time were fined 3 per cent of the total amount due.[67] Serfs who repeatedly failed to meet their obligations faced gaol, corporal punishment, conscription, and even exile.[68] The landlord

---

[65] H. E. Melton, 'Enlightened seignioralism and its dilemmas in serf Russia, 1750–1830', *Journal of Modern History* 62 (1990), pp. 675–708; Mironov, 'Local government in Russia', pp. 173–4, 195.

[66] Demographic behaviour on the Gagarins' Petrovskoe estate was also regulated. See Hoch, *Serfdom and social control*, pp. 87–8.

[67] RGADA, f. 1287, op. 3, ed. khr. 555 ('Instructions, 1796/1800').

[68] RGADA, f. 1287, op. 3, ed. khr. 1614 ('On the exile of serfs in arrears, 1843'). See also the discussion in chapter 4. It is difficult to say how these policies compared with those on corvée labour estates, since there are not, as of yet, any micro-historical accounts of the Sheremetyevs' corvée estates. And comparison with a corvée estate of another landlord – such as the Gagarins' Petrovskoe estate – would not suffice, as there is no way of

also levied taxes on land transactions, and charged serfs for the administration's contract enforcement services. Additional taxes were levied on serfs who engaged in conspicuous consumption. Serfs who owned 'several changes of the nicest sorts of clothing', as well as those who had luxurious houses and extravagant furnishings were scrutinised and penalised.

This pattern would have diminished the incentive to engage in the sort of entrepreneurial initiatives that played such an important role in the agricultural and industrial revolutions in early modern northwest Europe. Such initiatives could exist and even be quite successful in Russia where conditions were favourable, as – to some degree – on the Voshchazhnikovo estate. But the traditional confiscatory pattern survived there, too, even within a relatively stable administrative framework that made entrepreneurial initiatives possible. This framework of serfdom, then, forced entrepreneurial activity into the informal sector, discouraged investment, and thus economic development, even when a particular landlord was able to create an island of relative predictability and (internal) rule of law *within* the larger, informal framework.

As a result, the institutional framework outlined here imposed a sort of glass ceiling on economic development at Voshchazhnikovo, similar to that described by economists for modern economies in the developing world. As de Soto has argued, in order for societies to prosper, these so-called local social conventions must be integrated into a unified system 'from which general principles of law can be drawn'.[69] A formal system of enforceable property rights is crucial, since 'without formal property, no matter how many assets they accumulate or how hard they work, most people will not be able to prosper'.[70]

Russia had an opportunity to develop such a unified system in 1861. The monarchy certainly had the power that would have enabled it to promulgate and implement a legal system evolving toward the universal enforcement of contracts and property rights. But it did not. Instead, it created a system that handed many of the despotic rights of landowners over to a legally nebulous and ill-defined entity – the commune – which combined coercive powers over social issues, judicial conflicts, and land management.[71] All peasants (at least those who could not afford to

---

distinguishing the differences due to the corvée system from those due to differences in landlord policy. While it seems plausible that the administrative regimes on corvée labour estates were somewhat more coercive than on quitrent estates, the evidence for Voshchazhnikovo suggests that serfs on quitrent estates were hardly free from landlord interference in their economic affairs. They did not have to work on the demesne, but their behaviour was constrained in a number of other ways, through taxes, fines, and various coercive measures.

[69] De Soto, *The mystery of capital*, p. 167.   [70] *Ibid.*, p. 170.
[71] Crisp, 'Peasant land tenure', esp. pp. 40–5.

escape) had communal land – and thus communal obligations – forced on them. Those who had previously enjoyed some semblance of a rule of law found themselves, suddenly, not under the relatively impartial contract-enforcement regime of the Sheremetyevs, but rather subject to the arbitrary rule of a local elite with no chance of escape or appeal.[72] This is why historians such as Gerschenkron have suggested that the codification of communal land tenure and the strengthening of constraints on mobility in the post-Emancipation period undermined rural development and economic growth.

Even worse, none of these reforms was embedded in a universal and consistently enforced legal framework, a rule of law. Despite their rhetoric about integrating peasants into a formal legal framework, the reforms of the second half of the nineteenth century appear to have moved Russia even further away from resembling a society based on the universal rule of law. In place of serfdom, where at least the rules were known, the new dispensation declared that local decisions be based on peasant 'custom', a concept so vague and lacking in practical meaning that all parties to disputes were able to invoke it in their favour.[73] This absence of clear legal guidelines not only increased the discretionary power of petty officials – and was therefore guaranteed to reinforce the sort of systemic corruption described above – but may well have made investment even less secure than it had been under the informal regime *before* 1861.

Rather than apply a clearly articulated set of legal principles to all Russian subjects, the state took a haphazard approach to governing the countryside, marked by 'successive impositions of bits and pieces of contradictory legislation'.[74] Serfs were emancipated from their landlords, but bound to their communes. They were granted land, but in communal tenure, with communal restrictions on sales and mortgages. A rural court system was established, but judges could rule on the basis of 'custom'.[75] Recent research indicates that this pattern continued into the twentieth century: when a law was passed, it would soon be accompanied by others that undermined and contradicted it.[76] No one who wished to improve land, specialise in a market crop, start a business, or emigrate to follow the

---

[72] On the arbitrariness of local rule in the later nineteenth century, see Gaudin, *Ruling peasants*, esp. pp. 23–7, 47–61, and pp. 122–30 on the arbitrariness of the appeal process.
[73] *Ibid.*, pp. 110–30.   [74] *Ibid.*, p. 10.
[75] *Ibid.*, p. 18. See also G. Popkins, 'Peasant experiences of the late tsarist state: district congresses of land captains, provincial boards, and the legal appeals process 1891–1917', *Slavonic and East European Review* 78 (2000), pp. 90–114; and *idem*, 'Code versus custom? Norms and tactics in peasant volost' court appeals 1889–1917', *Russian Review* 59 (2000), pp. 408–24.
[76] This is one of the major themes that emerges in Gaudin's *Ruling peasants*.

best paid work could find solid ground under his feet. This was far removed from the kind of stable institutional framework with property rights that development economists have recognised as the precondition for sustained growth and industrialisation.

How Emancipation came to take this form is a different story, and a mysterious one, which lies outside the bounds of this discussion. But the Peasant Myth seems to have played an important role in the unfolding of the story.[77] Repeatedly, throughout the drafting process of the 1861 legislation, the disadvantages of communal landholding were urged by various participants.[78] But the officials in charge invariably deflected these 'merely theoretical' objections by referring to their original charter from the tsar and the minister Rostovtsev, in which the editorial commission was instructed *to maintain communal property-holding unchanged from its present (1857) state.*[79] This, in turn, was invariably interpreted to mean the peasant custom of collective and repartitional ownership of property as described by Haxthausen. The Peasant Myth – specifically, the notion that the newly liberated serfs were incapable of participating in market society, or were in some way resistant to it, and thus legal and economic change could only be introduced to them gradually – was then, in effect, the guiding constraint on the drafting process for the 1861 legislation. Ironically, it is quite possible that the resulting law actually did give rise to a rural society in Russia that corresponded much more closely to the Peasant Myth than other European societies, past or present – or than many regions and localities of Russia itself in the first half of the nineteenth century. Again, it is beyond the scope of the present study to assess this intriguing suggestion. But if it turns out to be the case, it would mean, as we have seen in this book, that the 1861 legislation fundamentally altered the nature of Russian rural society.

---

[77] Though there were clearly dissenting voices. For a more recent account, see I. A. Khristoforov, *'Aristokraticheskaia' oppozitsiia velikam reformam konets 1850–serediny 1870–kh gg.* (Moscow, 2002).
[78] Keussler, *Gemeindebesitz*, vol. I, pp. 134–43, 192–4.   [79] *Ibid.*, pp. 199–200.

Bibliography

ARCHIVAL SOURCES

SOUL REVISIONS

GAYaO, f. 100, op. 8, d. 647 (1816)
GAYaO, f. 100, op. 8, d. 2656 (1858)
RGADA, f. 1287, op. 3, ed. khr. 1941 (1850)
RGADA, f. 1287, op. 3, ed. khr. 2553 (1834)

PARISH REGISTERS FOR VOSHCHAZHNIKOVO PARISH

GAYaO, f. 230, op. 11, d. 1588 (1786–1826)
GAYaO, f. 230, op. 11, d. 1608 (1850–61)

HOUSEHOLD INVENTORIES

RGADA, f. 1287, op. 3, ed. khr. 1143 (1832/8)

DESCRIPTIONS OF ESTATES

RGADA, f. 1287, op. 3, ed. khr. 2320 (1858)

LANDLORD'S INSTRUCTIONS AND DECREES

RGADA, f. 1287, op. 3, ed. khr. 59 (1737)
RGADA, f. 1287, op. 3, ed. khr. 480 (1785)
RGADA, f. 1287, op. 3, ed. khr. 555 (1796/1800)
RGADA, f. 1287, op. 3, ed. khr. 677 (1808)
RGADA, f. 1287, op. 3, ed. khr. 714 (1816)
RGADA, f. 1287, op. 3, ed. khr. 848 (1822)
RGADA, f. 1287, op. 3, ed. khr. 867 (1821–2)
RGADA, f. 1287, op. 3, ed. khr. 934 (1825)
RGADA, f. 1287, op. 3, ed. khr. 991 (1827)
RGADA, f. 1287, op. 3, ed. khr. 1016 (1828)
RGADA, f. 1287, op. 3, ed. khr. 1305 (1764)

RGADA, f. 1287, op. 3, ed. khr. 1318 (1800)
RGADA, f. 1287, op. 3, ed. khr. 1584 (1842)
RGADA, f. 1287, op. 3, ed. khr. 1615 (1843)
RGADA, f. 1287, op. 3, ed. khr. 1684 (1845)
RGADA, f. 1287, op. 3, ed. khr. 1766 (1847)
RGADA, f. 1287, op. 3, ed. khr. 1942 (1850)
RGADA, f. 1287, op. 3, ed. khr. 1943 (1850)
RGADA, f. 1287, op. 3, ed. khr. 2212 (no date)
RGADA, f. 1287, op. 3, ed. khr. 2312 (1857)

CORRESPONDENCE BETWEEN THE CENTRAL ADMINISTRATION
AND THE ESTATE

RGADA, f. 1287, op. 3, ed. khr. 902 (1824)
RGADA, f. 1287, op. 3, ed. khr. 911 (1824)
RGADA, f. 1287, op. 3, ed. khr. 938 (1825)
RGADA, f. 1287, op. 3, ed. khr. 1713 (1846)
RGADA, f. 1287, op. 3, ed. khr. 2266 (1857)

PASSPORT LISTS

RGADA, f. 1287, op. 3, ed. khr. 131 (1746)
RGADA, f. 1287, op. 3, ed. khr. 262 (1760)
RGADA, f. 1287, op. 3, ed. khr. 271 (1762)
RGADA, f. 1287, op. 3, ed. khr. 272 (1762)
RGADA, f. 1287, op. 3, ed. khr. 776 (1820)
RGADA, f. 1287, op. 3, ed. khr. 957 (1825)
RGADA, f. 1287, op. 3, ed. khr. 958 (1825)
RGADA, f. 1287, op. 3, ed. khr. 1158 (1832)
RGADA, f. 1287, op. 3, ed. khr. 1246 (1834)
RGADA, f. 1287, op. 3, ed. khr. 2390 (1859–60)

COMMUNAL RESOLUTIONS

RGADA, f. 1287, op. 3, ed. khr. 141 (1750)
RGADA, f. 1287, op. 3, ed. khr. 174 (1754)
RGADA, f. 1287, op. 3, ed. khr. 275 (1763)
RGADA, f. 1287, op. 3, ed. khr. 323 (1775)
RGADA, f. 1287, op. 3, ed. khr. 496 (1786)
RGADA, f. 1287, op. 3, ed. khr. 525 (1787)
RGADA, f. 1287, op. 3, ed. khr. 565 (1791)
RGADA, f. 1287, op. 3, ed. khr. 652 (1804)
RGADA, f. 1287, op. 3, ed. khr. 1325 (1837)
RGADA, f. 1287, op. 3, ed. khr. 1590 (1843)
RGADA, f. 1287, op. 3, ed. khr. 1635 (1844)
RGADA, f. 1287, op. 3, ed. khr. 1789 (1847)
RGADA, f. 1287, op. 3, ed. khr. 2317 (1858)

RGADA, f. 1287, op. 3, ed. khr. 2518 (1791)
RGADA, f. 1287, op. 3, ed. khr. 2556 (1833)

CONTRACTS

RGADA, f. 1287, op. 3, ed. khr. 229 (1759)
RGADA, f. 1287, op. 3, ed. khr. 303 (1770)
RGADA, f. 1287, op. 3, ed. khr. 357 (1777)
RGADA, f. 1287, op. 3, ed. khr. 460 (1783)
RGADA, f. 1287, op. 3, ed. khr. 612 (1793)
RGADA, f. 1287, op. 3, ed. khr. 977 (1826)
RGADA, f. 1287, op. 3, ed. khr. 1108 (1831)
RGADA, f. 1287, op. 3, ed. khr. 1155 (1832)
RGADA, f. 1287, op. 3, ed. khr. 1336 (1837)
RGADA, f. 1287, op. 3, ed. khr. 1523 (1840)

ACCOUNT BOOKS

RGADA, f. 1287, op. 3, ed. khr. 189 ('Communal account books, 1754')
RGADA, f. 1287, op. 3, ed. khr. 294 ('Parish account books, 1764')
RGADA, f. 1287, op. 3, ed. khr. 530 ('Communal account books, 1787')
RGADA, f. 1287, op. 3, ed. khr. 608 ('Parish account books, 1793')
RGADA, f. 1287, op. 3, ed. khr. 921 ('Communal account books, 1824')
RGADA, f. 1287, op. 3, ed. khr. 944 ('Communal account books, 1825')

PETITIONS AND OTHER DOCUMENTS

GAYaO, f. 230, op. 1 ('Records of the Yaroslavl' consistorial court and other ecclesiastical institutions')
RGADA, f. 1287, op. 3, ed. khr. 103 ('On the distribution of flax, 1744–46')
RGADA, f. 1287, op. 3, ed. khr. 575 ('Monies collected from stallholders, 1792')
RGADA, f. 1287, op. 3, ed. khr. 588 ('Petition regarding credit, 1792')
RGADA, f. 1287, op. 3, ed. khr. 620 ('Petition regarding property dispute, 1787')
RGADA, f. 1287, op. 3, ed. khr. 628 ('Petition regarding inheritance dispute, 1795')
RGADA, f. 1287, op. 3, ed. khr. 629 ('Petition regarding credit, 1795')
RGADA, f. 1287, op. 3, ed. khr. 661 ('Punishments meted out to serfs, 1807')
RGADA, f. 1287, op. 3, ed. khr. 668 ('Petition against Slasnikov, 1807')
RGADA, f. 1287, op. 3, ed. khr. 706 ('Petition regarding credit, 1820')
RGADA, f. 1287, op. 3, ed. khr. 729 ('Petition regarding credit, 1819')
RGADA, f. 1287, op. 3, ed. khr. 739 ('Monies collected from stallholders, 1820')
RGADA, f. 1287, op. 3, ed. khr. 745 ('Petition regarding property dispute, 1820')
RGADA, f. 1287, op. 3, ed. khr. 766 ('Petition regarding property dispute, 1820')
RGADA, f. 1287, op. 3, ed. khr. 768 ('Petition regarding dispute, 1820')
RGADA, f. 1287, op. 3, ed. khr. 770 ('Petition regarding dispute, 1820')
RGADA, f. 1287, op. 3, ed. khr. 733 ('On the election of estate officials, 1821')
RGADA, f. 1287, op. 3, ed. khr. 843 ('Petition regarding credit dispute, 1822')
RGADA, f. 1287, op. 3, ed. khr. 844 ('Petition for poor relief, 1822')

RGADA, f. 1287, op. 3, ed. khr. 850   ('Petition for poor relief, 1849')
RGADA, f. 1287, op. 3, ed. khr. 864   ('On the letting of the market square, 1820')
RGADA, f. 1287, op. 3, ed. khr. 886   ('Petition regarding property dispute, 1824')
RGADA, f. 1287, op. 3, ed. khr. 898   ('Punishments meted out to serfs, 1823')
RGADA, f. 1287, op. 3, ed. khr. 912   ('Petition regarding household dispute, 1824')
RGADA, f. 1287, op. 3, ed. khr. 914   ('Petition from village of Malakhovo residents
        against Sal'nikov, 1825')
RGADA, f. 1287, op. 3, ed. khr. 930   ('Petition regarding land repartition, 1825')
RGADA, f. 1287, op. 3, ed. khr. 941   ('Petition against the serf Sal'nikov, 1825')
RGADA, f. 1287, op. 3, ed. khr. 993   ('Petition regarding inheritance dispute, 1828')
RGADA, f. 1287, op. 3, ed. khr. 994   ('Petition regarding property dispute, 1828')
RGADA, f. 1287, op. 3, ed. khr. 1022   ('On the election of estate officials, 1850')
RGADA, f. 1287, op. 3, ed. khr. 1030   ('Petition against poor relief, 1830')
RGADA, f. 1287, op. 3, ed. khr. 1070   ('Instructions from Rostov district, 1831')
RGADA, f. 1287, op. 3, ed. khr. 1119   ('Report on estate manufactories')
RGADA, f. 1287, op. 3, ed. khr. 1124   ('Petitions regarding marriage, 1832')
RGADA, f. 1287, op. 3, ed. khr. 1133   ('Petition regarding credit, 1832')
RGADA, f. 1287, op. 3, ed. khr. 1140   ('Petition regarding maintenance of parish
        church, 1832')
RGADA, f. 1287, op. 3, ed. khr. 1178   ('Petition regarding credit dispute, 1833')
RGADA, f. 1287, op. 3, ed. khr. 1181   ('Petitions regarding marriage, 1833')
RGADA, f. 1287, op. 3, ed. khr. 1227   ('Petition regarding credit dispute, 1835')
RGADA, f. 1287, op. 3, ed. khr. 1256   ('Petition against bailiff Tizengauzen, 1835')
RGADA, f. 1287, op. 3, ed. khr. 1283   ('List of trading peasants and guilds, 1836')
RGADA, f. 1287, op. 3, ed. khr. 1325   ('Punishments meted out to serfs, 1825')
RGADA, f. 1287, op. 3, ed. khr. 1336   ('Petition regarding land purchase, 1837')
RGADA, f. 1287, op. 3, ed. khr. 1345   ('Report on serfs' buildings, 1837')
RGADA, f. 1287, op. 3, ed. khr. 1385   ('Petition from merchant Sheshunov, 1838')
RGADA, f. 1287, op. 3, ed. khr. 1391   ('List of trading peasants and guilds, 1838')
RGADA, f. 1287, op. 3, ed. khr. 1434   ('Petition regarding labourer purchase, 1839')
RGADA, f. 1287, op. 3, ed. khr. 1435   ('Petition regarding labourer purchase, 1839')
RGADA, f. 1287, op. 3, ed. khr. 1438   ('Petition regarding property dispute, 1839')
RGADA, f. 1287, op. 3, ed. khr. 1492   ('Petition regarding land purchase, 1840')
RGADA, f. 1287, op. 3, ed. khr. 1563   ('Petition regarding land purchase, 1840')
RGADA, f. 1287, op. 3, ed. khr. 1568   ('Report on grain harvests, 1842–54')
RGADA, f. 1287, op. 3, ed. khr. 1598   ('On serfs' houses, 1843')
RGADA, f. 1287, op. 3, ed. khr. 1614   ('On the exile of serfs in arrears, 1843')
RGADA, f. 1287, op. 3, ed. khr. 1643   ('Petition regarding trade dispute, 1844')
RGADA, f. 1287, op. 3, ed. khr. 1646   ('Petition for household division, 1844')
RGADA, f. 1287, op. 3, ed. khr. 1745   ('Petition regarding officeholding, 1847')
RGADA, f. 1287, op. 3, ed. khr. 1764   ('Petition regarding credit, 1847')
RGADA, f. 1287, op. 3, ed. khr. 1774   ('Contributions to the estate granary, 1847')
RGADA, f. 1287, op. 3, ed. khr. 2058   ('Petition regarding land repartition, 1853')
RGADA, f. 1287, op. 3, ed. khr. 2232   ('On serfs in arrears, 1855–60')
RGADA, f. 1287, op. 3, ed. khr. 2241   ('Record of sums belonging to serfs')
RGADA, f. 1287, op. 3, ed. khr. 2280   ('Petition regarding savings, 1857')
RGADA, f. 1287, op. 3, ed. khr. 2518   ('Petition regarding property dispute, 1791')

SECONDARY SOURCES

Acemoglu, D., 'Constitutions, politics, and economics', *Journal of Economic Literature* 43 (2005), pp. 1025–48.

Acemoglu, D., Johnson, S., and Robinson, J. A., 'The colonial origins of comparative development: an empirical investigation', *American Economic Review* 91 (2001), pp. 1369–401.

Aleksandrov, V. A., *Sel'skaia obshchina v Rossii, XVII–nachalo XIX vv.* (Moscow, 1976).

'Typology of the Russian peasant family in the feudal period', *Soviet Studies in History* (1982), pp. 26–62.

Obychnoe pravo krepostnoi derevni Rossii, XVIII–nachalo XIX v. (Moscow, 1984).

Andorka, R., and Faragó, T., 'Pre-industrial household structure in Hungary', in R. Wall, J. Robin, and P. Laslett (eds.), *Family forms in historic Europe* (Cambridge, 1983), pp. 281–307.

Artynov, A. A., *Vospominaniia krest'ianina sela Ugodich, Iaroslavskaoi gubernii Rostovskago uezda* (ed. A. A. Titov) (Moscow, 1883).

Avdeev, A., Blum, A., and Troitskaia, I., 'Peasant marriage in nineteenth-century Russia', *Population* 59 (2004), pp. 721–64.

'Serfdom and state power in imperial Russia', *European History Quarterly* 33 (2003), pp. 29–64.

Bartlett, R., 'Introduction', in R. Bartlett (ed.), *Land commune and peasant community in Russia: communal forms in imperial and early Soviet society* (London and New York, 1990), pp. 1–6.

Bartlett, R. (ed.), *Land commune and peasant community in Russia: communal forms in imperial and early Soviet society* (London and New York, 1990).

Behrisch, L., 'Social discipline in early modern Russia, seventeenth to nineteenth centuries', in H. Schilling and L. Behrisch (eds.), *Institutionen, Instrumenten, und Akteure sozialer Kontrolle und Disziplinierung im frühneuzeitlichen Europa* (Frankfurt, 1999), pp. 325–57.

Belliustin, I. S., *The description of the clergy in rural Russia: the memoir of a nineteenth-century parish priest* (translated G. Freeze) (Ithaca, 1985).

Berlin, I., *Russian thinkers* (London and New York, 1978).

Birner, R., and Wittmer, H., 'Converting social capital into political capital: how do local communities gain political influence?', paper presented at the Eighth Biennial Conference of the International Association for the Study of Common Property (2000).

Blanchard, I., *Russia's 'age of silver': precious-metal production and economic growth in the eighteenth century* (London and New York, 1989).

Blanes Jiménez, J., 'Cocaine, informality, and the urban economy in La Paz, Bolivia', in A. Portes, et al. (eds.), *The informal economy* (Baltimore, 1989), pp. 135–49.

Blickle, P., *Kommunalismus: Skizzen einer gesellschaftlichen Organisationsform*, 2 vols. (Munich, 2000).

Blum, J., *Lord and peasant in Russia from the ninth to the nineteenth century* (Princeton, 1961).

Bobke, W., 'August von Haxthausen: eine Studie zur Ideengeschichte der politischen Romantik', unpublished Ph.D. dissertation (Munich, 1954).

Bohac, R., 'Family, property, and socioeconomic mobility: Russian peasants on Manuilovskoe estate, 1810–1861', unpublished Ph.D. dissertation (University of Illinois at Champaign–Urbana, 1982).

'The "mir" and the military draft', *Slavic Review* 47 (1988), pp. 652–66.

'Agricultural structure and the origins of migration in central Russia 1810–1850', in G. Grantham and C. S. Leonard (eds.), *Agrarian organization in the century of industrialization: Europe, Russia and North America*, Research in Economic History Supplement 5 Part B (Greenwich, CT, and London, 1989), pp. 369–88.

'Widows and the Russian serf community', in B. E. Clements, B. A. Engel, and C. D. Worobec (eds.), *Russia's women: accommodation, resistance, transformation* (Berkeley and Los Angeles, 1991), pp. 95–112.

Bourgholtzer, F., *Aleksandr Chayanov and Russian Berlin* (London and New York, 1999).

Bretell, C. B., *Men who migrate, women who wait: population and history in a Portuguese parish* (Princeton, 1986).

Briggs, C. D., 'Manor court procedures, debt litigation levels, and rural credit provision in England c. 1290–1380', *Law and History Review* 24 (2006), pp. 519–58.

Credit and village society in fourteenth-century England (Oxford, 2009).

Brown, J. C., and Guinnane, T., 'Regions and time in the European fertility transition: problems in the Princeton Project's statistical methodology', *Economic History Review* 60 (2007), pp. 574–95.

Burbank, J., *Russian peasants go to court: legal culture in the countryside 1905–1917* (Bloomington, 2004).

Burds, J., *Peasant dreams and market politics: labour migration and the Russian village 1861–1905* (Pittsburgh, 1998).

Bush, M. L. (ed.), *Slavery and serfdom: studies in legal bondage* (London and New York, 1996).

Bushnell, J., 'Did serf owners control serf marriage?', *Slavic Review* 52 (1993), pp. 419–45.

Carus, A. W., and Ogilvie, S., 'Turning qualitative into quantitative evidence: a well-used method made explicit', *Economic History Review* 62 (2009), pp. 893–925.

Chayanov, A. V., *The theory of peasant economy*, ed. D. Thorner, B. Kerblay, and R. E. F. Smith (Homewood, IL, 1966).

Chernukha, V. G., 'Pasport v Rossiiskoi imperii: nabliudeniia nad zakonodatel'stvom', *Istoricheskie zapiski* 122 (2001), pp. 91–131.

Clements, B. E., Engel, B. A., and Worobec, C. D. (eds.), *Russia's women: accommodation, resistance, transformation* (Berkeley and Los Angeles, 1991).

Coleman, J. S., *Foundations of social theory* (Cambridge, MA, 1990).

Confino, M., *Domaines et seigneurs en Russie vers la fin du XVIIIe siècle: études de structures agraires et de mentalités économiques* (Paris, 1963).

Systèmes agraires et progrès agricole: l'assolement triennal en Russie aux XVIIIe–XIXe siècles (Paris, 1969).

Crisp, O., *Studies in the Russian economy before 1914* (London and Basingstoke, 1976).

'Peasant land tenure and civil rights implications before 1906', in O. Crisp and L. Edmondson (eds.), *Civil rights in imperial Russia* (Oxford, 1989), pp. 33–64.

Crook, D., 'Freedom, villeinage and legal process: the dispute between the abbot of Burton and his tenants of Mickleover, 1280', *Nottingham Medieval Studies* 44 (2000), pp. 123–40.

de Custine, A., *Letters from Russia* (repr. New York, 2002).

Czap, P., 'The perennial multiple-family household, Mishino, Russia 1782–1858', *Journal of Family History* (Spring 1982), pp. 5–26.

'"A large family: the peasant's greatest wealth": serf households in Mishino, Russia, 1814–1858', in R. Wall, J. Robin, and P. Laslett (eds.), *Family forms in historic Europe* (Cambridge, 1983), pp. 105–51.

Dasgupta, P., *An inquiry into well-being and destitution* (Oxford, 1993).

Dennison, T. K., 'Serfdom and household structure in central Russia: Voshchazhnikovo 1816–1858', *Continuity and Change* 18 (3) (2003), pp. 395–429.

Dennison, T. K., and Carus, A. W., 'The invention of the Russian rural commune: Haxthausen and the evidence', *Historical Journal* 46, 3 (2003), pp. 561–82.

Dennison, T. K., and Ogilvie, S., 'Serfdom and social capital in Bohemia and Russia', *Economic History Review* 60 (3) (2007), pp. 513–44.

Drobak, J., and Nye, J., *The frontiers of the new institutional economics* (San Diego and London, 1997).

Druzhinin, N. M., *Voprosy sotsial'no-ekonomicheskoi istorii i istochnikovedeniia perioda feodalizma v Rossii* (Moscow, 1961).

Dyer, C., 'Memories of freedom: attitudes toward serfdom in England, 1200–1350', in M. L. Bush (ed.), *Serfdom and slavery: studies in legal bondage* (Harlow, 1996), pp. 277–95.

Easterley, W., *The elusive quest for growth: economists' adventures and misadventures in the tropics* (Cambridge, MA, 2002).

Eggertsson, T., *Economic behavior and institutions* (Cambridge, 1990).

Ekonomakis, E. G., *From peasant to Petersburger* (New York and London, 1998).

Elton, G. R., 'Happy families', *New York Review of Books* (14 June 1984), pp. 39–41.

Return to essentials: some reflections on the present state of historical study (Cambridge, 1991).

Emigh, R. J., 'Labor use and landlord control: sharecropping and household structure in fifteenth-century Tuscany', *Journal of Historical Sociology* 11 (1) (1998), pp. 37–73.

Emmons, T., *The Russian landed gentry and the peasant Emancipation of 1861* (Cambridge, 1968).

Engel, B. A., *Between the fields and the city; women, work, and family in Russia, 1861–1914* (Cambridge, 1996).

Engerman, D., *Modernization from the other shore: American intellectuals and the romance of Russian development* (Cambridge, MA, 2003).

Farnsworth, B., and Viola, L. (eds.), *Russian peasant women* (Oxford, 1992).

Fauve-Chamoux, A., 'The importance of women in an urban environment: the example of the Rheims household at the beginning of the industrial revolution', in R. Wall, J. Robin, and P. Laslett (eds.), *Family forms in historic Europe* (Cambridge, 1983), pp. 475–92.

Fedor, T. S., *Patterns of urban growth in the Russian empire during the nineteenth century* (Chicago, 1975).

Field, D., *The end of serfdom: nobility and bureaucracy in Russia, 1855–1861* (Cambridge, MA, 1976).

Figes, O., *Natasha's dance: a cultural history of Russia* (New York, 2002).

Frances, C. M., 'Networks of the life course: a case study of Cheshire, 1570–1700', unpublished Ph.D. thesis (Cambridge, 2000).

Frank, J., *Dostoevsky: the seeds of revolt, 1821–1849* (Princeton, 1976).

Frank, S., *Crime, cultural conflict, and justice in rural Russia, 1856–1914* (Berkeley and Los Angeles, 1999).

Freeze, G. L., *The Russian Levites: parish clergy in the eighteenth century* (Cambridge, MA, 1977).

    The parish clergy in nineteenth-century Russia: crisis, reform, counter-reform (Princeton, 1983).

Frierson, C., 'Razdel: the peasant family divided', in B. Farnsworth and L. Viola (eds.), *Russian peasant women* (Oxford, 1992), pp. 73–88.

Fyodorov, V. A., 'Vozniknovenie torgovogo ogorodnichestva v rostovskom uezde Iaroslavskoi gubernii (konets XVIII–pervaia polovina XIX veka)', *Vestnik moskovskogo universiteta* 6 (1962), pp. 49–68.

    'Naemnyi trud v zemledelii nakanune krest'ianskoi reform 1861 g. (po materialam tsentral'no-promyshlennykh gubernii)', *Vestnik moskovskogo universiteta* 3 (1968), pp. 85–96.

    'Zemlevladenie krepostnykh krest'ian v Rossii (po materialam tsentral'no-promyshlennykh gubernii)', *Vestnik moskovskogo universiteta* 1 (1969), pp. 47–67.

    Pomeshchich'i krest'iane tsentral'no-promyshlennogo raiona Rossii kontsa XVIII–pervoi poloviny XIX v. (Moscow, 1974).

    'Torgovoe zemledelie krest'ian Moskovskoi gubernii v pervoi polovine XIX v.', *Vestnik moskovskogo universiteta* 8 (2003), pp. 93–105.

Gatrell, P., *The tsarist economy 1850–1917* (London and New York, 1986).

Gaudin, C., *Ruling peasants: village and state in late imperial Russia* (DeKalb, IL, 2007).

Gerschenkron, A., *Economic backwardness in historical perspective* (Cambridge, MA, 1962).

    Continuity in history and other essays (Cambridge, MA, 1968).

Gestwa, K., *Proto-Industrialisierung in Russland: Wirtschaft, Herrschaft und Kultur in Ivanovo und Pavlovo, 1741–1932* (Göttingen, 1999).

Gill, A., *Rural credit markets: financial sector reforms and the informal lenders* (New Delhi, 2000).

Glickman, R., *Russian factory women: workplace and society, 1880–1914* (Berkeley and Los Angeles, 1984).

Goehrke, C., *Die Theorien über Entstehung und Entwicklung des 'Mir'* (Wiesbaden, 1964).

Gorshkov, B. B., 'Serfs on the move: peasant seasonal migration in pre-reform Russia, 1800–61', *Kritika: Explorations in Russian and Eurasian History* 1 (2000), pp. 627–56.

Gorskaia, N. A., *Monastyrskie krest'iane tsentral'noi Rossii v XVII veke* (Moscow, 1977).

Russkaia feodal'naia derevnia v istoriografii XX veka (Moscow, 2006).

Gottlieb, B., 'The meaning of clandestine marriage', in R. Wheaton and T. Hareven (eds.), *Family and sexuality in French history* (Philadelphia, 1980), pp. 49–83.

Grossman, G., 'Informal personal incomes and outlays of the Soviet Union population', in A. Portes, M. Castells, and L. Benton (eds.), *The informal economy* (Baltimore, 1989), pp. 150–70.

Guinnane, T., *The vanishing Irish: households, migration, and the rural economy in Ireland, 1850–1914* (Princeton, 1997).

Hagen, W., *Ordinary Prussians: Brandenburg Junkers and villagers, 1500–1840* (Cambridge, 2002).

Hall, R. E., and Jones, C. I., 'Why do some countries produce so much more output per worker than others?', *Quarterly Journal of Economics* 114 (1999), pp. 83–116.

Hajnal, J., 'Age at marriage and proportions marrying', *Population Studies* 7 (1953), pp. 111–36.

'Two kinds of preindustrial household formation system', *Population and Development Review* 8 (1982), pp. 449–94.

Hamburg, G. M., 'Peasant emancipation and Russian social thought: the case of Boris N. Chicherin', *Slavic Review* 50 (1991), pp. 890–904.

Hartley, J. M., *A social history of the Russian empire 1650–1825* (London and New York, 1998).

Hatcher, J., 'English serfdom and villeinage: towards a reassessment', *Past and Present* 90 (1981), pp. 3–39.

Haxthausen, A. F. von, *Studien über die innern Zustände, das Volksleben und insbesondere die ländlichen Einrichtungen Rußlands*, 3 vols. (Hannover, 1847–52).

Hellie, R., *Enserfment and military change* (Chicago, 1971).

The Muscovite Law Code (Ulozhenie) of 1649 (Irvine, CA, 1988).

The economy and material culture of Russia, 1600–1725 (Chicago, 1999).

Herzen, A., 'O sel'skoi obshchine v Rossii', in *Sochineniia v deviati tomakh* (Moscow, 1956), pp. 508–13.

'The Russian people and socialism: an open letter to Jules Michelet', reprinted in *From the other shore & The Russian people and socialism* (repr. Oxford, 1979).

Hoch, S. L., *Serfdom and social control in Russia: Petrovskoe, a village in Tambov* (Chicago, 1986).

'On good numbers and bad: Malthus, population trends and peasant standard of living in late imperial Russia', *Slavic Review* 53 (1994), pp. 41–75.

'The serf economy and the social order in Russia', in M. L. Bush (ed.), *Serfdom and slavery: studies in legal bondage* (London and New York, 1996), pp. 311–22.

'Famine, disease, and mortality patterns in the parish of Borshevka, Russia, 1830–1912', *Population Studies* 52 (1998), pp. 357–68.

Hoffman, P. T., *Church and community in the diocese of Lyon 1500–1789* (Yale, 1984).

Growth in a traditional society: the French countryside 1450–1815 (Princeton, 1996).

Hoffman, P. T., Postel-Vinay, G., and Rosenthal, J.-L., 'Information and economic history: how the credit market in old regime Paris forces us to rethink the transition to capitalism', *American Historical Review* 104(1) (1999), pp. 69–94.

Holderness, B. A., 'Widows in pre-industrial society: an essay upon their economic functions', in R. M. Smith (ed.), *Land, kinship and lifecycle* (Cambridge, 1984), pp. 435–42.

Ignatovich, I. I., *Pomeshchich'i krest'iane nakanune osvobozhdeniia* (Moscow, 1925).

Indova, E. I., *Krepostnoe khoziaistvo v nachale XIX veka po materialam votchinnogo arkhiva Vorontsevakh* (Moscow, 1955).

Johnson, R. E., *Peasant and proletarian* (New Brunswick, NJ, 1979).

Kabuzan, V. M., *Narodonaselenie Rossii v XVIII–pervoi polovine XIX v.* (Moscow, 1963).

Kahan, A., *The plow, the hammer, and the knout: an economic history of eighteenth-century Russia* (Chicago and London, 1985).

Russian economic history: the nineteenth century (Chicago and London, 1989).

Kanitschev, V., Kontchakov, R., Mizis, Iu., and Morozova, E., 'The development of family structure in Tambov region, 1800–1917', in P. Kooij and R. Paping (eds.), *Where the twain meet again: new results of the Dutch-Russian project on regional development 1750–1917* (Groningen, 2004), pp. 239–62.

Kanzaka, J., 'Villein rents in thirteenth-century England: an analysis of the Hundred Rolls of 1279–1280', *Economic History Review* 56 (2002), pp. 593–618.

Kapustina, G. D., 'Zapisnye knigi Moskovskoi krepostnoi kontory kak istocheskii istochnik pervaia chetvert' XVIII v', in *Problemy istochnikovedeniia*, vol. VII, (Moscow, 1959), pp. 216–73.

Kashin, V. N., *Krepostnye krest'iane-zemlevladel'tsy* (Moscow, 1935).

Kertzer, D. P., and Barbagli, M. (eds.), *The history of the European family*, 3 vols. (New Haven, 2001–3).

Kertzer, D. P., and Hogan, D. I., *Family, political economy, and demographic change: the transformation of life in Casalecchio, Italy, 1861–1921* (Madison, WI, 1989).

Keussler, J. von, *Zur Geschichte und Kritik des bäuerlichen Gemeindebesitzes in Rußland*, 3 vols. (Riga, Moscow, and Odessa, 1876–87).

Khristoforov, I. A., *'Aristokraticheskaia' oppozitsiia velikam reformam konets 1850–serediny 1870-kh gg.* (Moscow, 2002).

Kingston-Mann, E., *Lenin and the problem of Marxist peasant revolution* (Oxford, 1983).

Kingston-Mann, E., and Mixter, T. (eds.), *Peasant economy, culture, and politics of European Russia, 1800–1921* (Princeton, 1991).

Knack, S., and Keefer, P., 'Institutions and economic performance: cross-country tests using alternative institutional measures', *Economics and Politics* 7 (1995), pp. 207–27.

Knight, J., and Sened, I., *Explaining social institutions* (Ann Arbor, 1995).

Koenigsberger, H. G., 'The crisis of the seventeenth century: a farewell?', in *idem, Politics and virtuosi: essays in early modern history* (London, 1986), pp. 149–68.

Kolle, H., *Social change in nineteenth-century Russia: family development in a proto-industrial community* (Bergen, 2006).

Kollman, N. S., *Kinship and politics: the making of the Muscovite political system, 1345–1547* (Stanford, 1987).

Koval'chenko, I. D., *Russkoe krepostnoe krest'ianstvo v pervoi polovine XIX veka* (Moscow, 1967).

Koval'chenko, I. D., and Milov, L. V., 'Ob intensivnosti obrochnoi ekspluatatsii krest'ian tsentral'noi Rossii v kontse XVIII – pervoi polovine XIX v.', *Istoriia SSSR* 4 (1966), pp. 55–80.

Kussmaul, A., *Servants in husbandry in early modern England* (Cambridge, 1981).

Lanzetta de Pardo, M., Murillo Castano, G., and Triana Soto, A., 'The articulation of formal and informal sectors in the economy of Bogotá, Colombia', in A. Portes, M. Castells, and L. Benton (eds.), *The informal economy* (Baltimore, 1989), pp. 95–110.

La Porta, R., Lopez-de Silanes, F., Schleifer, A., and Vishny, R., 'The quality of government', *Journal of Law, Economics, and Organization* 15 (1999), pp. 222–79.

Laslett, P., 'The face to face society', in P. Laslett (ed.), *Philosophy, politics, and society*, First Series (Oxford, 1956), pp. 157–84.

'Introduction: the history of the family', in P. Laslett with R. Wall (eds.), *Household and family in past time* (Cambridge, 1972).

Family life and illicit love in earlier generations (Cambridge, 1977).

'The European family and early industrialization', in J. Baechler, J. Hall, and M. Mann (eds.), *Europe and the rise of capitalism* (Oxford, 1988).

Laslett, P., with Wall, R. (eds.), *Household and family in past time* (Cambridge, 1972).

Ledeneva, A. V., *Russia's economy of favours:* blat, *networking and informal exchange* (Cambridge, 1998).

Lenin, V. I., *The development of capitalism in Russia* (repr. Moscow, 1964).

Leonard, C. S., 'Landords and the "mir"', in R. Bartlett (ed.), *Land commune and peasant community in Russia: communal forms in imperial and early Soviet society* (London and New York, 1990), pp. 121–42.

Le Roy Ladurie, E., *The peasants of Languedoc* (Champaign, IL, 1977).

Lindenmeyr, A., *Poverty is not a vice: charity, society, and the state in imperial Russia* (Princeton, 1996).

Little, I. M. D., *Economic development: theory, policy, and international relations* (New York, 1982).

Macfarlane, A., *Reconstructing historical communities* (Cambridge, 1977).

The origins of English individualism: the family, property, and social transition (Oxford, 1978).

de Madariaga, I., *Politics and culture in eighteenth-century Russia* (London, 1998), pp. 124–49.

Mauro, P., 'Corruption and growth', *Quarterly Journal of Economics* 110 (1995), pp. 681–712.

Medick, H., *Weben und Überleben in Laichingen, 1650–1900: Lokalgeschichte als allgemeine Geschichte* (Göttingen, 1996).

Melton, H. E., 'Serfdom and the peasant economy in Russia: 1780–1861', unpublished Ph.D. thesis (Columbia University, 1984).

'Proto-industrialization, serf agriculture, and agrarian social structure: two estates in nineteenth-century Russia', *Past and Present* 115 (1987), pp. 73–87.

'Enlightened seignioralism and its dilemmas in serf Russia, 1750–1830', *Journal of Modern History* 62 (1990), pp. 675–708.

'Household economies and communal conflicts on a Russian serf estate, 1800–1817', *Journal of Social History* 26 (1993), pp. 559–85.

'The Russian peasantries, 1450–1860', in T. Scott (ed.), *The peasantries of Europe from the fourteenth to the eighteenth centuries* (London and New York, 1998).

'The magnate and her trading peasants: Countess Lieven and the Baki estate, 1800–1820', *Jahrbücher für Geschichte Osteuropas* 47 (1999), pp. 40–55.

Ménard, C., and Shirley, M., *Handbook of new institutional economics* (Berlin, 2008).

Milov, L. V., *Issledovanie ob ekonomicheskikh primechaniiakh k general'nomu mezhevaniiu* (Moscow, 1965).

Velikorusskii pakhar' i osobennosti rossiiskogo istoricheskogo protsessa (Moscow, 1998).

Mironov, B. N., 'Traditsionnoe demograficheskoe povidenie krest'ian v XIX – nachale XX v.', in A. G. Vishnevskii (ed.), *Brachnost', rozhdaemost', smertnost' v Rossii i v SSSR* (Moscow, 1977), pp. 83–104.

Vnutrennyi rynok Rossii vo vtoroi polovine XVIII–pervoi polovine XIX v. (Leningrad, 1981).

Khlebnye tseny v Rossii za dva stoletiia XVIII–XIX vv. (Leningrad, 1985).

'The peasant commune after the reforms of the 1860s', in B. Eklof and S. Frank (eds.), *The world of the Russian peasant: post-Emancipation culture and society* (Boston, MA, 1990), 7–33.

'Local government in Russia in the first half of the nineteenth century: provincial government and estate government', *Jahrbücher für Geschichte Osteuropas* 42 (1994), pp. 161–201.

'Work and rest in the peasant economy of European Russia in the 19th and early 20th centuries', in I. Blanchard (ed.), *Labour and leisure in historical perspective: thirteenth to the twentieth centuries* (Stuttgart, 1994), pp. 55–64.

Sotsial'naia istoriia Rossii perioda imperii XVIII–nachalo XX v., 2 vols. (St Petersburg, 1999).

Mironov, B. N., and Eklof, B., *The social history of imperial Russia, 1700–1917*, 2 vols. (Boulder, 1999).

Mitterauer, M., and Kagan, A., 'Russian and central European family structures: a comparative view', *Journal of Family History* 7 (1982), pp. 103–31.

Mitterauer, M., and Sieder, R., *Vom Patriarchat zur Partnerschaft: zum Strukturwandel der Familie* (Munich, 1991).

Moon, D., 'Reassessing Russian serfdom', *European History Quarterly* 26(4) (1996), pp. 483–526.

The Russian peasantry, 1600–1930: the world the peasants made (London, 1999).

The abolition of serfdom in Russia (London, 2001).

'Peasant migration, the abolition of serfdom, and the internal passport system in Russia, c. 1800–1914', in D. Eltis (ed.), *Coerced and free migration: global perspectives* (Palo Alto, 2002).

de Moor, T., and van Zinden, J.-L., 'Girl power: the European marriage pattern and labour markets in the North Sea region in the late medieval and early modern period', *Economic History Review* 63 (2010), pp. 1–33.

Morrison, D., *'Trading peasants' and urbanization in eighteenth-century Russia: the Central Industrial Region* (New York and London, 1987).

Muldrew, C., *The economy of obligation: the culture of credit and social relations in early modern England* (New York and Basingstoke, 1998).

Murav'eva, L. L., *Derevenskaia promyshlennost' tsentral'noi Rossii vtoroi poloviny XVII v.* (Moscow, 1971).

Newcity, M., 'Russian legal tradition and the rule of law', in J. Sachs and K. Pistor (eds.), *The rule of law and economic reform in Russia* (Boulder, 1997), pp. 41–53.

Nosevich, V. L., *Traditsionnaia belorusskaia derevnia v evropeiskoi perspektive* (Minsk, 2004).

Ogden, P. E., and Winchester, S. W. C., 'The residential segregation of provincial migrants in Paris in 1911', *Transactions of the Institute of British Geographers* 65 (July 1975), pp. 29–44.

Ogilvie, S. C., *State corporatism and proto-industry: the Württemberg Black Forest 1580–1797* (Cambridge, 1997).

'The state in Germany: a non-Prussian view', in J. Brewer and E. Hellmuth (eds.), *Rethinking Leviathan: the eighteenth-century state in Britain and Germany* (Oxford, 1999).

'The European economy in the eighteenth century', in T. C. W. Blanning (ed.), *The eighteenth century: Europe 1688–1815* (Oxford, 2000), pp. 91–130.

A bitter living: women, markets, and social capital in early modern Germany (Oxford, 2003).

'Communities and the second serfdom in early modern Bohemia', *Past and Present* 187 (2005), pp. 69–120.

'"So that every subject knows how to behave": social disciplining in early modern Bohemia', *Comparative Studies of Society and History* 48(1) (2006), pp. 38–78.

Ogilvie, S., and Edwards, J., 'Women and the "second serfdom": evidence from Bohemia', *Journal of Economic History* 60 (2000), pp. 961–94.

Ogilvie, S., Küpker, M., and Maegraith, J., *Community characteristics and demographic development: three Wurttemberg communities, 1558–1914*, Cambridge Working Papers in Economics (2009).

Owen, T., 'A standard ruble of account for Russian business history 1769–1914: a note', *Journal of Economic History* 49 (1989), pp. 699–706.

Page Moch, L., *Moving Europeans: migration in western Europe since 1650* (Bloomington, 1992).

Pallot, J., *Land reform in Russia, 1906–1917* (Oxford, 1999).

Pallot, J., and Shaw, D. J. B., *Landscape and settlement in Romanov Russia 1613–1917* (Oxford, 1990).

Pande, R., and Udry, C., 'Institutions and development: a view from below', in R. Blundell, W. K. Newey, and T. Persson (eds.), *Advances in economics and econometrics: theory and applications, Ninth World Congress* (Cambridge, 2006), vol. II, pp. 349–412.

Perrie, M., *The agrarian policy of the Russian Social-Revolutionary Party from its origins through the revolution of 1905–1907* (Cambridge, 1976).

Pipes, R., *Property and freedom* (New York, 1999).

Plakans, A., and Weatherall, C., 'Family and economy on an early nineteenth-century Baltic serf estate', *Continuity and Change* 7(2) (1992), pp. 199–223.

'Family and economy on an early nineteenth-century Baltic serf estate', in R. Rudolph (ed.), *The European peasant family and society* (Liverpool, 1995), pp. 165–87.

Polla, M. *Vienankarjalainen perhelaitos 1600–1900* (Helsinki, 2001).

'Family systems in central Russia in the 1830s and 1890s', *History of the Family* 11 (2006), pp. 27–44.

Popkin, S., *The rational peasant: the political economy of rural society in Vietnam* (Berkeley and Los Angeles, 1979).

Popkins, G., 'Code versus custom? Norms and tactics in peasant volost' court appeals 1889–1917', *Russian Review* 59 (2000), pp. 408–24.

'Peasant experiences of the late tsarist state: district congresses of land captains, provincial boards, and the legal appeals process 1891–1917', *Slavonic and East European Review* 78 (2000), pp. 90–114.

Popov, N. P., *The Russian people speak: democracy at the crossroads* (Syracuse, 1995).

Postan, M., *Fact and relevance: essays on historical method* (Cambridge, 1971).

Procaccia, U., *Russian culture, property rights, and the market economy* (Cambridge, 2007).

Prokof'eva, L. S., *Krest'ianskaia obshchina v Rossii vo vtoroi polovine XVIII–pervoi polovine XIX v.* (Leningrad, 1981).

Pushkarev, S. G., *Krest'ianskaia pozemel'no-peredel'naia obshchina v Rossii* (repr. Newtonville, MA, 1976).

Putnam, R. D., *Making democracy work: civic traditions in modern Italy* (Princeton, 1993).

Ray, D., *Development economics* (Princeton, 1988).

Rose, R., 'Getting things done in an antimodern society: social capital networks in Russia', in P. Dasgupta and I. Seregeldin (eds.), *Social capital: a multifaceted perspective* (Washington, 1999), pp. 147–71.

Rosenthal, J.-L, 'Rural credit markets and aggregate shocks: the experience of Nuits St. Georges, 1756–1776', *Journal of Economic History* 54 (1994), pp. 288–306.

Rubinshtein, N. A., *Sel'skoe khoziaistvo Rossii vo vtoroi polovine XVIII v.* (Moscow, 1957).

Rudolph, R. L., 'Family structure and proto-industrialization in Russia', *Journal of Economic History*, 40 (1980), pp. 111–18.

Rutherford, M., *Institutions in economics: the old and the new institutionalism* (Cambridge, 1994).

Sachs, J., *The end of poverty: economic possibilities for our time* (New York, 2005).

Sadoulet, E., de Janvry, A., and Benjamin, C., 'Household behaviour with imperfect labor markets', *Industrial Relations*, 37(1) (1998), pp. 85–108.

Saunders, D., *Russia in the age of reaction and reform, 1801–1881* (London, 1992).

Schofield, P., *Peasant and community in medieval England 1200–1500* (London, 2003).

Schultz, T. W., *Transforming traditional agriculture* (New Haven, 1964).

Scott, J. C., *The moral economy of the peasant: rebellion and subsistence in Southeast Asia* (New Haven, 1976).

Semevskii, V. I., *Krest'iane v tsartsvovanie imperatritsy Ekateriny II*, 2 vols. (St Petersburg, 1881–1901).

   Krest'ianskii vopros v Rossii v XVIII v pervoi polovine XIX veka (St Petersburg, 1888).

Shanin, T., *The awkward class: the political sociology of the peasantry in a developing society* (Oxford, 1972).

   'The nature and logic of the peasant economy', *Journal of Peasant Studies* 1 (1973), pp. 63–80.

   Russia as a 'developing society', 2 vols. (London and New Haven, 1985–6).

Shanin, T. (ed.), *Peasants and peasant societies* (Oxford, 1987).

Shchepetov, K. N., *Krepostnoe pravo v votchinakh Sheremetevykh* (Moscow, 1947).

   Iz zhizni krepostnykh krest'ian Rossii XVIII–XIX vekov: po materialam Sheremetyevskikh votchin (Moscow, 1963).

Shustrova, I., and Sinitsyna, E., 'Demographic behaviour in the Iaroslavl' loamy area: the results of cohort analysis for two typical rural parishes', in P. Kooij and R. Paping (eds.), *Where the twain meet again: new results of the Dutch-Russian project on regional development 1750–1917* (Groningen, 2004), pp. 7–24.

Sivkov, K. V., *Ocherki po istorii krepostnogo khoziaistva i krest'ianskogo dvizheniia v Rossii v pervoi polovine XIX veka* (Moscow, 1951).

Slicher van Bath, B. H., *The agrarian history of western Europe, A.D. 500–1850* (London, 1963).

Smith, A. K., 'Eating out in imperial Russia: class, nationality, and dining before the Great Reforms', *Slavic Review* 65 (2006), pp. 747–68.

   'Authority in a serf village: peasants, managers, and the role of writing in early nineteenth century Russia', *Journal of Social History* 43(1) (2009), pp. 157–73.

Smith, R. E. F., *The enserfment of the Russian peasantry* (Cambridge, 1968).

   Peasant farming in Muscovy (Cambridge, 1977).

Smith, R. E. F., and Christian, D., *Bread and salt: a social and economic history of food and drink in Russia* (Cambridge, 1984).

Smith, R. M., 'Some issues concerning families and their property in rural England 1200–1800', in R. M. Smith (ed.), *Land, kinship, and lifecycle* (Cambridge, 1984), pp. 1–86.

   'Further models of medieval marriage: landlords, serfs and priests in rural England, c. 1290–1370', in C. Duhamel-Amado and G. Lobrichon (eds.), *Georges Duby: l'écriture de l'histoire* (Brussels, 1996), pp. 161–73.

   'A periodic market and its impact on a manorial community: Botesdale, Suffolk, and the manor of Redgrave, 1280–1300', in Z. Razi and R. Smith (eds.), *Medieval society and the manor court* (Oxford, 1996), pp. 450–81.

de Soto, H., *The other path: the invisible revolution in the third world* (New York, 1989).

The mystery of capital (London, 2000).

Sreenivasan, G., *The peasants of Ottobeuren 1487–1726: a rural society in early modern Europe* (Cambridge, 2004).

Szoltysek, M., 'Rethinking eastern Europe: household formation patterns in the Polish-Lithuanian Commonwealth and European family systems', *Continuity and Change* 23 (2008), pp. 389–427.

Tanzi, V., 'Corruption: arm's length relationships and markets', in G. Fiorentini and S. Peltzman (eds.), *The economics of organised crime* (Cambridge, 1995), pp. 161–80.

Tarlovskaia, V. R., 'Rostovshchicheskie operatsii moskovskikh kuptsov i torgovyhk krest'ian v nachale XVIII v.', *Vestnik moskovskogo universiteta ser. istoriia* 3 (1977), pp. 44–55.

Tikhonov, Yu. A., *Pomeshchich'i krest'iane v Rossii: feodal'naia renta v XVII–nachale XVIII v.* (Moscow, 1974).

Tolstoy, L. N., *Anna Karenina*, trans. Louise and Aylmer Maude (Oxford, 1918; repr. 1980, 1992).

Troinitskii, A., *The serf population in Russia according to the 10th national census*, ed. E. Domar (Newtonville MA, 1982).

Troinitskii, N. A. (ed.), *Naselenie imperii po perepisi 28-go ianvaria 1897 goda* (St Petersburg, 1897).

Vdovina, L. N., *Krest'ianskaia obshchina i monastyr v tsentral'noi Rossii v pervoi polovine XVIII v.* (Moscow, 1988).

Venturi, F., *Roots of revolution: a history of the populist and socialist movements in nineteenth-century Russia* (Chicago, 1960).

Vovelle, M., *Piété baroque et déchristianisation en Provence au XVIIIe siècle: les attitudes devant la mort d'après les clauses des testaments* (Paris, 1973).

de Vries, J., *The Dutch rural economy in the golden age* (New Haven, 1974).

The economy of Europe in an age of crisis 1600–1750 (Cambridge, 1976).

The industrious revolution: consumer behaviour and the household economy 1650–present (Cambridge, 2008).

Wall, R., 'The composition of households in a population of 6 men to 10 women: southeast Bruges in 1814', in R. Wall, J. Robin and P. Laslett (eds.), *Family forms in historic Europe* (Cambridge, 1983), pp. 421–74.

Wall, R., Harevan, T., and Ehmer, J. (eds.), *Family history revisited* (Newark and London, 2001).

Wall, R., Robin, J., and Laslett, P. (eds.), *Family forms in historic Europe* (Cambridge, 1983).

Wegge, S., 'Chain migration and information networks: evidence from nineteenth-century Hesse-Cassel', *Journal of Economic History* 58 (4) (1998), pp. 957–86.

Whittle, J., *The development of agrarian capitalism: land and labour in Norfolk, 1440–1580* (Oxford, 2000).

Wolf, E., *Peasants* (Englewood Cliffs, NJ, 1966).

World Bank, *World development report 1989: financial systems and development* (Oxford, 1989).

Worobec, C., 'Victims or actors? Russian peasant women and patriarchy', in E. Kingston-Mann and T. Mixter (eds.), *Peasant economy, culture, and politics of European Russia, 1800–1921* (Princeton, 1991) pp. 177–206.

  Peasant Russia: family and community in the post-emancipation period (DeKalb, IL, 1995).

Wrigley, E. A., and Schofield, R. S., *The population history of England 1541–1871: a reconstitution* (Cambridge, 1981).

Index